AIR MOBILITY

Related Titles from Potomac Books

John Warden and the Renaissance of American Air Power
by John Andreas Olsen

A History of Air Warfare
edited by John Andreas Olsen

Global Air Power
edited by John Andreas Olsen

Air Mobility

A Brief History of the American Experience

ROBERT C. OWEN

Potomac Books
An imprint of the University of Nebraska Press

Library of Congress
Cataloging-in-Publication Data
Owen, Robert C., 1951–
Air mobility: a brief history
of the American experience /
Robert C. Owen.
pages cm
Includes bibliographical
references and index.
ISBN 978-1-59797-851-4
(hardcover: alk. paper)
ISBN 978-1-59797-852-1
(electronic)
1. Airlift, Military—United
States—History.
2. Transportation, Military—
United States—History. 3. United
States. Air Force—
Transportation—History.
I. Title.
UC333.O84 2013
358.4'40973—dc23
2013008393

First Edition

To
Professor Irvin Brinton (Bill) Holley Jr.,
"Dr. Doctrine"

He gave me my start and taught me the relevance
of old-school excellence in the new computer age.

And
Robert Reed Owen,
My Father

Hero at Midway, Iwo Jima, and many smaller fights,
and pioneer of modern flight test engineering.

Honor before Life

Contents

Acknowledgments

THIS STUDY IS a product of passion. Except for two educational assignments, I spent my entire air force career flying air transports or engaged in staff duties directly related to airlift and air mobility planning, doctrine development, and project management. In the course of all of that, I developed a passionate interest in the workings of the national air mobility system and a deep pride at being counted among those who moved the bullets, beans, and fuel of modern war. From that came my determination to capture the "personality" of air mobility and the essences of its operational, strategic, and theoretical characters.

So, my first debt of gratitude is to the community of air mobility practitioners that was my operational home and inspired me to write this book. I also owe thanks to my old colleagues at the Department of History at the Air Force Academy who nurtured my early skills as a military historian and theorist. I also would not be writing this had not Professor Irvin (Bill) Holley and Lieutenant General Anthony J. (Tony) Burshnick conspired together to get me into the Duke military history program in the late 1980s. Several of my colleagues at the Air Force School of Advanced Airpower Studies, particularly Professor Karl Muller (now at RAND) and Professor David Mets (now an honored emeritus), read my early writings on this subject and encouraged me to keep moving toward a book-length study. I've done that now, and I hope that the product honors their efforts.

Although this project has been on my desk or shelf for over twenty years, my duties in the Air Force and now at Embry-Riddle Aeronautical University have kept me from pursuing it continually. So it has been only in the past three years that I have been able to make the "death march" of getting everything together as a book. In this modern age of computers, I have no typists, research assistants, or editors to thank for the initial draft. They have all been replaced by Microsoft Office. But Timothy Henderson, my favorite literary critic, and General Arthur J. Lichte, former commander of the Air Mobility Command and mentor, generously read numerous chapter drafts and offered valuable criticisms. After that, the crew at Potomac Books provided most of the editorial support needed to turn this draft into a book. Thanks to all of them.

Beyond that, I have to say "thank you" again to all of the general officers, more junior military personnel, civilians, and fellow scholars who gave so generously of their time in formal interviews, telephone calls, and letters. I know that my findings in this book will not and could not in every case please them all. But I hope that their reading of it will reassure them that I took their time with gratitude and considered their inputs responsibly.

Last, I will never be able to thank enough my wonderful wife, Adrienne, and my two adult children, Heather and Robert, for putting up with this project and my frequent distractions from family duties for so many years. They are the safe harbor of home upon which my spirit floats.

Terms and Abbreviations

THIS LIST INCLUDES terms utilized in multiple chapters of this study. Terms used in only one chapter are defined at the first point of use. All terms are defined and presented with their abbreviations at the first point of use in each chapter. Some of the following terms correspond to terms defined officially in the U.S. Department of Defense Joint Publication 1-02, *Department of Defense Dictionary of Military and Associated Terms*, November 8, 2010. But, here, they are defined in reflection of their use in this study and for consistency with earlier forms of use.

ADMINISTRATIVE AIRLIFT	This is an airlift performed under secure conditions, usually at main bases and/or in aircraft loaded to take maximum advantage of their available hold volume.
AIR ASSAULT	During World War II an air assault referred to the delivery of troops into combat by parachute of gliders. Since the 1950s it also denotes the delivery of assault forces by helicopter.
AIR MOBILITY	Air mobility refers to the movement and delivery of personnel, cargo, or fuel by air transport and air-refueling aircraft.
AIR RESERVE COMPONENTS (ARC)	The ARC comprises the Air Force Reserve and the Air National Guard.
AIR TRANSPORT	As used in this study, this refers to the administrative movement of individuals or small groups of passengers and cargo by air, usually in support of operations by military forces deployed already.
AIR TRANSPORT COMMAND (ATC)	The Air Transport Command was the strategic air transport arm of the United States from 1942 to 1948. An earlier Air Transport Command (1941–1942) was responsible primarily for supporting army airborne training.
AIRBORNE	The definition of "airborne" is generally the same as for "air assault."
AIRDROP	An airdrop is the delivery of personnel and cargo from aircraft in flight, either with or without parachutes.

AIRLAND	This refers to the delivery of personnel and cargo from an aircraft that has landed or, in the case of helicopters, that remains in a hover.
AIRLIFT	As used in this study, this refers to the operational movement of military units into combat zones or theaters.
ARMY AIR CORPS	The Army Air Corps directed the equipping and training of all U.S. Army air units from 1926 to 1941. From 1935 it relinquished operational control of field units to General Headquarters Air Force.
ASSAULT AIRLIFT	Used through the 1960s, this term generally referred to the delivery of passengers and cargo into very short and minimally developed assault zones by fixed-wing aircraft.
ASSAULT ZONE	An assault zone was used for the landing of aircraft, usually helicopters, but was used also to describe short, rough fields suitable for use by fixed-wing assault transports.
BATTLEFIELD AIRLIFT	This term is used in this study to indicate U.S. Army Aviation forces and/or operational movements of ground combat forces by airlift units controlled organically by the moving units or by higher-level ground commanders.
CHANNEL AIRLIFT	A channel airlift is a regularly scheduled airlift mission or cargo, generally moving between established bases.
COMBAT AIR FORCES	These are air commands in the United States and overseas responsible for training air combat forces and commanding them overseas. Currently these include the Air Combat Command and air components of unified combatant commands, such as United States Air Forces in Europe and Pacific Air Forces.
COMBATANT COMMAND	A combatant command is a unified or specified command with a broad, continuing mission under a single commander reporting directly to the president through the secretary of defense.
COMMON-USER AIRLIFT	A common-user airlift is airlift and/or aerial refueling forces operated by a single organization to provide air mobility support to multiple user organizations in accordance with priorities and directives established by a superior military command.

DIRECTOR OF MOBILITY FORCES	This is a senior officer with extensive air mobility experience serving as the agent for air mobility operations within a combatant command or joint task force and who links the local air operations center and the Tanker-Airlift Control Center of the Air Mobility Command.
DROP ZONE	A drop zone is an area designated to receive personnel and cargo from airborne aircraft.
GENERAL HEADQUARTERS AIR FORCE	This controlled army air combat units within the United States from 1935 to 1941 and served as a template for expeditionary air forces, should they be required.
GLOBAL AIRLIFT	This term was coined in the early 1960s and connotes the ability to move and support complete air and ground combat forces over international and transoceanic distances by air.
INTERTHEATER AIRLIFT	This airlift is the movement of cargo and passengers by air between theaters and the continental United States and to other theaters.
INTRATHEATER AIRLIFT	This airlift is the movement of cargo and passengers within theaters of operation.
LANDING ZONE	A landing zone is used for the landing of aircraft, which may range from an open field for helicopters to a graded strip for fixed-wing aircraft. If the landing zone is paved, it usually is referred to as an airfield or runway.
MILITARY AIR TRANSPORT SERVICE (MATS)	This was the strategic air transport command of the United States from 1948 to 1967. It formed from a combination of the Air Transport Command and part of the Naval Air Transport Service.
NATIONAL AIR MOBILITY SYSTEM (NAMS)	This is the total combination of civil and military organizations contributing to the airlift and air-refueling capabilities of the United States.
NAVAL AIR TRANSPORT SERVICE (NATS)	This was the strategic and theater air transport arm of the U.S. Navy from 1941 to 1948.
OPERATIONAL AIRLIFT	An operational airlift is performed under combat conditions and/or in aircraft loaded to facilitate the arrival of units in readiness to commence combat operations.

ORGANIC AIRLIFT — This is an airlift and/or aerial refueling forces assigned directly to a using organization, primarily to support that organization's missions.

OUTSIZE CARGO — Outsize cargo includes items exceeding the dimensional and weight-carrying capacity of all aircraft except the C-5 and C-17.

OVERSIZE CARGO — Oversize cargo is too large to fit on a standard military 463L air cargo pallet but still small enough to fit into all standard military transports and most civil cargo aircraft.

REGIONAL AIR MOVEMENT CONTROL CENTER — This is an organization within an air operations center tasked with metering the flow of aircraft into specified airfields, usually during humanitarian relief operations.

SHORT TAKEOFF AND LANDING — This is a vague term that basically refers to operations on unusually short runways by specialized, fixed-wing aircraft. During the Vietnam era, this term referred roughly to takeoff and landing rolls of less than 2,000 feet. Later terms, "STOL-RF" and "Super STOL," referred to operations onto rough fields and rolls of less than 1,000 feet, respectively.

SPECIFIED COMBATANT COMMAND — A specified combatant command has a broad, continuing mission and is composed predominantly of the forces of a single military service.

STRATEGIC AIRLIFT — See "intertheater airlift."

STRATEGIC SUPPORT SQUADRONS (SSS) — These are organic air transport squadrons that were operated by the Strategic Air Command in the early 1950s.

THEATER AIR FORCES — See "combat air forces."

THEATER AIRLIFT — Theater airlifts are missions and operations involving administrative and/or operational air movements within theaters of operation and/or battle zones.

UNIFIED COMBATANT COMMAND — This command has a broad, continuing mission and is composed of the forces of two or more military services.

Introduction

GLOBAL AIR MOBILITY is an American invention. During the course of the twentieth century, other nations developed capabilities to transport supplies and personnel by air in support of military forces already on the battlefield. A few countries, mainly the Soviet Union, Nazi Germany, and Great Britain, fielded airlift forces capable of moving infantry divisions over distances of a few hundred miles and delivering them by parachute or directly from aircraft landed at rough forward fields. But only the United States mustered the resources and will to create a global force of transport and aerial refueling aircraft capable of moving whole air and ground combat forces of all types to any region of the world and then supporting them in continuous combat operations. The end product of nearly a century of operational and doctrinal experience and investment, these forces can lay down an "aluminum bridge" involving thousands of aircraft and the requisite support and control structures between the homeland and/or distant regions in mere days, even hours. No other country can do that or has even really tried.

Global air mobility changed the world. Most obviously, it elevated the American military's penchant for speed and maneuverability to an unequalled art. Since World War II, it is fair to say that every major U.S. strategic concept and regional war plan has presumed substantial reliance on air mobility. Whether contemplating a bomber campaign against the Soviet Union or halting another North Korean surprise attack, American war planners depended on transport and tanker aircraft to launch, reinforce, and sustain operations. Even privates know of no other way to travel between routine assignments or to go into battle over distances of a few hundred miles or so.

Less obviously, global air mobility changes the way the United States relates to the world. American leaders use air mobility to signal friends and enemies of their intent and ability to intervene, attack, or defend on short notice and powerfully. Air wings and armored brigades sitting in the United States on Sunday can be patrolling the air of any continent on Wednesday and taking up defensive positions on a friend's borders by Friday. The knowledge that the United States can do those things affects the diplomacy and the calculations of America and its friends and enemies alike.

It also is worth noting that the very possession of global mobility has made America the world's philanthropist. Knowing that the United States has the capability, the world expects that America will send military transport aircraft loaded with relief supplies and eager helpers wherever things go badly wrong in distant and remote places. Indeed, from their earliest days, American airlift forces have performed thousands of missions to deliver hay to snowbound cattle, get stranded pilgrims to Mecca, bring food and medicine to tsunami-stricken towns, and do a host of other things that no one could have anticipated before they happened. Tens, perhaps hundreds, of thousands of people owe their lives to the speed at which U.S. air mobility forces brought relief. Indeed, even though humanitarian operations are merely a by-product of capabilities developed for military purposes, they are a frequent and profoundly positive feature of America's outreach to the world.

There is more to the story. Beyond development and operations, the global airlift story includes protracted and convoluted themes of doctrinal and political dispute. Doctrinally, it took decades for the full potential and resource requirements of air mobility to become clear and, then, for a small community of proponents to influence defense policies accordingly. Senior air leaders stalled progress for several decades by refusing to acknowledge or fund airlift missions beyond providing logistics support to deployed forces and enhancing the mobility and striking power of strategic air forces. Frustrated by the Air Force's reluctance to maintain strong theater or battlefield airlift forces, the U.S. Army reestablished an aviation arm of its own in the 1950s that further complicated the political, not to mention the operational, scenes. Added to that, the airline industry and its supporters aggressively sought shares of the nation's airlift effort, since many peacetime and wartime airlift missions could be performed by civilians flying airliners. At times, therefore, airlift politics rose to national importance, were Byzantine in their complexity, and revealed much about the competing strategic priorities and the internal rivalries of the American defense community. No clear appreciations of the history and the potentials of global airlift are possible apart from these doctrinal and political stories.

Given all these themes and subplots, and despite its brevity, this study will cover a lot of historical and analytical territory. Some of it, of course, will tell the "drums-and-trumpets" stories of technology, operations, and people. The important contributions air mobility made and is making to the defense of the United States, and the deeds and sacrifices of air mobility warriors in the air and on the ground, call for no less. But given the important interconnections between the operational side of the air mobility story and the broader contexts of American culture, technology, and military strategy and politics, this study will examine those issues as well. In the end, this study aims to achieve the objectives of all good military histories: first, to satisfy our curiosity about the origins, rise, and nature of this amazing instrument of American power and, second, to provide some foundation for assessing its appropriate future and the requirements for its continued success.

The century-long duration and complexity of the air mobility story requires careful definition of some key terms. Over the decades, practitioners and theorists have used such terms as "air transport," "airlift," and "air mobility" differently to describe operations, missions, organizations, policies, and doctrines. So, to highlight the continuities of the air mobility story, this book will apply specific and consistent meanings to certain terms, even though they were not used with such consistency in every period. The most important of these include the following:

- *Air transport* is the administrative movement of individuals or small groups of passengers and cargo by air, usually in support of operations by military forces deployed already. Air transport is a peacetime and wartime function and can include nonmilitary operations, such as humanitarian assistance and support of civil and private agencies.
- An *airlift* is the operational movement of military units into combat zones or theaters. Such movements include airborne operations, in which units parachute into battle; airland operations, in which units arrive by transport aircraft landing at forward airfields; and subsequent resupply and support operations.
- *Strategic air transport and/or airlift* missions and operations involve administrative and/or operational air movements between the United States and distant theaters of operations and/or battle zones, or movements between those theaters and zones.
- *Theater air transport and/or airlift* missions and operations involve administrative and/or operational air movements within theaters of operation and/or battle zones.
- *Battlefield airlift* missions involve operational movements of ground combat forces by airlift units controlled directly by the moving units or by higher-level ground commanders.

- *Air mobility* is a term that describes the ability of forces to move by air and describes the combined mission of airlift and aerial refueling forces.
- *Common-user* airlift and/or aerial refueling forces are operated by a single organization to provide air mobility support to multiple user organizations in accordance with priorities and directives established by a superior military command.
- *Organic* airlift and/or aerial refueling forces are assigned directly to a using organization, primarily to support that organization's missions.

When appropriate, this book will introduce and use such terms as "troop carrier aviation," "tactical airlift," and "aviation" that have been used at different times to categorize air mobility missions and organizations. But when used, these terms also will be placed in the context of the previously described lexicon to maintain the continuity and clarity of the broader story. The value of imposing this somewhat strained discipline on the terminology of this history will become clearer as it progresses.

AIR MOBILITY

1. Discovering Air Mobility

Natural Idea with Many Skeptics

IT TAKES NO great leap of imagination to visualize military airlift. Certainly thousands of beleaguered soldiers and desperate commanders of the past wished for the ability to fly into battle or away from bad situations. Indeed, Frenchmen had barely invented practical balloon flight in 1783 when Benjamin Franklin penned the following to a friend:

> It appears, as you observe, to be a discovery of great importance, and what may possibly give a new turn to human affairs . . . five thousand balloons, capable of raising two men each, could not cost more than five ships of the line; and where is the prince who can afford so to cover his country with troops for its defence, as that ten thousand men descending from the clouds might not in many places do an infinite deal of mischief, before a force could be brought together to repel them?[1]

The French, at least, appeared to have listened to Dr. Franklin, since Napoleon's planners, or at least his publicists, briefly considered using balloon-borne troops as part of a planned invasion of England. There are drawings from the time showing giant balloons carrying infantry, horses, cannons, and the other impedimenta of war.[2]

Professional military men of the time never gave the notion of balloon assaults more than a quick look, if that, before dismissing the idea as folly. The obvious problem was technology. Armies were heavy, and balloons were small. Most balloons carried fewer than a handful of people. Even the biggest ones, such as the French Giant of the early 1860s, carried only a few tons of cargo and people. Worse, balloons could be navigated only imprecisely. Nineteenth-century balloonists became skillful at exploiting the varying currents of air at different altitudes. But, even so, they could go only where the winds carried them, and they could not return. Military ballooning, as a consequence, gave useful service in reconnaissance and signaling but had no obvious application to logistics and mobility.

The Franco-Prussian War of 1870–1871 provided the only opportunity in history to use balloon air transport on a significant scale. When the Prussian-led armies of the German states surrounded Paris, the small community of aeronauts entrapped in the city saw immediately that balloons offered a way to get mail, important people, and homing pigeons out of the city. Precise navigation wasn't a requirement, since balloons needed only to lift their precious loads over the besieging lines and deposit them somewhere in the surrounding regions of unoccupied France. Easily convinced of the value of at least trying the experiment, the authorities authorized the conversion of the city's unemployed rail stations into balloon factories. Hundreds of seamstresses sewed cheap cotton fabric into gasbags, while stranded sailors wove netting and passenger baskets. Experienced aeronauts began training novices to operate the balloons. Navigation was a chancy affair: one balloon landed in Norway, and others simply floated out to sea and were never seen again. But in the end, 66 balloons drifted out of Paris, carrying about 110 passengers, 400 pigeons, and around 3 million letters. Thousands of letters, reduced into an early form of microfilm, came back attached to the legs of the swift birds. Some of the better pigeons made four or five flights out and back into the city, ensuring that French authorities stayed in touch, and the citizens of Paris could send letters to the outside world.[3] Balloon air transport had found its niche in a great city under siege and nowhere else.

The appearance of dirigible balloons and airships at the end of the nineteenth century prompted some fanciful but little serious military discussion of invading armies arriving by air. By 1900 Count von Zeppelin's designs were carrying twenty passengers on sightseeing trips, and bigger ships were in the offing. But even ships carrying a hundred passengers each offered little promise as the means to lift the thousands of troops and thousands of tons of cargo needed to deposit and sustain a significant military force behind the lines. So the military missions of the airships entering service in Europe and the United States remained the traditional ones of observation and communications, with the cautious addition of bombardment and ground attack.

Few authoritative writers at the time expected much from airplanes either. Looking forward to the advent of heavier-than-air flight, most expected aircraft would be too small and underpowered to contribute greatly to military or even civil transportation. Only a few years before the Wrights flew, Octave Chanute wrote in his seminal study *Progress in Flying Machines* that aircraft "will seldom be built to carry more than from three to 10 passengers, and will never compete for heavy freights." Such aircraft, he argued, would be useful "for reconnoitering the enemy's positions and for quickly conveying information . . . although their limited capacity to carry weight will not enable them to take up a large quantity, nor to employ any heavy guns."[4]

The Americans Discover Airlift

American soldiers and early airmen, however, were not authoritative writers; they were pragmatists. So regardless of the economics of air transport, they were quick to understand the lift capabilities of the flimsy craft that began to show up after the Army bought its first plane in 1908. Early air leaders viewed reconnaissance and perhaps bombardment as the predominant applications of military aircraft. But even when army aircraft were scarcely capable of lifting a pilot and, perhaps, an observer, they also suggested that aircraft would be useful to perform "occasional transportation" and "rapid transportation of superior commanding officers."[5]

Consistent with these predictions, the Army sent the 1st Aero Squadron to Northern Mexico in 1916 to provide reconnaissance for the Punitive Expedition against Mexican revolutionaries who had violated the U.S. border. But the 1st expended most of its sorties on moving "mail and dispatches" between army base camps and field units. During much of the campaign, the squadron conducted a regularly scheduled airmail service linking major posts and maneuvering field units. It seems, however, that no superior commanding officers entrusted themselves to the underpowered and decrepit Curtiss Jennies flown at great personal hazard by the squadron's pilots.

World War I gave the Army its first opportunity to use air transport on a continual, albeit tiny, scale. During most major campaigns, the U.S. Air Service kept flights of "command airplanes" ready to fly dispatches, photographs, and other intelligence items between major headquarters. The Air Service routinely moved delicate instruments and other high-value items between supply depots and forward units.[6] Back in the States, the Army cooperated with the U.S. Post Office Department in the spring and summer of 1918 to fly a daily airmail service between New York and Washington, D.C. Overcoming the challenges of weather, inexperienced pilots, and balky airplanes, the Army made 270 flights during the spring and summer, lifting over twenty tons of official and private mail. While storms and mechanical problems obliged the young army pilots to make some sixty-nine forced landings, they all survived, and the mail moved with remarkable reliability.

America's most famous, albeit ineffective, air transport feat of the war was the attempt to drop relief supplies to the so-called Lost Battalion in early October 1918. When the remnants of several 77th Infantry Division units became surrounded during the Argonne offensive, aircrews of the 50th Aero Squadron attempted to find and resupply them with their De Havilland-4 light bombers. Flying low and slow into German ground fire, the 50th's pilots searched in vain for a view of the beleaguered Americans. In desperation, they dropped small packets of food and ammunition into the trees, but all were lost or fell to the Germans. Finally, in an act of courage and self-sacrifice, two fliers flew as slowly as possible at the very treetops to locate their comrades, mainly by observing from where ground fire was not coming. Mortally wounded and with their plane shot to bits, Lieutenant Harold Goettler and Lieutenant Erwin Bleckley crashed into French trenches, and Bleckley passed with his dying hand a bloody map marked with the battalion's position to a *soldat*.

Thus by the end of the Great War, the Army had discovered air transport. The experience base was sparse in the extreme, the product of on-the-spot innovation rather than of any systematic doctrinal or technical experimentation. Planes were available and things needed moving, so individuals and units just did the job. The whole process was so low key in fact that none of the Army's major end-of-war reports mentioned air transport or lessons learned about it, even as they lavished detailed attention on the combat branches of military aviation. There were lessons to be codified: the value of transports for keeping squadrons supplied in the field, the importance of aircraft capacity, the need for brave and determined crews and quality maintenance, and so on. At the time, air transport must have seemed too simple an idea and too secondary in importance to merit much attention, and it didn't get any. But it proved also to be too important to just go away.

2. Military Air Transport in the 1920s

THE FIRST DECADE of the Golden Age of Aviation was a busy time for the U.S. Army Air Service, which became the U.S. Army Air Corps after 1926. Almost daily, military airmen pressed the limits of aircraft performance, broke records, and discovered or refined their understanding of the roles aircraft could play in modern war. As warriors, they focused on building the Air Service's competency in bombardment, pursuit, and attack aviation. But airmen did explore the use of air transport to supply tactical squadrons at forward airfields and to provide liaison and medical evacuation support to field headquarters. The fledgling state of aviation technology and the penurious budgets of the U.S. Army during these years sharply limited the scope of these explorations. But by extracting double duty from bombers and purchasing small numbers of type-designed transports, army airmen proved the value of air transportation as a necessary adjunct to modern war.

Early Explorations

The Army entered the 1920s with no formal doctrine or professional writing on air transport. No major report on air operations in the Great War gave more than indirect and passing mention of the use of aerial transportation. True enough, the Air Service performed little organized air transport during the war. But it also dropped only about 138 tons of bombs. Furthermore, only weeks before the end of the war in November 1918, the endlessly visionary Brigadier General William (Billy) Mitchell proposed the use of Handley Page bombers to drop and resupply the entire 1st Infantry Division behind German lines as an opener for the expected Allied offensive in the spring of 1919. Despite this relative equality of experience, or rather inexperience, between bombardment and air transport, army airmen devoted hundreds of pages to the future of bombing operations and apparently none at all to Mitchell's grand plan or air transport in general.[1] Perhaps most surprising of all, the subject of air transport did not appear in the curriculum of the Air Service Tactical School (ASTS), activated in 1921 to train young officers in the ways of air warfare. There were lessons on bombardment and pursuit aviation, naturally, along with others on cavalry tactics and field sanitation. Major William C. Sherman, the first commandant of the ASTS, similarly overlooked transport aviation when he wrote the Air Service's first formal doctrine manual, *Training Regulations 440-15: Fundamental Principles for the Employment of the Air Service*, in 1923.[2] Indeed, only the Army's overarching *Field Services Regulation* had anything to say about air transport in its 1923 edition and then only to point out that it might be a useful way to augment surface transport modes in support of land operations.[3]

By their actions, however, army leaders in the early 1920s revealed that they were interested in air transport. Most important, the Air Service's first commander, Major General Mason Patrick, activated the so-called Model Airway in February 1921. Patrick saw the Model Airway as a valuable experiment in the conduct of sustained and reliable air transport. The initial route ran about 390 miles between McCook Field, Ohio, the Air Service's main matériel depot, and Bolling Field, across the Potomac from Washington, D.C. Physically, the airway consisted of a string of five main fields capable of providing fuel, servicing, and weather forecasting, plus ten secondary fields and about twenty emergency fields, which were little more than mowed, flat pieces of ground. Outside support for the project came from municipalities along the route that did such things as paint town names on the roofs of prominent buildings and from the Boy Scouts, who volunteered to monitor the condition of the emergency fields and to guard crashed airplanes.[4] Pilots on the route generally flew De Havilland-4 light bombers capable of carrying a passenger or several hundred pounds of cargo. They were supported by a weather service and guided by the first air service maps produced specifically for aerial navigation. The Model Airway closed in 1926, after carrying about 1,200 passengers and over thirty tons of cargo. Useful as it was, the airway several times almost ran out of money. But General Patrick always scraped enough from his puny coffers to keep it going.

If the Model Airway represented a step forward in the development of routine air transport, the deployment of air service squadrons to help suppress the West Virginia coal strikes of 1921 introduced the Army to air mobility, the movement of actual combat units by air. When striking coal miners threatened rebellion against the state of West Virginia, the Air Service ordered Brigadier General Mitchell to get two squadrons of attack aircraft and bombs from Langley Field, Hampton, Virginia, to Charleston as quickly as possible. Mitchell's squadrons made the 270-nautical-mile flight over a period of two days, suffering several accidents and injured crewmen along the way. Martin bombers brought the personnel, spare parts, medical supplies, food, and other necessities of the ground support echelon in their bomb bays.[5] Happily, the Air Service was not called on to bomb or gas American laborers protesting poor pay and harsh working conditions. Ultimately, the deployment of Mitchell's squadrons opened up a new vista of speed and flexibility in warfare.

Speed and flexibility held strategic importance for the Air Service. The Army's primary mission in peacetime was continental defense, securing America's borders from invasion. Given the large size of the United States in relation to the small size of the Army, this mission presumed that the Army's few divisions would have to move rapidly from their posts to threatened shores, perhaps hundreds, even thousands of miles away. Knowing that such movements could take days or even weeks, General Mitchell and other airmen argued that the Air Service should be the nation's first line of defense, since air units could cover the required distances much more quickly than ground units. Moreover, air service bombers could locate and strike enemy ships at sea, perhaps neutralizing an invading force before it came ashore.[6] In keeping with the importance of the mission, air service leaders initiated many operations to develop the technologies and techniques needed to deploy aircraft over long distances. These included the Kelly-Macready nonstop transcontinental flight of 1923, the World Flight of 1924, and several air-refueling experiments beginning in 1923 and culminating in 1929 with the famous *Question Mark* endurance flight.

Despite the obvious need for air transport support for such long-distance deployments, the cargo aircraft available to the Air Service in the early 1920s lacked the range, speed, and numbers needed to support long-distance unit deployments. In 1919, the service acquired a single copy of the T-1, powered by two 400-horsepower Liberty engines and capable of carrying twelve passengers at seventy-five knots for 400 nautical miles.[7] Later, in 1922, the Air Service took delivery of just two Fokker T-2s, each capable of carrying ten passengers at about seventy knots for 350 miles. A very reliable monoplane design, the T-2 was chosen by Lieutenants Oakley G. Kelly and John Macready to make their 2,740-mile flight across the United States in 1923. But, otherwise, these planes were too limited in number and too awkward in their cargo-loading characteristics (they loaded through a hatch in the floor) to provide much logistic support to forward-deployed air service field units. Beyond these three aircraft, the Army did whatever air transport it did with standard or slightly modified single- or two-engine bombers. Things began to pick up in 1925, when the Air Service acquired twenty-seven Douglas C-1s, its first specialized transport produced in quantity. Powered by a 435-horsepower version of the Liberty, the C-1 could carry six to eight passengers or equivalent cargo about 350 miles at seventy knots. The planes came with three-feet by five-feet cargo doors in their fuselages that greatly facilitated loading, but they still lacked the performance needed to carry squadron supplies and support personnel across the continent.

As the C-1s were settling into operations, air service leaders began to consider even greater expansion of the air transport force. In 1926 Major William C. Sherman, now an instructor at the Army War College, suggested that squadrons of transports should be attached to large combat units to ensure a steady flow of supplies and critical spare parts until surface transportation links could be established or reestablished as those units moved from base to base. Sherman did not see the need for many transport squadrons, however, since they could be augmented by bombers and since units moving about the continental United States would be able to forage locally for most of their victuals, shelter, and even gasoline.[8]

In keeping with Sherman's vision, air transportation played increasingly important roles in air service exercises. The final report of the Air Service's 1925 maneuvers declared that "air transports are essential for the movement of an air force."[9] During the 1927 annual maneuvers, C-1s and C-2s linked rear depots with deployed air bases. A year later, the Second Bombardment Group employed fourteen bombers to lift thirty-three tons of supplies in five hours between Langley Field, near Hampton, Virginia, about twenty miles to an expeditionary field near Virginia Beach. Reporting on the experience, the group commander, Major Hugh J. Knerr, suggested that future army transports should be based on standard bombers modified with larger fuselages.[10]

Beyond its role in air combat, the Air Service discovered that air transport was an important element of its day-to-day operations, both for routine logistics missions between bases and depots and to mitigate the consequences of natural disasters. In an early example of such disaster relief, army bombers dropped hay to cattle stranded by winter storms. Later, in 1927, crews from the U.S. Army, Air Service, and Air National Guard led rescuers to thousands of stranded people during the great Mississippi flood of 1927 and in the aftermaths of several hurricanes.

Perhaps the largest disaster relief air transport mission of the decade came in 1929, when the Army and the Navy put out a maximum effort to locate and provide assistance to victims stranded in the flooded countryside of southern Alabama, centered on the town of Elba. Over a period of five days, the Air

Corps brought together some thirty-eight aircraft at Maxwell Field and flew at least 296 sorties to deliver over fifty tons of supplies. The Navy provided 113 sorties from Pensacola, Florida. Air corps pilots dropped burlap sacks of food and water directly onto rooftops. They also brought in several thousand pounds of mail and newspapers and even dropped an outboard motor by parachute. In addition to saving hundreds of desperate citizens and bringing relief to thousands more, these flights demonstrated the potential of air transport as an element of military logistics.

These relief operations also revealed the dangers of flying even air transport sorties in an era when air crashes were a routine element of any type of flying. One pilot during the Alabama floods, Lieutenant W. H. Higgins, recounted the consequence of the engine failing in his O-11: "We hit the water at only about 60 miles per hour . . . and no sooner than the plane touched it whipped over on the back. This threw Corporal Woodward out and clear of the ship, but I was trapped in the cockpit with my parachute." After an exhausting struggle in the cold waters, Lieutenant Higgins and his observer were rescued.[11] But, for anyone paying attention, this kind of event showed that transport flying was not for the weak of heart, for it shared dangers with combat flying.

While the Army's air arm was not involved in any combat operations in the 1920s, the U.S. Marines were, and their experiences spoke to the value of air transport in the realm of counterinsurgency operations. Roughly from 1910 to 1933, marines were present in Nicaragua almost continuously, with combat and transport aircraft becoming an increasingly important part of their operations after the mid-1920s. Writing in 1930, at the end of his tour as the air commander of the intervention, Colonel Thomas Turner reported that he operated as many transport aircraft as combat aircraft and that his transports underpinned the effectiveness and morale of his units by carrying ammunition, medications, food, and mail out to the field and injured troops back to main bases. Often air transport was the only link that jungle-bound marine base camps had with the outside world, since ground transport was too difficult or dangerous. Between 1927 and 1930, the dozen or so Ford trimotors, single-engine aircraft, and small amphibians lifted some 1,500 tons of cargo, air-dropped over 75 tons of food to isolated posts, and transported 7,789 individuals around the country.[12]

Fully aware of their own service's experiences and the implications of those on the outside, army airmen continued to invest in modern air transport aircraft, though still on a scale inadequate to its needs. In 1926 and 1927, the Army acquired three Fokker-Atlantic Aviation C-2s and eight C-2As, respectively. In

1928 and 1929, it added eight Ford C-3s, followed by eight Ford C-8s and eleven Fokker-Atlantic C-7s. Each of these aircraft was powered by three 225- to 300-horsepower engines, carried ten to fourteen passengers, and cruised around 100 to 115 knots for three to four hours.[13] They were as modern as the aircraft manufacturing industry could produce at the time. But even if the Air Corps could concentrate these aircraft into a single effort, they still would be too few to support the movements of its combat groups. The challenge was to find more transports, without diverting critical funding away from its combat groups.

It was just at this time that the sudden expansion of the U.S. airline industry into passenger operations offered a potential source of augmentation to the Army's air transport capability in wartime. Prior to 1925, there was no airline industry in the United States to speak of. Then, with the passage of the Kelly Air Mail Act in 1925, a series of airlines formed to compete for lucrative government airmail contracts. A subsequent amendment in 1928 encouraged these carriers to acquire multiengine passenger aircraft to subsidize their incomes from carrying the airmail. All this corresponded to a surge in the numbers of Americans willing to risk their necks by traveling routinely by air, a surge fueled by Charles Lindbergh's heroic transatlantic flight in 1927 and by marked improvements in aircraft safety and all-weather reliability. Rising to the opportunity, the commercial airline industry grew from about 128 aircraft in service in 1927 to 600 in 1930. But even at the end of the decade, most of the aircraft in airline service were single-engine mail planes. Recognizing the latent potential of this fleet and its workers, former chief of the Air Corps General Mason M. Patrick suggested that the airlines must be considered a military reserve of aircraft, pilots, and support personnel.[14]

As the decade of the 1920s ended, army airmen were fully cognizant of the value of air transport as an adjunct of combat air operations. But that is about as far as their vision went in this period of primitive aircraft and stingy budgets. Apart from articles written by marine veterans of operations in Nicaragua, there was little if any discussion of air transport in support of land operations. This lack of serious discussion probably reflected the realization of the difference between transporting the spare engines, toolboxes, tentage, and rations of a fighter group and transporting the tens of thousands of tons of people and equipment in an infantry division. Serious consideration of airlifting trucks, artillery, tanks, tactical bridges, and so on would have to wait for the development of aircraft far more capable than the Army's little Ford and Fokker trimotors droning through the skies of the latter 1920s.

3. Civil Aviation between the Wars

BY THE MID-1920S, military-minded leaders in the United States saw an obvious connection between the commercial airline industry and national defense. Transmitting the thoughts of President Warren Harding, Fiorello H. La Guardia told fellow congressmen that "the outstanding weakness in the industrial situation . . . is the inadequacy of facilities to supply Air Service needs. . . . To strengthen [the commercial] industry is to strengthen our national defense." Other countries, La Guardia went on, already promoted their airlines as adjuncts to national airpower.[1] Always the zealot for airpower, General William Mitchell urged the government to organize a "system for the development of commercial aviation" and to provide a larger industrial base and mobilization reserve of skilled personnel for the military.[2] The President's Air Policy echoed Mitchell's statements, declaring that a strong commercial industry would create "a reservoir of highly skilled pilots and ground personnel . . . [that] will make it easier to rapidly build up an expanded air power if an emergency arises."[3]

The problem for all the advocates of airline expansion was the lack of an industry to promote during the 1920s. Every company that had formed thus far to conduct scheduled passenger operations had gone under quickly. The aircraft available were small, slow, and too unreliable to provide routine service at a profit, even if enough daredevil passengers could be found willing to fly in them regularly. In any case, first-class travel on the railroads was cheaper, often faster, and certainly more comfortable than anything an aircraft of that time could offer. So, by mid-decade, the commercial aviation industry consisted of local air express operators and barnstormers performing circus stunts and selling airplane rides to anyone daring enough to ride along. In national aggregate, these tiny express operators transported a daily traffic of about two tons of "gold and currency, financial documents, jewelry and precious metals, plans and specifications . . . and other articles needed in a hurry."[4] At the time that Mitchell and La Guardia voiced their visions, therefore, commercial aviation in America amounted to a recreational activity, plus transportation activities equal to the capacity of a few small trucks.

The airmail service of the U.S. Post Office Department stood in bright contrast to the flickering prospects of commercial aviation. Well financed by tax money and the postage of the millions of letters it carried, the airmail service was noted for its expert pilots, well-maintained aircraft, and organized routes of airports, emergency strips, and beacon lights stretched out like a necklace across the countryside. Its trunk route, the "Columbia Line," stretched 2,680 miles from New York to San Francisco. By 1924 relays of airmail pilots provided daily service on this line, crossing the country in about thirty-four hours, a third of the time required by rail. By the standards of the time, the airmail service also was safe. Airmail pilots suffered a fatal accident for about every 463,000 miles they flew, while a barnstormer or a passenger died for about every 13,500 miles flown.[5] Appropriately, an airmail pilot, Shirley J. Short, received one of the first Harmon trophies for aerial achievement for flying 2,169 hours in all kinds of weather, mostly at night, without a single mishap.[6]

For those dreaming of a strong commercial airline industry, the lessons of the government airmail experience were obvious. First, reasonably safe and routine flying at night and in poor weather was feasible if operators were financed adequately and disciplined in their operations. Second, the government could help finance such safe and routine operations by transferring responsibility for carrying the airmail to civilian airline companies. That was the purpose of Fiorello La Guardia's comments: to get Congress to move the airmail through civil companies, just as it contracted with the railroads to move surface mail. He was echoed by many, including the Department of Commerce and the American Engineering Council, which jointly pressed the post office to contract out the mail "as rapidly as it is possible" to support both the national economy and the national defense.[7]

Congress listened. In 1925 it passed the Air Mail Act, which authorized the postmaster general to "contract with any individual firm . . . for the transportation of air mail by aircraft between such points as he may designate." In the next year, Congress passed the Air Commerce Act, which laid the regulatory foundations of a disciplined interstate airline industry. Henceforth, all commercial carriers flying across state borders would have to certify their aircraft with the Department of Commerce, and their pilots would have to hold federal licenses. The act also empowered the commerce secretary to regulate air operations to ensure their safety. Now, with money at hand and a firm regulatory basis in the offing, everyone waited for the airline industry to take off.

In the short run, existing express companies and newly formed airlines snapped up airmail contracts all over the country. But most were reluctant to start passenger operations. Simply put, there was profit to be made in the mail, and there was money to be lost in passengers. In 1929 carrying 200 pounds of mail across the country—about the weight of a single passenger and baggage—could generate $900 in revenue. At the same time, Transcontinental Air Transport (TAT) charged only $350 to carry a passenger from New York to Los Angeles. Though it was the first airline to provide a transcontinental air service, TAT was obliged to cap its fares in relation to those charged for first-class rail service in order to draw a steady market of repeat passengers. Even then, TAT planes rarely flew full, and the airline went out of business after only sixteen months.[8] These economic realities, coupled with the post office's decision to let contracts only for short "feeder" routes, while continuing to operate the Columbia route itself, meant that the nascent airline industry quickly became a hodgepodge of small companies. Since the route structures of these little airlines linked only to the Columbia route, which did not carry passengers, they hardly composed the foundation of a regional and national air passenger service.

Technologically, the aviation industry was poised to undertake scheduled, long-distance flying. Most important, the new Pratt & Whitney Wasp and Wright Whirlwind radial engines, which appeared in 1926 and 1927, respectively, profoundly increased the power, efficiency, and reliability of the engines available for commercial aircraft. Manufacturers soon mounted two or three of these power plants to aircraft capable of carrying mail and passengers for 300 to 400 nautical miles between stops. Notable among these designs were the eight-passenger Fokker F.VII (1926), the fourteen-passenger Ford 4AT (1929), and the twelve-passenger Curtiss Condor (1930). All of these aircraft came equipped with receivers for loop-range navigational radios and gyroscopic artificial horizons and compasses, which enabled pilots to navigate at night and in all but the worst conditions of icing, turbulence, and poor visibility. In just a few years then, the airline industry found itself with aircraft that could carry the mail, which paid most or even all operational costs, and passengers, whose tickets covered remaining expenses and, hopefully, provided a margin of profit.

Then, suddenly, a lot of people were ready to fly. The event that inspired many of the rich, famous, or merely adventurous to give air travel a try was Charles A. Lindbergh's courageous solo flight across the Atlantic in May 1927. Lindbergh's heroism in daring the fog and ice of the North Atlantic sky for thirty-three hours between New York and Paris marked him as a hero who people wanted to emulate. His feat also assured many that flight had become safe enough to be done routinely. If an aircraft with a single Whirlwind engine could carry a lone flier across the Atlantic, then how much safer would a flight be in an aircraft equipped with two or three of the same engines in the hands of two highly skilled pilots? Wrote the *Literary Digest* a few weeks after Lindbergh landed in Paris, "By the success of his transatlantic flight [Lindbergh] has . . . dispel[ed] the timidity of American capital and of the American people in their attitude toward commercial aviation." Reflecting the general excitement, the *Digest* predicted a time not far off when 100-seat airliners would cross the Atlantic daily at 100 to 200 miles per hour.[9]

For the future of the airline industry, the man of the moment turned out to be Postmaster General Walter Folger Brown. Convinced that only large and well-financed companies could establish transcontinental air routes and run them safely, Brown proposed to transform the airline scene from one of numerous small carriers engaged in "destructive" competition to one of a few large carriers subsidized by contracts to carry the mail. Since only they would receive such subsidies, these big carriers would have little to fear from upstart competitors, which could not hope to operate profitably without mail contracts. In 1930, therefore, Brown called together the presidents of the airmail carriers and advised them of the new order of things. Then, without much input from anyone, he divided future airmail contracts between four airlines he liked—namely, American Airways, United Air Transport, Eastern Air Transport, and Transcontinental and Western Air—and left the others to either sell out to the "Big Four" or just go out of the airline business. Without airmail subsidies to gird their ledger books, they had no other choice.

The Airmail Crisis and Restoring the Status Quo

Postmaster Brown's heavy-handed actions set the stage for the Airmail Crisis of 1934. From the start, his actions raised protests inside and outside the airline industry. None had effect until Franklin Roosevelt became president in March 1933. Senate hearings into Brown's tactics were under way already and produced a report that rebuked the former postmaster and recommended handing the airmail routes to the Army Air Service until more proper proceedings could award new contracts to commercial carriers. In full accord with the Senate's recommendation, the new postmaster general, James Farley, persuaded the president to cancel all commercial airmail contracts and hand the job over to the Army on February 9, 1934. With only days to prepare, the Army found itself carrying the mail for the next several months. But equipped with combat aircraft and possessing few pilots trained for night and foul-weather operations, the Air Service's contribution proved to be expensive in lives and money. Twelve of the Air Service's pilots died carrying the mail. Economically, its efforts cost the government an average of $2.21 per aircraft mile flown, compared to $0.54 per mile paid to the carriers in 1933. In the end, events proved that Brown had been right: the country needed large and subsidized airlines if it wanted safe, reliable, and economically efficient airmail and air passenger services.

Congress bowed to reality in June 1934 by passing a new Air Mail Act, which empowered the postmaster general to award contracts "between points as he may designate . . . to the lowest responsible bidder." The proviso of "lowest *responsible* bidder" gave Farley broad powers to assign contract awards on the basis of criteria other than lowball bidding. When the dust finally settled, the Big Four once again ran the transcontinental and East Coast routes, though under slightly different corporate names and with different senior officers.

By 1935 the industry had stabilized on the lines drawn originally by Postmaster Brown: the government subsidized the carriers, which, in return, provided mail and passenger services along prescribed routes. Flying for government airmail contracts that paid only about half as much as those paid before 1934, the carriers didn't make big profits. But they stayed in business and were protected from competition, and passenger traffic surged. In 1935 the major airlines flew 314 million revenue passenger miles, with a rate of growth of about 20 percent for each of the next several years.[10]

The DC-3 and Protecting Vested Interests

The Douglas DC-3 upset Brown's tidy arrangements. Appearing in 1936, the soon-to-be-legendary plane threatened the ability of the post office to control competition through allocations of airmail contracts. Embracing a host of technologically advanced features—metal construction, retractable gear, deicing equipment, controllable-pitch propellers, streamlining, all-weather navigation equipment, and so on—the DC-3 could carry twenty-one passengers in reasonable comfort at about 140 knots. The net effect of all these features was that it was the first plane capable of carrying passengers at a profit, so long as it flew full or at least nearly full. Consequently, any new airline company equipped with DC-3s could challenge established companies for passenger traffic on any busy, or "cherry," route. In the face of such a potentially destructive frenzy of competition, the loose regulation of the industry through control of airmail contracts would soon become ineffective.

Seeking to encourage "the present and future needs of the foreign and domestic commerce of the United States, of the Postal Service, and of the national defense," Congress passed the 1938 Civil Aeronautics Act to regain control of competition within the airline industry. Still seeking to protect the Big Four and some regional carriers from unfettered competition, the act established the Civil Aeronautics Authority (CAA) and empowered it to set the "fair and reasonable" rates airlines could charge their customers. Furthermore, the new law gave the CAA authority to determine which airlines were "fit, willing, and able" to provide schedule service on any interstate route. Since only those carriers would receive the "certificates of common carriage" needed to operate on those routes, all other carriers would be locked out.[11] Blatantly anticompetitive, the Civil Aeronautics Act, in essence, set up the CAA as the board of directors for the airline industry, with broad powers over its corporate strategies, operations, and finances. Some complained. But others, like Edgar S. Gorrell, president of the Air Transport Association, declared, "The government could carry no more worthwhile activity than to encourage air transport efficiency as a national defense measure and peacetime necessity."[12]

Already growing rapidly, the airline industry did well under the tight regulation of the Civil Aeronautics Act. Passenger traffic increased almost logarithmically, reaching 1.4 billion passenger miles in 1940, roughly equal to four thousand transcontinental passenger boardings per day. Projections at the time called for the number of travelers to double in 1941.[13]

To handle this rapid market growth, the airlines and their manufacturing partners exploited their modest profits and guaranteed markets to finance development of a new generation of large, four-engine aircraft. For beauty and performance, the Boeing 314 flying boat was the queen of the airline fleet. Entering with Pan American World Airways with service between San Francisco and Hong Kong in January 1939, these "clippers" came with four 1,600-horsepower Wright engines. They could accommodate seventy-four day passengers or forty night passengers in great comfort, while cruising at 160 knots for up to 3,100 nautical miles. Then, in 1940, the Boeing 307 ushered in a new era of pressurized passenger aircraft able to fly "above the weather." Powered by 900-horsepower Wright engines, the 307 carried thirty-three passengers at 190 knots for up to 2,100 nautical miles. Finally, the DC-4 was just entering production when the Japanese attacked Pearl Harbor. Aerodynamically efficient and powered by

1,450-horsepower engines, the DC-4 cruised at 195 knots and could carry fifty passengers from San Francisco to Honolulu, the longest overwater route in the world without the possibility of an intermediate landing. The new Douglas plane was the first commercial aircraft that literally could go anywhere on the planet.

Thus, on the eve of its entry into World War II, the United States possessed a commercial airline industry that was large, technologically advanced, and operationally sophisticated. Through purposeful legislation, happenstance events, and technological progress, the country had come into possession of airline companies and equipment capable of moving large masses of people and matériel over great distances and of providing a mobilization reserve of pilots, mechanics, and airplanes in the early days of a war. The challenges facing military and governmental leaders were determining how to mobilize such an asset for greatest effect and then learning to leverage its unique capabilities to maximize its contribution to victory in a future war. But, at least, they had something to work with.

4. Military Air Transport in the 1930s

DURING THE 1930S army air corps leaders reversed the relationship between the air transport *doctrines* and the air transport *capabilities* of their service. At the start of the decade, they knew a lot more about the uses and operational nature of air transport than their tiny fleet of single- and three-engine cargo aircraft could handle. But transport aircraft technologies advanced profoundly in the coming years, spurred mainly by the rapid growth of the civil airline industry. From operating a few handfuls of Ford Tin Gooses and fabric-covered biplanes, the industry grew to hundreds of all-metal aircraft, mostly twin-engine Douglas DC-2s and DC-3s. The Army also acquired significant numbers of modern transports, mostly derivatives of the DC-2. But air corps leaders failed to build up a community of officers and technicians experienced with air transport and a body of appropriate doctrines. These failures limited the service's ability to exploit the full capabilities of air transport and to expand its air transport arm in the event of war. Thus, as World War II stalked nearer, America had unprecedented military air transport capabilities and potentials at hand, but army air corps leaders possessed only the most rudimentary ideas of how to use them.

Continued Experimentation and Discovery

As they had since 1927, air corps commanders continued to integrate air transport operations into their annual exercises. During the 1930 exercise, army transports provided deployment support and logistical air service from San Francisco and San Diego to Mather Field, near Sacramento, the main operating base for about 250 bombers and fighters defending against an "enemy" invasion.[1] In the next annual exercise, the Air Corps established a Provisional Air Transport Group of forty-eight aircraft to supply over 670 combat aircraft in their maneuvers from Dayton, Chicago, New York, Boston, Atlantic City, Philadelphia, and Washington, D.C.[2] In 1935, Major Byron Q. Jones choreographed the operations of eight transports to enable a provisional wing of twenty-nine bombardment and forty-four pursuit aircraft to shift their operating bases rapidly between Miami, Tampa, Tallahassee, New Orleans, and

Montgomery. Reporting on the exercise, Jones called for the acquisition of a large fleet of specialized military transports.[3] Following another exercise in 1937, Jones calculated that deployed fighter and bomber groups required 53 and 193 tons of aerial resupply per day, respectively, plus munitions and fuel. In a war involving many combat groups, Jones concluded that the Air Corps' small transport fleet fell well short of need.[4] His reports succinctly summarized two continuous themes of the use of air corps transports during this period. First, commanders employed them exclusively in support of maneuvering *air* combat forces, and second, there were never enough of them to go around.

The Airmail Crisis

It was a setup for disaster. On February 9, 1934, President Franklin Roosevelt gave the Army Air Corps just ten days to take over the national airmail system from the commercial airline industry. Scrambling to satisfy such an urgent tasking, Chief of the Army Air Corps Major General Benjamin Foulois and his staff faced daunting challenges.[5] They had no money; Congress had not yet made the necessary appropriation. Beginning with squadrons and groups concentrated at main bases, they had to disperse, operate, and supply people and planes in small packets at dozens of locations. The winter weather was unusually atrocious, and most army fliers were capable of flying only in the clear skies required for the conduct of combat operations. Air corps leaders anticipated these operational dangers and directed that the young pilots arriving at their airmail stations practice instrument flying and that the depots improve the instruments and radios in as many aircraft as possible. But ten days wasn't much time, so the small teams of airmen arriving at their stations came without proper clothing and equipment and had no per diem money for food and shelter or even tents and rations. The pilots generally took off in inadequately equipped aircraft and sometimes into stormy weather that pounded them right back out of the sky.

Fortunately for the nation, the Army's airmen were better than their leaders deserved. They set up operations in back rooms and spare offices, slept in hangars or the spare bedrooms of sympathetic citizens, and ran up tabs at greasy-spoon restaurants near their fields or simply heated cans of beans over blowtorches. Pilots flew in open-cockpit planes and suffered from extreme cold. One lieutenant, Norman Sillin, became hypothermic in minus-sixteen-degree weather, began hallucinating, and recovered only at the last moment to avert a crash. Twelve pilots died. But others flew nearly 15,000 hours with a 99.33 percent mission success rate and lost not a single piece of the public's mail.[6] When they could, pilots attended classes and made training flights to improve their foul-weather flying. Some benefited from management and training help provided by the very airlines they were supplanting. Others simply learned by doing and not dying in the process. Gradually, they matured their operation from one of unprepared risk taking to one approaching airline levels of regularity and safety. By May 8, when the commercial carriers began taking back the airmail under new contracts, most airmen felt that they had the problem well in hand and could have gone on indefinitely.

For all of the determination and skill of army fliers, however, anyone could see that the Air Corps had neither the right equipment nor the support and control facilities to conduct daily long-distance transport flights on a sustained basis. The service possessed few actual transport aircraft—a dozen or so single-engine Bellanca C-27s and a handful of trimotors—and used them to provide logistic support to dispersed units, not to actually fly the mail. One historian of the event suggests that the Army left these aircraft and their highly experienced enlisted pilots out because it didn't want the "embarrassing publicity" of having sergeants climb out of the cockpits of aircraft engaged in such an important mission.[7] It may also have been that C-27s and Ford trimotors simply were slower and shorter in range than the multiengine bombers and sleek pursuit and observation ships available in much larger numbers. Moreover, once junior officers flying those combat aircraft became proficient at foul-weather flying, the bombers and observation aircraft, but not the fighters, proved adequate to move the mail. Combat aircraft were, however, an expensive means for moving the mail. Prior to losing their contracts, airmail contractors were charging the government an average of $0.54 for each aircraft mile they flew, while the Army came in at $2.21 per mile. Air transport clearly wasn't a forte of the Air Corps.

Expanding Transport Capabilities

The War Department's initial response to the Air Corps' poor showing was to charter a study of its general condition and future requirements under the leadership of former secretary of war Newton Baker. While the Baker Board spent most of its time considering air warfare theories, combat aviation technologies, and the organizational relationship of the Air Corps to the Army, it also gave some attention to air transport. The board acknowledged the crucial role that air transport would play in future wars and called for significant expansion of the Air Corps' cargo fleet. Bowing to fiscal realities and the presumption that the principal role of air transport was to deploy and sustain air corps combat units, the board also recommended that the Army fill its requirements by purchasing commercial-type aircraft and/or by modifying bombers to carry cargo and passengers. Acquiring airliners and modifying bombers, the board believed, would provide suitable aircraft cost effectively and facilitate the mobilization and employment of the airlines in the event of a major war.[8]

The best commercial plane around was the DC-2. Compared to other transports available at the time, the DC-2 was a leap ahead in capacity, reliability, performance, and safety. The plane first flew in 1934. Powered by two 710-horsepower engines, it cruised at around 140 knots\ while carrying fourteen passengers or 3,600 pounds of cargo for about 900 miles. The DC-2's improved performance stemmed from the integration of these engines and a host of new technologies into a balanced design that included streamlined structure, NACA engine cowls, retractable gear, controllable-pitch propellers, deicing equipment, and modern navigation instruments. In combination, these features produced an aircraft unequalled in its ability to carry passengers and cargo over transcontinental distances in all but the foulest weather. In army air corps service, the plane could enhance the mobility and logistics of aviation combat forces anywhere in the country or within an overseas zone of operations. It may have been for the DC-3, a much-refined derivative of the DC-2, to revolutionize *commercial* air travel, with its unprecedented ability to carry passengers at a profit, but it was the DC-2 that projected *military* air transport into a new era.

The Army's confidence in the DC-2 translated into significant purchases from 1935 to 1939. In September 1935, the service acquired a test model in normal airline configuration that it designated the XC-32. Given its comfortable interior and seating, this aircraft became a flying office for senior commanders, complete with radios, office furniture, typewriters, and a buffet.[9] Satisfied that the plane met its promise, the Air Corps acquired eighteen DC-2s with stripped-down interiors that it designated C-33s and two more standard models for VIP travel, designated as C-34s. Equipped with a large loading door and cargo tie-down equipment, the C-33s were capable of carrying most of the field equipment and spare engines required by combat squadrons. Finally, the Army bought thirty-five C-39s in 1938 and 1939. These models came with 975-horsepower engines and could carry two tons of cargo for about 1,100 nautical miles.

Seeking an alternative to buying expensive commercial planes, air corps leaders directed the Materiel Division to explore the modification of bombers for duty as transports.[10] In response, the division modified a B-18 in 1937 for cargo operations. But the modifications actually cost more than a new C-32, and they produced an aircraft that was unsafe to fly. Although derived from the C-32—its wings, undercarriage, and engines were the same—the B-18's fuselage was designed to carry a dense load of bombs at its center of gravity, not a dispersed load of people or cargo. Following evaluation of the aircraft, General Augustine Robins, the Air Corps' Materiel Division commander, recommended that the Air Corps undertake the "regular procurement of transport planes" to meet its needs.[11]

While air corps leaders worked to expand the military transport fleet's capabilities affordably, the growing airline industry offered an obvious and otherwise unmatchable source of mobilization capacity, seemingly without cost. As early as 1925, the president's Air Policy Board declared that "commercial aeronautic activity . . . creates a reservoir of highly skilled pilots and ground personnel . . . [that] will make it easier to rapidly build up an expanded air power if an emergency arises."[12] Year after year, thereafter, government and private studies reaffirmed the likely value of the commercial industry in future wars.[13] Indeed, the 1938 Civil Aeronautics Act declared that the roles of the new Civil Aeronautics Authority were "the encouragement and development of an air transportation system properly adapted to the present and future needs of the foreign and domestic commerce of the United States, of the Postal Service, and of the national defense."[14] Flying some 500 aircraft and boarding 1.6 million passengers in 1938, the airline industry's mobilization value was unmistakable.

Naturally enough, industry and military leaders approached the mobilization issue from different perspectives. As experts in getting the most productivity from their aircraft, airline executives sought a plan that kept their companies intact and serving future war efforts through military contracts. This was the plan put forward by Edgar S. Gorrell, the president of the Air Transport Association, in 1938. Gorrell's plan maintained the corporate integrity of the airline companies but placed all of their personnel and resources under military direction, either directly through contracting or indirectly through the establishment of priority lists to control their use.[15] Informally, the War Department offered a different plan. Although never endorsed officially, its planners called for full impressment of the airlines into military service at the beginning of the next war. From a military perspective, this approach offered assurance that airline personnel would do their duties reliably in the face of combat, since they would be functioning under military discipline. Essentially, the airlines would disappear as commercial organizations for the duration of a conflict. Given the fundamental conflict between these industry and military mobilization concepts, the War Department seemed to have shelved its transport mobilization planning until the actual start of the war, probably to concentrate on issues that the looming war made more pressing.[16]

As the size and capabilities of the air transport fleet grew, Materiel Division commanders continued to centralize their control over operations and to reinforce the manning of their transport units. In 1932 Brigadier General H. Conger Pratt organized four transport squadrons, each assigned to a major depot and operating three planes. The aircraft available to these units were capable only of linking their depots with airfields in their regions of service. Inter-depot and long-distance transportation was accomplished by rail, which was cheaper, more reliable, and often faster.[17] Over the next several years, General Pratt and his successor, General Robins, increased the authorized strengths of these depot squadrons several times.[18] Recognizing the need for efficient management of the increasingly capable fleet of DC-2 derivative aircraft, the assistant chief of the Air Corps, General Henry H. (Hap) Arnold, consolidated these squadrons into the 10th Air Transport Group in April 1937.[19]

Things Not Done: Doctrine and Personnel

Army airmen in the 1930s only rarely spared systematic thought for air transport. No official army or air corps publication discussed air transport in any level of detail beyond, perhaps, mentioning its importance. At the Air Corps Tactical School, where the service trained its future leaders, only one student seems to have chosen transport aviation as his research topic.[20] Few authoritative airmen wrote on the issue with any rigor. B. Q. Jones, Augustine Robins, Conger Pratt, Hap Arnold, and a few staff officers probably filled the list. For airmen, it seems, transport aviation was too simple a concept to merit much intellectual energy. In their minds, it had only two missions: supporting the maneuvers of combat squadrons and linking them to their bases of supply and command. The simplicity of that perspective did not produce the conflicting priorities, issues of ownership, and complex tactical procedures that tend to inspire most doctrinal writing.

General Arnold was the most important contributor to discussions about air transport during the latter part of the decade, and he didn't say much. In 1938 he declared, "Air transport is absolutely essential for the operation of the Air Corps . . . [so] it behooves the Air Corps to organize, train, and equip at least a nucleus of this organization for peace operations."[21] A few years later, now as chief of the Army Air Forces (AAF), Arnold declared, "The cargo plane . . . must always be considered as an integral and important part of any well-rounded and completely developed air force."[22] Beyond these general declarations, however, Arnold wrote nothing about tactics, logistics, operational priorities, manning, or the host of other issues important to effective operations. Thus, on the eve of war, virtually all of the Air Corps' experience with and knowledge of air transport resided mainly in the heads of the small body of airmen and officers actually flying and maintaining transports.

The rub was that almost all of the people flying and maintaining army transports were from the enlisted ranks, apart from a handful of mid-grade officers directing them on a part-time basis. All of the pilots permanently assigned to the Materiel Division's transport squadrons and the 10th Air Transport Group were sergeants. Sergeants more often than not also flew the transports assigned to field units. They were a sort of underclass of "hack" pilots who seldom held billets in combat aircraft; instead, they flew transport "milk runs," towed aerial targets, flight tested repaired aircraft, and so on.[23] When an officer flew a transport in those days, he usually did so as a lark, to run some sort of experiment, or, if he was young, perhaps to build a little flight experience under the tutelage of a seasoned sergeant.

Air corps leaders saw the concentration of its enlisted pilots in transport squadrons as natural and desirable. Sergeant pilots, with their lower pay scales, were a necessity in the impoverished Air Corps. But given the social and professional gaps between them, the Army preferred to separate sergeant and officer pilots as much as possible. Officers flew as "knights of the air" in bombers and fighters, while sergeant pilots flew unglamorous transports.[24] In truth, army leaders viewed transport flying as beneath the dignity of good officers. In 1925 the Air Corps' chief of personnel dismissed plans to commission mobilized airline pilots, pointing out that they would require significant training in formation flying, tactics, and "general military principles" before they would be suitable for service. He went on to say that the service already had plenty of old pilots available to fly its few transports. Years later, General Arnold condescended to not-so-skilled student pilots that "not every pilot can measure up to the standards required of our fighter pilots . . . it takes a little more aggressiveness and a slightly quicker reaction time to fly single-seaters than big planes."[25] Put in unadorned terms, the Air Corps put sergeant pilots and old officers into transport units because it thought this simple and lackluster mission was suited to their unscrubbed natures and/or declining skills.

There were two predictable consequences of concentrating sergeant pilots into transport units. The first was that these sergeants became excellent pilots, flying for years longer than typical officer pilots, who often were diverted into staff and educational assignments where they flew little, if at all. Epitomizing the skills of sergeant pilots, the eight enlisted pilots of the 3rd Transport Squadron flew their new C-33s for 5,511 hours in 1936–1937 without a single accident or loss of a passenger.[26] They made this record at a time when the airlines were in the midst of a major safety crisis while flying the same type of aircraft. The second consequence was that the Army was approaching a new world war without the personnel foundation for a balanced expansion on a large scale. There were no deeply experienced mid-grade officers, majors, and lieutenant colonels ready to rise to command transport groups or fill senior staff. There also were no lieutenants or captains prepared by their educations and experience to set up and lead new line squadrons and training units. The sergeants were there, of course. They were dedicated and skilled fliers, but they had not undergone the university, tactical school, exercise leadership, or other forms of professional education and experience that normally went into the preparation of a junior officer for command. When war came, therefore, the Air Corps would have to build its air transport forces on the foundation of a small number of technical experts and a scratch team of leaders with little or no experience in such operations.

By 1939 the Air Corps controlled a fleet of markedly more effective aircraft than it had at the start of the decade, and the Materiel Division had centralized its control and management arrangements substantially. But there weren't enough of these aircraft to meet wartime requirements, and no arrangements were in place to mobilize the airline industry to make up the shortfall. Of even greater portent for future mobilization, the Air Corps had not nurtured the rise of a professionally balanced body of experts or the doctrinal guidance needed to expand its airlift arm rapidly and cohesively. These shortfalls in the matériel and human requirements for war would shape the expansion of American airlift forces throughout World War II and for decades thereafter.

5. Mobilizing Air Transport for Global War

AMERICAN AIR TRANSPORT capabilities grew more proportionately than any other arm of military airpower during World War II. In 1940 the Army Air Corps and the Navy possessed decades of experience in combat aviation—pursuit, attack, and bombardment—and they had operational units, training exercises, and doctrine libraries to show for it. Nothing similar existed for air transport. The Air Corps possessed fewer than a hundred transport aircraft, flown mostly by sergeants, while the Navy and Marine Corps together fielded fewer than twenty modern cargo planes. Neither the Army nor the naval services possessed a body of senior officers experienced in such operations. Yet by 1945, the United States would field around 8,000 transport aircraft in numerous commands, flying passengers and piece cargo all over the world, parachuting whole divisions behind enemy lines, and even keeping an entire country, China, in the war. By then air transportation was an integral feature of modern war.

As War Loomed

In 1940 the Army Air Corps' air transport organization was grounded on two informal doctrines. The first was that the primary mission of air transport was to enhance the mobility of bomber, pursuit, and attack units. When combat units moved to new fields, their crews flew their planes, and transport units brought along their ground personnel, tentage, tools, spare parts, rations, and the other impedimenta needed to start operations on arrival. Once ground lines of supply caught up with these units, air transport continued to link them to rear area depots, headquarters, hospitals, and the like. The second informal doctrine thought these "tactical" and "supply train" missions differed enough from each other to justify the establishment of separate organizations and chains of command to accomplish them.[1] Accordingly, the 10th Air Transport Group operated about thirty new C-39s to provide lift for unit moves and link air corps supply depots to field units. Meanwhile the tactical command of the Air Corps, General Headquarters Air Force (GHQ AF), allocated its older C-33s in ones or twos to each of its nine combat groups to provide on-call linkage to rear area support. Area commands in Hawaii, Panama, and the Philippines and GHQ AF also possessed small flights of transports for their use.[2]

Preparations for likely involvement in the expanding war in Europe brought changes to the Army's air transport program. The most obvious change was an increasing flow of new aircraft into the service, with 164 delivered in 1940 and 745 more ordered for 1941.[3] Most of these new aircraft were C-47s, military versions of the DC-3, and larger C-46s, derived from the Curtiss CW-20 airliner. To accommodate so many new aircraft, the Air Corps activated two air transport groups, the 62nd and 63rd, in January 1941 and placed them and the 10th Air Transport Group under the 50th Air Transport Wing, which also stood up at that time. Furthermore, in the late spring of 1941, General Henry H. (Hap) Arnold, the chief of the Air Corps, activated the Air Corps Ferrying Command to assist with the delivery of American-built aircraft through Canada and on to Britain and, later, Russia. Beginning in July, Ferrying Command also flew about a half dozen flights per month between the United States and Britain, mostly carrying returning ferry pilots and military and civil leaders on observation and diplomatic missions. The command used modified B-24 bombers for these flights. Chosen because of their long range, these aircraft came equipped with plywood floors and metal bucket seats carefully designed, it seemed, to torment their bundled passengers in freezing discomfort as they crossed the North Atlantic.

The Army's experimentation with parachute troops pushed the Air Corps into a new mission of airlifting airborne units, perhaps whole divisions, into battle. This was a large mission, one that could require acquisition of thousands of specialized transports and development of the new doctrines, equipment, and tactics needed to put paratroops on the ground quickly and in fighting condition. No one in the Army Air Corps knew how to do that. Apart from some brief and very small-scale experiments by General William (Billy) Mitchell right after World War I, no one had explored the concept between the wars. Nevertheless, General Arnold shared the Army's new vision that delivering infantry by parachute or by landing aircraft behind enemy lines would be an important part of future war.[4] Accordingly, he activated a new organization, the Air Transport Command, on April 30, 1941, and assigned to it the entire 50th Air Transport Wing with the dual missions of airlifting parachute units and enhancing the mobility of air combat units.

Establishing Air Transport Forces in the Frenzy of War

Only days after the Japanese attack on Pearl Harbor, the Navy took the first big step to expand its transport forces for war by activating the Naval Air Transport Service (NATS) on December 12. Building from a small number of DC-2s and amphibian patrol bombers, NATS steadily expanded with the additions of mobilized airline personnel, including several senior executives; all of the big flying boats of Pan American Airlines; and land planes taken up from the airlines and other sources. Its first two squadrons, VR-1 and VR-2, were activated in March and April, respectively, and VR-2 was flying from California to Hawaii in May. By war's end, NATS grew to ten transport squadrons, distributed among its Hawaiian, West Coast, and Atlantic wings. At its peak, the service included over 26,000 military and civilian personnel operating 540 aircraft predominantly over the Pacific but also over the Atlantic and down into Latin America.[5]

The real priority at the time was getting the hundreds of modern transports and thousands of skilled personnel of the commercial airlines into the war effort, and fortunately there was a plan. In preparation for mobilization, Edgar S. Gorrell, the president of the Air Transport Association, and General Arnold had been collaborating informally since 1936 on a plan to bring airliners into the war effort with as little as twenty-four hours' notice.[6] While all of the presidents of the big carriers supported the plan, its strongest proponents were Edward (Eddie) Rickenbacker, a Medal of Honor fighter pilot in World War I and the president of Eastern Airlines, and Cyrus R. Smith, the president of American Airlines.[7] At its core, the Gorrell-Arnold plan presumed that the airlines could give their best service if they remained organizationally intact and under their civilian managers. Those managers would operate their companies under contract on routes and schedules and in accordance with priorities set by the military. Arnold's satisfaction with the airlines' response to the military's initial calls for support and his confidence in the airline presidents were such that he made no effort to draft any part of the industry.[8] The airlines repaid General Arnold's confidence by putting themselves and their resources at the military's convenience from the first day of the war.

Despite the willing contributions of the airlines, War Department planners sought initially to draft them wholesale. Seeking immediate support from the industry, Secretary of War Henry Stimson sent a draft executive order to President Roosevelt authorizing a call-up of whichever parts of the airline industry the military deemed necessary.[9] Arnold and Gorrell intervened with the president on December 13, as the order lay signed on his desk. Convinced by their arguments, Roosevelt tore up the paper and allowed the Army, Navy, and airlines a free hand to work out contractual arrangements for airline mobilization. But when it became obvious in the following April that some airline personnel and aircraft were needed to prime the establishment and/or expansion of army and navy air transport commands, the president authorized the military to draft all but 200 of the airline industry's DC-3s.[10]

In return for control of the manner in which airline resources were mobilized, Gorrell offered a balanced call-up that would preserve the productivity of the airlines for the war effort and also provide the personnel and planes needed to jump-start the military's air transport units. To begin the process, senior airline executives met at the Wings Club in New York and either volunteered up front or drew lots to see who would go into uniform to help the military organize its global air transport system. Over thirty went into service immediately; others went later.[11] Cyrus Smith supervised the execution of Gorrell's plan and then put on an army air forces uniform himself. Later, when the president ordered the partial call-up of their aircraft in April 1942, industry leaders essentially acted as their own draft boards, determining which of their flight, maintenance, and support personnel would enter service or remain in airline "colors." Most of the industry's major repair facilities also went into military service, repairing the planes of their parent airlines only when military demands allowed. By June the airlines actually had exceeded the president's directive by selling 193 of their prewar stock of 359 DC-3s to the Army, Navy, and Marine Corps.[12]

By the summer of 1942, it was time to organize the Air Force's long-range air transport more appropriately for America's increasingly global involvement in the war. Although not organized or supplied with the headquarters staff and field facilities to perform the task, Ferrying Command continued to function as the long-range air transport arm of the Army Air Forces, which had replaced the Air Corps in the summer of 1941. With robust assistance from the commercial carriers, the command opened and/or expanded routes from the United States to Alaska, Australia, Europe, Latin America, North Africa, and India. But the task was becoming overwhelming, and cargo was backing up at Ferrying Command bases. So in June 1942, General Arnold activated a *second* Air Transport Command consisting of separate divisions for ferry operations and air transport. To give the command the expertise needed to mobilize what in essence was a military airline, Arnold gave command of the Air Transport

Command to Brigadier General Harold Lee (Hal) George, a noted air planner and bomber commander, and enticed Cyrus Smith to take leave from American Airlines and become George's deputy. In Arnold's view, "the two officers complemented each other in ability, experience, and judgment—they made a perfect team."[13]

The activation of a second Air Transport Command in June 1942 obliged the Air Force to do something about the one established in January 1941 to train army paratroopers. General Arnold was ambivalent about even continuing an organization that demanded so many resources and was dedicated to such a specialized mission. There is no direct historical record of where his thinking was going at this time, but he did have the old 10th Air Transport Group as a possible model to guide his thoughts. If the 10th Air Transport Group could carry the dual missions of providing general logistics support and mobility support for air corps field units, then perhaps the new Air Transport Command could provide both global logistics and on-call support for parachute units in overseas theaters. Whatever Arnold's thoughts on the matter, his executive officer, Lieutenant Colonel Ray Dunn, rendered them moot. An enthusiast for air transport—he had helped design the Army Airways system in the early 1920s and set up the Materiel Division's first air cargo operations a decade later—Dunn signed an order establishing I Troop Carrier Command (I TCC) while Arnold was away on a trip. Angry, Arnold banished Dunn from the Pentagon. But the Army was too deeply committed to its new airborne divisions for him to reverse the action.[14]

Activating on July 1, 1942, I TCC had two missions: supporting paratroop training in the United States and preparing other troop carrier units for deployment overseas. Based at Stout Field, Indiana, I TCC ultimately organized six troop carrier wings (TCWs). Four—the 50th, 51st, 52nd, and 53rd—served overseas while the 60th and 61st stayed in the States to command troop carrier training units and groups organizing for overseas service. An additional wing, the 54th, activated in the Southwest Pacific theater to consolidate operational control over a number of squadrons and groups operating there already. Once these units arrived in a combat theater, they fell under the troop carrier command assigned to the numbered air force conducting operations there. For example, when the 52nd TCW deployed to North Africa in May 1942, it became part of the XII TCC of the 12th Air Force. Later, in February 1944, the wing relocated to England and passed to the IX TCC or the 9th Air Force. The strength of troop carrier commands and wings rose and fell as the Army Air Forces headquarters added or subtracted troop carrier groups (TCGs) from them in keeping with the evolution of combat operations in their theaters. In all, the Army Air Forces activated twenty-eight TCGs during the war, plus four smaller combat cargo groups in the China-Burma-India theater of operations.[15] On average, each group fielded about 100 transport aircraft and 1,800 officers and men for the troop carrier groups, and about half that many for combat cargo groups, which came with very small maintenance establishments.[16]

The marines also developed an air transport arm during the war. By participating in the draft of airline pilots and aircraft in the spring of 1942, the marine air transport force grew from two DC-2s and a handful of smaller aircraft to several squadrons in just a few months. The initial echelon went into Marine Air Group 15, which trained transport crews for overseas duty and provided lift for the 1st Marine Parachute Regiment that was then in the process of working up. By May, Marine Transport Squadron (VMJ)-253—a small squadron of C-47s and seaplanes—was flying between Hawaii, Midway, and other points in the mid Pacific. VMJ-142 activated in the Southwest Pacific in June, just in time to support marine operations in Guadalcanal. As the war progressed, the marine air transport fleet in the Pacific grew to six squadrons, plus the usual scattering of aircraft assigned directly to combat air groups and headquarters units. By 1945 these units all fell under an air transport group. But, along the way, marine transport squadrons also were attached to small Combat Air Transport Commands organized for the Southwest Pacific, later the Solomon Islands (SCAT), the Central Pacific (CenCATS), and briefly the Samoan area (also SCAT).[17]

The Logic of Duplication

Although the rapid stand up of so many air transport commands, units, and service elements produced much operational duplication and inefficiency, it made more organizational sense at the time than might be obvious in hindsight. Most important, interservice cooperation was an unrefined art in the early 1940s. Until that time in American military history, coastlines demarcated distinct operational zones for the Army and Navy. Except for amphibious operations, with which the United States had little experience, naval transport of army supplies, and perhaps the coastal defense of the United States, the two services rarely intermingled operationally or logistically. So when the time came to set up air transport units in the rush and confusion of war, both services and their principal subordinate units, the Army Air Forces and the Marine Corps, naturally enough viewed them as extensions of their normal organic logistics arrangements. Under those circumstances, the overlapping routes and base infrastructures of the Air Transport Command and NATS and the potential operational overlaps between marine and troop carrier commands in the Pacific were less important than establishing operations expeditiously and in accordance with the organizational and doctrinal cultures of each service.

Technology also reinforced the logic of the Army's and Navy's fractionated organization of air transport. During the war, the U.S. military took delivery of about 14,000 large transports (C-46s, C-47s, and C-54s) and another 9,000 miscellaneous and smaller designs.[18] There were, consequently, a lot of aircraft to go around and little incentive to save a few aircraft by consolidating large organizations that most senior commanders thought of as naturally separate. Furthermore, the principal operational advantages of consolidation, flexibility, and mutual support weren't practical. Generally, the available aircraft didn't have the "legs" to shift rapidly between theaters. The theater mainstay, the C-47, had a maximum ferry range of about 1,500 miles at 140 knots. Also, since the support echelons of C-47s moved by surface means, movements of complete units could take months, regardless of how far and fast their aircraft flew. Last, it was doubtful that the radio teletype and grease board command-and-control "systems" available could have planned and directed such agile transtheater operations if anyone had tried.

So the United States organized its transport forces for World War II in a rush and on the basis of expediency. The result was a hodgepodge of units serving specific services and commands and probably hundreds of penny-packet flights of smaller aircraft attached to headquarters units, logistics commands, hospitals, communications units, and so on. At least in the minds of the people rushing to fight the Axis powers, the inherent wastage of this setup was a small price to pay in return for expedient and reliable access to a suddenly indispensable new capability.

6. Air Transport in World War II

"MORE, PERHAPS, THAN any other single organization," wrote the Air Transport Command (ATC) historian, "the Command reflected the global character of the war."[1] He could have been writing just as well for the Naval Air Transport Service (NATS). Among the major operational commands of the Army and the Navy, ATC and NATS were the only ones with planning and operational purviews that extended around the globe. In contrast to theater-assigned combat air forces, fleets, and land forces, the aircraft and personnel of the two organizations moved routinely across theater boundaries to link them to the homeland and one another. Air transport routes and planes stretched out to wherever military operations required, and the weight of the global transport effort could shift just as quickly as theater battle tempos rose and fell across the globe. Thus, while most combat commanders necessarily focused on events within their areas of operations, NATS and especially ATC leaders watched the whole war and managed their commands and resources in response to the grand strategies of the Joint Chiefs of Staff in Washington.[2]

The Airline Contribution

As discussed in the previous chapter, the airlines stood ready under the Gorrell-Arnold plan to mobilize wholesale for military service at the outbreak of hostilities. But integration of the airlines into the defense effort began even before the United States entered the war actively. Beginning in February 1940, Pan American Airways employees were opening and/or expanding a string of bases down the Atlantic coast of South America with an eye to immediate commercial and later military needs.[3] This secret effort expanded in August 1941, when the War Department contracted Pan Am to open a ferry and air transport route from Lagos, Nigeria, to Khartoum, Sudan. At the outbreak of hostilities, the industry executed the Gorrell-Arnold plan. Within days, the airlines were flying routes and booking passengers in accordance with military directions and priorities. The Army and the Navy impressed all fifteen four-engine seaplanes and land planes in commercial service but contracted their original civilian crews to fly them. Gradually, the military brought increments of aircraft and airline personnel into military service. By June 1942, about half of the approximately 450 two-engine airliners were available, and thousands of pilots, mechanics, and staff personnel were in uniform.[4] The airlines also dedicated their heavy maintenance depots to military use and opened up several schools for mechanics and pilots learning to fly large aircraft in instrument conditions. To minimize disruption of the civil airline service in the United States, the Army and the Navy allowed airline executives to manage most of the mobilization process themselves, determining which aircraft and even which employees entered the service. Following their planes and people, about seventy senior executives volunteered for military service, often being commissioned as senior unit commanders and staffers at ATC and NATS headquarters. These included Cyrus Smith and Robert Six, president of Continental Airlines. Two board chairmen, twelve vice presidents, and three airline regional managers went into service as well. NATS got four vice presidents and Commander Clarence H. Schildhauer, a navy reservist, record-holder seaplane pilot, and Pan American operations manager.[5]

The infusion of commercial personnel into ATC and NATS was natural, since both would function essentially as military airlines. Their role would be to move passengers, mail, delicate equipment, medical supplies, and other high-value piece cargoes through a global route system connecting the far-flung military forces of the United States. Airline executives knew, and military air transport leaders would soon learn, that transport aircraft gave their best service in such operations when flown individually, safely, for as many hours per day as possible, and on schedules designed to use maintenance and support facilities efficiently. Individual aircraft keeping schedules facilitated the efficient use of ground-support personnel and facilities. Safety was essential to preserve people and aircraft for the long haul.[6] Heightened emphasis on safety was possible, because few transport missions were so essential that they could not be delayed for a day or so until technical problems could be fixed, weather got better, or the military situation along their routes improved. This mind-set of managing a fleet for long-term productivity did not come naturally to military airmen used to taking great risks to accomplish life-or-death missions in their fighters and bombers. But it was second nature to airline operators and completely appropriate to all but the most exceptional transport operations of ATC and NATS.

The quest for long-term productivity brought airline operating techniques into ATC and NATS that were distinct within the general realm of military aviation. Their operating patterns and resulting manning levels were a particularly thorny issue. Most combat units flew as units in surges. A fighter escort squadron, for example, might fly an eight-hour mission every few days or so. In between, its pilots would rest, and its mechanics would repair and service aircraft for the next mission. Consequently, such a unit would be manned with one pilot and a handful of mechanics and armorers per aircraft. In comparison, a transport unit was a black hole for personnel. The modern aircraft available to ATC and NATS, with their all-metal construction, reliable engines, and poor-weather navigation capabilities, could fly a lot of hours. But over time individual pilots were capable of flying an average of only two or three hours per day. They might fly twelve hours on a given day. But rest periods, leave times, sickness, and mandatory safety limits sharply reduced their availability. Thus, to get the most from their aircraft, ATC and NATS learned from the airlines to man their units with three or four crews per plane and enough mechanics to keep them in the air. ATC and NATS also quickly distinguished themselves by adopting safety standards that were exceptional within the general military culture of the time, though common to the airlines. As the war progressed, ATC achieved accident rates that were less than half of those for heavy bombers and as little as a tenth of those for fighters and light bombers.[7]

The global perspectives and commercial practices of ATC and NATS created some friction with their counterparts in the combat theaters. Combat commanders accustomed to the single pilot/crew manning of fighter and bomber units complained often about the diversion of so many aircrew and maintenance personnel to transport units. In the press of combat, overseas commanders also took to shanghaiing transport aircraft, using them for their own missions. This practice obliged the Army Air Forces and the War Department to issue several directives ordering local commanders to let ATC aircraft pass through their areas unmolested.[8] Commanders also viewed the transport community's focus on safety as an inappropriate import from the airlines that pampered crews and reduced available airlift support. The common sight of transport crews enjoying the comfort, safety, and recreational opportunities at the established bases and exotic towns along their routes only increased commanders' umbrage. Worse for the reputation of transport crews was the sight of them winging back to the homeland, as the passengers they had just dropped off at forward fields prepared to move ever closer to their destinies in the combat zones. The common perception that transport crews had things a little too cushy was reflected in irreverent renderings of ATC and NATS as "Association of Terrified Civilians" and "Never Around Tough Situations," respectively.

In reality, transport flying was dangerous in World War II. Natural hazards were bad enough. Airplanes often disappeared on long and lonely flights over the oceans and inhospitable jungles, deserts, tundra, and ice caps that stretched below them. Every ATC command eventually stood up rescue services and survival schools for its crewmen. Transport crews also faced military hazards when they flew near or even over enemy-controlled areas. German submarines broadcast bogus navigation signals to draw transports away from remote Ascension Island, a refueling point in the South Atlantic, and North Atlantic bases in Greenland and Iceland. The ditty "If I don't make Ascension, my wife will get my pension" was born in these times. Japanese fighters shot down dozens of aircraft over the jungles of Burma, and German patrol aircraft got a few over the North Atlantic. Here and there, ATC aircraft were fired on and sometimes shot down by Allied ships at sea or intercepting fighters. Unfortunately for the reputations of transport crewmen, most things happened well away from witnesses who could report their loss or give credit for their sacrifice. Bomber crewmen and fighter pilots might go down before the eyes of squadron mates in battle formations. Transport crews often just didn't make their next stop.

The Hump

The air movement of troops and matériel over the Himalayan "Hump," between India's Assam Province and western China, was the penultimate example of how ATC operated. This was a vital operation, since the Hump air bridge was the only means of moving war matériel and personnel to Chinese and American combat units operating in the region. The American 10th Air Force began the airlift in the spring of 1942. Augmented by fresh drafts of airline personnel and aircraft that summer, the 10th overcame daunting barriers of poor logistical support and appalling weather to reach a throughput of about 1,000 tons per *month* by the fall. In November 1942 ATC received responsibility for the route. The command sent out a succession of its best commanders and such resources as it could scrape together to increase throughput.[9] One after the other, the commanders wore out, and their personnel endured appalling living conditions, malaria, and polluted drinking water and local foods that knotted their guts to raise the daily lift to around 1,000 tons per *day* by the fall of 1944.[10] They paid a high price, as hundreds of planes and crews were lost to nightmare winds and turbulence over the mountains, stalking Japanese fighters, and poor flying and decision making born of exhaustion, hypoxia, disease, and flagging morale. Then, when ATC's India-China Division seemed near a break down, Tunner arrived.

Brigadier General William H. Tunner was a phenomenon. Three years before arriving in India, he was a captain in an obscure posting at army air corps headquarters. But he had a reputation as a hard-charging doer who was unintimidated by rank and who put in man-killing weekdays at his desk and then took a break by ferrying aircraft back and forth across the country on the weekends. Frankly, he was a workaholic and unsympathetic to those who weren't. Colonel Robert Olds snatched Tunner in the summer of 1941, putting him to work coordinating the daily flight operations of the new Ferrying Command. Energetic and brash, Tunner quickly rose in responsibilities and rank. When ATC stood up in June 1942 under the command of Major General Hal George, Colonel Tunner commanded its Ferrying Division; he was thirty-six years old and in charge of a global operation with 50,000 members, including over 8,000 pilots. Married with two sons, he might as well have been overseas, since he worked fifteen-hour days, never took a day off, traveled continually, and learned rapidly from experience and the airline executives that flowed into ATC headquarters.[11]

Perhaps nothing illustrated Tunner's unblinking focus on accomplishing his mission more than the role he played in bringing women into military flying. Beginning in late 1939, the famous aviator Jacqueline Cochran pestered General Arnold to use her and other women pilots to ferry aircraft for the Army Air Corps. Recognizing the contemporary social mores such an action would challenge, the air corps commander demurred for over two years, despite a growing shortage of male pilots. Meanwhile, in the summer of 1942, Nancy Harkness Love, a pilot and wife of an ATC staff officer, made a similar appeal to General George and General Tunner. Tunner, struggling every day to find competent or at least nearly competent pilots to ferry the thousands of aircraft coming out of American factories, and hardly a slave to social convention, was a ready convert to Love's vision.[12] Thus, after a few more months of dithering at air force headquarters, the first class of women began training as ferry pilots in the fall of 1942, and 1,074 ultimately would serve as Women Airforce Service Pilots (WASPs). Initially, the Air Force allowed new graduates to fly only trainers and small liaison aircraft. But the women proved their skills quickly, and their duties expanded to include ferrying combat aircraft, towing aerial targets, conducting flight tests, operating aerial drones, and testing new flight-training syllabi. There was danger in the mission, of course. Thirty-seven WASPs died in training and operational accidents, and another thirty-six were injured.

Despite the service of the WASPs, Congress blocked the Air Force's efforts in the summer of 1944 to induct the WASPs into active service with officer commissions similar to those held by army nurses.[13] The problem wasn't that the WASPs weren't doing a good job. Official air force studies would verify what anyone connected directly with these women knew already: they were physically capable of flying anything the Air Force had, and they performed their duties as well as male pilots did.[14] But WASP pilots had the bad luck of being women holding jobs that men suddenly wanted. As ever-larger groups of pilots returned to the States from completed combat tours, the Air Force needed places to put them. At the same time, the steady reduction of pilot training after mid-1944 released thousands of civilian pilots from their flight school positions and, it followed, from their draft deferments. Suddenly faced with the prospect of finding new civilian flying jobs with the military or being drafted into the infantry, these pilots became vociferous in their defamatory criticisms of the WASPs and the "injustice" of letting these women fly when men were available to take over. Their complaints played into the hands of several congressmen and newspaper columnists critical of the moral dangers of pants-wearing women flying military aircraft, now that the emergency of the war's early days was past. General Tunner and his boss, General George, fought hard for the program but were silenced eventually by General Arnold, who saw the writing on the wall.[15] Arnold disbanded the WASPs in December 1944, even as he acknowledged that they could "handle our fastest fighters, our heaviest bombers . . . [and were] capable of . . . countless other activities."[16] Officially never more than civilian contract employees, the women went home at their own expense and received no military recognition, honors, or benefits. But for two years they were a mainstay of ATC's success.

By the time the WASP program entered history, Tunner was the unchallenged expert on aircraft ferrying operations and had learned a lot about transport flying. Everyone knew he was a bit mercurial, but he always got things done, no matter the challenges. Consequently, he was ATC's best choice to take over the troubled Hump operation. Still, Tunner was surprised and dismayed when General George gave him the mission. Like many in the command, the young brigadier general viewed the India-China Division as an operational backwater, a dumping ground for misfit officers and men and a potential graveyard for the career of an otherwise promising officer. He also knew that under the prevailing circumstances, the simultaneous challenges of increasing tonnage on the route and improving safety "could be considered diametrically opposed to each other." But always a good soldier, he submitted gracefully and took the assignment.[17]

The general found his new command in crisis. Despite the best efforts of his predecessors and their men, the grueling pace, high accident rate, heat, rain, bad food, and demeaning living conditions of the operation had beaten them down. His immediate subordinates were demoralized and working at cross-purposes. Junior officers and enlisted personnel were unkempt, even unwashed, and tired to the point of being numb to their conditions and to military courtesies, and their productivity was in decline. The India-China Division operated an inadequate fleet of aircraft. Its mainstay was the two-engine Curtiss C-46 Commando, which could carry four to six tons across the mountains. But it was difficult to fly and often was a death trap when an engine failed. The only four-engine aircraft on the route were modifications of the B-24, the C-87 for cargo and passengers, and the C-109 for carrying fuel. They carried about the same payloads as the C-46 but were difficult to fly, and the C-109s had such a reputation for blowing up in the air that they had an unofficial designation as "C-One-o-Booms." On top of everything, more senior air commanders in the theater were demanding an immediate increase in tonnage, even if that meant subjecting Tunner's crews to higher accident rates.[18]

Even without the additional pressure, the Hump was a dangerous place to fly. Accidents and aircraft disappearances were daily events, with as many as nine in a single day of particularly bad weather. Hump pilot Otha Spencer captured the violence of the weather: "Suddenly, the plane shuddered and almost rolled over . . . fifty- and sometimes hundred-mile-an-hour winds created violent updrafts in the mountains . . . we were thrown five hundred feet upward . . . a downdraft dropped the plane back down to twenty thousand . . . sometimes planes were broken in two and we read about it on the operations bulletin board."[19] Going down in the jungle carried its own terrors; getting out could be a nightmare of walking for days, while hungry and evading Japanese patrols. Tunner was troubled in particular by the fate of one young crewman who, having parachuted from his plane and become suspended from a tree upside down and attacked by ants, finally shot himself.[20] To improve everyone's chances, Tunner directed the activation of jungle survival schools at each of his bases and assigned several of his best crews and flight surgeons to a jungle rescue service. Even then, the Hump swallowed at least 590 aircraft and 1,659 crewmen. Almost 1,200 other crewmen went down, but they were recovered.

Tunner charged into his new command with characteristic energy and impatience. He saw that the deteriorating state of the airlift was the sum of many small and big problems, and he wanted them all fixed, now! Addressing his human problems from his first day in charge, he drove his base and unit commanders to build new living quarters, clean up and drain cantonment areas, improve messing facilities, stock base exchanges with more necessities and minor luxuries, and do whatever else they could do to make life in the theater more bearable. By clarifying and enforcing the rotation policy, he quickly sent the most exhausted and demoralized individuals home and gave all others firm and fair return dates. In return for improving their living conditions, the general demanded good order, military courtesies, pride, and disciplined flying from his officers and men. To get the most from his aircraft, Tunner initiated production line maintenance, a process in which tractors towed aircraft through a series of cleaning, maintenance, servicing, and loading stations to get them ready for their next missions as quickly as possible.[21] Better rested crews and robust maintenance ultimately allowed the India-China Division to get an average of 11.7 flight hours per day from its C-54s and similar utilization rates out of its other aircraft. Tonnage over the Hump went up steadily, reaching 71,042 tons for the peak month of July 1945 alone.[22]

General Tunner and his command had refined military air transport to the highest art achieved in World War II. The general viewed airlift as "Big Business" and demanded that every aspect of the India-China Division's organization, policies, and operations was disciplined to the overarching task of producing maximum tonnage while flying safely. Everything, from aircrew scheduling to spark plug cleaning, went before his statisticians, efficiency experts, and daily staff meetings to ensure that it was being conducted for optimal efficiency in its own right and in the context of the overall operation. Laying some of the foundations of modern safety science, Tunner also turned his commanders and statisticians loose on every accident suffered by the division. They examined details as diverse as the flight experience of the crewmen involved to the actions of every mechanic that had come in contact with an accident aircraft. Flight surgeons examined every pilot before every mission.

The cumulative effects of all these actions were astonishing; in just a few months, the Hump accident rate dropped by an order of magnitude, from 2.0 to 0.24 accidents per thousand flying hours. This reduction equated to the survival of hundreds of airmen who otherwise would have died in preventable accidents.[23] Planes moved over the Himalayas with a staccato rhythm that reached intervals of less than three minutes on most days. On the busiest day of the lift, August 1, 1945, the India-China Division made 1,118 trips over the mountains, delivered 5,327 tons of cargo, and did not suffer a single accident.[24]

The flexibility and responsiveness of the lift also improved, as commanders learned that it was easier to redirect the efforts of a transport fleet moving at maximum effort than to increase and decrease the pace of operations in concert with shifting demands and unexpected delays. The division's repertoire of missions also grew to include transporting Chinese infantry divisions into Burma and back into China and augmenting local theater transport forces in supporting U.S. and British incursions into Burma.

Impacts

Mission 75, the airlift of initial U.S. occupation forces into Japan, revealed as well as any one event the full scope of American air transport capabilities and strategic importance at the very end of World War II. General Douglas MacArthur's staff first advised ATC of the mission on August 9, 1945. In the next three weeks, ATC drew C-54s from Africa, Europe, the States, and the Hump to concentrate 202 of them at a newly constructed base at Kadena, Okinawa. To put the undeveloped base into operation, ATC set up tower, weather, billeting, and maintenance facilities in a matter of days. Far East Air Forces (FEAF) contributed over 300 C-46s and C-47s to the force as well. Thereafter, ATC flew 1,336 C-54 sorties in and out of Japan without a single loss between August 30 (three days *before* the formal surrender of Japan) and September 12. Augmented by the FEAF transports, the big Skymasters lifted the combat elements of the 27th Infantry and 11th Airborne Divisions and advanced headquarters units—23,000 troops—along with over 1,200 vehicles and 900 tons of rations and ammunition into Japan.[25] In concert with seaborne troop insertions, Mission 75 ensured that the occupation of Japan was rapid and comprehensive, minimizing the vulnerability of occupation troops to local, diehard resistance and maximizing the psychological impact of the American arrival. Also, rapidly arriving troops were able to liberate Allied prisoners of war throughout the country and thereby minimize the risk that their erstwhile captors would kill them in revenge for Japan's defeat or to cover their war crimes. If the Hump airlift demonstrated the ability of sustained airlift to supply a whole theater of war, Mission 75 showed the capacity of a globally articulated airlift command to concentrate vast capabilities quickly for strategic effect.

The globally articulated air transport arms of the United States had come a long way since June 1942. From a hodgepodge of airliners and converted bombers, NATS and ATC had grown profoundly by August 1945. ATC embraced over 300,000 personnel and 3,224 aircraft, over 1,000 of which were C-54s and variations of the B-24.[26] NATS at that time controlled over 26,000 personnel and 540 aircraft. During the last six months of the war, ATC alone transported 2,957,000 passengers and 1.3 million tons of cargo. Through the course of the war, the commercial carriers grew to nearly 1,000 planes in operation and contributed about 1.1 billion cargo ton miles and 4.1 billion passenger miles to the war effort.[27] The implications of these staggering figures for the future of military air transport and the airline industry were not clear, of course. But army air forces commander General Henry H. Arnold saw enough of the future to advise his successor, General Carl Spaatz, to maintain "an integrated autonomous single Air Transport Command," one capable, among other things, of "moving . . . one Army Corps and its essential equipment from the United States to its most distant bases within seventy-two hours."[28] This was a huge task, and Arnold knew that the airlines would play a critical role. The airlines, much enlarged and just then starting to equip with a new generation of larger and faster aircraft, had the potential of living up to the task. The future promised great things.

7. Troop Carrier Aviation in World War II

Varsity: The Biggest of Them All

The Wehrmacht troops deployed in and around the Diersfordter Wald expected the attack to come straight at them. The wald, a four-square-mile patch of forest stretching in a westward-facing arch around the village of Diersfordt, sat on a low ridge that sloped gently down to the Rhine River, two to three miles farther to the west. For days, German intelligence reports had confirmed that the 2nd British Army planned an assault across the river, somewhere between the town of Wesel, a few miles southeast of the wald, and the larger town of Emmerich, about fifteen miles to the north, at the Dutch border. In the early morning of March 24, 1945, the axis of the British attack, code-named Plunder, clearly pointed straight at them. In the darkness of the previous night, Allied bombers had leveled Wesel, and at 2200 hours, British assault boats began crossing the river. With the coming of daylight, the German units deployed along the edge of the wald and in a defensive belt of farmhouses and fighting positions to the east of it could see events along the river only sporadically. Dust and smoke blowing on a steady south wind from Wesel and from British smoke pots along the river obscured visibility to as little as a few hundred yards. But British infantry clearly were in control of several pockets along the east bank. Knowing that the offensive would reach them later in the day, the waiting *soldaten* could only hope that their artillery firing from within the woods and from fields farther to the east would prevent the English from throwing tactical bridges across the river and thereby reinforce the attack with tanks.

The airborne attack came as a surprise, at least tactically. German commanders knew that a landing by two or three divisions was part of the Allied plan. But based on previous operations in Normandy and Holland, they had good reason to expect that the drops would happen some miles behind the immediate assault zone.[1] So confident were they that the Allies would not dare to drop right among their units, the Germans had not constructed antiglider obstacles in the fields on either side of the Diersfordter Wald. So when transport aircraft, parachutes, and gliders began to appear out of the smoky murk, landing near and on their positions, the German soldiers and tactical unit commanders were caught off guard and ill deployed to launch a coordinated defense and strong counterattacks against the American and British parachute and glider troops, who seemed to attack from everywhere as they landed.

It was the effect that Allied planners had hoped to achieve when they made the decision to insert the British 6th and the American 17th Airborne Divisions directly into the jaws of battle, in daylight, rather than adhere to the usual procedure of dropping or landing airborne troops in the night or at dawn some distance away from enemy strong points. The airborne commanders believed that immediate effect was more important than gaining a little time to organize before commencing combat. Determined to rob the Germans of the height and cover of the Diersfordter Wald before their guns could delay construction of the tactical bridges, the Allies put their parachute and glider troops into the fields directly east of the woods, with the intent of clearing them from behind.

To achieve the necessary strength, American air force lieutenant general Lewis H. Brereton, commander of the 1st Allied Airborne Army, organized the largest and most-rapidly delivered airborne assault of the war. Demanding maximum effort from the IX Troop Carrier Command and the 38th and 46th Transport Groups of the Royal Air Force (RAF), he dispatched some 1,156 transport aircraft and 1,348 gliders to put over 16,000 airborne soldiers, over 1,300 vehicles, and 109 guns onto the battlefield in two and a half hours.[2] In addition, more than 2,000 glider pilots would organize on the ground for the first time as fully equipped light infantry companies able to conduct defensive tasks, such as guarding prisoners, manning roadblocks, and defending headquarters. This unprecedented "density" of delivery was essential to ensure that the airborne regiments would have the strength and organization to enter battle on landing, conduct their assaults, and defend against enemy counterattacks that could come at any time.

Initially, Operation Varsity, the code name for the airborne portion of Plunder, went very well. Aided greatly by daylight and clear weather, the transport squadrons took off as scheduled from a dozen fields in East Anglia and another dozen around Paris. Navigation was precise; the two streams of planes and towed gliders merged over Wavre, Belgium, and flew the remaining 100 nautical miles side by side to their drop and landing zones on time and generally in good order, apart from occasional overruns by rearward formations of those in the lead. Upon the squadrons' crossing the Rhine, however, the dense smoke and dust over the battlefield made navigation difficult for the last few miles. Most formations did manage to find the final checkpoints visually and make accurate drops or landings. But others were forced to navigate by headings and elapsed time and then release their paratroops and glider men over uncertain terrain. Despite the confusion and rapidly increasing enemy fire, most regiments arrived on or very near their objectives, though a few were blown several miles north of their intended zones but still within the boundaries of the overall assault area.

As anticipated, Varsity turned out to be a tough fight for the airborne soldiers, who suffered about 20 percent casualties, and for the transport and glider crews, who did not fare much better. Quickly getting over their shock, the German troops initially put up strong resistance. Dispersed for a defense in depth against a ground assault, they held farmhouses, other buildings, and fighting positions all over the battlefield—nowhere in strength, but everywhere that a parachutist or glider might touch down. As a consequence, transport aircraft and gliders began falling to antiaircraft guns, infantry machine guns, and even rifle fire before they dropped their loads or landed. Gliders also were shattered by 88mm antitank guns and raked by small arms fire as they made their landing rolls. One gun piled up eight big Horsa gliders with white phosphorus shells, incinerating all of the big wooden planes and the British soldiers inside.

Many glider pilots found themselves in combat as close as any faced by the infantry. The copilot of a British Horsa glider shot it out with a four-barrel 20mm antiaircraft gun as his landing airplane rolled by, wiping out the entire German crew with just his Sten gun. On another landing zone, Lieutenant Walter Price chased down and killed a fleeing German soldier by landing on him with his CG-4 glider.[3] Transitioning instantly from flying in combat to close quarters fighting on the ground, Flight Officer George Julian crash-landed his glider on the battlefield and took immediate fire from a nearby farmhouse:

> Julian and his copilot . . . could hear the loud whack of German rifle bullets. . . . He dived down to the nearest field, crashed deliberately . . . and hooked the port wing on a brick house. The glider slewed around and came to an abrupt halt. . . . Julian instructed a bazooka gunner lying near him to pump a round into the house. Using the bazooka fire for cover, Julian ran up to the front door . . . and threw a grenade inside. As soon as it exploded he dashed inside, expecting to see dead German soldiers.[4]

Later that night, in the Battle of Burp Gun Corner, a platoon of glider pilots, all of them officers, fought off German probing attacks at a key road junction, killing dozens of soldaten and forcing them to abandon two tanks. Before evacuating from the battle area, 71 glider pilots were killed in Varsity, with another 373 missing, wounded, and injured, along with 191 casualties in the powered transports.[5] Fortunately, most of the missing wandered back to their units as the exigencies of wartime travel allowed.

Origins

Operation Varsity was the capstone airborne operation of World War II and unequalled in its scale since. The transport and glider stream passing over France and Belgium on its way to Germany took over two hours to pass a given point in a revelation of power and operational sophistication that struck many of the soldiers and civilians watching along the way with awe. For those familiar with the origins and buildup of the American and British airborne forces, the assault was doubly impressive, since it was the result of less than five years of experimentation and operational experience, which began with activation of the U.S. Army's first parachute test platoon in June 1940. For its part, the Army Air Forces did not activate a dedicated air transport force for airborne operations, Troop Carrier Command (TCC), until two years later, in July 1942. Prior to that, the air arm provided airlift to army jump experiments and training as an adjunct to the duties of existing air transport and bomber squadrons. This small-scale and somewhat haphazard commitment had been acceptable in the first two years of the airborne program, since the Army planned to employ the new parachute infantry battalions only as independent raiding forces to capture airfields, destroy key enemy installations, or perhaps take and hold key points such as road defiles and bridges.[6] But when the Army began to activate the 82nd and 101st Airborne Divisions, AAF commanders somewhat reluctantly set up TCC and its training arm, the First Troop Carrier Command (I TCC), to prepare the many specialized squadrons of aircraft and gliders needed to lift such huge units. Thus, the transformation of the airborne program from one contemplating company-size raids to one with the capability to put a whole corps of parachute and glider troops behind enemy lines took less than three years. Given that, not only was Varsity simply awesome, it bordered on the miraculous.

The U.S. Army developed its airborne capabilities and doctrines incrementally in response to military developments and its own discoveries about the technical and operational possibilities of large-scale assaults. The Army's parachute test platoon activated on the same day that France's formal surrender to Germany went into effect, June 25, 1940. On the basis of Germany's use of parachute commandos in the Battle of France, the U.S. Army began test jumps later that summer and activated the 1st Parachute Battalion on November 16. The Army continued to expand its airborne force through 1941, even as its new airborne command continued to test new parachutes, aircraft loading procedures, tables of organization and equipment, doctrine manuals, and training schedules for the new mode of war. Following the German employment of a full division of parachute and glider-borne troops during the invasion of Crete in May 1941, the Army and the Air Force began considering the employment of units larger than battalions and the use of gliders to follow up parachute assaults with additional infantry and heavy weapons. By November 1941, the Army possessed four independent parachute battalions at nearly full strength. In the same month, it set up the 501st Parachute Infantry Regiment as its first large-scale airborne tactical unit capable of conducting independent operations for more than a few hours. More regiments followed in the spring, and in July 1942 the War Department authorized the establishment of the 82nd and 101st Airborne Divisions. By the end of the war, the Army's airborne force included five divisions, six separate regiments, and four separate battalions, plus a number of supporting artillery, engineer, transportation, medical, and other units.

Struggling to prepare their own forces for the looming war, the army air corps and, after the reorganization of June 20, 1941, army air forces commanders tried to support airborne experiments with as little disruption of routine operations and the buildup of combat air forces as possible. Sharing the Army's early expectation that airborne assaults would be company- and maybe battalion-size raids, the Air Corps initially assigned the combined airborne training mission to its one large air transport unit, the 15th Air Transport Wing (ATW). Already fully employed in its primary mission of supporting military aircraft production by shuttling parts between factories, the 15th routinely left army requests for paratroop training flights unsatisfied.[7] In some early exercises, army parachutists jumped from B-18 bombers in the absence of transport aircraft. In response to growing demands for airborne training, the Air Corps activated the Air Transport Command on April 30, 1941, which absorbed the 50th Wing and all its missions. The shortage of planes to support army airborne training remained acute as more parachute battalions and, later, regiments came on line.

Once the Army decided to field entire airborne divisions, the Air Force had no choice but to put its part of the mission on a more solid footing. Recognizing the pressing need for a dedicated air transport establishment to team with airborne units, the Air Force renamed the Air Transport Command as TCC in July 1942 and made airborne operations its primary mission. While TCC headquarters worked on building the force, developing tactics, and writing doctrine, the I TCC prepared tactical units for combat and deployment overseas. Ultimately, I TCC would put some 4,500 transport crews and 5,000 glider pilots through training programs it modified continually in response to overseas battle reports.[8] Once combat ready, the Air Force assigned these units to troop carrier commands assigned to theater commands. Thus, troop carrier units sent to North Africa fell under the XII TCC of the 12th Air Force, while those going to the European theater of operations were assigned to the IX TCC of the 9th Air Force. By the time the war ended, the Air Force possessed some twenty-eight troop carrier and four smaller combat cargo groups worldwide. The largest TCC, the IX TCC in Europe, included fourteen groups and over 2,000 aircraft and gliders.

Organization

No other operational element of the Army Air Forces was integrated more closely to the tactical combat requirements and battle ethos of the Army than Troop Carrier Aviation. Put simply, troop carrier existed because airborne existed, and army airborne units derived their tactics, military usefulness, and very reason for being from the mobility provided by troop carrier. Their relationship approached symbiosis. From the earliest combat exercises, army air and ground commanders worked to integrate their efforts as closely as possible.[9] The need for integration and close teamwork only increased as airborne assaults grew from battalion size to regiment size and to corps size in scale and became complex choreographies of such things as route and drop zone selections, detailed intelligence assessments of enemy and friendly fire threats, diversion and deception operations, counterintelligence procedures, air interdiction missions to isolate drop zones from enemy counterattacks, the setting up of whole systems of radio navigation aids, air-sea rescue operations, the training and combat experience of individual battalions and regiments, and many others. Consequently, troop carrier and airborne commanders and personnel worked and trained together for prolonged periods of time, socialized together, briefed together prior to missions, and shared the risks of battle together. They knew and identified with each other in an unusually close community of airmen and soldiers.

In Europe, the need for close teamwork became so compelling that Supreme Allied Headquarters set up the 1st Allied Airborne Army on August 2, 1944, to plan and command the in-flight and initial assault phases of future airborne operations. The air force commander of the 1st AAA, Lieutenant General Brereton, exercised command over all Allied air transport and ground units assigned during the training for and execution of airborne assaults. These units included U.S. IX TCC (50th, 52nd, and 53rd Wings) and XVIII Airborne Corps (17th, 82nd, and 101st Divisions), British airborne-qualified air transport groups (38th and 46th), 1st Airborne Corps (1st and 6th Divisions), and the 1st Special Air Service Brigade; and the Polish 1st Independent Parachute Brigade.

Wings were the administrative building blocks of troop carrier commands. Normally, they consisted of four to five troop carrier groups, each possessing three to four flying squadrons. For the main, troop carrier wing commanders and staffs managed the personnel of their subordinate units, oversaw training, and planned major operations. Wing commanders and their judge advocates also handled major discipline cases and punishments. Wing commanders routinely led their units in combat, but their presence was more about morale than actually directing operations in the air. With their planes and gliders stretched out in formations fifty or more miles in length, they could share risks with their subordinates, but they could do little to observe or direct events once their units were in the air. Tactical leadership in troop carrier missions came from squadron and group commanders. Wing commanders kept things running between operations and boosted the morale and determination of their crews by fighting alongside them.

Groups were the building blocks of troop carrier air assault operations. Typically, groups could put up fifty to sixty aircraft and, if necessary, a similar number of gliders towed behind them. In combat, a group formation would stretch over two to five miles of airspace, depending on whether its aircraft were carrying paratroops or towing gliders. There was a much more immediate relationship between group commanders and the combat crewmen in the squadrons. Normally, a group headquarters and its squadrons were assigned to a single base, and all personnel used the same messing, recreational, chapel, exchange, and other facilities. Group staffs worked with squadron personnel to plan the tactics of forthcoming missions and to coordinate planning with supported ground units. Since a group's aircraft generally were capable of dropping or airlanding the 500 to 600 men, heavy weapons, and equipment of an airborne infantry battalion and, perhaps, a "slice" of regimental or divisional support personnel and/or weapons, the basic planning units for airborne operations were group-battalion teams that sometimes carried through more than one operation.[10] Group commanders usually briefed the pilots and navigators from all squadrons en masse and then flew with them on big operations. But, in contrast to wing commanders, their aircraft were plainly visible to their entire formation. Perhaps not surprisingly, therefore, virtually all troop carrier "memory books" from World War II are based on groups, sometimes squadrons, but never on wings.

Squadrons were the military "neighborhoods" of troop carrier units. Since each squadron maintained its own barracks, maintenance areas, and limited recreational facilities, their personnel spent most of their working and flying hours with their squadron mates or in squadron training formations in the air. In combat, a troop carrier squadron typically could put up sixteen to eighteen aircraft in a "serial" of several smaller formations. If squadron aircraft were carrying paratroops into battle, they usually flew in three-aircraft Vs, with either five or six Vs flying in trail with a couple of hundred feet between each, or in two Vs of Vs, involving six or nine aircraft each. If towing gliders, squadrons usually flew in sequential echelons of two to four aircraft, with each echelon forming a line slanted back to the right or left. The close proximity of squadron aircraft in combat allowed crews in a serial to be aware of the performance and fate of their comrades and to even look into one another's faces in flight. Life, skill, the terrors of battle, success, and death were communal events in line squadrons, and they forged relationships of intensity difficult to describe to individuals who never served in a combat unit. As in all combat units, their sense of mission and fear of letting one another down in the midst of battle kept troop carrier crewmen pressing forward. The fighting spirit of troop carrier was borne in its squadrons.

Aircraft

Throughout the war, airborne troops and their matériel were carried into battle in a modified airliner or a flimsy glider. The airliner was the DC-3, which first flew in 1935. Modified with a large cargo door, fold-down bucket seats, and fittings for securing cargo, the DC-3 became the C-47, of which the military acquired over 10,000 during the war. Carrying only eighteen paratroops and with a typical cruise speed of around 140 knots, the C-47 was painfully small and slow in relation to the demands placed on it. But it began the war with the important virtues of coming off an existing production line, being unusually rugged, and, if its unprotected fuel tanks did not explode, being capable of absorbing an amazing amount of battle damage and still stay in the air. Flown by a good pilot, the Gooney Bird also could get in and out of a rough landing strip of about 1,200 feet in length.

The glider was the Waco CG-4, 13,909 of which were built during the war. Boxy and based on a tubular steel frame covered in doped fabric, the Waco was not a pretty aircraft, but it was useful. A C-47 could tow one easily and two with difficulty, each loaded with thirteen troops or a prescribed maximum cargo load of 3,750 pounds. In reality, CG-4s often carried heavier loads, which could include a jeep and 37mm antitank gun or a 75mm pack howitzer. Handling of these light vehicles and bulky items was eased by a flip-up cockpit, which exposed the full cross section of the cargo area for loading and unloading. Besides bringing in heavy weapons, these aircraft were particularly useful for delivering medical supplies and personnel, communications equipment, small bulldozers, and many other items or personnel not suited or trained for parachute drops. Their honeycomb plywood floors were strong enough to handle these loads, but their overall structure was weak, and many gliders broke up in flight from heavy turbulence or enemy gunfire. As an indication of the hazards of landing these planes on rough fields under fire, later models came with a cable rig to attach their cockpits to the rear of their cargo loads. So if the load plunged forward in a crash, the cable would snap the cockpit and pilots up and out of the way of being crushed.[11]

Efforts to provide troop carrier squadrons with more suitable aircraft during the war received low priority from the Air Force and met with limited success at best. At the end of the war, during the Wesel drop only, a few squadrons received the C-46. But while post-action studies showed that these aircraft were more efficient and no less safe than C-47s, aircrews distrusted their flying characteristics and damage tolerance.[12] In 1941 the Air Force also funded development of three aircraft designed specifically to meet troop carrier needs better than the C-47 could. Seeking aircraft able to drop paratroops, land on rough airfields of 1,200 feet, and load medium-size vehicles and artillery, the service also required the manufacturers to use nonstrategic materials. Accordingly, the Budd Streetcar Company constructed the C-93 Conestoga with stainless steel, Curtiss-Wright used wood for its C-76 Caravan, and Fairchild used plywood and steel to prototype its C-82 packet. Ultimately, the C-76 and the C-93 were failures, with the former being grossly unsafe to fly and the latter having range and payload characteristics inferior to those of the more conventional C-46s and C-47s. The C-82 effort was on the verge of failure until the Air Force allowed Fairchild to switch to aluminum construction.[13]

The redesigned C-82 reached operational status too late to see active service in the war, but its design layout opened a new era in troop carrier capabilities.

Equipped with two 2,100-horsepower engines, the new plane could carry forty-two troops or 10,000 pounds of cargo for 1,200 nautical miles at 190 knots.[14] Perhaps most important, its pod-type fuselage was suspended under the wing and between two booms carrying the engines and tail and had clamshell doors in the rear that could be opened to the full profile of the fuselage on the ground or removed altogether prior to flight. This feature facilitated truck-bed-height loading at forward airfields and offered the possibility of air-dropping small vehicles and artillery pieces by parachute. This ability to drop heavy equipment by parachute, rather than deliver it at great hazard by glider, portended significant change in the way airborne units would go into battle.

Glider development projects met with little more success. Troop carrier units in Europe did receive several thousand Horsa gliders from the British. Of wholly wooden construction, Horsas were larger than CG-4s, carrying twenty-five to thirty troops or around 5,000 pounds of cargo. But towing them placed C-47s under severe strain, American glider pilots disliked their flying characteristics, and they had an unfortunate tendency to shatter into deadly splinters if they crashed. By late 1943 the United States was testing three glider designs that were substantially larger than the CG-4. These were the CG-10, CG-13, and CG-16. CG-10s saw limited use during the Wesel drops, and at least one CG-13 served in the Philippines. The CG-16 was an unorthodox twin-boom design that crashed in testing and did not reach production. Each of these aircraft had rear-loading doors and could carry over forty troops or 10,000 pounds of cargo. Had they been available in quantity before the war ended, they would have greatly improved the firepower and mobility of parachute units by bringing in medium artillery, light tanks, two-and-a-half-ton trucks, and so on.

Operations

Troop carrier commands participated in major airborne assaults in North Africa, Europe, the Pacific, and Burma. The 60th Troop Carrier Group and the 2nd Battalion of the 502nd Parachute Infantry Regiment (PIR) opened the American airborne war on November 8, 1943, with a desperate and somewhat haphazard operation near Oran, Algeria. There followed several other battalion-size operations over the next few weeks to capture airfields in the region. In July 1943, the five groups of the 50th Troop Carrier Wing inserted the 505th and 504th PIRs into Sicily on two successive nights. The results of these drops were generally poor, due mainly to decisions to drop at night, inadequate combined training of the airborne force, and serious friendly fire incidents. By the invasion of France in June 1944, the three wings of the IX TCC could drop the 82nd and 101st Airborne Divisions on the same night. Better planning and training virtually eliminated friendly fire hazards, but the challenges of navigating and dropping at night and through unexpected cloud banks still undermined the overall effectiveness of the operation. Consequently, the two largest airborne operations of the war—Market Garden, September 1944, and Wesel, April 1945— flew and dropped in daylight. Drop accuracy in both missions was generally very good, and aircraft losses to antiaircraft fire were not much different from those suffered in the earlier night drops. Airborne operations in the Pacific were less frequent and on a smaller scale than those in Europe, highlighted by an assault by most of the 503rd PIR at Nazdab, New Guinea, September 1943, and at Corregidor, the Philippines, February 1945. In Burma, Operation Thursday, March 1944, began with a battalion of glider-borne infantry taking a landing zone deep behind Japanese lines that was then used to airland several brigades of British and colonial infantry.

For all of the dash and importance of airborne operations, the main contribution of Troop Carrier Aviation to American victory turned out to be logistics, the simple transport of matériel and personnel from airfield to airfield. While air transport was one of its missions, part of the rationale for establishing troop carrier as a separate command was the presumption that combined airborne training and operations would consume most of its sorties. Instead, even in the European campaign, there were months between airborne assaults, during which troop carrier aircraft by the hundreds were available to move supplies and people. Theater commanders soon realized that, expensive as it was in relation to other transportation modes, air transport could be an invaluable or even indispensable link between rear supply depots and frontline units.

Troop carrier air transport capabilities were particularly valuable in situations where rapidly advancing units outstripped their surface supply lines or where they were operating in terrain and climatic conditions that rendered surface transportation impractical or impossible. Between the breakout from the Normandy peninsula and VE day, for example, troop carrier groups, with some augmentation from RAF and other U.S. transport units in the theater, delivered 232,000 tons of supplies—primarily fuel, ammunition, and rations— to the advancing divisions of the 12th Army Group. In the war's last days, the troop carrier effort reached over 2,000 tons per day outbound, plus "backhaul" of thousands of wounded soldiers, returning prisoners of war, and high-value cargo items.[15] In remote jungle areas, such as New Guinea and Burma, air transport was the only practical way to sustain combat units advancing behind the lines or just out beyond the last road. Following the Nazdab drops, for instance, 5th Air Force C-47s were the sole logistical pipeline for the Australian 7th Division as it advanced up the Markham River valley, deep in the interior. In 1943 and 1944, 10th Air Force transports, augmented by Air Transport Command planes assigned to the Hump operation, sustained a half dozen British brigades maneuvering through deep jungle for months.[16]

In the European theater of operations, the competing demands for logistics air transport and the airlift of airborne units became an acute operational issue for theater commanders. As early as preparation for the invasion of Italy in September 1943, the airborne commander complained that preparations were hampered by the XII TCC's relocation of its groups from North Africa to Sicily, requiring transportation of thousands of personnel and hundreds of tons of equipment to activate twelve new bases in the weeks prior to the operation.[17] Even the Air Force recognized that the most "persistent difficulty" in preparing for airborne operations in Europe was the "drain" on troop carrier resources by the requirements for air transport of supplies to the rapidly advancing armies.[18] From the other side of the dilemma, ground commanders of nonairborne units were acutely aware of the impact of shifting troop carrier lift away from their units racing across northern France toward Germany. Planning and training for Operation Market Garden alone, in September 1945, reduced the available logistics lift from 45,000 tons to 20,000 tons, with significant impact on the ability of the Army to maintain its offensive.[19]

The most obvious implication of the practically infinite demands for troop carrier's finite assets was recognition that "Troop Carrier aviation [was] a theater of operations force . . . [to be] controlled by the highest agency . . . with jurisdiction over all land, sea, and air forces."[20] Consequently, once operations had begun on the continent, theater airlift in Europe ran on the principles that the "decision as to employment of troop carrier aircraft as between air transport . . . and airborne training and/or combat . . . must be that of the theater commander. Operation of air transport should be under the air commander."[21] Put another way, once the Supreme Allied commander, General Dwight D. Eisenhower, apportioned theater airlift capacity to given users for particular operations or time periods, the Allied Expeditionary Air Force (AEAF) commander, British Air Marshal Trafford Leigh-Mallory, was responsible for allocating actual American and British transport units to fill their requirements.

In practice, after August 1944, two organizations supervised day-to-day air transport operations on behalf of the AEAF commander. During the run-ups to major operations, the IX TCC, under Major General Paul L. Williams, oversaw the preparation and training of units. A highly respected combat leader, Williams flew with his forces in major operations, though his actual ability to direct 150 miles of transports, once launched, was limited at best. Consequently, direction and control of ongoing airborne and air transport operations was handled by the Combined Air Transport Operations Room (CATOR), which functioned within the headquarters of the 1st Allied Airborne Army.[22] Working within the apportionment decisions of the theater commander, CATOR assigned specific units to provide preplanned and/or emergency air transport support to authorized airborne and other army ground units and to relocating air units and forward air bases. CATOR also tracked ongoing operations and made necessary cargo-handling, ground-servicing, and other support arrangements for transports landing at forward fields.[23]

Theater commanders took numerous actions to ease the burden on the IX Troop Carrier Command. As General Williams briefed aspiring air force staff officers just after the war, he and other commanders learned to use their forces with ever-greater efficiency. During the run-up to the Wesel drops, he reported that his crews practiced tactical procedures during routine transport sorties. Instead of simply droning through the sky between airfields, they flew in formation, practiced run-in navigation procedures and "slow ups," and made practice parachute drops along the way. Consequently, final preparations and conduct of the actual drops consumed only a few days of dedicated effort.[24] Help also came from the 302nd Air Transport Wing (Special), which normally provided personnel and logistics lift for the 8th and 9th Air Force Service Commands. But in the latter months of the war, the wing's 27th and 31st Air Transport Groups made their seven transport squadrons available to move passengers and cargo into the forward areas. On occasion, the 8th Air Force also made B-24 bombers available to drop parapacks of supplies or to deliver fuel to forward airfields. Air Transport Command's European wing also operated regular services to major cities, particularly Paris, as the war progressed. Although not always closely coordinated with one another, the operations of these various organizations and units emphasized two important realities: first, modern warfare used a lot of air transport; and, second, the somewhat haphazard mobilization of American air transport forces early in the war had produced complicated and overlapping activities and lines of command in the theaters of operation.

Battle

*Inside the burning plane 1st Lt. John P. Goodwin of the 95th Squadron was fighting
to hold his scant 100 feet of altitude. The port side of the cabin had been blown out,
both engines were blazing and the wind screens and roof of the cabin were gone. . . .
With its port engine still functioning, the plane hit the choppy water of the channel
at 80 miles an hour. The three men fought their way out of the smoke filled cabin.
. . . Looking down into the fuselage; they could see the bodies of the crew chief . . . the
radio operator . . . the war correspondent . . . and an enlisted man of the 101st.*[25]

Violent action, courage, and high casualties characterized the signature mission of Troop Carrier Aviation: the aerial delivery of army paratroopers and glider troops onto contested ground. From failures in the North Africa and Sicily drops, troop carrier crews and planners had learned that the only way to put airborne units down on the ground in reasonable order and readiness to fight was to bore into their objectives at low altitude and slow airspeeds and without taking evasive action. So they went in at altitudes of 300 to 750 feet, at speeds of 95 to 120 knots, and in tight formations. From the moment they crossed enemy lines, they were ducks in a shooting gallery for every soldier on the ground with an antiaircraft gun, a machine gun, a rifle, or even a pistol. What saved most of them from certain death was surprise, the usual inaccuracies of fire delivered under combat conditions by frightened men, and the fact that transport aircraft had lots of empty volume through which projectiles could pass without damaging critical structural components or detonating their fuel or sometimes explosive cargoes. Even when death seemed inevitable, most pilots pressed ahead, determined to get their troopers or loads in before they were shot down. Wrote one pilot after a supply drop into Normandy in June 1944,

> "I was mesmerized by the fire coming up at our planes . . . —couldn't take my eyes off it. I could see the bullets finding the range of the leading elements. I felt that in a few minutes that I would be dead. . . . One consolation: it seemed to me that most of the gliders from the lead elements were going to make it down near the LZ [landing zone]."[26]

This was tough fighting, equivalent to the massed bomber formations bulling through the skies of Germany and Japan, with hundreds of planes, thousands of men, pushing in, no matter what. There were differences between airlift and bomber missions, of course. Troop carrier crews had nothing with which to shoot back. They flew low enough to be shot at by everything that bombers faced plus every other weapon an infantry unit could carry. Troop carrier planes did not have self-sealing fuel tanks. So a hit by anything could set them afire, and they were already too low for anyone to bail out. Moreover, for glider pilots, their airland missions ended with them picking up their carbines and bazookas, forming into platoons, and spending the next few days fighting as commissioned officer infantrymen alongside their former passengers.

Troop carrier airmen, consequently, thought of themselves less as transport pilots than as combat personnel who happened to fly aircraft. They operated over "enemy territory" while Air Transport Command crews just "hauled freight."[27] Glider pilots were fond of saying that the big G engraved on the shield of their wings stood for "guts," not just "gliders." Troop carrier crewmen—pilots, navigators, and engineers—do not seem to have come up with a similar declaration. But there was no doubt in their minds that they were a different breed of transport pilot, with more kinship to fighter and bomber crews than to ATC or NATS fliers. It was a sense of identity that would characterize their attitude and relationship to the world of airlift and the Air Force for decades to come.

8. Airlift Consolidation in the 1940s

IT WAS PREDICTABLE that, in the later years of World War II and immediately thereafter, military planners began to consider the proper distribution of control over air transport forces. Given the expense and insatiable demand for transport aircraft from so many organizations, the logic of gathering long-range aircraft into a single command charged with providing "common-user" service made sense to many. The pressure for consolidation increased after the war, when all transport arms demobilized. The Air Transport Command (ATC), for example, shrank from over 3,000 aircraft and 314,000 personnel at the end of 1945 to about 500 transports and 47,000 personnel in just two years.[1] At the same time, Troop Carrier Command strength dropped from 32 groups to 10, and the Naval Air Transport Service (NATS) reduced from almost 500 transports at the end of the war to less than 200 in 1948.[2] Given the necessity of maintaining large forces overseas, the airlift drawdown was not matched by a proportional reduction in demand.

The challenge faced by airlift planners considering consolidation was complex and thorny. Every U.S. service and major overseas command operated air transport forces and preferred to exercise direct control over them. Any effort to take transport units away from them would engender major turf battles that undoubtedly would involve the president and Congress. In reflection of these realities, efforts to merge ATC and NATS stalled, until the president, Congress, and the first secretary of defense forced the Army and Navy to stop squabbling and activate a centralized command. The resulting Military Air Transport Service (MATS) did activate in June 1948 as an air force major command. But unwilling to relinquish direct control of its organic airlift, the Navy released only personnel and squadrons it considered surplus to its core needs. MATS, therefore, was little more than a renaming of ATC, the symbol but not the substance of organizational consolidation.

The Logic of Consolidation

The central logic of consolidation—that it would reduce redundancies and costs—carried only limited weight in relation to long-range air transport. In the first place, the missions of ATC and NATS were different. ATC provided common-user service on behalf of the Joint Chiefs of Staff, including the "ferrying of all aircraft within the United States and to destinations outside the United States . . . [and] transportation by air of personnel, materiel, mail, strategic materials, and other cargoes for all War Department Agencies . . . and for any Government agency . . . subject to established priorities."[3] NATS, in contrast, provided ferrying and transport services specific to the requirements of the Navy. Unavoidably, the routes and bases of the two commands overlapped since the Navy fought in the same theaters as everyone else. But the Navy operated its transports with reasonable efficiency, so the degree of wastage was limited and hard to quantify. Even an ATC report done in late 1945 to justify consolidation acknowledged that ATC would require 450 aircraft to replace the 500 held by NATS, a 10 percent savings in the best of circumstances. The limited promise of savings, contrasted to the Joint Chiefs of Staff's position that "air transport requirements of the Navy vary greatly from those of the Army . . . [and] can best be met by the Department involved," severely weakened the argument for consolidation.[4]

Consolidation probably made the most sense in the context of the confusion of air transport and airlift commands operating overseas theaters of operation. Troop carrier commands operated in all major theaters, flying hundreds of transports in support of airborne operations and, more frequently, providing logistics support to the Army, Army Air Forces, and sometimes the Navy. In addition, air force service commands in most theaters operated transport squadrons for logistics support to forward bases and air combat units. U.S. Marines had transport squadrons in the Pacific, while dozens of tactical and support units in all services possessed transport aircraft for use in support of their own missions. These small detachments might include "staff transports" assigned to very senior commanders, a "hack" or two attached to or scrounged by a fighter group, a flight of small planes moving patients and medicines for a medical command, and many, many other bits and pieces that might or might not show up on an official table of organization. In truth, the U.S. military would have been pressed to say just how many transport aircraft it was operating. But it could say that there were a lot of them, they worked for many different bosses, and they were not subject to centralized coordination or review of their operations.

The absence of centralized oversight of all these transport units was a matter of concern on at least two accounts. First, local combat commanders had no way of knowing if transports passing through their bases were on missions of equal priority to their own needs. To them, planes carrying aircraft parts and staff officers looked like a proper opportunity to "divert" them to move more important things, such as ammunition, medical supplies, rations, and the wounded. Diversions of ATC aircraft, in fact, became commonplace at the beginning of the war, prompting the commander, Major General Harold L. George, to advise his boss, General Henry H. Arnold, that his operations were suffering "due to orders from Commands operating on the premise that transport operations which traverse their areas are under their complete control while within such areas."[5] Second, the lack of visibility over all air transport operations left senior commanders to wonder if they were getting the best use out of these scarce assets. Transport commands in one theater might be stretching like Atlas to undergird campaigns and battles, while those operating in quieter areas might be engaged in routine logistics missions or even junkets.

There also was the matter of strategic vision. As American airmen gained experience and confidence in the effectiveness of moving large ground units and the ground echelons and supplies of air combat groups, their vision of its future uses grew. At the end of the war, General Arnold exhorted General George to protect ATC's knowledge, capabilities, and overseas bases as much as possible during the postwar demobilization of the Air Force.[6] Furthermore, Arnold advised his replacement, General Carl Spaatz, to maintain an airlift force able to lift an army corps to any point on earth in seventy-two hours.[7] Even considering the newest aircraft coming off American production lines, Arnold was proposing something huge: moving perhaps 40,000 soldiers, tens of thousands of tons of equipment and supplies, plus their air support and logistics establishments with aircraft capable of carrying only about 100 troops or fifteen tons of cargo for 2,500 miles or so. Even a few quick calculations on a napkin would reveal that ATC would have to control many hundreds of aircraft and strings of robustly supplied bases to make such a plan work. Such a force could be had only through careful management and operational control of the entire American military and civil air transport establishments. Nothing could be misdirected or squandered by haphazard, decentralized management.

Early Initiatives

Historically, armies and navies rarely found it necessary to coordinate their operations except at the level of strategy making or for the conduct of amphibious assaults along the marches of their otherwise separate realms. At the beginning of World War II, however, long-range transport aviation opened up a new frontier of interservice coordination. So it was that barely two weeks after Pearl Harbor, U.S. Army and U.S. Navy leaders found themselves dividing up the paltry fleet of four-engine land planes and seaplanes then composing the long-range air transport capability of the entire country. In an agreement made on December 22, 1941, the Army's Ferrying Command retained the eleven converted B-24s already in its possession, along with five Boeing 307 Stratoliners from Trans World Airlines (TWA) and three Clipper flying boats from Pan American Airways. The Navy took up Pan Am's remaining seven flying boats.[8] In addition, both services relied on Edgar S. Gorrell, the president of the Airline Transport Association, to modulate the flow of commercial aircraft, pilots, mechanics, and other personnel into their otherwise separate, distinct, and independent air transport services.

And that was about it, for the situation was not so desperate that the two services would even consider jointly managing their day-to-day transport operations, let alone actually merging Ferrying Command and NATS. The chairman of the Civil Aeronautics Board L. (Lloyd) Welch Pogue made such a suggestion in the spring of 1942, recommending the establishment of a single War Transport Command to absorb all long-range aircraft. As chairman of the organization overseeing the economics and competitive environment of the airline industry, Pogue believed that a single command could manage aircraft acquisition programs, daily operations, and movement priorities more effectively than several competing organizations. Service leaders gave his ideas no more than a nod. Stretched as they were for resources, they had no intention of giving up their direct control of what was fast becoming an indispensable adjunct to their combat effectiveness.[9]

The bosses of Ferrying Command and NATS, Major General Robert Olds and Captain John P. Whitney, saw the need for at least some coordination of their activities. So beginning in July 1942, they chartered an informal committee "to discuss common problems arising in connection with contracts with commercial air carriers."[10] They formalized this arrangement as the Joint Army-Navy Air Transport Committee (JA-NATC) in September. The deputy chiefs of ATC and NATS usually chaired its meetings. Although the JA-NATC wielded no formal power, its accomplishments included agreeing to reduce some overlapping routes, drafting joint movement priority lists, and creating standardized procedures to contract and pay for the services of civil operators.[11] Though JA-NATC was a deliberative body only, with no independent authority to direct anything, its membership, the rapidly increasing flow of resources into both commands, and perhaps the wartime spirit of cooperation made it work so long as the issues before it did not impinge on the organizational survival of ATC or NATS.

Faced, perhaps, by more desperate shortfalls in available capabilities, theater commanders made several experiments with consolidated control of their airlift forces. The South Pacific Combat Air Transport Command (SCAT) was particularly notable, if only because it involved actual interservice cooperation. Marine Transport Squadron (VMJ)-253 of Marine Air Group 25, Lieutenant Colonel Perry K. Smith commanding, hastily deployed from California to New Caledonia in late August 1942 to alleviate the critical supply situation of the 1st Marine Division operating on Guadalcanal and to establish other routes in the Southwest Pacific theater. The twelve planes of VMJ-253 immediately began transporting munitions, aircraft fuel, mail, medical, and hygiene supplies to the largely isolated marines, and picked up wounded soldiers. Flying and even landing under fire or air attack were common events. VMJ-152, Major E. W. Seeds commanding, joined the effort in late October. When the 13th Troop Carrier Group began flying in support of growing army operations in the Southwest Pacific area, army, navy, and marine commanders decided to join all air transport operations under SCAT. The Navy directed activation of SCAT on November 24, 1942, and requested that the Army assign "air transport squadrons to the operational control of [SCAT]."[12] Integrated operations began in November, and the command was organized fully by January, with Colonel Smith in command. While all units remained under their parent service chains of command, Smith's multiservice staff, en route support bases, and maintenance organizations assigned missions to SCAT aircraft and kept them flying on a coequal, common-user basis.

SCAT earned a hard success. Starting with about thirty-six aircraft, the command grew to six flying squadrons before it was inactivated in February 1945. Salted heavily in its early days by marine reservist airline pilots and stewardesses, who put their registered nurse credentials to work as flight nurses, SCAT fliers were noted for their audacity in getting loads into battle zones and the wounded back to rear area hospitals. Official inspectors noted that SCAT's operational élan was accompanied by indifferent staff procedures, including patchy record keeping and a "lack of adequate planning and proper traffic coordination and control."[13] The paperwork eventually got organized, and in its first eighteen months of operation, SCAT transported about 220,000 passengers and 15,000 tons of cargo and was credited with saving several cutoff units with supply drops under fire.[14]

The scale of transport operations in Europe was significantly greater than that in the Southwest Pacific, but the shortfall of available capacity compared to demand was no less acute. In absolute terms, there were a lot of transports in the theater. The IX Troop Carrier Command alone included fourteen groups assigned to three wings and was capable of putting almost 3,500 aircraft and gliders into the air for a single mission. Next in size were the Royal Air Force's 38th and 46th Air Transport Groups, with about 500 aircraft plus twice that many gliders. The 27th and 31st Air Transport Groups, assigned to the Air Support Commands of the 8th and 9th Air Forces, respectively, fielded four to seven transport squadrons between them.[15] ATC and NATS also operated in England and on the continent as the campaign progressed.[16] Demand for transport support was no less staggering. Airborne commanders needed continual support for training and actual drops. Field army commanders relied on air transports to augment their tenuous surface supply lines to maintain their mechanized advances. Fighter groups based at advanced airfields depended on a steady stream of airlifted fuel, munitions, rations, and even construction material to sustain their part of the war.

To bring order and tighter control to this cacophony of demands and protests, General Dwight Eisenhower, the supreme commander of the Allied Expeditionary Forces, directed his air component, the Allied Expeditionary Air Force (AEAF), commanded by Air Marshal Sir Trafford Leigh-Mallory, to establish a department to direct air transport operations in support of all military activities on the continent apart from airborne missions. Mallory's solution was the Combined Air Transport Operations Room (CATOR). Then, in August 1944, General Eisenhower transferred CATOR to 9th Air Force, which, as a component of the 1st Allied Airborne Army, became responsible both for planning airborne operations and for servicing the demands coming from all other commands for airlift. General Eisenhower and his supply staff worked to ensure that the conflict of interest in CATOR's position as a user and supplier of air transport capacity did not result in its inefficient or strategically inappropriate use. They did this mainly by providing general guidelines, or "apportionments," of airlift capacity to the various users in accordance with the unfolding strategic priorities of the European campaign. In keeping with this evolving general guidance, CATOR would allocate missions to specific units and make the necessary cargo-handling and aircraft-servicing arrangements.[17] So if the supreme commander authorized a major airborne assault, CATOR would commit virtually all available lift to the operation, but as soon as the airborne surge was over, it would reapply its groups to fly supplies to advancing ground units and forward air bases. Despite occasional efforts by other commands to influence CATOR operations, the Army's official history indicated general satisfaction with the placement of CATOR under the air force theater command.[18]

This Far and No Farther

The clear implication of these limited forays into coordinated air transport operations encouraged several senior commanders to propose more concrete organizational consolidations. Most suggestions were for "lateral" consolidations of ATC and NATS and of theater-operating organizations. A few visionaries recommended bringing all air transport capacity under one roof. But these early recommendations ran into implacable resistance from any command that expected to lose direct control of its existing airlift capabilities.

In February 1943, the deputy commander of ATC, Brigadier General Cyrus R. Smith, advised consideration of the "advantages of consolidating the Air Transport Command and the Naval Air Transport Service into one Government Air Transportation System (GATS)." As the president of American Airlines, Smith viewed the growing redundancies in ATC and NATS operations as wasteful and was in full support of similar suggestions then being made by the Civil Aeronautics Board chairman, L. Welch Pogue. Smith argued that a consolidated command would use people, aircraft, and bases more efficiently than two smaller commands and would please Congress with its cost-cutting results. Thinking even further ahead, he suggested that the GATS "would be one step forward" in the Air Force's march to independence from the Army and that it would undergird America's domination of international air travel after the war.[19]

Smith's and Pogue's advocacy produced limited but useful results. In May 1944, the Joint Chiefs of Staff strengthened the JA-NATC by requiring regular meetings, making it a formal arm of the Joint Chiefs of Staff, and directing it to reduce overlaps in air transport operations.[20] At the same time, the Joint Chiefs of Staff released a directive limiting the operational portfolio of NATS to providing specialized air transportation for the Navy only. ATC alone would have interservice responsibilities to move people and matériel.[21] Also responding to the ideas of the two civil air transport leaders, General Lauris Norstad,

AAF assistant chief of staff for plans, released a report in September 1945 recommending consolidation of ATC and Troop Carrier Aviation.[22] Under Norstad's
plan, the training and foreign air transport divisions of a new ATC would conduct all training and overseas flights, while its troop carrier groups would operate under the operational command of theater air commanders.[23] These arrangements amounted to a groundbreaking suggestion that a single air force
operational command would function as a military service in miniature. Like
the Air Force, the new ATC would have a global operational portfolio, including the preparation and management of tactical forces transferred to overseas
combat commands. This was a truly global concept, the first published in relation to air transport.

But those limited doctrinal and process reforms were as far as airlift policy
advanced in response to Pogue's and Smith's recommendation. Most important, and despite his enthusiasm for air transport and his public criticisms of
the coexistence of ATC and NATS, General Arnold stopped short of advocating any form of airlift consolidation. Unshakable in his belief that the "authority of the Theater Commander in his area is paramount," Arnold, on the same
day that he told General Spaatz to maintain a powerful air transport arm after
the war, also disapproved Norstad's plan.[24] Consistent with this view, the 1946
revision of Army Air Forces Regulation 20-44, *Responsibilities for Air Transportation*, reaffirmed that ATC's mission was "air transport services between
different overseas area commands" and did not include "intratheater services
required by overseas commanders." In short, the different operating realms of
ATC and Troop Carrier Command mandated separate organizational status.[25]

Unsurprisingly, the leaders of the other services and airlift commands wanted
nothing to do with any elevation of ATC's status. As General Smith recognized,
the debate over consolidation was influenced by the "pride factor" of the people
in ATC and NATS and the determination of the Army and the Navy to hang
on to them.[26] In 1944 the commander of I Troop Carrier Command, Brigadier
General William Old, declared that consolidation would undermine the troop
carrier mission. His successor, General Paul L. Williams, actually stated that all
overseas unit movements should transfer to Troop Carrier Command, while
ATC should shrink to a rump organization moving individual passengers, mail,
and piece cargo.[27] The Navy simultaneously stonewalled a Joint Chiefs of Staff
proposal to create a joint task force to rationalize and supervise army and navy
air transport operations. Immediately after the war, the Navy also sponsored a
memory book, *Operation Lifeline*, recounting NATS's World War II exploits

and asserting that an integrated "air transport nucleus" was essential to naval operations and could not be replaced by a "supermonopoly [sic] controlled by one service."[28] Even the Army weighed in, rejecting any absorption of troop carrier by ATC, preferring instead to preserve the close Troop Carrier Command–Airborne association pioneered by the 1st Allied Airborne Army.[29] "It is absolutely necessary," declared a report of the General Board of the European Theater Forces Command, "that airborne divisions must have attached to them . . . sufficient troop carrying airplanes for their exclusive use."[30]

Beyond official resistance, troop carrier pilots and personnel did not want any part of ATC. Combat-seasoned troop carrier veterans viewed ATC pilots and ground personnel as spoiled civilians and felt obliged after the war to correct "people who confused us with the Air Transport Command. . . . TCC served in combat and ATC did not."[31] Lecturing other officers in 1946, Major John McVay extolled Troop Carrier Command as "one of the mightiest fighting units in the Army Air Force" and then expressed his relief that "no longer would Troop Carrier crews be confused with ATC crews," who saw no combat and mainly flew "all over the world . . . building up valuable transport time for airline flying after the war."[32]

Last, the air force leaders backed away from airlift consolidation, because they were not sure that ATC would not be replaced by commercial contract operations after the war. Articulating that concern in 1946, General Robert M. Webster, who took command of ATC in September 1946, argued, "[ATC's] continued existence . . . as a convenience for military activities, is questionable since such transportation service can eventually be provided . . . by the civil air transport industry." In other words, if ATC's mission remained simple air transport and did not include a combat component, it was doomed to fade away in favor of commercial carriers that could move most of the military's routine traffic. Webster argued, therefore, that ATC's mission should be the "provision of strategic concentration, deployment, and support, by air, for the Army Air Forces and the War Department"—global *airlift*, not just global air transportation.[33]

Even then, senior air force leaders might moot the need for improved aircraft if they embraced a vision of future wars based on fleets of atomic-armed bombers rather than airborne divisions.[34] Such a force of bombers would not be effective, Lieutenant General Elwood R. Quesada, commander of the Air Force's new Tactical Air Command, told Congress, "unless it has the Air Transport Command to carry its mechanics, its bombs . . . and all needed equipment until the land and sea lines of communications are established."[35] Since civil carriers would not be a reliable source of airlift under such conditions, Quesada presumed that ATC would do the job. But since everything that the bomber fleet needed would fit into commercial-type aircraft, Quesada's concept implied that the military command would continue to be equipped with airliners rather than with aircraft specialized for broader military mobility requirements.[36]

By 1947 development of a policy of airlift consolidation had stagnated in the face of unsettled strategic and technological questions and by opposing institutional interests. No one yet knew whether the United States would deploy balanced land and air forces to fight future wars or send out the Strategic Air Command to incinerate future enemies under nuclear fires. There was reason also to question the ability of any airlift force to move air and land forces overseas, since the long-range aircraft available could not carry more than light vehicles and artillery, and the new generation of more capacious theater airlift aircraft, mainly the C-119, lacked suitable range. ATC's existing fleet could perform the bomber deployment mission, and beginning in 1946, that was the only "combat" mission it practiced routinely. Neither the Army nor the Navy liked the idea of consolidation, and the Air Force needed the acquiescence of both if it was to gain institutional independence. Independence was the highest priority of air force leaders at the time, so they simply dropped the consolidation issue like a hot rock and let it be.[37] To settle the internal issue of Troop Carrier Command and ATC, General Spaatz set up the new Air Force to include ATC as a separate command and assigned the 3rd Air Force (Troop Carrier) to Tactical Air Command, an organization "equipped and trained to perform joint air-surface training and field exercises with the surface forces."[38]

The Power of Illusion: MATS

Defense reorganization and politics revived air transport consolidation. Signed by President Harry S. Truman in that year, the National Security Act of 1947 charged the new secretary of defense, James V. Forrestal, with taking "appropriate steps to eliminate unnecessary duplication or overlapping in . . . transportation." The act also created the U.S. Air Force. Taken together, these two provisions put air transport consolidation back on the table and gave air force leaders the freedom to press the issue, without fear of its impact on their quest for independence. Five months later, President Truman released *Survival in the Air Age*, a report prepared under the direction of Thomas K. Finletter. Among many provisions aimed at strengthening American commercial and military aviation, the so-called Finletter Report called for "the consolidation of ATC and NATS into one Military Air Transport Service to handle all scheduled military transport services."[39]

Any impression that the Finletter Commission's transport recommendations might have ATC "fingerprints" on them would be correct. Cyrus Smith, back in his job as president of American Airlines, consulted extensively with the commission. Furthermore, he received informational and staff support on a daily basis from John F. Shea, ATC's chief of plans and programs. A former ATC statistical officer, Shea was just beginning a four-decade career as the intellectual lodestone of airlift reform and policy.[40] These two men did as much as anyone to shape the airlift recommendations of the Finletter Report.

With the intent of the president and Congress clear, Secretary Forrestal moved quickly to put planning under way for a new ATC. In December 1947 he directed the Air Force and the Navy to start planning.[41] After some quibbling—the Navy wanted a Joint Airlift Task Force, not a consolidated command—Forrestal directed the two service chiefs to set up an Armed Forces Air Transport Service as an air force major command. In early February the Air Force and Navy's planning group proposed establishment of MATS. Forrestal approved the plan, and MATS activated on June 1, 1948, under the command of Major General Laurence S. Kuter.

In reality, MATS was far less a triumph of joint military planning and cooperation than it was an expedient renaming of the ATC. Like ATC, the new command was responsible for "the transportation by air of personnel . . . materiel, mail, strategic materials and other cargoes for all agencies of the National Military Establishment and . . . all other government agencies." Again like its army air forces predecessor, MATS would oversee the design of new military transport aircraft, contracting with civilian airline and air cargo companies and ensuring that its "aircraft and crews . . . [would] not be delayed or diverted by Theater, Area, Fleet, Air Force, or similar Commanders unless . . . [necessary] for the security of MATS aircraft and crews."[42] In continuation of preexisting arrangements, MATS received no authority over "the tactical air transportation of airborne troops and their equipment, the initial supply and resupply of units in forward combat areas, or that required by the Department of the Navy for internal administration."[43] As a consequence, the Air Force's large troop carrier force and the many packets of air transports operated by other commands, bases, and units remained independent of MATS control. For its part, the Navy was obliged only to move forty-four of its large transports to MATS while keeping forty in its Fleet Logistics Groups (FLOGs). Even then, the activating directive explained, "The personnel, property and facilities furnished by the Navy will be used to provide air transport of primary interest to the Navy insofar as practicable."[44]

In sum, the foundation of MATS was little more than a symbolic action to show the mettle of the new Defense Department. It gave the illusion of consolidation without actually having to fight with any service or major command over things it wanted to keep.[45] The Army got the assurance that Troop Carrier Command remained under the Tactical Air Command, its nominal teammate on the battlefield. By keeping all of its non-ATC airlift assets out of the new command, the Air Force actually made a proportionally smaller contribution to MATS than did the Navy.[46] For its part, the Navy didn't give up anything it felt it needed for its own use. It viewed the squadrons going into MATS as beyond its organic needs and had been starving them for manpower and matériel for months.[47] Senior NATS leaders even took consolidation as an opportunity to advise surplus pilots and navigators to seek air force commissions "in view of the uncertain future facing you as a Reserve Officer in the Navy."[48] If MATS offered anything new to American defense, it was a bully pulpit for a new, but still very small, cohort of airlift "true believers" who saw a big future for the size, mission responsibilities, modernization, and combatant status of the American airlift arm.[49] Just what zealots such as William Tunner, Cyrus Smith, General Kuter, John Shea, and others hovering just outside of the airlift spotlight would do with this pulpit would become evident in the next two milestones of the air mobility story—the Berlin Airlift and the Korean War.

9. The Berlin Airlift

BERLIN WAS LOST, of course. When the Russians blocked the railroads and highways connecting the city to the outside world on June 24, 1948, there was no diplomatic or military option available to the United States, Britain, and France—the Western powers sharing governance of the city with the Soviets—that seemed capable of saving it from starvation and eventual takeover. Geography alone made the city's situation tenuous; its three Western-occupied zones sat as an island in a sea of Soviet-occupied German territory. A hundred miles or so separated it from the main American and British zones of occupation in Western Germany, and the 6,500 Western troops in the city were incapable of defending it against the 16,000 troops in the Soviet zone of the city. An immediate diplomatic solution seemed unlikely, given the sharp differences between the Soviets and the other powers over occupation policy in Berlin and Germany as a whole. Attempting to reopen the routes with armed convoys also was out. In the likely event that the Soviets resisted an incursion, a world war could break out. There was a possibility of airlifting supplies through three air corridors into the city that remained open under provisions of a separate agreement with the Soviets. But no one at the time, certainly not the Russians, could conceive of an airlift capable of feeding 2.5 million Berliners, let alone of bringing in enough fuel and other necessities.[1] So by any reasonable calculation, Berlin was doomed to fall under Soviet control.

But General Lucius DuBignon Clay disagreed, and that made all the difference. An imperious and strong-willed decision maker of overweening self-confidence, he had been the U.S. military governor of Germany since March 1947, and he did not intend for the Russians to achieve a strategic victory on his watch. Retreat from Berlin, he knew, would only prompt further Soviet adventurism and undermine America's long-term security. So despite countervailing recommendations from his staff and superiors in Washington, Clay proposed staying. Since his boss, Secretary of the Army Kenneth Royall, had told him on the first day of the blockade that the ground convoy option was out, Clay on his own authority ordered his air commander, Major General Curtis E. LeMay, to start an airlift.[2] Neither Clay nor LeMay thought an airlift could feed the city, but starting one at least would show resolve and maybe buy a little time. So LeMay's C-47s were flying into the city the next day, June 26, even as President Harry Truman convened the National Security Council (NSC) to discuss the crisis and Clay's precipitous action. When Royall tried to discuss abandoning Berlin to the Soviets, Truman cut him off with an unequivocal "we're staying" and directed the Joint Chiefs of Staff to put Clay's airlift on a "full-scale organized basis."[3] Thus, unfazed by the dithering of his staff and superiors, Lucius Clay had preempted national policy and set his country on a strategic course to save the city.[4]

The man charged with running the airlift, Curtis LeMay, had earned a reputation for decisiveness and force of will during World War II. Now, as the commander of the U.S. Air Forces in Europe (USAFE), he wasted no time getting operations under way. On the 26th, USAFE got thirty C-47s into the air, delivering eighty tons of cargo to Tempelhof, the American air base (AB) in Berlin. British transports actually began flying the previous day into Gatow, their small airfield in the city. Realizing that he would need a lot more lift to have any real impact on the supply situation in Berlin, LeMay that same day asked the Air Force to send as many C-54s as could be made available. On the 27th, the air force chief of staff, General Hoyt S. Vandenberg, notified LeMay that an initial four squadrons of the big planes—fifty-four in all—would be coming from troop carrier groups in the United States, Panama, Hawaii, and Alaska. Also on the 27th, the USAFE commander ordered the 60th Troop Carrier Group to move from Kaufbeuren AB in southern Germany to Weisbaden AB, located much nearer to the entrance of the southern air corridor to Berlin. The 60th was flying out of Weisbaden on the next night. The first C-54s began arriving on July 1, and they and their tired crews were dispatched immediately into the south air corridor leading to Berlin. The Royal Air Force's airlift, mainly through the north corridor, also was increasing steadily in scale and cargo throughput.

There was plenty of confusion, of course. No one knew how long the lift would last. The USAFE staff knew all about fighter and bomber operations but had few officers knowledgeable of air transport. At the beginning, the airlift's cargo planner didn't even know the carrying capacity of a C-47.[5] Their oversights became evident as soon as operations began. Crews poured into bases before arrangements to billet, feed, and bathe them decently had been made. Flight scheduling was chaotic, as crews waited for hours, sometimes a day or more, after their scheduled flight times before they received clearances to take off in aircraft actually loaded with supplies. Load management was an unknown art, as some planes took off with flour and coal while others went with tons of mimeograph paper and bushes for Berlin's reforestation program. Other planes took off overloaded with high-density loads, like canned foods and gasoline, while others flew stuffed to their cabin roofs with cartons of macaroni that weighed only a fraction of their carrying capacity. Only after several days would cargo planners learn to put dense loads on the floor and top them with light materials to ensure that every plane flew loaded and everything got to the city in proper order. On arrival at Berlin, pilots sometimes waited again for hours to get their planes unloaded, stood in line for weather briefings and flight clearances or even just to buy a cola and a hot dog at a snack bar. Even LeMay was delayed almost two hours, waiting for takeoff clearance out of Rhein-Main on the 29th. Disturbed by that and the disorganization he witnessed at Tempelhof, he ordered operations personnel to bring flight plans, weather reports, and food out to the crews in their planes, and he returned to Weisbaden determined to put someone in charge.[6] His choice was Brigadier General Joseph Smith, headquarters commandant of the Weisbaden military area.

Joseph Smith Becomes an Airlifter and Gets Things Going

At first glance, Brigadier General Joseph Smith's record might leave the impression that he was the wrong officer to set up an air transport operation that would either buy time for diplomacy or trigger World War III. He had never commanded an operational unit larger than a squadron. In fact, he had built his career as a staff officer. From the time Lieutenant Joe Smith left West Point in 1923, he performed well enough in his line duties, first as a cavalry officer and then as an aviator, but he had shined in a sequence of increasingly important adjutant, education, staff director, and planning assignments. Before coming to Wiesbaden in March 1947, Smith had served as the staff director of the 8th Air Force as it relocated from England to Okinawa in August 1945 and then as the deputy commander of the Air University. As the Wiesbaden commandant, he supervised the discipline, security, finances, and support of airfields, billeting facilities, depots, and service organizations scattered as much as forty miles from the city.[7]

Smith also could be something of a gadfly within the good-old-boy environment of the postwar Air Force, particularly in occupied Germany. He was long noted for his acute sense of professional propriety, peppery temper, and conviction that everyone should play by the book.[8] As evidenced in the pages of subsequent oral history interviews in 1976 and 1991, Smith's punctilious sense of integrity placed him at odds with several senior officers, most important, LeMay. Even after the passage of many years, Smith remained hot at LeMay's disdainful treatment of him in meetings and failure to back him on several disciplinary complaints against senior USAFE officers. Smith recorded in the earlier interview that his boss had the "finest combat records . . . but he lacked any respect for his subordinates . . . [and] he had absolutely no social graces."[9]

Just why LeMay picked Smith for the job, then, probably had more to do with expediency than professional respect. The two evidently didn't like each other very much. LeMay also had alternatives at hand. Experienced colonels commanded his two troop carrier groups. Colonel Bertram C. Harrison commanded the 60th Group, operating about thirty-six C-47s and just completing its move from Kaufbeuren to Weisbaden, and Colonel Walter Lee commanded the 61st, operating another thirty-six C-47s and a couple of C-54s just down the road at Rhein-Main AB. In addition, LeMay's chief of staff, Brigadier General August W. Kissner, was a longtime confidant and had commanded the Central Atlantic Wing of the Air Transport Command during the war. Why not send him? The most likely reason was that LeMay at the start thought the airlift would be no more than a small-scale and short-lived demonstration of American resolve and, therefore, wasn't worth disrupting his own staff or the two flying units to operate. So he sent Smith to do a minor job, a job so minor that LeMay had Kissner pass the word rather than tell the thoroughly surprised headquarters commandant himself.[10] Smith, in short, probably received command of the first military operation of the Cold War because LeMay thought he was good enough to handle such a small thing.

General Smith surprised the daylights out of everyone. The airlift didn't go away, and as it continued to expand, Joe Smith revealed that fine commanders sometimes come in unexpected packages. A bit nonplussed by an assignment to command something he knew almost nothing about, and reluctant to be an "empire builder," Smith decided he only needed a staff of a couple of operations planners and a maintenance officer to direct the operation.[11] He thus went into the unknown with fewer staff officers than would be assigned to a single air transport squadron of a dozen planes. Empowered by how little he really knew about air transport operations, Smith told his little staff to get going and advise him of any support requirements. He then focused on getting the 60th TCG moved into Wiesbaden AB and its arriving crews retrieved from bars and other recreation facilities and put on rosters and schedules.[12] Despite the potential for chaos, Smith, the troop carrier commanders, and various service organizations got the crews in hand, planes serviced, cargo loaded, and more and more planes on their way to Berlin every day.

Despite his understated approach to leadership, Joe Smith had some experience with managing transport operations during the airmail crisis of 1934 and some vicarious knowledge of the Hump Airlift and of transport planning in the Pacific. From this tenuous experience base, he adapted quickly to the demands of the current airlift, which he dubbed Operation Vittles on his first day in charge. Knowing that the notoriously foul weather of northern Germany could disrupt operations at any time, Smith worked with the USAFE communications officer to install a continuous line of radio navigation aids along the routes from Weisbaden and Rhein-Main to Berlin. He also moved to put air traffic control procedures on an unprecedented footing. At a time when controllers expected to separate aircraft by twenty-five minutes when they were operating under instrument procedures along the same route, Smith began sending out his transports at three-minute intervals, separating them by differences in their cruising altitudes rather than longer time intervals. When Frankfurt air traffic controllers balked at handling returning aircraft on such close timing, Smith asked General LeMay to put them under his authority, which LeMay did. As C-54s began arriving, Smith concentrated them at Rhein-Main, sent all C-47s to Weisbaden, and asked the Military Air Transport Service to loan him Colonel Glen R. Birchard, commander of the MATS wing at Wiesbaden. Birchard, well versed in C-54 operations, smoothed the bed down of the planes at Rhein-Main and worked out procedures to integrate the bigger and faster aircraft into the flow of C-47s already winging to and from Berlin.

The results of Smith's innovations and willingness to reach out for help from any source were impressive. By the middle of July, scarcely three weeks into the operation, he commanded over 150 aircraft that were moving an average of about 1,000 tons per day into the city. In a day of clear weather on July 12, Smith's crews and ground teams put 240 flights and 1,249 tons into Tempelhof. This still amounted to less than a third of the 4,500 tons per day of food, coal, fuel, and other supplies that planners estimated were required to sustain the city. But the airlift was still getting organized, and more planes and people were coming in from the States. Operation Vittles was exceeding everyone's expectations and giving reason for the Western allies to stand tough against the Russians.

The strategic moment came on July 22, 1948, at a meeting of the National Security Council at the White House. Over the pessimism and objections of almost every cabinet member and military service chief present, General Clay argued urgently for staying with the people of Berlin. By flying eighty C-47s and fifty-two C-54s from two to three sorties each per day, his airmen were transporting about 2,500 tons per day into the city. With seventy-five more C-54 Skymasters, he believed he could go to 3,500 tons per day. That, plus the thousand tons a day being delivered by the RAF, would sustain the city indefinitely. General Vandenberg greeted Clay's implied request with strong opposition. That many planes could come only from MATS, the air force chief argued, and stripping MATS of so many planes would pose unacceptable strategic risks. If the Russians went to war, they could all be destroyed, and even if they weren't, they would not be available to support the emergency movements of bomber and fighter escort units in the early days of a conflict.[13] To Clay's relief, President Truman listened to all arguments and then directed Vandenberg and the rest of the Joint Chiefs of Staff to give the airlift the fullest support possible, including the additional C-54s.

At that point, Joseph Smith became a victim of his own success. With so much now riding on the operation, army Lieutenant General Albert C. Wedemeyer strongly advised the president and the NSC to hand over leadership of the airlift to Major General William H. Tunner, the deputy commander of the Military Air Transport Service. Wedemeyer knew Tunner well. During wartime service as the commander of U.S. forces in China, he had been the primary beneficiary of the Hump Airlift under Tunner's command. Wedemeyer argued that the increased scale and strategic importance of the Berlin Airlift called for the most capable commander available, and that commander was Tunner. General Vandenberg dismissed the need for Tunner, saying, "Any of my senior officers could handle such an operation."[14] Perhaps he shared LeMay's and Joseph Smith's initial presumptions that it could not really be all that difficult to run something as simple as an airlift. At any rate, given Tunner's proven ability to squeeze productivity out of transport aircraft, Vandenberg had no choice but to send him out to LeMay, who was no more excited about receiving an outsider to "save" his operation.

Tunner Takes Charge and Finishes the Job

Bill Tunner was waiting for the call. From his position at MATS headquarters, he chaffed at not being in what was shaping up to be the biggest event in the short history of airlift. Tunner being Tunner, he believed unabashedly that Berlin would not be saved unless more aircraft went to Germany, along with him to regiment every aspect of the airlift—planes, maintenance, people, cargo handling, ground infrastructure, and support activities—to produce the absolute maximum flow of tonnage into the two airfields available and any others that perhaps might be built. Eager to the point of professional indiscretion, he wrote a letter to his boss, Lieutenant General Laurence Kuter, to volunteer and "show him that I was serious." Reluctant to champion the request, Kuter told his deputy to "relax . . . that's not the way to do it, Bill. . . . Let's just sit tight and see what happens."[15] Tunner wisely accepted Kuter's advice and did not press to relieve LeMay and Smith of their missions in the midst of crisis and their growing success. Justifiable or not, air force leaders would have taken such a direct intervention as disruptive and self-serving. Instead, Tunner focused on setting up logistics and maintenance support for the airlift, while keeping a close eye on its progress and Pentagon assessments of what to do about it. It was a frustrating time for him, but he had no choice but to wait for events to make his case.[16]

Considering the importance of what Tunner was setting out to do, and the fact that the airlift would still be a USAFE operation, the twenty airlift experts in his entourage when he arrived at Rhein-Main on July 28 should have found frantic arrangements under way to ensure their success. LeMay and Smith should have met him at the plane, with positive assurance that he would have all the support they could muster. They should also have introduced Tunner's officers to several bright USAFE counterparts responsible for facilitating their support requests and coordination in an unfamiliar theater. Finally, in an occupation environment where the Americans could commandeer anything they needed, the Air Transport Command team should have found adequate quarters and organized, fully equipped office space waiting for them or in the midst of hurried completion. The national interest demanded no less.

Instead, Smith and LeMay gave Tunner and his cohort cold greetings and a grudging level of support seemingly designed to make their work as difficult as possible. General Smith, naturally enough hurt at losing command of the airlift, generally shunned Tunner, whom he thought came with an overly large staff, "made many demands," and set up the airlift command "for his own glorification."[17] LeMay, obliged by air force headquarters to accept Tunner, waited for him in his commandeered, servant-filled, 102-room mansion in Weisbaden. He greeted and, basically, dismissed Smith's usurper with a gruff "I expect you to produce." Tunner left LeMay's palace to find that his own room was in a rundown hotel with a makeshift bathroom. He soon discovered that USAFE had found offices for him and his staff in a gutted building empty of furniture, telephones, lights, and anything else needed to get organized.[18] Neither shaken nor probably surprised by the frigid nonsupport forthcoming from the command whose mission he was serving, Tunner put a few members of his staff to organizing the building and sent the rest of his officers into the field to discover the state of the airlift and identify any problems that needed fixing.[19]

Tunner and his staff moved quickly, building on the procedural foundations laid by Generals Smith and LeMay but tightening up everything and innovating in a hundred ways. They made General Smith's three-minute interval a fetish. Tunner demanded that pilots begin their takeoff roles on the scheduled second, climb at precise airspeeds on precise routes, make accurate position reports, and adjust their flight speeds to ensure that they crossed checkpoints three minutes after the preceding aircraft made its position report. To ensure that everyone was flying at the same speed, he had several F-51s equipped with calibrated airspeed indicators fly in formation with each transport to give its crew an opportunity to check their instruments' reading against a common standard. Piggybacking on LeMay's directive that crews would stay with their airplanes at Tempelhof, Tunner ordered his pilots to stay in or next to their planes, period. Flight dispatchers and weathermen passed briefing documents to them via clothespins on the end of sticks. Refreshments also came to the planes in canteen trucks manned by the prettiest young women the Red Cross could recruit at Tunner's behest. Crewmen feeling the call of nature were obliged to wait until they were airborne again and could use their aircraft's relief tube.

Then a near disaster showed Tunner that his reforms had not gone far enough. Arriving over Berlin on September 13, he found the operation a shambles. Weather on the ground was at minimums. Consequently, controllers had stacked dozens of aircraft in holding patterns to await opportunities to land, and more were arriving every three minutes. Worse, individual pilots had pressed in anyway, resulting in one aircraft crashing and burning at the end of Tempelhof's runway, another sitting on the runway with blown tires from overbraking, and another stuck in the mud of a construction area on the field. Horrified at the danger and furious at the controllers for letting the situation develop, he went on the radio and, in a tone that booked no argument, told the shocked controllers, "Tunner talking, and you listen. Send every plane in the stack back to its home base." Having cleared the pattern, he put in practice that time-honored privilege of all military commanders to kick ass and take names. Before he left Berlin, he ordered his two best operational planners, Lieutenant Colonels Red Foreman and Hal Sims, to stay there until they worked out procedures to make sure nothing like that happened again.[20] On returning to Weisbaden, he sent a request to General Kuter to find him some controllers who were able to handle high-density traffic.

The problem was more about philosophy than procedures. From their first days in training, military pilots are imbued with and promoted upon their individual initiative and determination to accomplish their assigned missions. For the most part, those are good things. But in the relatively packed air traffic environment of the airlift, unfettered individualism was hazardous and inefficient. At peacetime airfields socked in by poor weather, transport pilots who went into holding patterns or made multiple approaches until they found "holes" in the clouds and landed were just doing what they were selected and trained to do. Traffic controllers also were trained to facilitate the requests of such pilots, either to get them back into the traffic flow or to put them into holding until things got better. But in the skies of Berlin, such individual efforts created significant risk of collisions and further disrupted the flow of aircraft. In this case, pilot individualism and initiative had to be disciplined in light of the greater need to keep the metronomic flow of aircraft as rhythmic and unbroken as possible. Individual mission accomplishment was less important than keeping the city alive. So, as Tunner later assessed, "I insisted on complete regimentation in every aspect of flying for every pilot . . . no variations. I wanted no experimenting on anyone's part."[21]

Knowing their commander's mind, Foreman and Sims set out to regiment the airlift to a degree heretofore common to combat flying, with its mass formations and interdependent operations, but not so far imposed on operations by transport crews. They began by drafting a plan of precise routes into and out of Berlin's airports that would govern the path of every single aircraft in the system—no deviations allowed in place, time, or speed from takeoff to landing. On arrival in the Berlin area, all pilots, regardless of the weather, were ordered to operate under the observation and guidance of radar controllers. Even on days as clear as crystal, they would follow the heading and speed directives of ground control approach controllers right down to landing. The controllers, not the pilots, would determine if cloud ceilings and visibilities were sufficient for an approach. Whenever controllers advised pilots that the weather was below minimums, they were required to follow other precisely defined procedures to begin an immediate flight back to their home bases, with no opportunity to request a second chance. Maintaining the operational rhythm, even for unsuccessful approaches, was the fulcrum of the new scheme. Despite their professional desire to get their loads in, pilots who were forced by weather or poor airmanship to break off an approach went home with their loads. Tunner endorsed this procedure, because he knew that the overall productivity of the airlift would be served better by keeping the flow going rather than by breaking the rhythm to give unlucky or badly flown planes another go.[22]

The innovations of Tunner and his staff went beyond procedural details to include infrastructure and logistics improvements. In August, he ordered construction of a third airfield in the Tegel suburb of Berlin, which, at 5,500 feet in length, would have been the longest runway in Europe. He combed the Air Force and the Navy for qualified and almost-qualified pilots to increase the daily utilization (ute) rate of his aircraft. Eventually, he ended up with a third of all the flyable C-54s in the Department of Defense and two-thirds of its qualified crews.[23] The average ute rate for Vittles' C-54s reached over four round-trips per day per aircraft. Taking advantage of some more pioneering by General Smith, Tunner got permission from the British and General LeMay to bed down a group of incoming C-54s to Fassberg, a Royal Air Force (RAF) base near the western end of the north corridor and closer to Berlin. To reduce the time his aircraft spent in the routine but labor-intensive inspections they required after every 200 hours of flying, Tunner prevailed on USAFE and the Air Force to reactivate a World War II maintenance depot at Burtonwood, England. Despite persistent manpower and supply shortages, Burtonwood eventually could put a half dozen C-54s through their 200-hour inspections every day. With an eye to future airlift operations, Tunner also brought in one of the Air Force's eleven C-74s to fly some demonstration missions into Tempelhof. The big plane was over twice the weight and carrying capacity of a C-54 and was hard on Tempelhof's runway. But in twenty-four sorties, the plane delivered 429 tons of cargo (equivalent to at least forty-three C-54 loads) and demonstrated the greater efficiency of larger aircraft in operations aimed at putting high tonnages into a limited number of airfields.[24]

Knowing that the morale of the personnel under his command would be a fragile but vital element of the airlift's success, Tunner worked tirelessly to take care of their physical needs and to reinforce their sense that they were doing something important and recognized. He and his staff pushed USAFE continually to upgrade their living quarters, food, and recreational opportunities. When the USAFE staff scheduled a "Berlin Airlift" tour by Bob Hope and other entertainers just about everywhere but the airlift bases, Tunner went to LeMay with an ultimatum to either reschedule or disassociate the tour from the airlift. LeMay agreed and let Tunner reschedule the tour's stops to match the work schedules of his people.[25] Tunner orchestrated morale-building publicity with virtuoso skill. His publicity officer, Captain Raymond Towne, put out a daily *Task Force Times* with stories and news clippings about the operation, the daily statistics of tonnages flown, and sometimes biting and always irreverent cartoons by his personal radio operator, Technical Sergeant John "Jake" Schuffert.

When Tunner discovered that one of his pilots, Lieutenant Gail Halvorsen, was making unauthorized drops of candy attached to handkerchief parachutes to children gathered at the edge of Tempelhof, he chose to exploit the publicity value of the young officer's generosity rather than punish him for violating regulations. Halvorsen became the personification of the airlift's humanitarian goals and of the thousands of American servicemen enduring hardships and danger to preserve the lives and freedom of the trapped people of Berlin. With a big smile and quiet decency, the lanky pilot also became the link between average Americans, the great rescue operation under way, and ultimately the people of Germany. Following a quick publicity tour back in the States, Halvorsen began to receive tons of candy and thousands of parachutes from individual Americans and confectionary companies that he and other "Candy Bombers" began delivering by hand and parachute to the children of Berlin. Living conditions and the pace of work remained demanding throughout the airlift, but Tunner's morale and welfare initiatives, and the self-sacrificing dedication of airlift personnel, kept morale positive if not always high.

In his zeal to make the airlift successful and to prove the strategic value of military airlift in general, Tunner stepped on toes. Never satisfied with the support he received from USAFE, and not given to patience, he made a habit of going directly to MATS, the Air Materiel Command, or any other source of needed support. General LeMay, a pragmatist himself, generally accepted Tunner's circumvention of normal channels. At Tunner's request, he willingly agreed to merge the American and British airlift efforts under the direction of a Combined Airlift Task Force (CALTF), commanded by Tunner and his RAF deputy, Air Commodore J. W. F. Merer. In theory, the agreement abridged USAFE's direct control of the American part of the airlift, but it also promised to improve efficiency, and that is what interested LeMay.

LeMay's replacement in October 1948, General John K. Cannon, was far less tolerant of Tunner's expediencies. He opened their first meeting by demanding an explanation of the CALTF arrangement, which he didn't like at all, and then ordered his airlift commander to make all further requests for outside help through the USAFE staff. Tunner was able to convince Cannon of the need for the CALTF, but his superior's insistence on working through regular staff channels remained in place.[26] Thereafter, relations remained cold and resentful between Cannon, an older, combat commander determined to run things in his theater, and the much younger transportation specialist, equally determined to keep control of Operation Vittles.[27]

Chaffing under Cannon's edict to work through the USAFE staff, which he considered as unsympathetic to the needs of his personnel and of the airlift itself, Tunner jumped at the first opportunity to air his problems above his boss's head. The opportunity came when the secretary of the Air Force, Stuart Symington, inspected the airlift in December 1948. After updating the secretary on the operational details and accomplishments of John K. Cannon, Tunner took him on a tour of all major airlift bases to see how it worked. Symington saw it all, not only the ticking regularity of operations but also the dismal living conditions of the airmen, sailors, and soldiers making it work and the severe supply shortages hampering their efforts. In one famous incident at Rhein-Main, a young mechanic explained that he had been forced by supply shortages to buy a handful of "not worth a damn" tools at his own expense to perform his duties. The fact that such a basic shortfall existed some five months into the operation amounted to a harsh indictment of the effectiveness, perhaps even the attitude, of General Cannon and his staff. But all the USAFE commander could do was to listen as the astute and now very alert secretary probed his subordinate for the full scope of his supply and support problems. At Symington's request, Tunner later provided him with a folder of lists and reports enumerating his immediate needs and also encouraging the Air Force to begin developing a large cargo aircraft.[28]

Apart from Tunner's testy relations with USAFE, there was no denying that his methods were producing results that bordered on the incredible. In August 1948, while Tunner was still getting a handle on the airlift, the aircraft and crews put in place by General Smith moved 74,000 tons of supplies into the city— impressive but still well short of the 4,500-tons-per-day goal. By December, the CALTF operated about 200 American and 100 British aircraft and transported 115,000 tons into the city. Although this was still below the predicted requirements, refinements in load packaging, food dehydration, and the like had substantially increased the net value of a ton of lift. By the spring, the American transport planes, virtually all of them C-54s, were flying an average of about four trips per day into the city and produced a daily throughput of 5,000 to 6,000 tons. In a maximum effort surge on Easter Sunday 1949, Tunner's transport units, competing like rival sports teams, put 1,398 flights and 12,941 tons of cargo into the city. The fervor of that lift was such that one unloading team at Tempelhof raced to retrieve the coal from a plane that lay upside down and broken beyond the end of the runway, with its dazed crew still crawling out of the wreckage.[29] Tonnages mounted steadily, with July 1948 setting a final record of 202,000 tons out of a grand total of 2,325,509 tons of cargo and 227,655 passengers carried into and out of Berlin. By that time, the lift was not only feeding the city but also bringing in raw materials and flying out manufactured goods to help return its economic life to normal.

Changing the World

Watching the Berlin Airlift could not have been exciting for long; it was just airplanes being loaded, flying the corridor, unloading, flying back, and starting over again. Except in emergencies, individual missions in the necklace of planes thrumming through the corridors were hardly distinguishable from one another. But it was when one considered the importance of the event at the moment and for the future that its real significance and excitement came to light. The Berlin Airlift was a world-changing event. Taken as a whole, it saved Berlin, changed the way the East and West related strategically, and midwifed the rebirth of the German state and the moral rehabilitation of the German people. It also sparked a reassessment of airlift doctrine that would shape national military strategy and relations between the Army and the Air Force, even if it produced no measurable policy changes in the short term.

Most important at the time, Operation Vittles humiliated the Soviets and forced them to back down from their goal of starving Berlin into submission. Within a few weeks of slamming shut the gates into the city, they became unhappy witnesses to a growing stream of transports that undermined and eventually made a mockery of their strategy. Worse, the humanity and technical majesty of Vittles cast a harsh and scornful light on the barbarity and stumbling brutality of their blockade, and the world was watching. General Tunner and others believed that Soviet leaders finally lost hope when the Easter Parade signaled clearly that the Allies were prepared to fly the corridors indefinitely and were capable of making Berlin thrive.[30] So without fanfare, the barriers on the roads and rail lines going into Berlin came up on May 12, 1949, less than eleven months from the start of the blockade and just over three weeks after the parade. The communist leaders never explained or apologized for their act; they just gave up and glared out at a world that had just bitten back.

The success of the airlift also revived and rehabilitated the people and state of Germany. In stunning contrast to Soviet expectations, the Berliners did not capitulate. They endured and spoke defiantly of their intention to "offer resistance," even if the Allies did not stand with them. When the Allies did stand with them, the Berliners in the Western sectors voted in a new government, and they energized German politicians to write a new constitution for a new state, West Germany, crafted from the French, British, and American zones of occupation. The noncommunist world generally accepted this new democratic state and, in so doing, marked the political and humanitarian rehabilitation of the West Germans from defeated minions of an odious dictatorship to the citizens of modern Europe. Bitterness and suspicion remained in the hearts of many Europeans who had suffered at the hands of Nazi Germany. But the establishment of West Germany marked the de facto end of World War II and started the country down the road to membership in the North Atlantic Treaty Organization (NATO) and the formal end of the occupation in 1955.

Berlin also turned around the relationship of Germany and the United States. As late as 1946, gangs of Nazi diehards, "Werewolves," were attacking occupation forces and German officials cooperating with them. Even in early 1948, Americans in Germany were cautious about traveling alone or at night for fear of attacks by opportunistic thugs. During the airlift, active German resistance ended. America was now the defender of West Germany's freedom, and Americans became a large and generally accepted minority in German society. During the ensuing four decades of the Cold War, American military communities sprang up all over the southern half of the country, and millions of American soldiers and their families, civilian employees of the government, and members of the business community experienced years of life in Germany and among the Germans. Perhaps nothing revealed the strength of the esteem Germans granted to the leaders of the airlift than the sight of Gail Halvorsen, the beloved Candy Bomber, carrying the team placard for Germany at the Munich Olympics in 1972. For opponents in two world wars, the two countries became remarkably linked, to their mutual benefit and the consternation of their Soviet enemies.

The triumph of Berlin also fanned a burst of debate in the Department of Defense over future airlift policy. While Tunner was in Europe, he was uncharacteristically circumspect in his promotion of airlift interests. But he did tell the readers of *Time* magazine that the airlift was "an exercise in the technique of using big airplanes in a manner hitherto unknown."[31] He also spoke frequently of the need for a new transport aircraft, larger and more suited to military requirements than even the big C-74s then available. Using the C-74's operating characteristics to illustrate his point, Tunner reported that 68 of them could replace a fleet of 178 C-54s to move 135,000 tons per month into Berlin while burning less than half the fuel. Beyond a few such official inputs, however, the unstinting demands of directing the airlift restricted Tunner to conducting quick interviews with visiting reporters, during which he usually focused on the workings of the operation and its potential value. The value of larger aircraft became the grist for almost every interview Tunner gave to the press during this period, and he sent several reports to the Pentagon pushing for their development.[32] As soon as he got home, however, he began writing and speaking frequently on the subject.[33]

The real push for the modernization and reorganization of airlift forces came from MATS headquarters, where General Kuter and his deputy, Rear Admiral John P. Whitney, had greater freedom to speak out in military and public forums. General Kuter was committed to the fundamental tenets of the global airlift vision: consolidation of airlift forces, modernization, and recognition of airlift as a combat arm of the U.S. Air Force.[34] In August 1948, while the airlift was still in its desperate first months, he pressed the Department of Defense to assign all of its airlift arms—MATS, Troop Carrier Aviation, navy Fleet Logistics Groups (FLOGS), marine transport squadrons, Strategic Air Command (SAC) Strategic Support Squadrons, and so on—to MATS. Such a force, he reasoned, would be powerful, be able to use all its assets rationally and efficiently, and be flexible enough to be "diverted to other priority requirements after SAC is deployed and adequately supported by surface means."[35]

Kuter was a little more circumspect in public forums. Speaking to an Air War College class in February 1949, for example, he declared that MATS was a military command providing "strategic airlift" to the Strategic Air Command and other users. But he stopped short of calling for consolidation or any expansion of his command's missions beyond air transport.[36] Similarly, Admiral Whitney the next month regaled a gathering of the Society of Automotive Engineers with details of the airlift and declared that "no longer . . . is there the danger that our nation will . . . be hamstrung because of the inadequate support of second-rate air transport." But he avoided any mention of such controversial topics as consolidation and combatant status at such a public podium.[37]

Among others, army leaders were observing the Berlin Airlift carefully and drawing their own conclusions about its implications for their service. Even civilian reporters were quick to draw a connection between an ability to feed 2.5 million people and, perhaps, the ability to deploy and support an army fighting deep into a continent and far from the sea.[38] This was an attractive notion to an army confronted by the likelihood that future enemies armed with atomic bombs would certainly target the port facilities and lines of communications of an advancing American army. If a significant force, perhaps even a corps or field army, could leap over those points and directly attack important objectives, it could inflict decisive harm to future enemies, perhaps before they could react. Numerous army officers discussed such "airhead" operations even before Berlin. But the chief of Army Field Forces, General Jacob L. Devers, publicly made them an official area of study as a direct result of the Operation Vittles experience. Vittles, Devers wrote in *Military Review*, undermined any objections to his earlier statements that entire field armies could be inserted into and supported through airfields located in a large airhead area. Newly developed air force transport aircraft, he noted, gave "every reason to believe that . . . a combat effective infantry division, less medium tanks, can be completely transported by air." Most important among these aircraft were the C-119B, which could drop paratroops and land on short runways, and the C-124A, a substantial modification of the C-74, which had an integral loading ramp in its nose and could carry "all but a few items of equipment of a field Army." The Army, Devers reported, was examining all of the Air Force's "records, statistics, studies, and findings" on the airlift and applying them to "the problems which might be expected to arise."[39]

Air force leaders probably were aghast. Given an extremely tight defense budget projected for 1950, service leaders planned to reduce the size of the MATS fleet and operations, not undertake a major expansion to accommodate the Army's vision.[40] In a systematic attack on the practicality of the airhead concept, an Air War College professor of logistics, Colonel Jasper N. Bell, argued that "an air transportable operation of corps size is loaded with limiting factors." A corps comprising one airborne division, two infantry divisions, and appropriate supporting units, he estimated, would consist of 72,150 personnel; initially require the delivery of 50,790 tons of personnel, equipment, supplies, and airfield construction materials; and require a daily resupply lift of 4,791 tons plus additional fuel and munitions if it went on the offensive. The initial movement of this force would require 9,728 aircraft sorties and another 938 resupply sorties each day. Given imponderables, such as bad weather and enemy action, Colonel Bell questioned whether the effort expended would be worthwhile, "as long as there is a more effective way of neutralizing the enemy."[41]

The "more effective way" to which Bell was alluding was a bomber fleet armed with atomic bombs. Since the end of the war, senior air force leaders had been clear in their belief that a strong and quickly deployable bomber fleet had to be at the heart of the national defense.[42] Discussing the airlift implications of that strategic concept in late 1947, the commander of the Tactical Air Command, Lieutenant General Elwood R. Quesada, advised Congress that the Air Transport Command existed to support the long-range striking force, "carry[ing] its mechanics, its bombs . . . and all needed equipment until the land and sea lines of communications are established."[43] Happily, for the Air Force at least, bomber deployments placed much smaller demands on Air Transport Command than would deployments of land forces. During one exercise in 1946, for example, five C-54s moved the ground personnel and equipment required by eight B-29s flying from Fort Worth, Texas, to Panama.[44] Moving a ground combat unit, this little flight of C-54s would have been hard pressed to lift much more than a fully armed infantry company. For the same investment in airlift, therefore, the Air Force felt it could position a force capable of leveling cities and destroying armies or move a ground unit capable of holding a hill or conquering a village. It was not surprising, then, that General Muir Fairchild, the vice chief of staff, advised Tunner that a truly modern transport design would not be funded anytime soon.[45] The best the Air Force could do was to develop the C-124, a modified version of the C-74 that boasted more powerful engines, a larger payload, and improved loading characteristics.

It turned out, then, that the experience of the Berlin Airlift galvanized thought on the elements of the global airlift model but had virtually no impact on policy. The Air Force was seeking an atomic-based strategy and force structure that called for neither an expansion of its airlift capabilities nor even energetic modernization. Thus, while a few new C-124s and C-119s began to flow into MATS and troop carrier units, respectively, the Air Force "ruthlessly cut" MATS operations and force structure overall. By April 1950, General Kuter was obliged to warn Congress that his command possessed only 290 "C-54 equivalents" of lift in a mixed fleet of C-54s, C-74s, Boeing C-97s, and Douglas C-124s. These 290 C-54 equivalents fell well short of the 2,500 called for in various war plans.[46] In response to these dire numbers, the Air Force directed MATS to reduce its flight schedules even further and close several routes in May.[47] Before these reductions could take effect, however, the United States found itself at war in far-off Korea.

10. The Korean War

CLAY BLAIR OPENED his history of the Korean War by saying that, while the conflict was little more than a "phrase in history books" for many Americans, its "impact . . . on the United States government and society was profound." Blair made his point by listing the intensification of the Cold War, acceleration of the U.S.-Soviet nuclear arms race, and encouragement of McCarthyism among the war's impacts on American national security and political affairs.[1] Much the same thing could be said about the impact of the Korean War on air mobility policy and affairs. In the early months of the struggle, Major General William H. Tunner invented modern theater airlift by requesting and getting command over all air force transport organizations in the theater and operating them on a "common-user" basis. Meanwhile, the Military Air Transport Service (MATS) refined the efficiency and capacity of its transpacific routes and integrated a new category of civil air carriers, the so-called nonskeds, into the military air transport effort in a first step toward establishing the modern Civil Reserve Airlift Fleet. Most important and for the first time, all of the major elements of America's modern air mobility capabilities—airlift, air refueling, and battlefield airlift—conducted combat operations simultaneously, if not in coordination with one another. These organizations and events would shape American air mobility affairs and policy from then to the present.

Operation Swarmer

Speaking at the U.S. Air Force Academy in 1978, General Theodore Ross Milton described Operation Swarmer as a prelude to the organization and conduct of theater airlift during the Korean War. As the chief of staff for General William H. Tunner's Combined Airlift Task Force during the Berlin Airlift, holding the same position for Swarmer, and MATS director of operations at the start of the Korean conflict, Milton spoke with authority. Berlin was the model for the air transport phase of the exercise, he told gathered air force historians, and in turn became the model for theater airlift operations in Korea.[2] What Milton did not have time to relate during his brief talk at the academy was that Swarmer also marked a number of "firsts" in airlift history, making it an important event in its own right. So, though often lost as a footnote between accounts of the Berlin Airlift and the Korean War, Swarmer was the proximal beginning of the Korean War, at least for airlift operations and policy.

New planes and the Berlin Airlift planted the intellectual seeds of Operation Swarmer. During World War II airborne units were obliged by their equipment and limited resupply to conduct defensive operations in place once they were on the ground. Equipped only with what could be dropped by parachute or delivered in relatively small gliders, they did not have the tanks, trucks, artillery, and engineer equipment needed to strike out from their drop zones against strong enemy resistance. But by early 1950 the Air Force and Army had developed equipment and techniques to parachute heavy equipment and weapons out of the large cargo openings in the rear of the Air Force's C-82s and growing fleet of larger C-119s. Using these capabilities, the Air Force could strengthen parachute infantry units with at least some artillery and antitank guns during their initial assaults. Then, if those units established an airhead by capturing one or more airfields, transport units could employ the traffic control procedures developed for the Berlin Airlift to quickly land the personnel and combat equipment needed for offensive tactics. C-124s, which also were becoming available, could strengthen the offensive by delivering light tanks, such as the twenty-five-ton M24.

Swarmer, then, was the first test of inserting and sustaining an airborne force into an airhead to launch a sustained ground offensive. On April 28, 1950, following a four-day preliminary air campaign, the 187th Regimental Combat Team (RCT) dropped adjacent to Mackall Army Airfield on the west side of the huge Fort Bragg military reservation. Three hours later, the field having been secured, a stream of cargo aircraft began landing at ninety-second intervals day and night. Mirroring Berlin control procedures, these aircraft flew precise routes and approach procedures into the airport under radar guidance. On the ground, several thousand troops of the 11th Airborne Division debarked from their planes, while loading teams extracted cargo trucks, fire trucks, bulldozers, bridging equipment, radio transmitters, medical teams, howitzers, and other impedimenta from dozens of other planes. Even as the transport stream continued into Mackall, three regimental combat teams jumped along the line of advance to strengthen the offensive toward Pope Air Force Base (AFB), about thirty miles east of Mackall. In the five days of the exercise, the transport force delivered over 26,000 soldiers by parachute or by off-loading them on the ground, 3,098 heavy weapons and vehicles, and almost 3,000 tons of supplies.[3]

Swarmer also marked the first time that Air Transport Command and Troop Carrier Command forces were integrated in a tactical operation. Given their atrophied state in the wake of postwar demobilization, the Air Force had little choice in the matter. As *Time* magazine pointed out in its preview of the exercise, "The simulated attack on a peaceful section of North Carolina will involve just about all the Sunday punch the U.S. can mobilize." Not only were the Army's postwar airborne divisions understrength, continued *Time's* essay, but the operation involved "virtually all the troop-carrier and cargo planes that would be available if the U.S. were attacked this week," or barely enough to drop one regiment at a time.[4] This was a paltry force, indeed, compared to the one that dropped whole divisions during World War II.

Even with MATS and Troop Carrier Command joined, Swarmer posed serious challenges. One of the most immediate ones would be building movement plans around a mismatched assortment of transports that included fifty-one C-46s, ninety-one C-54s, forty C-82s, seven C-74s, forty-five C-119s, and a handful of developmental aircraft, including C-122, C-123, and C-125 assault transports and the huge C-124.[5] Next, once the airdrops were accomplished, the Swarmer plan merged troop carrier units into the clockwork stream of transports flying into Mackall. This was new territory for troop carrier crews. Normally, they flew either in large, highly regimented formations or as individual transports with minimal outside control while in flight. On their part, transport crews understood regimentation, but they were not used to coordinating with air defense controllers and fighter escorts or worrying about "enemy" ground-based air defenses.[6]

Knowing that scheduling discipline and centralized control would be essential to the success of the exercise, the air force commander of the exercise, General Lauris Norstad, took the controversial step of naming General Tunner as the airlift commander.[7] Under Tunner, Brigadier General Milton would command air transport operations, the bulk of all sorties, while Major General Willard R. Wolfinbarger would direct troop carrier forces during airborne drops. All the choices made sense on paper. Tunner was the most capable airlift efficiency expert in the world. Milton had been Tunner's trusted right arm during the airlift and, as commander of the Tactical Air Command, Wolfinbarger controlled troop carrier units stationed in the continental United States. But, as Milton noted later, the selection caused some "evident dismay" among "grizzled troop carrier types."[8] Tunner's sudden waltz into the heart of what they considered their business carried unwelcomed institutional and doctrinal implications for Troop Carrier Aviation. Feelings were so strong that when Milton tried to brief Wolfinbarger's boss, General Ennis Whitehead, commander of the Continental Air Command, on the operation, the senior officer cut him off and stormed out of the briefing room.[9] Once again, Tunner had become a lightning rod of intraservice turf and doctrinal battles.

To no one's surprise, Swarmer exposed significant shortfalls in the American airlift program. Most involved were concerned by the artificialities of the exercise. To keep the airlift flow moving, General Norstad restricted "enemy" forces from disabling Mackall, and exercise umpires limited the successes of opposing fighter attacks on transports. Such limitations made sense in a test environment, but there was good reason to think that they would not pertain in actual war. The C-119 also showed great promise for delivering trucks and howitzers by parachute and unloading on the ground. But its design also proved to be too weak for operation on rough fields with heavy loads.[10] All recognized that airliner-derived designs, mainly the C-54 and C-74, were difficult to operate and unload at forward fields.[11] Numerous observers also worried that the Air Force's apparent failure to lift even "light" tanks into the Swarmer airhead left friendly troops vulnerable to enemy armored assaults several times during the exercise.[12] Finally, as noted by airpower theorist Alexander de Seversky, Swarmer "showed that to move a single corps and its supplies called for an airlift greater than that represented by the equipment of our entire domestic and foreign airlines system." A strong proponent of strategic airpower, de Seversky also argued that any effort to extend the "Army's strategic airlift" would undermine national security.[13] But before detailed assessment of Swarmer's implications could get under way, North Korea preempted the whole issue by launching its invasion of South Korea.

The Korean War: General Tunner Invents Theater Airlift

No war ever caught the United States more by surprise or unprepared than North Korea's invasion of South Korea on June 25, 1950. In comparison, the Japanese attack on Pearl Harbor was a surprise in terms of time and place but not as the start of a conflict that most in American military and political authority had known was coming. No American leader in authority, except perhaps the U.S. ambassador to Korea John J. Muccio, sensed the danger of a North Korean attack. Confronted with a simmering civil war throughout the Korean Peninsula and North Korea's general bellicosity, Muccio had warned Congress earlier in June of some vague "imminent threat." Unfortunately, neither he nor any other U.S. intelligence source picked up the political or military signs that the communist government of the north had decided to invade.[14]

So things immediately went to hell in a hand basket. Facing a North Korean Army of 89,000 troops supported fully by tanks, artillery, and Yak fighters, the Republic of Korea (ROK) Army fielded only 38,000 soldiers, a battery of howitzers, and no tanks or combat aircraft. Not surprisingly, the ROK Army began to lose cohesion and fade to the south in a matter of hours. By the second day of the war, the retreat was beginning to look like a rout. In the face of North Korea's naked aggression and the certain loss of South Korea, the United States and the United Nations (UN) committed themselves to the defense of Korea. The problem was that the only reinforcements immediately available were American occupation troops in Japan, and they were inadequately trained and equipped for conventional conflict. But there was no time to prepare, so the United States began committing units to combat, hoping to improve their equipment and supply stocks in time to halt the North Korean tide surging southward.

Under those conditions, air transport was vitally important. From the first day, transport aircraft assigned to MATS and the 5th Air Force in Japan began flying over 500 American civilian evacuees out of South Korea while bringing some military supplies into the country. On June 30, C-54s from the 374th Troop Carrier Group (TCG) lifted the first U.S. combat unit into the battle. Named Task Force (TF) Smith, after its commander, Lieutenant Colonel Charles B. Smith, this unit consisted of two infantry companies supported by an artillery battery, totaling 540 soldiers. In a delaying action against about forty tanks and 5,000 infantry, TF Smith disrupted the North Korean advance for a few vital hours, giving other elements of the 24th Infantry Division time to organize a stronger defensive position to the south. Over the next two months, as American and UN military units consolidated a defensive salient in the southern part of the Korean Peninsula, transport aircraft based in Japan moved thousands of tons of supplies and troops to augment the main flow of resources through the port of Pusan. Under the direction of Brigadier General Edward J. Timberlake, the 5th Air Force vice commander, the airlift stream into Pusan replicated the procedures refined during the Berlin Airlift and Swarmer, with an aircraft arriving every twenty minutes and returning directly to base if it missed its approaches in poor visibility.[15] Given the limited number of transports available—two squadrons of C-54s in the 374th TCG, augmented by a squadron of C-47s and some C-46s—Timberlake's accomplishment was impressive and necessary.

As planning began for a counteroffensive in the fall, the need for stronger airlift capabilities became obvious. The rugged geography of Korea, essentially an unbroken mix of mountains and ridgelines interspersed with narrow valleys, would be a logistical challenge in the best of conditions. But the advancing UN forces would not be operating under the best of conditions. Roads in Korea were few and generally more suited to ox carts than cargo trucks. The North Korean Army also had proven adept at guerrilla operations, so roads would be subject to interdiction and convoys at risk of ambush. Thus, while most bulk requirements would have to move by road, airlift would be needed to move delicate and high-priority cargoes—radios, engines, medical supplies and equipment, and so on—and to move essential personnel and wounded and sick soldiers rearward. Moreover, the 187th Regimental Combat Team was coming to the theater in late September, adding large-scale airborne assaults to the theater airlift schedule.

General George E. Stratemeyer, the commander of the Far East Air Forces (FEAF) and the air deputy of General Douglas A. MacArthur's Far East Command (FEC), acted quickly to strengthen the organization and leadership of his airlift forces.[16] As soon as the war began, he called on the Air Force for additional transport units, though the first unit, the 314th TCG with seventy-seven C-119s, could not arrive until early September.[17] Meanwhile, FEAF scrounged up about twenty C-47s and handfuls of C-46s and C-54s from air force units and headquarters in Japan and the Philippines. In late August, Stratemeyer also asked for the loan of the most capable air transport officer he knew, William H. Tunner. Serendipitously General Tunner was in Japan at the time, inspecting MATS operations in the theater. Following quick consultations with Stratemeyer, he made a marathon four-day round-trip back to the States to close out his report to MATS, get instructions from the air force chief of staff General Vandenberg, make caregiver arrangements for his two young sons, and report back to Tokyo, ready to go. Stratemeyer briefed him immediately on his new responsibilities—improving the efficiency of the logistics lift and preparing to drop the 187th RCT.

General Stratemeyer also placed Tunner in command of a wholly new organization, the Far East Air Forces Combat Cargo Command (FEAF CCC). Stratemeyer activated FEAF CCC on August 26, 1950, to consolidate all theater airlift operations under a single commander, who would operate under FEAF on a coequal basis with the 5th Air Force. Tunner's new command included the 374th TCG; the 1st TCG (Provisional [P]), also activated on August 26 to absorb the C-47s and C-46s drawn in from other commands; and the 314th TCG on its arrival a few weeks later. Tunner was excited and gratified by the independence of his command and his freedom from supervision by "tactical air people [who] just don't understand air transport."[18]

With about as free a hand as a subordinate military officer could expect, Tunner set about organizing and conducting Korean airlift operations his way. Knowing that a number of C-47s were still scattered around in the personal service of the 5th, 13th, and 20th Air Force commanders, several senior army headquarters, and the U.S. ambassadors to Japan and Korea, and to the 5th Air Force Air Service Command, Tunner launched a campaign to get them all into the 1st TCG (P). When the marines committed Transport Squadron (VMR) 152 to the theater, Tunner prevailed on General Stratemeyer to press for its attachment to Combat Cargo. Probably to the surprise of many, the marines readily agreed, and through the fall and winter, VMR-152 committed five of its ten C-54s daily to Combat Cargo tasks, moving over 2,500 tons of cargo and evacuating over 4,000 casualties in the process.[19] Despite efforts by senior commanders—notably Major General Edward M. Almond, commander of the X Corps—to get some of their planes back, General MacArthur and General Stratemeyer defended Tunner's control.[20] As Tunner recorded in his memoirs, "I was persistent. When the protestations ended, I had the planes—all of them."[21]

Tunner and the Air Transport Command staff officers he brought with him were masters at organizing big airlift operations at a run, and the results were clear. As soon as he took over his headquarters at Ashiya AFB, Japan, Tunner prevailed on MacArthur and Stratemeyer to streamline the procedures by which available airlift capacity was matched with the requests of the major air and ground commands. Under the new arrangement, the FEC Joint Air Priority Board, representing General MacArthur's priorities, allocated available capacity in percentages to the Army and the Air Force every month. Usually, the Army got 70 percent of the available airlift while the Air Force got 20 percent and FEC HQ held back 10 percent as a reserve for unforeseen requirements.[22] With these guidelines in hand, a Joint Airlift Control staff based at Ashiya would make day-to-day determinations of which command's cargo and personnel would be moved and with what priority. As Tunner desired, the only job of Combat Cargo was to move tonnage; he had no role in telling more senior commanders what he would and would not do for them. With typical flair, he worked every possible detail to smooth his operation and keep productivity at a maximum. Even hosting a visit by Stratemeyer was a choreography of a "delicious lunch" and "one of the finest briefings that [Stratemeyer had] ever attended."[23]

The first test of General Tunner's battlefield leadership came on September 15, 1950, when the U.S. Marines landed at Inchon, the port of Seoul, as one prong of the United Nations' counterattack to drive the North Korean Army back north. Plans for the operation called for Combat Cargo to drop the 187th RCT at Kimpo Airfield, about ten miles inland from Inchon. But the aggressive marines took Kimpo on the 19th, obviating the need for an airborne assault. In response, FEC directed Tunner to airland the 187th and its 5,000 tons of equipment at Kimpo. Within minutes of the field falling into marine hands, Combat Cargo aircraft began flowing in with loads of paratroopers and equipment, often at intervals as short as two minutes between planes. Flying in with the first formation, Tunner observed that the flow of marine supplies was bottlenecked by the great mud flats and high tides of Inchon Harbor. So, on landing at Kimpo, he found the marine commander and promised to "bring in all you want, right now." Running the airlift from a makeshift command center in his C-54 parked at Kimpo, Tunner coordinated marine and other requests in near real time and made airlift the primary source of supplies for several days.[24] For almost two weeks, Combat Cargo made the difference between a stalled offensive and moving forward.

Then Tunner was called on to do something that no one thought he could do: he directed the planning and execution of a major airborne operation. At that moment, even advocates of airlift consolidation admitted their conviction that "the one big training problem is that of producing commanders and staff officers who can see the implications of this total [global airlift] mission and not be swayed by their loyalties to either Troop Carrier or MATS."[25] Opponents of the idea stated flatly, "Each type [of] air transportation effort requires a specialist. The jack-of-all-trades cannot be depended upon when the chips are down."[26] So when it came time to drop the 187th RCT north of Pyongyang, the North Korean capital, the interest in how Tunner, an air transport man, would handle this signature element of theater airlift must have been acute, at least within the airlift community.

Tunner and his staff took it all in stride and rewrote the book on airborne operations. The specific mission was to put paratroopers and their heavy equipment down on drop zones at the villages of Sukch'on and Sunch'on to block the escape of enemy troops and perhaps rescue a train full of UN prisoners of war. Both villages were located about thirty-five miles north of Pyongyang, each astride one of the main highway/railway routes north. During the planning phase, Tunner broke with World War II precedent by standing down the seventy-one C-119s and forty C-47s committed to the drops for only two days, rather than weeks, to prepare crews and planes for the drops. Meanwhile, Tunner continued to use his C-54s and C-46s to move other critical personnel and cargoes around the theater. The drop at Sukch'on went in on October 20, 1950, with 1,470 men, followed for the first time in combat by parachute drops of jeeps, 90mm antitank guns, 105mm howitzers, and their ammunition. Minutes later, a similar force jumped into Sunch'on, about seven miles to the east, complete with its own complement of vehicles and heavy equipment. Combat Cargo conducted additional personnel and supply drops over the next two days, bringing the total personnel dropped to about 4,000 and over 600 tons of equipment.[27] In a display of initiative and courage that would earn him the Distinguished Service Cross, General Tunner had gone ahead of the main formation alone to make a final check of weather and defensive threats, and then hovered over the drops in his C-54 to observe results.[28] In further demonstration of his ability to lead and juggle the many competing demands on his forces, Tunner had most of his aircraft back in the logistics flow within twenty-four hours of the main drops.

Barely two months after the Sukch'on and Sunch'on drops, UN forces were retreating before a massive counterattack launched across the Yalu River by communist China on November 25. Over the next three months, as UN units struggled to extricate themselves from entrapment by the fast-moving communist forces and to establish a new defensive line farther south, the air transports of Combat Cargo command made a vital contribution to strategic success. In the northwest corner of Korea, air transport was the sole source of supply and evacuation for UN troops assigned to the U.S. X Corps fighting and then retreating along a seventy-six-mile road from the Chosin Reservoir to the port of Hungnam. C-47s flew through enemy fire at two strips, one only 2,300 feet long and the other even shorter, to bring in supplies and fly out thousands of wounded or ill soldiers. C-119s parachuted hundreds more tons of supplies, including the sections of a prefabricated treadway bridge, to the retreating American marines and soldiers and South Korean soldiers as they fought their way through Chinese roadblocks and attacks. Kept alive by airlift and a constant stream of close support aircraft, the UN forces eventually made it to Hungnam on December 11, still intact and in fighting order. In all FEAF Combat Cargo Command aircraft flew 1,608 sorties to bring almost 5,300 tons of supplies to the beleaguered UN forces and move 14,518 passengers into and out of the battle zone.[29]

By February 1951, the battle lines had stabilized into a near stalemate close to the original borders of North and South Korea, creating an opportunity to put theater airlift on a more permanent footing. On February 8, Tunner relinquished command of FEAF CCC and returned to MATS. His replacement was Colonel John P. Henebry, an air hero of World War II. Henebry had just returned to active duty, as commander of the Air Force Reserve 437th Troop Carrier Wing. On February 25, FEAF deactivated the provisional Combat Cargo Command and transferred all its resources to the new 315th Air Division (Combat Cargo). In March, General Stratemeyer placed the 315th under the 5th Air Force, essentially returning theater airlift to the organizational status it had at the beginning of the war. CCC and Tunner had dealt with the initial emergency, and now things could return to traditional and comfortable organizational, operational, and doctrinal patterns.

The 315th Air Division, generally still referred to as "Combat Cargo," continued to provide vital logistics support to UN forces in Korea. During the course of the war and with an average strength of only 140 aircraft, the command flew 210,343 sorties, evacuated 307,804 patients, and transported 2,605,591 passengers and 391,763 tons of freight. Over 18,000 tons of that freight was airdropped, often to units under severe enemy attack.[30] Much of this lift also supported the movement of whole fighter wings, including the bulk of their vehicles and heavy equipment. Army planners grew so confident of the availability of airlift support that they incorporated it routinely in the logistics of future operations and presumed that it mitigated the risks of enemy surprises. Thus, to an unprecedented degree, airlift had become a central element of the American way of war, not just a logistical adjunct to trucks, trains, and ships.

For all of the success of theater airlift during the Korean War, it was plagued from the beginning by an operationally awkward and technologically obsolescent fleet of aircraft.[31] Hardly designed for rough operations at forward fields, four of the five major transport types employed by Combat Cargo—the C-46, C-47, C-54, and C-124—were derived from commercial airliner designs. Designed at a time when paved runways were not common, the first three aircraft could operate on the sod and dirt runways that could be found or built quickly in battle areas. The C-47's ability to operate into rough fields less than 2,000 feet in length was critically valuable for supplying surrounded units and evacuating their wounded. But, otherwise, the low-wing designs and side-loading cargo doors of these aircraft rendered them slow to load and unload and sharply limited the dimensions and weight of the cargo items they could carry. The C-124, with its forward cargo ramp, freight elevator, and thirty-ton payload, was a much more useful aircraft for moving vehicles and equipment. But its ninety-ton gross weight tended to crush ordinary runways of dirt or thin concrete surfacing, so it was used only on the strongest runways at major airfields. On paper, the C-119 was better suited to parachute drops and operations at forward fields than any of the aircraft. Its high-wing design lowered the fuselage to truck-bed height, greatly facilitating loading, unloading, and air-dropping large items through its rear cargo door, which opened to the full profile of its cargo deck. But the "Dollar-nineteen" also was so underpowered at high gross weights, prone to structural damage from rough landings, and subject to engine failures that FEAF allowed only parachute-equipped passengers to ride in it. In the end, Combat Cargo accomplished its missions but only through astute management of the strengths and weaknesses of the individual aircraft in its overly complicated order of battle.

MATS and the Transpacific Lift

The outbreak of war did not present MATS with any unfamiliar operational problems or opportunities for pioneering doctrinal innovation. By that time, transpacific civil and military transport operations had been a matter of routine for over a decade, and MATS had access to bases along both a Central Pacific route to Japan via Hawaii and the North Pacific route through Alaska. But, like the rest of the Air Force, MATS wasn't ready for war. Even as the Berlin Airlift and Operation Swarmer were demonstrating the future importance of air transport, air force austerity measures had reduced the command to just over 200 four-engine transport aircraft, each with only one crew assigned. At that level of manning, the command overall was flying its aircraft less than three hours per day, and its average traffic across the Pacific was about one aircraft per day, for a total of several hundred passengers and seventy tons of cargo moved per month. From that limited base, the Joint Chiefs of Staff directed MATS on July 20, 1950, to increase its traffic to seventy-three tons per day.[32] Faced by this 3,000 percent increase in its responsibilities, MATS leaders were obliged to investigate every possible source of reinforcement and improved operational efficiency for the Pacific routes.

The first order of business was to put all available military capacity on the Pacific routes. The need for quick action was acute. In the first weeks of the war, the demand for high-priority movements, ranging from heavy bazookas to aircraft engines, far outstripped the capacity of the sixty C-54s assigned to MATS's Pacific Division. In response, MATS planners shifted available personnel and planes into the Pacific region. To get more crews on line and thereby increase the daily utilization, or "ute," rate of its aircraft, MATS accelerated its training programs. Air force chief of staff General Vandenberg helped by placing two troop carrier groups, with seventy-five C-54s, under Kuter's command. The 426th Squadron of the Royal Canadian Air Force began helping in July, flying its North Stars, improved versions of the DC-4, between McChord Field, near Seattle, and Tokyo's Haneda Airport.[33]

Although an obvious source of immediate relief, the new generation of pressurized transport aircraft in the scheduled airline industry proved a difficult resource for MATS to access. Compared to the C-54, the DC-6s, Boeing Stratoliners, and Lockheed Constellations flown by American Airlines, Pan American Airways, and other carriers were sixty to eighty knots faster and carried substantially more passengers and cargo. Pressurized, they also flew at higher and more comfortable altitudes. But it was summer, and the big carriers balked at taking their best planes off their routes at the height of tourist season. Eventually, MATS would get some of their aircraft, but the American airline industry clearly wasn't as eager to help as it had been at the start of World War II.

That left charter cargo carriers to pick up the load. These carriers included airlines like Transocean, California Eastern, and Seaboard, survivors of a crop of about 2,700 "fly-by-night-airlines" that sprang up at every airport in America after the war and were operated by veterans flying surplus military aircraft. Economics and the attentions of Civil Aeronautics Authority (CAA) inspectors quickly drove all but a few dozen of these marginal and often unsafe operators out business. As charter carriers, most of the surviving airlines operated under Part 145 of CAA regulations rather than the Certificates of Common Carriage issued to major airlines conducting scheduled flights. Consequently referred to as "Part 145s," "non-certs," and "nonskeds," some of these companies operated C-54s in generally good condition, employed two or three crews per aircraft, and were hungry for air force business. Wasting no time, the Air Force authorized MATS on June 25, 1950, to charter aircraft as needed to support the war effort, the number of which eventually settled out to about ten carriers flying sixty C-54s.[34]

The results of all these efforts were impressive in absolute numbers. By managing its resources carefully, the Pacific Division increased its ute rate to six hours per aircraft per day by the end of 1951.[35] On high-priority operations, such as the deployment of the 508th Fighter Escort Wing (FEW) from Turner AFB, Georgia, to Japan and the countermovement of the 27th FEW from Japan to Bergstrom AFB, Texas, participating MATS C-54s and C-97s each flew an average of seventeen hours per day. Improved military productivity and steady use of contract aircraft brought the average daily throughput from the United States to Japan and Korea to about seventy tons and 150 passengers. In the peak month of October 1951, MATS launched 548 transport sorties—including 118 by the military, 389 by contractors, and 41 from other nations—to the war zone in a fairly typical ratio throughout the war.[36]

In relative terms, however, the accomplishments of MATS tended to highlight the expense and limited capacity of long-range air transportation. During the war, for example, the Military Sea Transportation Service (MSTS) activated or chartered some 255 ships to bring supplies and most troops to Korea and to provide direct support to major amphibious operations, such as the Inchon invasion and the evacuation of Hungnam. Formed in 1950 as the naval equivalent to MATS, the MSTS carried a total of 54 million tons of cargo, 22 million tons of petroleum products, and almost 5 million passengers to and from Japan and Korea during the war. In that same period, MATS transported 214,000 passengers and 80,000 tons of cargo, or about 4 percent of the total logistics effort. Indeed, with some 20,000 personnel and over 200 aircraft assigned, the Pacific Division was hard pressed to get a dozen planes a day into the theater, carrying a load equivalent to that of a single railroad car and four buses. Planes simply couldn't compete with ships in throughput and cost. A typical freighter of the time might carry 10,000 tons of cargo at 12 knots, thus producing 120,000 ton miles per hour of lift, or 2.8 million ton miles per day (MTMD). By comparison, even a large C-124 carrying 25 tons at 180 knots for 12 hours per day produced only 0.18 MTMD. Air transports were a necessary means for getting high-priority people and matériel out to the war. But military airlift was a long way from being able to move combat units and their supplies over transoceanic distances.

Air Refueling Goes to War

At the start of the Korean War, the Air Force had only just begun to field effective air-refueling units. Development began in the late 1940s, when air force leaders realized a need to extend the range of bombers and escort fighters in the event of war with the Soviet Union.[37] Since the only source of proven and patented air-refueling kits was a British company, Flight Refueling Ltd. (FRL), the Air Force purchased thirty-eight sets of "looped-hose" systems from it in March 1948, along with drawings, manufacturing rights, and technical assistance. The looped-hose system involved a receiving aircraft snagging a hose towed by a refueling aircraft, winching it in through the tail, and then connecting it manually to its fuel system. The Air Force installed these kits in B-29s; refuelers were designated B-29Ms and receivers as B-29Ps. A year later, in September 1949, FRL installed a new and more practical "probe and drogue" system on three air force B-29s and two F-84E escort fighters. In this system, the aerodynamic drag of a small, parachute-like drogue held the refueling hose steady behind the refueling aircraft, allowing an appropriately equipped aircraft to fly up and insert a probe mounted on its wing or nose into a valve on the end of the hose. The success of air refueling was such that by the end of 1950, the Air Force had twelve squadrons of tankers on strength, some of them fully equipped and combat ready.

Given the priority demands of Strategic Air Command, the use of air refueling in Korea began slowly and remained on a small scale. The Air Force sent an experimental flight of three drogue-equipped aircraft, now known as KB-29Ms, to Japan in the spring of 1951. One refueled three RF-80A fighters on July 6 over the Sea of Japan, the first such operation under combat conditions. The RF-80s did not have the fuel system connections to fill their internal tanks in the air, so they used wing-tip auxiliary tanks equipped with short probes, which allowed them to replenish at least part of their fuel load. The pace of operations picked up from May to July 1952, when ten KB-29s supported strike operations by the 136th Fighter Bomber Wing based in Japan. Like the RF-80s, the F-84Es of the 136th carried probe-equipped tip tanks. A year later, however, the Air Force had F-84Gs on line, upgrades of the E-model plumbed to fill all of their tanks in the air. So between July 4 and 16, 1952, in an exercise called Fox Peter 1, the 31st Fighter Escort Wing flew from the Georgia to Japan, using air refueling on the Georgia–California and California–Hawaii legs. All aircraft made the flight safely and arrived in fighting order. This performance was a great improvement over the usual method of shipping aircraft on the decks of aircraft carriers, a process that took ten to twelve weeks and often delivered aircraft with significant damage from sea air, ship motion, and rough handling. By 1953 the use of air refueling to move F-84 and B-29 units across the Pacific was a matter of routine, though tanker operations in support of tactical operations in Korea remained episodic. It was a small beginning, but it was one that inspired the Air Force to activate the first air-refueling unit for its tactical air forces, the 421st Air Refueling Squadron (Medium), which came on line in Japan in July 1953.

Battlefield Airlift

The addition of battlefield airlift to the equation of American warfare was the most transformational air mobility innovation of the Korean War. Its ability to move combat units and matériel within forward combat zones with virtually no restrictions on their points of pickup and delivery changed things from the day the first helicopter air transport unit arrived in the theater. The need for the helicopter's unique capability was particularly acute in Korea, where the predominant geography of steep hills and narrow valleys, frequently shifting battle lines, enemy guerrilla units, and artillery fire made motorized transport for the last few miles to the front always difficult and dangerous and sometimes impossible. Commanders saw the value of helicopters immediately and applied the handfuls coming into the theater to supply forward units, to spare their wounded bone-jarring and frequently fatal ambulance rides, and then to move whole companies and battalions into combat. These applications quickly altered the Army's and marines' notions of time, space, battle rhythm, and risk.

The Marine Corps led the way. In September 1946 the Navy formed an experimental helicopter squadron, VX-6, to explore the utility of these new aircraft in naval and amphibious operations. Experimentation and doctrine developed rapidly, and in May 1948 the corps conducted its first amphibious exercise featuring helicopters ferrying combat troops ashore from a small escort aircraft carrier, the *Palau*. In that exercise, Packard II, five small helicopters flew fifty sorties to carry sixty-six assault troops some twelve miles from the carrier to a point behind the assault beach. In anticipation of more capable aircraft becoming available, marine doctrine writers published *Amphibious Operations— Employment of Helicopters (Tentative)* in November 1948 and in the following March began preparing a table of organization and equipment for an assault transport helicopter squadron. The necessary aircraft became available in 1950. This was the Sikorsky HRS-1 (called the H-19 in the Army and Air Force), which cruised at eighty knots and carried a maximum payload of about 2,000 pounds or, more normally, 1,200 pounds (six troops) for about 160 nautical miles. With fifteen HRS-1s on strength, the corps activated Marine Transport Helicopter Squadron 161 (HMR-161) in January 1951 and deployed it to Korea in August, manned mostly by ex-fighter pilots and under the command of Lieutenant Colonel George Herring.[38]

HMR-161 became a star of marine combat operations. When it unloaded at the port of Pusan on September 2, 1950, all the services had units of small two- and three-seat helicopters wop-wop-wopping around the hills of Korea, rescuing downed aircrewmen, evacuating casualties, spotting for artillery, carrying dispatches, and so on. The Air Force's 3rd Air Rescue and Recovery Squadron had been the first in the theater, followed by Marine Observation Squadron 6 (VMO-6) in August 1950 and then by the 2nd Army Helicopter Detachment in December. But, in comparison to the HRS-1, these aircraft were ballerinas flitting around stevedores come to do some heavy lifting. As a warm-up to bigger operations, HMR-161 began the first helicopter combat airlift in history on September 13, when it moved almost nine tons of supplies in twenty-eight flights from a forward supply point some seven miles to the 2nd Battalion, 1st Marine Regiment on the front line. On the 21st, the "windmills" made the first helicopter assault in history, transporting 224 fully equipped marines and nine tons of equipment to relieve a South Korean infantry unit occupying an isolated position on a steep hill. Since the helicopters could not land, the marines lowered themselves by climbing down knotted ropes, and their supplies came in on slings beneath the Sikorskys. Similar operations followed in quick succession, culminating in Operation SwITCH on November 11, 1951, during which twelve HRS-1s flew 262 round-trips in one day to move two battalions, or 1,902 marines, some fourteen miles. Fourteen miles actually was a longer distance than traversed by most battlefield airlift missions, but the difference between a twenty-minute helicopter ride and a day of dangerous trekking up and down the hills of Korea was of great tactical and morale advantage for the units involved. The lesson was taken to heart, and by the signing of the armistice in July 1953, HMR-161 had conducted 18,607 flights, flown 16,538 hours, carried 60,046 passengers, and carried over 3,700 tons of cargo. Together with VMO-6, it also evacuated 9,815 sick and wounded soldiers to rear area hospitals, saving thousands of lives in the process.[39]

The Army lagged behind the Marine Corps in the introduction of battlefield airlift units to Korea, but as a consequence of bureaucratic impediments rather than any lack of desire. Unlike the Marine Corps, which was free to develop whatever aviation elements it needed to accomplish its mission, the Army was dependent on the Air Force for its air support. Following the reorganization of the Army and the Army Air Forces in June 1942, the Army activated an aviation arm equipped with light aircraft to perform some of the tasks formerly accomplished by air force observation squadrons. These tasks included observation, artillery spotting, carrying dispatches and commanders between tactical headquarters, carrying emergency medical supplies to forward hospitals, and laying communication wires. The Air Force remained responsible for all other forms of aerial support—most important, air transportation and close air support. The joint services' Key West Agreement of 1948 reaffirmed the Air Force's responsibility "to furnish close combat and logistical air support to the Army."[40] A May 1949 agreement between the two service chiefs of staff further limited the Army to acquiring aircraft of no more than 2,500 pounds gross weight and helicopters of no more than 4,000 pounds to perform "direct support" missions, such as frontline surveillance, messenger service, and "limited aerial evacuation."[41] Service leaders, at least air force leaders, deemed such small aircraft sufficient for the limited missions assigned to Army Aviation. The fly in the ointment was that senior army leaders at least wanted to experiment with short-range air transport operations, even though the Air Force did not endorse the mission or want to divert aircraft manufacturers from the production of fighters, bombers, and larger transport aircraft.[42]

The outbreak of hostilities broke the logjam. In 1951 and 1952 Frank Pace and Thomas Finletter, the secretaries of the Army and Air Force, respectively, signed two agreements that in combination eliminated the weight ceiling on helicopters and raised the ceiling for fixed-wing aircraft to 5,000 pounds. To avoid operational overlaps with air force operations, the 1952 agreement restricted routine Army Aviation operations to a "battle zone" extending no more than 100 miles behind friendly lines.[43] In August 1952, army headquarters authorized activation of twelve helicopter transport battalions.[44] But even at forced draft, the Army's acquisition and training programs could not turn out a field-ready helicopter transportation unit until the 6th Transportation Helicopter Company arrived at Chunchon, Korea, in January 1953. When the 13th Transportation Helicopter Company arrived in May, both units were assigned to the 1st Transportation Army Aviation Battalion (Provisional) (TAAB [P]). Both companies performed yeoman duty, serving on several occasions as the primary supply conduits for multi-regiment forces. In a preview of the future importance of helicopter transportation, the 1st TAAB(P) and HMR-161 combined forces in Operation Byway in September and October 1953, during which they made 1,288 flights with twenty-eight HRS-1s/H-19s to lift over 6,000 troops from a carrier in Inchon Harbor to a landing zone some thirty-four miles inland.

Outcomes

Most obviously, air mobility emerged from the Korean War as a much more complex organizational realm than it had been at the start. The old Naval Air Transport Service was gone, of course, but MATS remained, and it had a navy component and an admiral serving as second in command. The Navy also maintained Fleet Logistics Squadrons for its own use, and the Marine Corps had transport squadrons assigned to each of its air wings. Troop carrier units remained scattered among the Tactical Air Command, Air Force Reserve, and Air National Guard; each was responsible for preparing units for combat and among the Air Force's major overseas commands, which had the role of employing forces in combat. The Army's aviation units were divided among various training organizations, the Transportation Corps, and every corps, division, and some regiments. No one yet understood the connections between air refueling and airlift, but the fierce competition for resources and the possibility of acquiring tanker-transport aircraft would soon establish their relationship in policy and doctrine.

The overlapping involvements of so many organizations created a snake ball of perspectives on the policy implications of the Korean air mobility experience. Air force leaders worried over the diversion of resources into the air transport program. MATS and the troop carrier community wanted new aircraft of increased capacity and operational flexibility. MATS still wanted to absorb the Troop Carrier Command, and Troop Carrier Command just as fervently wanted to stay independent. Army leaders were excited about the potentials of the helicopter, but they and troop carrier leaders were starting to worry about the boundaries between their capabilities. Moreover, all of these perspectives and vested interests had civilian participants in academe, the press, industry, and government. In short, preexisting institutional identities and the Korean War had created a large community of interest in air mobility affairs, created and/or left major doctrinal questions unsettled, complicated the competition for resources, and put zealots afoot. In other words, all of the elements of a ferocious doctrine and policy fight were in place.

11. Troop Carrier Aviation in the 1950s

ATOMIC BOMBS WERE pretty good for Troop Carrier Aviation. Happily, the things were never used after World War II. But their existence pushed the Army and the Air Force's Tactical Air Command (TAC) into operational concepts that demanded a lot of theater airlift. Adoption of these concepts, particularly by the Army, pressed reluctant air force leaders to expand and modernize troop carrier forces, despite their general reluctance to divert funding away from the nuclear strike and air defense programs of the Strategic Air Command (SAC) and the Air Defense Command. Dragging their heels at every turn, air force leaders sized and modernized troop carrier to support TAC's atomic-armed fighters and light bombers only. They left the Army's much larger requirements largely unaddressed. Frustrated army leaders eventually complained to Congress and turned to the Military Air Transport Service (MATS) for future strategic airlift support. But the decade ended before this turn of events could have much impact on troop carrier affairs.

The Fruits of War

When the North Korean Army lunged southward on June 25, 1950, Troop Carrier Aviation was in the doldrums. It had no organizational core and no money. To redirect personnel from what it considered a secondary mission, the U.S. Air Force (USAF) disbanded the 3rd Air Force (Troop Carrier) in 1946 and in 1948 reduced 3rd Air Force's parent command, TAC, to a lightly manned planning headquarters of the Continental Air Command (CONARC). CONARC assigned its three active duty troop carrier wings (TCWs) to the 9th Air Force, which embraced a mixed force of fighters, light bombers, and transports dedicated, more or less, to fulfilling the Air Force's statutory obligation to provide close support for the Army. These organizational arrangements left responsibility for organizing, training, and advocating Troop Carrier Aviation scattered among individuals and offices at air force headquarters, CONARC, 9th Air Force, overseas air forces, and various group headquarters in the reserve components—the Air National Guard and Air Force Reserve. Funding shortages were reflected in the war-battered C-46s, C-47s, and C-54s equipping most active component and all reserve component transport units. Two active wings were equipping with new C-119s, and CONARC had put in a request for some of the big four-engine C-124s under development. Beyond that, troop carrier affairs were adrift in a Sargasso Sea of institutional and budgetary neglect.

The North Korean attack broke the calm. Suddenly awash in war supplemental funding and reminded of their responsibility to support the Army, air force leaders blew people, money, and new planes into troop carrier. In October 1950, they selected the Chase/Fairchild C-123 Provider as the Air Force's first assault transport to replace C-46s and C-47s.[1] In December, the Air Force reactivated TAC as the trainer and provider of theater combat forces. TAC then stood up the 18th Air Force (Troop Carrier) in March 1951 to advocate, organize, and train theater airlift forces under the initial command of Major General Robert W. Douglass Jr. That same month, TAC issued a request for proposals to replace the C-119 with an aircraft of greatly improved productivity, safety, and ability to operate from forward fields, to lift twelve tons from San Francisco to Hawaii, to cruise at 250 knots, to land on airstrips of 3,500 feet or less with a full load, and to air-drop vehicles and equipment.[2] In September 1951, the 62nd Troop Carrier Wing became the first 18th Air Force unit equipped with C-124s. By the signing of the Korean truce in July 1953, therefore, air force troop carrier forces in the Continental United States (CONUS) and overseas were booming along in following winds of institutional interest and funding.

The 18th Air Force expanded rapidly in force structure and operational responsibilities. Initially focused on activating reserve units and preparing them for deployment to Korea and Europe, the 18th Air Force soon grew to ten TCWs and became a major airlift operator in its own right. Providing airlift support for army airborne training and exercises consumed a lot of its efforts. In addition, TAC and the 19th Air Force needed a lot of airlift for their experiments with long-distance unit moves. In September 1951, the 60th TCW began equipping with C-124s and soon began regular logistics flights to Japan and Korea. Most of these movements carried urgently needed tactical air force supplies, such as drop tanks, engines, and aerial munitions. But there was no escaping the fact that troop carrier operations were engaging in missions and on routes normally reserved for MATS by Department of Defense policies.[3] The pace of operations was such that, by 1956, 18th Air Force crews had flown 83 million plane miles, 391 million passenger miles, and 241 million ton miles to move 407,000 tons and 884,000 passengers.[4]

The C-119 was the heart of troop carrier's modernization program, though by 1950 its shortfalls as a theater transport were evident. The plane had many desirable attributes, including a twin-boom tail and high-mounted wing that lowered its full-profile and a rear cargo door to truck bed height for easier loading. Derived from the C-82, the "Dollar-Nineteen" shared its predecessor's ability to air-drop medium trucks, howitzers, self-propelled antitank guns, light engineering equipment, and so on—an attribute that greatly enhanced the maneuverability and hitting power of parachute units. Powered by two 3,500-horsepower engines, C-119s could carry up to twelve tons of cargo or sixty troops, though eight tons for 1,500 miles was a more typical load. These attributes, however, could not hide the fact that C-119s were dangerous airplanes to fly. Their fragile tail booms bent and buckled in hard landings on rough strips. They shed parts and even engines in flight with regularity. Even well below gross weight, C-119s often could not fly on one engine, even if their undersized rudders could maintain directional control, which they didn't do very well. Low-budget and inadequately tested expansions of the C-82 design, they were the best cargo planes the Air Force was willing to pay for in the late 1940s, but they could be no more than a stopgap in TAC's airlift plans.[5]

In contrast, the C-123 was popular from the start. The Provider came with two 2,400-horsepower engines and could lift about eight tons for 1,000 nautical miles. Equipped with a full-profile clamshell-type rear door and ramp, which could be opened and closed in flight, the plane could carry and air-drop similar loads to the bigger C-119 and could land and take off in less than 2,000 feet at full gross weight. Impressed by the Provider's ruggedness and short-field capabilities, the Air Force's evaluators in the assault airlift competition believed it was "well-suited to the requirements of troop carrier on rough terrain."[6] The C-123 had one other important attribute: it was an aerodynamically clean aircraft and visually well proportioned, making it much better looking and confidence inspiring than its bigger partners in the troop carrier fleet, the C-119 and slab-sided C-124.

The C-124 Globemaster II was a candidate for the "homely aircraft" prize. It was derived from Douglas Aircraft's first DC-7 design, only eleven of which were produced as the C-74. The C-124 kept the low-mounted wings and empennage of the airliner but replaced its efficient round fuselage with a hulking, rectangular thing that seemed too high for its length. Worse, the Globemaster's nose bulged larger than the fuselage behind it to get the cockpit above the cargo deck and to provide space underneath for an extendable vehicle-loading ramp. Besides limiting the C-124's cruise speed to a ponderous 180 knots, the ramp's seventeen-degree slope made loading slow and awkward. Designed for logistics operations, the plane's airdrop capabilities were limited to two paratroop doors and a large hatch in the floor through which it could drop bundles. It was, however, the largest cargo plane available at the time, powered by four 3,800-horsepower engines, and able to lift thirty-eight tons, maximum, or about twenty tons over the 2,200 nautical miles between California and Hawaii. With a cargo deck measuring 13 feet by 13 feet by 77 feet, the plane could lift any air force vehicle and 94 percent of those in an infantry division. Unfortunately, the remaining 6 percent included all of a division's tanks, heavy artillery, and bridging equipment. Called Old Shaky by its crews for its tendency to groan and rattle while flying even in calm skies, the C-124 amounted to another low-budget stopgap, one that took seventy flying hours and eight to ten days to make the round-trip from California to Japan.[7]

Although still a couple of years away from flying, the winning design for a new medium transport quickly replaced the Boxcar as the heart of troop carrier modernization. To achieve the performance and safety margins called for in the Air Force specifications, Fairchild suggested an enlarged version of the C-119, perhaps powered by four 2,500-horsepower radial piston engines. But by 1952 the Air Force had lost faith in the core design and rejected the notional C-119H in favor of a more ambitious proposal from Lockheed. Referred to as the XC-130, Lockheed's design would mount four turboprops of 3,000 or more horsepower and would exceed all of the Air Force's requirements while also improving operational safety and reducing maintenance costs. As the first air force transport designed from the ground up for turbine power, the XC-130 was a revolution in the making, with its rugged construction, nearly twenty-ton cargo capacity, accessible rear cargo-loading door, and impressive abilities to operate into and out of runways 2,000 to 3,000 feet long. Accordingly, the Air Force pressed Lockheed in 1952 to get the aircraft into production as soon as possible.[8]

The Fruits of Strategy: Assured Mission, Assured Support

Probably without realizing that he was doing so, President Dwight D. Eisenhower underwrote troop carrier's good fortune when he signed National Security Council (NSC) Paper 162-2 in late 1953. As a response to the president's direction to take a "new look" at American strategy, NSC 162-2 endorsed the preeminence of atomic bombs as the bulwarks of American defense. Given the rapid expansion of the Soviet Union's long-range bomber forces and the ability of communist bloc nations to field giant armies, the so-called New Look strategy called for breakneck expansion of America's own atomic capabilities. Implicitly, the costs of this expansion would be offset by reductions in army and navy nonnuclear forces and greater reliance on American allies to provide for their own defense.[9] In the event that the Soviets or Soviet-sponsored insurgents attacked allied states, New Look postulated that those states would defend themselves pending support by American units deployed rapidly in their reinforcement.[10] In a veiled threat to employ nuclear weapons in such situations, NSC 162-2 and American leaders repeatedly asserted that the United States would reply to communist aggressions by means and at places of its choosing.[11]

Air force leaders trumpeted New Look as appropriate to the strategic circumstances and as a triumph of their long-held belief that strategic bombardment was the decisive element of modern warfare. USAF vice chief of staff General Thomas D. White wrote that the strategy was recognition that atomic weapons made the Air Force "an instrument of national policy."[12] White's boss, General Nathan F. Twining, only worried that national leaders might recoil from using the bomb in defense of an ally facing local attack. Declaring that failure to "rely primarily on our ability to counterattack . . . with weapons of concentrated power" would force the United States to fight at a disadvantage, Twining encouraged national leaders to use atomic weapons in any type of conflict.[13] Writing in support, Brigadier General Dale O. Smith, a frequently published airpower doctrinalist, declared that nuclear weapons would return the initiative to American forces responding to Soviet-sponsored surprise attacks. "Obviously," Smith concluded, "no restrictions should be placed on the kinds of munitions . . . applied from the air."[14]

Though less confident in the universal usefulness of nuclear weapons, TAC's top commanders saw the writing on the Air Force's doctrinal and budgetary walls: get on board or wither away. Flexibility and atom bombs were TAC's new watchwords. Speaking in 1956, the TAC commander, General Otto P. Weyland, told military and civilian leaders that TAC had become "a versatile 'jack of all trades' . . . prepared to do a variety of tasks . . . at a moment's notice, anywhere in the world, with an appropriate degree of force." By "appropriate degree of force" Weyland was suggesting a primary reliance on a new family of tactical nuclear weapons to redress communist advantages in conventional forces and manpower. Atomic-armed tactical aircraft, he believed, must be "the theater commander's *primary strategic* weapons [emphasis in original]." Recognizing that decision makers outside the Air Force might reject the use of nuclear weapons in "periphery wars," Weyland asserted that "we must maintain . . . proficiency in the delivery of both non-atomic and nuclear weapons," but he left no doubt as to which category of weapons he believed would be most useful.[15]

The instrument of TAC's vision was the Composite Air Strike Force (CASF). Beginning just before and then during the Korean War, CONARC and then TAC developed and refined the art of using aerial tankers and troop carrier aircraft to support rapid deployments of fighter units overseas. By the summer of 1955, the command could move an entire fighter bomber group nonstop from the West Coast to the East Coast of the United States entirely by air, deliver it and its supplies to a bare base, and have it in operation just hours after arriving.[16] At the same time, TAC reactivated the 19th Air Force as a small headquarters responsible for supervising the organization, training, and dispatch of TAC squadrons identified as elements of CASF. Acting as a subordinate planning element of the 9th Air Force, the 19th Air Force consisted of fewer than a hundred individuals. There was, then, no standing CASF unit, merely a pool of squadrons from which the 19th Air Force would draw to tailor CASFs as needed to engage in peripheral conflicts and other crises. Once CASF squadrons arrived in a theater, they would fight under the theater air commander, probably as a cohesive unit led by the 19th Air Force commander. Anticipating that CASFs would operate in a wide range of conflicts, TAC prepared CASF-designated squadrons to deliver conventional and nuclear weapons. The program matured rapidly and exercised for the first time in Operation Mobile Baker, September 1956, when the 19th Air Force deployed a squadron each of F-100s and F-84s and flights of B-66s and RF-84s.[17]

As TAC developed its long-range deployment capabilities, army leaders were exploring the relationships of atomic weapons and air mobility in future wars. Much had been learned already from Operation Swarmer, May 1950, and the Korean War about the ability of robust, centrally controlled airlift forces to sustain offensive and defensive maneuver by ground forces.[18] During 1951, the Department of Defense contracted the California Institute of Technology to conduct Project Vista, an analysis of the impact of atomic weapons on the future defense of Western Europe. Among its numerous findings, the Vista report proposed the establishment of two airborne corps, one in Europe and one as a reserve in the United States, and to provide for their strategic and tactical mobility by acquiring 400 C-124 and 800 C-123 aircraft.[19] Once freed from the demands of the war in Korea, the Army acted on the provisions of the Vista report by activating the XVIII Strategic Army Corps (STRAC) in 1955 and, in the next year, committing to the conversion of its infantry and armored divisions to the "Pentomic" model, which was designed to achieve greater flexibility, in part, through aerial resupply.[20]

Conducted in November and December 1955, Operation Sagebrush was the milestone in the Army's experimentation with atomic warfare, both operationally and politically. The exercise involved two divisions, the 1st Armored and 3rd Infantry, organized specifically for operations on atomic battlefields. The 82nd Airborne Division also participated, as did most of TAC's assets, including all of its troop carrier units. The exercise swept across much of central Louisiana and emphasized the rapid concentration and dispersal of ground combat units. On numerous occasions, "atomic simulators" created bright flashes and small mushroom clouds at concentration points, bridgeheads, and so on to indicate the hazards of slowing down or concentrating fighting units for too long at any one place. Flying in World War II–style V formations, TAC C-119s dropped 82nd Airborne Division units in several places, while C-123s made their operational debuts delivering troops and supplies to forward landing zones. In a first, an experimental Sky Cavalry troop used its own helicopters to place reconnaissance squads and antitank and artillery direction teams all over the "battlefield."[21]

The Army's use of helicopters to maneuver beyond the battle lines raised the ire of General Weyland, who told the XVIII Airborne Corps commander, Major General Paul D. Adams, that for such deep operations, the Army could use only air force aircraft, including the H-19s and H-21s of the newly activated 516th Rotary Wing Assault Group of the 314th TCW. Their confrontation boiled all the way up to the service secretaries, who agreed to let the Army run the experiment its way. Interpretations of the exercise results varied as to the ability of ground units to operate and survive in a "tactical" atomic environment. But no doubt existed after Sagebrush that the Army needed lots of airlift support and had taken control of at least part of its short-range requirements.[22]

At times, the Army's vision of how much airlift it needed seemed to ignore fiscal and technological realities. In 1951, for example, the Army told the Air Force that it needed enough airlift to drop two and two-thirds airborne divisions simultaneously and enough extra to lift an entire division by air to any point on the globe.[23] Two years later, the airborne adviser at the Air Force's Air University declared that the Army's requirement for enough air transports to lift three divisions simultaneously and to move six divisions from the United States to Europe in twenty-four to seventy-two hours "must be met within the immediate future."[24] Given the 180-knot cruise speeds and thirty-ton capacities of the largest aircraft available at the time, such requirements translated into fleets of thousands of transport aircraft and chains of well-supplied bases and depots along their deployment routes. Even after several years of sharp debate with the Air Force over the issue, army leaders still wove visions of air mobility that simply were unattainable technologically, let alone economically. In 1957 Major General Earle G. Wheeler told army commanders that 300 C-124s would be needed to carry the combat elements of an airborne division to Japan or Taiwan in ten to twelve days.[25] This was a good estimate of the deployment requirement, perhaps, but it is not clear that he understood that the same fleet of aircraft, operating on a ten-day cycle between the United States and Asia, likely could not have supplied that division in combat. As in any form of rapid mobility—horses, trucks, or airplanes—airlift presented maneuver opportunities that it then could not sustain.

Regardless of their operational details and logistical nuances, the CASF and STRAC concepts were good news for Troop Carrier Aviation. As an irreplaceable element of air force and army strategic concepts, troop carrier received a steady flow of funding that took it from being a neglected backwater in 1950 to a robust and still-growing combat arm in 1955. The first C-130 Hercules and C-123 flowed into TAC in 1955, and by 1960 those types would equip all active wings. As TAC's C-119s became surplus, they went to reserve units, which grew from 199 C-46s and 38 C-119s in 1956 to 667 C-119s and 47 C-123s assigned to fifteen wings in 1960.[26] The Air National Guard also had a few transport squadrons.

The Army Protests, and Congress Intervenes

For all of the growth in troop carrier forces, army leaders had numerous reasons for concern. In the first place, TAC commanders unabashedly asserted primacy of claim to "their" organic airlift arm, which they felt was "available within TAC to aid in deploying and supporting the [CASF]."[27] Active component TCWs trained regularly with the Army, but, reported the 18th Air Force historian, "the 18th has put in more flying hours airlifting TAC combat units with atomic capability than it has in transporting Army personnel."[28] Even on the flight line, 18th Air Force crews had no doubt that TAC's mobility needs had higher priority "first, last, and always."[29] Army tensions heightened in 1954, when the Air Force decided to redirect funding from a planned purchase of fifty-three C-124s, which had mobility value in land warfare, to buy instead seventy-three C-118s, which, as minimally modified versions of the DC-6B airliner, offered little value to ground units.[30] As if oblivious to army anxieties, the Air Force next decided to transfer all C-124s to MATS.[31] The Air Force took this action as an economy move. But by putting all of the Air Force's transoceanic lift capacity into a command clearly focused on SAC, the action left the Army with no ensured source of airlift other than, perhaps, the comparatively obsolescent C-119s in the reserve units.

Army leaders criticized the situation often and pointedly. In 1954, Secretary of the Army Robert T. Stevens complained that the lack of theater airlift was hobbling the Army's mobility and called for the Air Force to acquire 300 large transports for intertheater deployments and 625 C-119s to lift the assault elements of an airborne division.[32] Chief of Staff Matthew B. Ridgway simply resigned in protest over the Army's declining share of the defense budget and consequent difficulties in fielding viable military capabilities. In his closing letter to the secretary of defense, Ridgway linked airlift to his service's strategic future, advising Secretary of Defense Charles E. Wilson to "make full provision . . . [for] an increase in the readiness and strategic mobility of uncommitted United States and British Commonwealth Forces."[33] A year later the staff of *Army Magazine* acidly wrote that the consequences of the Air Force's doctrinal confusion and neglect "would be chaotic" as the services "presented high-priority demands for far more strategic airlift than presently exists."[34]

But leaders and publicists for the Air Force weren't buying, at least not any transport aircraft beyond the requirements of SAC and TAC. While senior commanders usually were somewhat circumspect in their pronouncements, airpower hard-liners minced no words in declaring that support for the Army largely was wasted effort. "In a war of thermonuclear missiles," wrote the staff of *Air Force Magazine* in 1956, "the question of close air support for the infantry fades in importance . . . [whether for] 'battlefield mobility,' tactical airlift, [and] short-range reconnaissance."[35] Clearly, for all the improvements being made in troop carrier forces, the Army and the Air Force remained deadlocked, and the increasingly rancorous debate could only attract outside interest, worst of all from Congress.

Senator William Stuart Symington (D-MO) spotlighted the deadlock in airlift policy during hearings he directed as chair of the Air Force Subcommittee of the Armed Services Committee. As part of a broad inquiry into the state of American airpower, the senator discovered that neither MATS nor TAC took responsibility for providing overseas lift for army combat units. Knowing that MATS functioned in theory as the long-range transport arm of the Joint Chiefs of Staff, the senator asked Lieutenant General Joseph Smith if his command could do the job. Smith's reply was predictable; his priority was on moving SAC, and moving the Army was TAC's job. When given the same question,

General Otto P. Weyland replied that TAC could not lift the combat elements of a single airborne division and that the transoceanic mission belonged to MATS anyway.[36] So MATS had the mission of moving the Army over the oceans but hid behind the Joint Chiefs of Staff's priorities, while TAC truly never had the mission but army commanders thought it did. So who was going to take the Army to the dance?

Over in the House Army Subcommittee hearings, Major General Hamilton H. Howze, the director of Army Aviation, didn't claim to know, but he did see "a discernable trend in the Air Force brand of aviation—as the aircraft have increased in size, speed and complexity, a sort of vacuum has appeared in the support of aircraft for the Army." One of the areas suffering from air force neglect, Howze reported, was in airlift.[37] Howze was speaking to a receptive congressman, Daniel J. Flood, a Democrat representing the Wyoming Valley of Pennsylvania. A former vaudeville actor and World War II infantryman, Flood was a crusader for his former service and outspoken in his dislike for "slick" air force generals. Outraged by Howze's report, Flood took his crusade to the concurrent Air Force Subcommittee hearings to plead the Army's case and lambaste the plan to buy "plushed up" C-118s instead of C-124s.[38]

For the moment, the results of the Army's protests and congressional scrutiny were indecisive. The report of the Symington committee included recommendations to expand and modernize the Air Force's airlift forces, and Daniel Flood got some more time in front of the microphone. But they should have been a message to the Air Force that the heat was on and that Congress would be back again to pry into its airlift affairs. Before air leaders could absorb the message, presuming they were inclined to—which they weren't—TAC sent out two CASFs to quell regional crises.

The Year of the CASFs: 1958

A looming civil war in Lebanon, incited in part by the interventions of surrounding Arab states, was the trigger for the first CASF deployment.[39] The Lebanese president asked for outside help on July 14, 1958, following protracted riots in Beirut and aggressive posturing by Iraq. A marine landing force, which had been waiting offshore for the call, went over the beach that same day. Anticipating possible counterinterventions from Lebanon's neighbors, President Eisenhower directed the Air Force and the Army to reinforce the marines. The next day, TAC launched CASF-Bravo, a four-squadron force, from the United States to Incirlik Air Base in south-central Turkey. Sixty 18th Air Force C-130s supported the movement, lifting a total of 860 personnel and 220 tons of equipment. Meanwhile MATS C-124s, with some help from USAFE units, carried 3,200 army troops and 2,300 tons of army matériel from Europe to Incirlik and then on to Beirut.[40] To the anger of army observers, TAC withdrew its C-130s to the United States during these movements, leaving an airborne battle group waiting for airlift from Germany to Lebanon.[41] In total, MATS airlifted 5,500 tons of cargo and 5,400 troops from the United States and Europe to Lebanon, dwarfing the contribution of TAC's organic C-130 units.

CASF-B was hardly in place when intensifying fighting between communist China and nationalist China obliged the United States to send another CASF to Taiwan. On August 18, the People's Liberation Army began shelling nationalist positions on the islands of Quemoy and Matsu. As tensions increased, TAC formed CASF X-Ray–Tango and sent C-130s out into the Pacific to preposition maintenance and support personnel along the anticipated deployment route. X-Ray–Tango moved out on August 29, when the communists seemed on the verge of invading the two small islands. As they had for the Lebanon deployment, TAC tankers and C-130s supported the movement of the CASF's six squadrons and their support echelons, while 144 MATS flights moved most ground support equipment, supplies, munitions, and follow-up personnel. MATS also established a regular, transpacific shuttle to sustain the deployed units, and in a first, its C-124s carried twelve partially disassembled F-104 interceptors to the island. Together, TAC and MATS airlifted 1,718 people and 1,088 tons of cargo into the theater.[42]

Not surprisingly, the Air Force and the Army assessed the Lebanon and Formosa deployments differently. General Laurence Kuter, commander of the Pacific Air Forces and former commander of the Air Transport Command, summarized the rapid arrival of powerful American air units as "effective deterrence . . . the basic lesson of Taiwan."[43] The 19th Air Force commander, General Henry Viccellio, said simply that the commitment of the CASFs "helped immeasurably to halt these flare ups before worldwide nuclear exchange became a possible result."[44] Less impressed by the Air Force's crowing, the Army found itself looking at MATS with new interest. Army officers valued TAC's C-123s and C-130s, but they also feared that there weren't enough of them to satisfy theater mobility needs and that they offered no transoceanic capacity. Only MATS seemed to have the aircraft needed to move divisions to flaring brushfire wars. So by 1959 army leaders were calling for joint exercises of MATS and the Strategic Army Corps. Such exercises, they expected, would test and refine the Army's long-range deployment concept and help MATS "learn what its job really is in the field."[45]

And, suddenly, MATS was receptive. General Joseph Smith, who had commanded MATS since 1952 and who had never taken much interest in army requirements, retired.[46] General William H. Tunner, "Mr. Airlift" and the successful commander of Combat Cargo Command in the first months of the Korean War, took his place. Tunner had an agenda, and it included the Army. As the inveterate visionary of global airlift, his abiding objective was to see the day when all airlift forces were consolidated under MATS or a successor organization and operated flexibly in support of every service in accordance with national strategic priorities. In a stump speech he gave in many venues, Tunner declared that "[MATS] . . . must be an integrated system working in harmony with all the military services . . . as well as the Strategic and Tactical Air Commands."[47] Knowing full well that his air force superiors were committed to preserving MATS as SAC's reserved airline, Tunner was prepared to build an alliance with the Army to pursue his dream. This union of a bureaucratic insurgent within the Air Force and the Army on the outside would change the world of Troop Carrier Aviation fundamentally.

At Decade's End

In 1960 Troop Carrier Aviation was riding on the fair winds of a hurricane's eye. In terms of force structure and modernization, things were going well. TAC fielded eight wings of C-123s and C-130s, while MATS operated four wings of former TAC C-124s, which were still designated for theater missions. Of these wings, the 18th Air Force controlled two medium (C-130) and two assault (C-123) wings. United States Air Forces in Europe had two medium wings and a squadron of MATS C-124s, and Pacific Air Forces had a medium wing and two squadrons of C-124s.[48] In addition, the Air Force Reserve fielded fifteen wings of C-119s, most of which were less than ten years old. Troop carrier's vital role to both TAC and the Army seemed to secure its institutional status and access to a share of the Air Force's budget. But swirling just over the horizon was a political storm that could threaten troop carrier's close connection to the Army and thereby its distinctiveness and organizational independence from MATS. For years air force and army leaders had talked past each other regarding theater airlift requirements, and, now, the Army and William Tunner were conspiring to jam a new airlift dispensation down the Air Force's institutional throat.

12. Army Aviation in the 1950s

BETWEEN THE END of the Korean War and the beginning of active American military involvement in the Vietnam War, the Department of Defense gave the U.S. Army broad latitude to develop its aviation arm. Held back only by the limitations of contemporary technology, budgets, and air force doctrinal prerogatives, army aviation experts largely were free to take their experiments and developments wherever they wanted. In a few short years they transformed Army Aviation from a tiny but valued adjunct of ground formation into a central element of army war-fighting doctrines and capabilities. Battlefield airlift—the movement of combat units and their matériel within or in the immediate vicinity of the battlefield—was a major component of this transformation. By the early 1960s, it had grown into a force involving thousands of turbine-powered, all-weather aircraft, manned and supported by tens of thousands of soldiers and an infrastructure of research and development, logistics, and training facilities. As such, battlefield airlift at the end of the decade was on the verge of changing the way the Army and its enemies would make war.

A Vision of War

Hanson Baldwin probably got it first. Writing for *Life* magazine while the ashes of Hiroshima and Nagasaki still smoldered, the Pulitzer Prize–winning military journalist realized that atomic bombs would change the conduct but not the fundamentals of land warfare. In the future, he prophesied, wars would be decided by atomic-armed robot bombers and ballistic missiles. They would be "push button" wars, fought by men in bunkers in defense of factories and cities dispersed and perhaps even buried for protection. But for all the power of atomic weapons, Baldwin reasoned, the Army's strategic role would remain important, though "more limited and specialized." "The plane, the robot and the rocket," he wrote, "can destroy and devastate, but cannot occupy, hold and organize the earth on which men live. . . . Men on the ground must do this . . . [in] an Army trained in wide dispersion, rather than close concentration . . . whose principal transport may be aircraft."[1] While admitting his limited ability to "plumb an unknowable future," Baldwin saw clearly that stealth and movement would be life for armies fighting under the threat of nuclear attack.

Not that the Army was inclined or even able to do much about Baldwin's vision at the time. Focused on demobilization, organizing the occupations of Germany and Japan, and facing penurious peacetime budgets, it had little time to worry about future atomic wars. Besides, the Air Force was responsible for providing such air transportation that the Army might need in future wars. Even after the Army finally excised its troublesome air arm in September 1947, the Air Transport Command and Tactical Air Command (TAC) retained responsibility for providing most long-range air transport and for organizing troop carrier units to lift army airborne units and provide emergency aerial resupply capabilities in theaters of operation.

The Army did have a small aviation element, but it was neither funded nor intended to provide air mobility. Established in June 1942 to compensate for the Army Air Forces' deactivation of divisional observation squadrons, Army Aviation grew to 1,600 light civilian-type aircraft by the end of World War II. The Army assigned these aircraft to division headquarters and to artillery, signal corps, engineer, intelligence, and other battalions. As integral or organic members of those units, army airmen spotted for artillery, surveyed lines of advance, searched out enemy threats, laid signal wires, chauffeured senior commanders, moved mail, evacuated the wounded, and did other things of indispensable value to ground forces.

Recognizing that these roles were outside the general support responsibilities of the Air Force, the Army's chief of staff, General Omar Bradley, and his Air Force counterpart, General Hoyt S. Vandenberg, agreed in 1949 that the Army should have all the aircraft it needed, so long as they did not exceed 2,500 pounds in weight for fixed-wing aircraft and 4,000 pounds for helicopters and operated only in the immediate vicinity of the front lines. Such aircraft and operating restrictions were adequate to perform the Army's organic aviation missions, even to lift some emergency supplies over short distances.[2] But they also were small enough to dull any temptations that might arise to replicate air force capabilities, notably in theater air transport and tactical air support.

Initially, the Air Force seemed to take its obligation to provide airlift support of the Army seriously. In 1946, the Air Materiel Command began experimenting with parachute drops of palletized heavy equipment from the rear cargo doors of C-82 Packets. This line of development promised to improve the flexibility and capacity of Troop Carrier Aviation to reinforce airborne infantry with vehicles and heavy weapons while dispensing with the vulnerable assault gliders used in World War II. Then, in 1948, the Air Force began seeking an assault transport, a rugged aircraft that could operate into short and rough frontline airstrips. Competing for the developmental contract, Fairchild Aircraft offered a modified C-82, Northrop the C-125 Raider, and Chase Aircraft put forth the C-122 Avitruc and C-123 Provider. The winning aircraft was to complete the replacement of combat gliders in the airborne role and to enhance the Air Force's ability to deliver and pick up personnel and cargo at austere airfields near or at the battle lines.

But by the end of 1949, any confidence ground leaders had in the Air Force's willingness to meet their air mobility needs was on the wane. Most important, the Air Force downgraded TAC from an independent major command to a mere planning headquarters of the Continental Air Command. Focused on the air defense of the United States, CONARC put its troop carrier, fighter, and light bomber units earmarked for army support into the 19th Air Force and then began integrating the fighters into air defense operations. Having just lost its personal piece of the Air Force, the Army also found itself in deep disagreement with the Air Force over the best aircraft for the assault transport role. The Army liked the three-engine C-125 from the start for its extreme ruggedness and ability to get six tons or thirty troops in and out of open fields as short as 800 feet in length.[3] With somewhat greater payload and range characteristics, the Chase Avitruc also attracted army evaluators, though they were concerned that the aircraft required twice the runway as the Raider and was not built as ruggedly. For its part, the Air Force set its sights on the C-123. Able to carry 12.5 tons or sixty troops for 1,000 nautical miles, the Provider was slightly faster than the other two designs, could operate into 1,500-foot fields, and had superior loading, unloading, and airdrop characteristics. The Provider's greater size also offered an opportunity to satisfy the Army's needs with fewer aircraft and less diversion of personnel and funding away from bomber and fighter programs.[4]

As the assault program bogged down in indecision, two events further heightened the Army's interest and anxieties over airlift. The first was the explosion of an atomic bomb by the Soviet Union at its test site at Semipalatinsk, Kazakhstan, on August 29, 1949. Suddenly, Hanson Baldwin's vision of atomic-armed robot planes and armies scurrying about like cockroaches to avoid their fire seemed a pending reality. The second event was the Air Force's refusal to let the Army acquire the new Sikorsky H-19 helicopter for air mobility experiments. The H-19 first flew in November, came with a 600-horsepower engine, and could carry about ten soldiers or 2,000 pounds of cargo at eighty knots for about a hundred miles in sea-level conditions of temperature and atmospheric pressure. Despite its smallness in comparison to fixed-wing air transports, the H-19 offered the Army the first rotary-wing aircraft able to move squads of soldiers, light artillery, and such from virtually anywhere on the battlefield to anywhere else. Painfully aware that the U.S. Marines had been experimenting with ship-to-shore helicopter mobility for several years, army leaders believed the time had come for them to explore the use of the machines in sustained land warfare. Empowered by their ignorance of land warfare, however, air force leaders could not or would not acknowledge the tactical value of such flexibility. Their opinion was important, because they controlled army aircraft production and refused to divert H-19 production from its rescue, medical evacuation, and VIP transport squadrons.[5]

During the Korean War

The Korean War unstuck army helicopter aspirations more or less instantly. With their troops engaged in desperate battles and supplemental war funding available, army leaders wasted no time making demands for significant changes. In September 1950, the House Armed Services Committee announced that it would consider a plan to place air force tactical aviation back under the doctrinal, operational, and procurement control of the Army. Simultaneously, the Army announced that it wanted to raise the weight limitations on its aircraft and put institutional arrangements in place to give its requests for transport, fighter, and bomber design features greater authority in air force planning.[6] Ground service leaders next protested the Air Force's selection of the C-123 as its next assault transport in October, followed by what they saw as "long, unnecessary delays" in getting the aircraft into production.[7] In November the Army activated the 1st Transportation Helicopter Company at Fort Sill, planning to equip it with twenty-one H-19s and two small H-13s. In response to the Air Force's protests that air transport was its business, the Army's chief of staff called for outright elimination of all weight restrictions on aviation aircraft and hinted at plans to buy a test batch of C-122s.[8]

Undoubtedly, army leaders were engaged in a little horse-trading at this time, or demanding a lot to set up a "compromise" later that gave them as much as they reasonably could want or expect to get. Having only just recently disencumbered themselves of the Air Force and its airmen, army leaders could not seriously have wanted, let alone thought they had the political support needed, to bring tactical airpower back into the fold or to build a large fixed-wing air transport force of their own.[9] Despite outside pressures for the reincorporation of tactical air force units into the Army, leaders were careful to reaffirm their intent to remain dependent "upon USAF for major airlift and tactical support" and that they would not buy "aircraft in such large numbers that they infringe upon USAF roles and missions."[10] It seems reasonable to presume, then, that they were using proposals of takeovers and air transports to coax the Air Force into making more robust provisions for army air transport needs and to stop obstructing the development of organic aviation. If these were in fact their goals, this would not be the last time that army leaders would use diversionary tactics to extract major concessions from the Air Force regarding aviation.

Regardless of whether they were good horse traders or just lucky, army leaders and aviation advocates got pretty much what they could have wanted. In March 1951, the Army announced that its aviation budget would increase to $100 million each for fiscal years 1951 and 1952, up from about $10 million in 1949.[11] In an effort to avoid duplicative efforts, Secretary of the Air Force Thomas Finletter and Secretary of the Army Frank Pace signed a memorandum in October 1951 that lifted all weight restrictions on army aircraft and allowed ground commanders to employ them in a battle zone stretching fifty to seventy-five miles behind friendly lines. Taking advantage of the opening, the Army announced in August 1952 that the Transportation Corps would establish twelve helicopter transportation battalions of H-19s or larger aircraft over a period of five years, a program equating to about 750 aircraft on the line. The Air Force responded to the Army's plan by ordering 163 H-21B transport helicopters in April and then activating its first troop carrier (assault rotary wing) squadron in December 1952. To avoid further duplication, Secretary of Defense Robert Lovett directed Pace and Finletter to meet again. The result was another compromise in favor of the Army's aspirations. Signed in November 1952, the new agreement did reimpose the 5,000-pound weight limit on fixed-wing aircraft, but it left helicopters alone and extended the Army's aerial battle zone to 100 miles behind friendly lines.[12] Apparently reconciled to the inevitable, the Air Force offered no resistance to a decision in 1953 to expand Army Aviation from 1,800 to 2,200 helicopters.[13] Wholly confident in the power of nuclear weapons to decide all future wars, air force leaders saw little military value in any expansion or modernization of the Army. But so long as the aviation program remained focused on tasks it believed were appropriate to the Army's assigned missions, air leaders devoted themselves to the defense of American cities from Soviet bombers and on building up the Strategic Air Command.[14]

While always at pains to avoid or at least choose the timing of their doctrinal battles with the Air Force, Army Aviation leaders energetically exploited their new freedom to explore the potentials of rotary-wing air transport. In September 1952 they publicly demonstrated the impressive ability of even small numbers of helicopters to move combat units during an exercise at Fort Bragg. Flying before army brass and civilian VIPs, twelve H-19s clattered in low to mask themselves behind trees and terrain. Dropping off two infantry platoons in good order and in just a few seconds on an open field, they immediately cycled back to a pickup point for their next load. A few minutes later, the helos reappeared, carrying a battery of howitzers and cannoneers. Again, the helicopters cycled away and came back with ammunition and picked up a couple of "casualties" for rearward movement. Thus, the helicopters had repositioned a protected and ready-to-fire artillery battery to an open field in a tactically useful space of time and could move it away again before it became a target for counter-battery fire.[15] No fixed-wing unit, whether Army or Air Force owned, could have done the job.

Of course, the Fort Bragg exercise did not suggest any reduction in the Army's need for long-range, fixed-wing air transport support. Compared to aircraft like the Air Force's C-119 and C-124s, H-19s and any new helicopters on the developmental horizon were profoundly small in their lift capacity and limited in their range. Although not described by the reporter observing the exercise, the distance between the pickup and delivery points at Bragg could only have been a few miles to allow multiple shuttles so quickly and apparently without any refueling of the aircraft. Helicopters were limited in their long-range deployment capabilities, as well as their tactical operating ranges. During the 1953 Desert Rock exercise, for example, a company of H-19s took nineteen days to cover the 4,000-nautical-mile round-trip from Fort Benning, Georgia, to Nellis AFB, Nevada, for an average of less than three flight hours per day. A dozen C-124s, each carrying two partially disassembled C-19s, personnel, and equipment, could have moved the company each way in a day. The same C-124s also could have deployed the ground echelon of a Strategic Air Command bomber unit; that was why the notion of moving a few army helicopters in the early days of a war was so unacceptable to air force leaders. Nevertheless, the future of army air transport clearly lay in striking some sort of balance in capabilities and doctrines that exploited the advantages and compensated for the disadvantages of rotary- and fixed-wing transports in coordinated operations.

By the signing of the Korean truce in July 1953, then, a robust aviation program had come to stay in the Army. On the battlefields of Korea, H-13s were the ubiquitous aerial ambulances of the battlefields, saving thousands of soldiers. Two companies of H-19s were demonstrating the value of helicopter air transport daily, lifting whole battalions from where they disembarked from air force transport aircraft or army trucks to their forward fighting positions. The helos also moved thousands of tons of supplies, sparing men, mules, and drivers the exertions and dangers of transporting material through mountainous terrain and under enemy fire. Helicopters remained limited in performance and difficult to maintain. Whoomp whoomp whoomping under their whirling blades, they simply shook their bolts, connections, and parts loose from one another and, along with the normal hazards of combat flying, gave their mechanics endless opportunities to hone their skills. But the things were so useful tactically that the Army had dug deeply and painfully into its budget, which was the smallest of the three services', to build its aviation strength to 3,000 aircraft by the end of 1953 and to put a new generation of more capable aircraft on order.

Most important among these new aircraft were the H-21 and the H-34. Notionally able to carry twenty troops but usually carrying about half that number, the H-21C Shawnee was a twin-rotor design powered by a single 1,425-horsepower radial engine. Having two centers of lift, one at each end of the aircraft, eased a major challenge in helicopter flight—that is maintaining stability when the aircraft's center of gravity shifted. So, though ponderously slow—it cruised at eighty knots—the Shawnee entered service in early 1955 and served well for over a decade. The more important new aircraft, however, would be the CH-34 Choctaw, which first flew in March 1954. The Army acquired a test batch of H-34As from the Navy in time for the November 1955 Sagebrush exercises, but the aircraft did not enter the fleet in large numbers until after 1956. When it did, the Choctaw became the Army's mainstay battlefield air transport, able to carry up to sixteen troops or equivalent cargo at 100 knots over distances of about 100 nautical miles or less. Interestingly, the H-34 solved the stability problem by putting its principal centers of mass, its 1,525-horsepower engine and the tail rotor assembly, in the extreme nose and at the end of a long tail. Thus positioned, they acted as counterweights to mitigate the impact of cargo and passenger movements in the fuselage on the center of gravity. However they achieved stability, the two aircraft greatly improved the Army's ability to move large units over battlefield distances.

The Takeoff: 1954–1960

Nuclear war was the operational theme of aviation development between 1954 and 1960. Growing fears that the Soviets, now armed with atomic bombs, might be on the verge of attacking Europe led the Department of Defense in January 1951 to charter the California Institute of Technology to study strategic and technological options for fending off numerically superior communist forces. Conducted under tight security in the Vista Hotel in Pasadena, California, Caltech presented the so-called Project Vista report to the military in January 1952. The study team recommended strengthening the U.S. Army in Europe and equipping it with small atomic weapons and increased troop carrier airlift support.[16] In parallel to Caltech's top secret report, a number of aviation-minded army officers called for reinforcement of Army Aviation's ability to move large units from where air force airlift capabilities terminated at forward airfields to where army units actually did their fighting.[17]

But there was more in the minds of army aviators than simple air transportation. In April 1954 Lieutenant General James M. Gavin, the Army Director of Operations, let the cat out of the bag in an article published by *Harper's Magazine* titled "Cavalry, and I Don't Mean Horses." Without actually saying so, Gavin's article revealed the broad conclusions of a series of classified operational studies, which indicated that Army Aviation was ready for more direct combat roles. In the near term, Gavin proposed the organization of "Sky Cavalry" units to perform the traditional missions of cavalry—observing, doing reconnaissance, controlling artillery fire, and conducting local blocking actions—but at speeds appropriate to the scale of the atomic battlefield.[18] Perhaps more out of recognition of the Air Force's likely reaction of any proposal to arm army aircraft, Gavin focused his proposal on the movement of ground teams to observation points from where they could locate enemy units and direct artillery, tactical air, and/or nuclear fires down on them. But given that two of the cavalry's most important roles were doing armed reconnaissance behind enemy lines and blocking enemy breakthroughs, the need for arming some of the aircraft in these Sky Cavalry units lurked just beneath the surface of Gavin's writing.

The problem for the Army was that all these thoughts about "traditional missions," organic air transport, and Sky Cavalry were out of step with the strategies and priorities of the Department of Defense, the Joint Chiefs of Staff (less the army chief, perhaps), and the Air Force. In early 1954, President Dwight D.

Eisenhower and Secretary of State John Foster Dulles had positioned the Air Force and its long-range bombers at the dead center of their New Look national defense strategy. Under New Look, the president anticipated that the United States would rely on nuclear-armed bombers to deter and, if that failed, defeat major enemies—namely, the Soviet Union. As a corollary to what Eisenhower hoped would be the resulting nuclear stalemate, New Look also proposed that the United States would help allied nations build up their forces to deal with local conflicts. If necessary, the United States could stiffen these forces either with nuclear threats and even attacks or perhaps with small doses of U.S. troops. The Army's role under New Look, therefore, was secondary. Defense budgets after 1954 reflected this reduced role, as the Army's share declined steadily, forcing reductions in manpower and limiting modernization. By 1957 the Army's chief of staff General Maxwell D. Taylor estimated that his service needed 1.5 million troops and twenty-eight combat-ready divisions to do its job; his budget only funded the equivalent of about twenty-two divisions, a number of which were not manned fully or mobile.[19]

There were critics of New Look from the start. Even the New Look strategy document, National Security Council Paper 162/2, hedged its bet on nuclear weapons by suggesting that a review would be necessary if Soviet nuclear capabilities grew to the point that they would "neutralize" U.S. nuclear forces.[20] Some civilian defense scholars raised questions about New Look from the start, but army leaders, understandably, were tempted to the point of mutiny by what they considered the willfully shortsighted folly of the strategy. General Gavin later wrote that he was stunned by the Department of Defense's continued reliance on strategic nuclear weapons. He and his compatriots were convinced that conventional forces and tactical nuclear weapons in overseas theaters would be just as important to the national defense as strategic weapons based in the homeland. Angry at what he saw as the "deception and duplicity" of the senior Pentagon leaders defending the new strategy, Gavin reserved special vitriol for Secretary of Defense Charles E. Wilson, whom he considered "the most uninformed man, and the most determined to remain so, that has ever been Secretary."[21] When Gavin's boss, Army Chief of Staff Matthew B. Ridgway retired in June 1955, he was only slightly less damning in his assessment of New Look and Secretary Wilson. On his way out, Ridgway wrote an open letter to Wilson in which he argued at length about the importance of preparing to win local wars without the employment of "global" nuclear weapons. As a consequence of the Department of Defense's emphasis on air force bombers, Ridgway declared,

"United States military forces are inadequate in strength and improperly proportioned to meet . . . requirements."[22]

Despite the Army's desperate shortage of funds, General Taylor came in as Ridgway's replacement, determined to prepare the Army doctrinally and structurally for future wars fought with or under the threat of nuclear weapons. Doctrinally, he briefed his staff on a new concept, "Flexible Response." Whether the Department of Defense liked it or not, Taylor believed that the Soviets would employ local aggressions by proxy states and insurgents to achieve their goals and avoid triggering a mutually destructive exchange of strategic nuclear weapons with the United States. Some of these wars would employ conventional forces only, and others might involve the use of theater atomic weapons.[23] Taylor told his staff to prepare for all types of war and directed a revision of the basic army operations doctrine, Field Manual 100-5, to emphasize limited war. Structurally, Taylor announced that all army divisions would be reorganized on the so-called Pentomic model. As the name suggested, the combat elements of Pentomic divisions would be parceled out to five combined-arms battle groups, each consisting of infantry, artillery, mechanized, and engineer companies as appropriate to the type of division. Each battle group would consist of about 1,500 soldiers and would be capable of operating independently and of moving rapidly when necessary to concentrate for attacks or to scuttle away before enemies could strike back with nuclear weapons. Organic aviation would provide mobility for infantry and artillery units and logistics support for all, including mechanized units. Thus supported, these units would have the stealth and speed of movement needed to fight and survive on battlefields pockmarked by atomic blasts.[24]

Knowing that Pentomic soldiers would depend on air transport for their lives, army leaders stretched their resources to build up the aviation arm.[25] Late in 1955, army headquarters and various field commands developed a comprehensive plan for the expansion and reorganization of aviation over the next several years. Besides calling for acquisition of new aircraft, the plan also recommended making improvements in the management of army aviators, transfering training and logistics functions from the Air Force to the Army, and creating an aviation center to handle training, doctrine writing, and research and development. Probably to avoid another fuss with the Air Force, the Army's chief of staff did not formalize the plan with his signature but nevertheless made it the aviation blueprint for the next several years.[26] Even as the aviation plan was under development, the Army assigned responsibility for creating a

U.S. Army Aviation Center (USAAVNC) at Camp Rucker, Alabama, to Brigadier General Carl I. Hutton. An aviation zealot, Hutton organized the center
through 1955 and exploited the post's isolation from prying air force eyes to
develop doctrines and technology for what he and like-minded generals called
an air fighting army. In this concept, Hutton proposed that the role of aviation
would move beyond transportation to include the integration of "fighting vehicles" to provide organic air assault and fire support capabilities to combat units.[27]
He was assisted in his efforts by General Gavin and Brigadier General Hamilton Howze, who directed the G-3 Aviation Branch and who, in January 1956,
became the first director of Army Aviation.

The Pentomic and Sky Cavalry concepts themselves went on public display
in November and December 1955 during Operation Sagebrush. Held over vast
stretches of Louisiana, Sagebrush involved 110,000 army troops and 30,500
airmen, including virtually every troop carrier unit in the United States, and
three divisions, including the 1st Armored and 3rd Infantry organized as Atomic
Field Army divisions, precursors to the final Pentomic concept. Drawn from
the 82nd Airborne Division, the Airborne Reconnaissance Troop (Provisional)
composed the Sky Cavalry test unit. Supporting the "aggressor" forces in the
exercise, the troop included a large aviation company of twenty-nine aircraft,
including fourteen H-21s, and platoons of jeep and light tank-mounted reconnaissance troops, armored artillery, and infantry. Its mission was to "obtain
information quickly, to surprise the enemy behind his own lines and to get
back with accurate data."[28] The unit also inserted its infantry platoon several
times as a blocking force to bunch up enemy units for exploitation by aggressor artillery and tank units. Simulated atomic weapons played a focal role during the exercise, with almost 150 set off in the vicinity of important targets, like
troop columns, bridgeheads, supply dumps, and headquarters units.[29]

To all practical purposes, Sagebrush also marked the end of the Air Force's
effective resistance to the expansion of Army Aviation. General Otto Weyland,
the commander of the Tactical Air Command and the exercise commander,
attempted to block the use of the Sky Cavalry unit behind enemy lines and the
transport of army units in army aircraft, saying that such activities duplicated
air force capabilities. Army exercise commanders protested Weyland's position
as intrusive and not supported by the existing Pace-Finletter and other agreements. Eventually, to head off the issue before it went to higher levels, army
and air force secretaries met and agreed that the Army was correct in its plan
to use its new CH-34s to move troops beyond the front lines and that the Sky

Cavalry experiment could proceed. From that point on, official and unofficial spokespersons for the Air Force complained often and sometimes bitterly over the Army's program but without much effect on policy. The Army Aviation program continued to struggle for funding but mainly because the Air Force was winning the overall budget battle and not because it was winning any doctrinal points.

Exploiting the momentum gained from Sagebrush, the Army pressed even more insistently and confidently for freedom and funding to build up Army Aviation. General Taylor wrote and spoke frequently on the critical importance of aviation in the Army's ability to fight modern—that is, "atomic"—wars.[30] More substantively, the secretary of the Army pushed Secretary of Defense Charles Wilson to drop all restrictions on the size, weight, and capabilities of Army Aviation. Though skeptical of the Army's aspirations, Wilson overrode vehement air force objections and eliminated the weight restriction on helicopters. He preserved the 5,000-pound limit on fixed-wing aircraft but also authorized the Army to buy a test batch of five De Havilland of Canada DHC-4 Caribous. With two 1,425-horsepower piston engines and gross weights approaching 28,500 pounds, these aircraft could carry up to thirty-two troops at 150 knots for over 1,000 nautical miles. They also could operate from fields of less than 1,000 feet in length. All things considered, Wilson's permission for the Army to acquire them vitiated the weight restriction and gave ground commanders an aircraft with capabilities similar to those of the earlier C-122 and that significantly overlapped those of the C-123. Tacitly recognizing this, Wilson went even further, clearing the Army to operate its planes throughout an operational zone extending from 100 miles behind to 100 miles beyond the front lines. In keeping with its growing technological capabilities and doctrines, Army Aviation was becoming an air force in its own right.

In 1956 the Army acquired one aircraft type and put another one on order that, taken together, presaged another leap in its aviation capabilities. In the summer of that year, the first CH-37s began to enter army transportation helicopter battalions. Called the Mojave, this aircraft had two 2,100-horsepower piston engines and could lift twenty-eight troops and three tons or more of cargo or small vehicles for about 130 nautical miles. The Mojave had clamshell doors and a short cargo ramp in its bulbous nose that made it the first helicopter able to carry vehicles and artillery pieces internally. As an indication of the mobility value of these machines, three companies, or fifty-one aircraft, could lift an entire infantry battalion in a single lift of more than 196 tons of people, weapons, vehicles, and supplies. Later in the fall, the Army's first turbine-powered helicopter, the Bell XH-40, made its first flight. Designed primarily as a medical evacuation (medevac) aircraft, the XH-40 came with a 700-horsepower engine and could carry four passengers or a couple of litter patients. Soon redesignated as the HU-1, for Helicopter Utility-1, the aircraft went through several upgrades in power and size over the next several years. The Huey, as it became known, would greatly improve the operational and logistical capabilities of Army Aviation and become the iconic symbol of the Vietnam War.

In that same year, the USAAVNC began to experiment with armed reconnaissance and transport helicopters. Once again sensitive to a potential air force backlash, senior commanders gave the experiment director, Colonel Jay D. Vanderpool, an iconoclastic genius, freedom to conduct the tests, but they also made no official announcements of the experiments or issued formal orders to the center or Vanderpool. Keeping a low profile, Vanderpool proceeded with the help of volunteer pilots and mechanics—"Vanderpool's Fools"—who modified the aircraft and conducted their tests on their weekends and other free times. Cautious in their uncertainty of what would happen to a fragile helicopter under the strain of cannon recoil and missile back blasts, the experimenters started with H-13 helicopters restrained on wooden platforms and then moved on to flight tests with increasingly large aircraft and more powerful weapons. Eventually, they blasted their way through gunnery ranges with H-34s carrying batteries of .50–caliber machine guns and 20mm aircraft cannon and bristling with launch tubes for rockets as large as five inches in diameter and packing sixty-pound warheads. These aircraft could do a great deal of damage, if their slow speeds and mechanical vulnerabilities didn't get them shot down first.[31]

Arming transport helicopters and, perhaps, their escorts had profound operational and doctrinal implications. Operationally, it gave transports engaged in assault operations the ability to provide for their own preplanned and emergency fire support. As in the case of armored personnel carriers and navy landing ships, guns were what transformed helicopters from mere logistics carriers into mobility weapons able to fight their way onto contested ground and deliver their loads of soldiers and supplies. Unquestionably, artillery and air force attack aircraft could soften up future helicopter landing zones. But in the last few hundred yards of an aerial assault, those weapons would be too inaccurate and dangerous to allow their use in proximity of assaulting helicopters. For those minutes when army helicopters came under close fire, they would have to provide for their own defense, because nothing else could.[32] There could be no doubt that arming helicopters was both an indispensable step toward General Hutton's vision of an air fighting army and a serious intrusion into what air force leaders considered to be their business. But if the Army was going to move troops by air into combat, it had to have the ability to shoot it out at close range, instantly, and with organic weapons.

By 1959 Army Aviation was becoming an all-turbine-powered fleet and no longer under significant threat of having its way forward blocked by bureaucratic or political action. By that time, the aviation fleet contained some 5,500 aircraft, with authorizations for 6,500. During the year, the Army ordered 159 Caribous to equip six transport companies and ordered the first five of what would become a fleet of hundreds of CH-47 helicopters. Powered by two 2,200-horsepower (later 2,850-horsepower) turbine engines, the Chinook carried loads similar to the Caribou's and at similar speeds, though for shorter distances.[33] Meanwhile, a program to convert the HU-1 design into an assault aircraft capable of carrying an entire infantry squad was well under way, and the Army would begin buying thousands of them in 1960.

Galvanized in November by the obvious implications of these enhancements to army battlefield airlift capabilities, the Air Force's chief of staff, General Thomas D. White, directed talks between the Tactical Air Command and the Continental Army Command to clarify the Army's limited war requirements for the Air Force and the operational boundaries between the two services. White's later presentation to the House Appropriations Committee revealed the Air Force's cooperative posture when he declared, "We are accused of not providing airlift . . . there are even suggestions that the airlift functions should go to some other service. . . . I say we want it and cannot get it. . . . If there is to be more airlift, the only question is to establish a requirement for it and provide the funds."[34] Regardless of where the doctrinal and operational boundaries wound up being drawn, White's statement and other developments ensured that the whole spectrum of the Army's airlift requirement—battlefield, troop carrier, and strategic—was going to receive serious, though perhaps still reluctant, treatment by the Department of Defense and the Air Force.

As the years of peace and experimentation between the end of the Korean and Vietnam Wars began to close, therefore, the rise of Army Aviation presented an impressive story of the abilities of service leaders to marshal technological developments, doctrinal studies, organizational reforms, and astute politicking to profoundly transform the Army's operational character. From an army whose operations were characterized by ground maneuver and episodic airborne operations, it had become an army organized to exploit aerial mobility and resupply and for which such operations were a matter of daily routine. As it turned out, happily, this new army would never be tested in the crucible of an atomic battlefield, for which it had been invented. No one would know for sure whether the idea of maneuvering heliborne or helicopter-supported battle groups among the towering mushroom clouds of nuclear battle was a good idea or a really crazy one. Instead, by 1960 the Army was shifting its focus to conventional low-intensity conflict, mainly the simmering insurgency in South Vietnam. Analysis showed that heliborne mobility would be even more central to American counterinsurgency operations, so the Army conducted several assessments of future requirements in 1960 under the leadership of Lieutenant General Gordon B. Rogers. These studies recommended the continued modernization of Army Aviation and the creation of a test division to explore the fullest potential of air mobility.[35] A year later, in November 1961, three helicopter transport companies of H-21s went to South Vietnam, and the Army was back in a war, a war that would prove the value of the military helicopter if not the wisdom of intervening in a foreign insurgency.

13. Air Transport in the 1950s

THROUGHOUT THE 1950S, the Military Air Transport Service (MATS) operated under continual doctrinal and institutional duress. Each military service, the Joint Chiefs of Staff (JCS), the scheduled and unscheduled airline industries, different groups in Congress, and other interests all had differing views of the proper roles, the operational priorities, and even the very need for the command. According to its charter, MATS was the common-user air transport service of the military. Its capabilities were available to all services in accordance with priorities set by the JCS, and no other military service was authorized to replicate them. In peacetime, MATS exercised with the Strategic Air Command (SAC) and provided scheduled transportation for military personnel, their dependents, and high-priority cargo. In wartime, at least at the beginning of the decade, the JCS and air force commanders agreed that the primary role of MATS was to provide mobility for the bomber units of SAC. Army leaders challenged this focus as the decade advanced, claiming that they too would require robust airlift support in the event of major war. The Air Force's continued acquisition of commercial airliner–type aircraft for MATS increased army frustrations since these aircraft offered little mobility to ground combat units. Looking like an airline in its equipage and daily operations, MATS also drew the ire of the commercial airline industry, which saw MATS as an illegal government competitor performing services it could offer more cheaply. All of these perspectives had champions in Congress. This perfect storm of conflicting service, commercial, and governmental perspectives on the proper utilization of MATS (i.e., over doctrine) energized a series of congressional hearings that, by 1959, poised national policy to either reform or disband MATS.

Open Debate

Prior to and during the first year of the Korean War, air transport leaders pressed an unwilling Air Force to expand and modernize airlift as a flexible arm of national strategy. In 1946 the Air Transport Command commander, Major General Robert Webster, warned that since contract carriers could perform most of Air Transport Command's air transport roles, the continued existence of the command rested on its "provision of strategic concentration, deployment, and support, by air, for the Army Air Forces and the War Department."[1] The Department of Defense responded by reinforcing the status of MATS as a general transport organization, with no authority over "the tactical air transportation of airborne troops and their equipment, the initial supply and resupply of units in forward combat areas, or that required by the Department of the Navy for internal administration."[2] Later, General Laurence S. Kuter, the first commander of MATS, told Air War College students in 1949 that MATS was not an airline but an "air route command . . . which can be expanded rapidly in time of national emergency."[3] Building on the global airlift vision of a consolidated command serving all services, Kuter later pushed the Department of Defense and Air Force to transfer all long-range transports currently assigned to air force troop carrier units, navy Fleet Logistics Groups, marine assault aviation, and SAC Strategic Support Squadrons to MATS. Only with complete control of these assets, Kuter argued, could MATS support the strategic bomber force in the opening days of a major war and then lift other air and ground forces as directed by the JCS.[4] Just on the eve of war in Korea, Kuter resubmitted his plan, with a promise to release units temporarily to SAC and overseas air forces when needed. He also offered to establish a subordinate "Tactical Air Transport Command" to preserve troop carrier's identity and expertise.[5]

A few months later, in February 1951, Kuter's zealous operations deputy, Major General William H. Tunner, closed his temporary command of theater airlift forces in Korea with an end-of-tour report designed to "put in a blow for airlift consolidation."[6] Believing that he had demonstrated conclusively the ability of a single commander to direct both global and theater air transport operations, Tunner declared, "We must prepare to use all available air transportation to the maximum extent, by integrating [it] into one organization which will have the mission of standardizing . . . equipment, units and technique." He also called for development of a four-engine version of the C-119 or a larger aircraft to increase the safety and flexibility of the theater airlift fleet.[7] Like his boss, Tunner's mantra was "modernize and consolidate, modernize and consolidate."

One Step Forward, One Step Back

The outbreak of war obliged the Air Force to modernize its airlift forces. Reminded by the near disaster in Korea of its obligations to support the Army and flush with war supplemental funding, the service proposed to expand

MATS to thirty transport squadrons and to begin replacing its World War II–vintage C-54s, the bulk of the fleet, with more capable aircraft. Accordingly, in 1951, the service bought an initial batch of C-118s, military versions of the DC-6B freighter, and received enough C-124s to equip a wing.[8] The Air Force also initiated programs to develop turbine-powered transports. Seeking initially to control costs, the service chartered Douglas Aircraft in July 1950 to design a turboprop-powered version of the C-124. Then, when Douglas reported in February 1953 that a turbine-powered C-124 was not practical, the Air Force agreed to fund two other long-range transport projects.

The first of the developmental aircraft, the XC-133, was a transitional design. Basically, Douglas hung four 6,000-horsepower turboprop engines on the C-124's wing and moved it to the top of a more streamlined and pressurized fuselage. Its designers expected the aircraft to carry about fifty tons and cruise at around 260 knots. Its low-slung fuselage would allow loading and unloading at truck-bed height through its full-profile rear cargo door and ramp.[9] Given its more capacious fuselage, the C-133 would carry some loads that would not fit in a C-124. But for the Army, it offered no really new capability, since it carried only the trucks, light tanks, towed artillery, and engineering equipment already lifted in the Globemaster. Most important, it could not carry a battle tank, the essential ingredient of army mobile warfare.

In comparison to the C-133, the other aircraft, the XC-132, could change the airlift world. Powered by four 15,000-horsepower engines, the swept-wing aircraft's designers expected it to cruise at 400 knots while carrying a maximum load of 100 tons, or 50 tons for 3,500 nautical miles.[10] More to the point, it would be able to lift all major combat and support equipment items in the Army's inventory, including battle tanks, atomic canons, and air defense missiles on their launchers. Also, since the giant planes would cycle between the homeland and overseas theaters in a third of the time required by C-124s, they could generate vastly increased airlift flows over great distances. For the first time, then, military air transport would be able to lift fully equipped army divisions into combat theaters in tactically useful time frames.

Despite the necessity of buying new transports, the Air Force saw no need to adjust the organization or status of MATS. Responding indirectly to Kuter's memo on consolidation in September 1950, Secretary of the Air Force Thomas K. Finletter told a gathering of aviation writers that the air transport and troop carrier missions were vital and distinct and often would occur simultaneously; therefore, their consolidation into a single command would not be practical or productive.[11] Meanwhile, the commanders of SAC and the Tactical Air Command (TAC) pressed the Air Staff to reject General Kuter's consolidation memo more directly. TAC sought to preserve Troop Carrier Aviation's separate identity, and SAC was determined to retain control of its three Strategic Support Squadrons, which carried atomic weapons and other equipment for the command. General Joseph Smith, the initial commander of the Berlin Airlift and now the air force director of plans, was their point man in the Pentagon.[12] In a telling move, air force leaders elevated TAC from its position as a subordinate element of the Continental Air Command (CONARC) to that of a separate Air Force Major Command (MAJCOM) in December 1950. In the following March, TAC placed troop carrier units based in the continental United States (CONUS) under the 18th Air Force. The 18th Air Force quickly grew from three to ten wings, began preparing troop carrier units for overseas deployments, and started transoceanic air transport operations along routes already flown by MATS.[13]

Kuter and Tunner pushed back, naturally, but got nowhere. In response to their complaints that troop carrier's foray into transoceanic operations was redundant and robbed MATS of long-range capability, the TAC commander, General John K. Cannon, asserted that the 18th Air Force's new C-124s were necessary to provide long-range transport to army and air force combat units. Writing General Tunner separately, Cannon declared, "Any proposal to merge troop carrier and air transport units . . . is basically in error in that it combines combat functions with service functions." Cannon's position conformed exactly to that of Air Force Chief of Staff Hoyt S. Vandenberg, who said at about the same time that the business of MATS was routine air transport and to support SAC, for "without this type of support the strategic bombing force is neither truly strategic nor potent."[14] The decisive moment came in November 1951, when the Air Force selected Lieutenant General Joseph Smith, instead of Major General Tunner, to replace Kuter as the commander of MATS. Unmistakably, the Air Force was finished with the debate and wanted everyone to get in line and do their jobs.

From the Air Force's perspective, Smith was an outstanding choice. His service record revealed unusually strong staff and adequate operational experience. His rapid stand-up of the Berlin Airlift demonstrated that he understood many essentials of air transport. Moreover, Smith's immediate past assignment as the deputy chief of staff for plans put him in touch with the Air Force's deepest secrets and objectives and had given him an opportunity to show his read-

iness for higher command. Perhaps most important for air force leaders looking to shepherd the transport community back into the fold, Smith was not a
grandstander and had no hidden agendas. He was a confident leader, but he
was also quiet by nature and ethically averse to anything that smacked of self-
promotion. Not given to what he viewed as Kuter and Tunner's "empire building," he planned to make the Air Force's priorities those of MATS as well.[15]

Kuter and Tunner did not share the Air Force's view of Smith's suitability. As
a zealot who had appeared on the cover of *Time* as "Mr. Airlift," Tunner felt he
was more qualified for the job. But as a subordinate officer now under Smith,
he could only bide his time and nurture his grudge. As Smith's coequal, Kuter
was freer to indulge his anger. In their first meeting, Kuter told Smith that he
was persona non grata at MATS headquarters for taking the command billet
in place of Tunner. At the change of command, Kuter and his staff left Smith
standing at the Andrews AFB Officers' Club while they slid out and motored
over to the flight line for the parade. Incensed, Smith flagged down a "god-
damned bread truck" to get him to the ceremony in time to take command and
review his troops. The next day he discovered that the Kuters had taken the
government furniture from his official residence to their new digs at Bolling
AFB. Smith also learned that Kuter had assigned several key colonels from
MATS headquarters to field assignments, leaving substitutes behind who the
new commander felt lacked the attitude and preparation for senior staff duties.[16]
It took little imagination to realize that he was being set up to fail.

General Smith Takes Charge

Failure, however, was not something that Joe Smith did very well. In military
parlance, he might not have been a "show dog," but he knew operations, rel-
ished command, and could scrap with the best of them when needed. When
Kuter told him he was not liked at MATS headquarters, Smith blasted back,

> Anybody who doesn't want to serve with me because you say I am per-
> sona non grata, run for the rat holes and get the hell out as fast as they
> can, because I will kick them out. . . . I am in control, and I am going to
> mark that outfit until they know Joe Smith has command of it.[17]

Smith then promptly dragged Kuter's liberated staff officers back from the field
and told them to keep the command running while he learned the ropes. He
called the supply officer at Andrews and told him to get his furniture back from
Kuter, and he did. By the time General Tunner left in February 1952 to become

the vice commander of the Air Materiel Command, Smith had the reins of MATS firmly in hand.[18]

Smith wasn't impressed by what he saw at the other end of the reins. Speaking of his staff, he later recalled, "MATS people were pretty mediocre." Worse, he was "shocked" at the sloppy discipline and deteriorating safety record of his field units. In one case of criminal irresponsibility, a pilot in the Air Rescue Service, a subordinate component of MATS, had raced his HU-16 amphibian up a water ramp at night and destroyed five aircraft in the parking area.[19] In other incidents, two aircraft collided in clear weather while conducting training in the traffic pattern of their base, killing both crews, while another crew nearly ran out of gas carrying the newly designated army chief of staff, General Matthew Ridgway, from Japan to Hawaii. In Smith's first six months on the job, his command racked up eighty-six aircraft accidents, resulting in thirty-nine fatalities and many more injuries.[20]

Taking on the safety issue, Smith began pulling the wings from pilots who damaged planes through "stupid errors," like landing short of a runway. Unit commanders learned that their jobs depended on their safety training and accident rates.[21] Smith's efforts produced results. By May 1952 the accident rate dropped from thirty-four major accidents per 100,000 flying hours to ten. As the safety record improved, insurance companies began selling flight insurance to MATS travelers at the same rates offered to commercial passengers.[22] Nevertheless, the accident rate in the subordinate commands of MATS—the Air Route Communication Service, Air Weather Service, and Air Rescue Service— remained as high as five times the air transport rate. There was still a lot to do to make MATS a safe command.[23]

During his first year in command, General Smith also guided his staff through a fundamental revision of the MATS fleet modernization plan to bring it into compliance with air force priorities. The plan he inherited from General Kuter aimed to improve mobility support for both the Air Force and the Army. It proposed increasing MATS's transport strength to fifty-eight squadrons by 1955, including thirty squadrons of C-124s. Once the C-124s were on line, the existing plan called for a slow replacement of C-54s by C-118 Liftmasters. But viewing the smaller and faster C-118s as more useful than C-124s for many bomber support and routine transport missions, Smith asked the Air Force in 1952 to convert a pending order for forty-eight C-124s into one for seventy-three C-118s.[24] Thinking along the same lines at the end of the year, General Smith also articulated the need for a high-wing, jet-powered cargo aircraft capable of carrying fifteen tons of "people and high-priority cargo" at about 550 knots for 2,500 miles. In response to criticisms that such specialized aircraft would be expensive and unattractive to civil airlines, Smith responded, "MATS is not so much a mover of bulk loads as [it is] a rapid transit system for personnel and relatively small high value bits and pieces."[25] What Smith could not say, since the mission was classified, was that his focus was on getting the personnel and equipment of SAC reconstitution teams to overseas bomber recovery bases as quickly as possible in wartime, not to move passengers in peacetime or army equipment in wartime. Given the priorities laid out for him by the Air Force, the smaller jet transport made good sense to Smith.

General Smith's preference for the C-118 over the C-124 was a matter of priorities. When MATS acquired the Liftmaster, there were larger and faster aircraft coming available, such as the DC-7 and Lockheed Constellation. But the DC-6 was cheaper to acquire and noted already for its reliability and low operating costs. Its four 2,500-horsepower engines produced a cruise speed of about 250 knots and enabled it to carry ten tons from California to Hawaii. Most C-118s came as "triple-threat" aircraft, capable of quick conversion for cargo, passenger, or medical evacuation missions. Some also had the comfortable interiors of commercial airliners, complete with coach class seats, lavatories, galleys, and even bulkhead brackets to hold infant bassinets.[26] Military travelers and their families praised the comfort and service on these aircraft; they were a far cry from the conditions on the frosty, unpressurized, bare metal cargo decks of most of the other transports in the MATS fleet. The planes also gave excellent support to SAC's reconstitution teams, which normally consisted of personnel, tool kits, parts bins, and light support equipment. If a reconstitution team deployed to a "bare base," one not occupied already by an air force contingent, it might also bring along light vehicles, cargo trucks, and even fire trucks, which would be carried by C-124s. General Smith did recognize that the C-118 offered little to the Army, since it had no airdrop capabilities and could not load vehicles or other large items. But he also considered his responsibility to the Army as secondary to his much greater responsibility to provide maximum support to SAC at minimum cost to the Air Force.[27]

Through the 1950s, then, MATS was SAC's airlift arm. It planned its fleet of C-118s and C-124s precisely to carry the bomber fleet's logistical tail to war. As Smith told Congress in 1958, MATS needed exactly fifteen C-124s and twenty C-118s to move the reconstitution elements of a bomb wing in one lift.[28] Parts of the MATS fleet stood alert, along with bombers and tankers, to ensure that the support teams made it to their overseas operating locations before the bombers limped in from their first strikes. Meanwhile the rest of the fleet either exercised with SAC or flew routine logistics missions. The SAC exercise mission consumed an increasing portion of MATS's flying hours, growing from a total of 39,000 passengers and 7,000 tons of cargo in 1954 to 55,000 passengers and 9,000 tons in 1958.[29] Throughout this same period, MATS did not conduct a single exercise with the Army.

Building Criticisms of General Smith's Handiwork

While General Smith did what he felt called to do by national strategic priorities and the directives of his superiors, he could not please everyone. Most important, the Army was confused. Under Department of Defense guidelines, MATS was supposed to be its primary source of long-range air transportation.[30] But from 1951 and onward, the 18th Air Force and Air Force Reserve troop carrier wings seemed to have that mission, though in aggregate they were inadequate to the task. A whole series of army studies made that case, culminating in the 1954 Project Vista study, which proposed that the deployment and support of a strategic army corps would require the dedicated support of 400 C-124s and 800 C-123s.[31] These were disheartening figures, given that the Air Force at the time possessed only about 560 medium transports, 90 C-124s, and a couple hundred airliners.[32] Smith's decision to acquire more C-118s and fewer C-124s, and the increasing focus of the 18th Air Force on moving TAC's new Composite Air Strike Forces, only increased the Army's anxiety and resentment.[33] To the Army's complaints, airline industry leaders added harsh criticism of MATS as a coddled competitor for the peacetime logistics mission, which they felt they could handle more efficiently than the Air Force.

Smelling an opportunity to reduce government spending, both President Eisenhower and Congress chartered military air transport studies in 1954. The first study, directed by Robert B. Murray, chairman of the president's Air Coordinating Committee, was released in May.[34] The congressional study, under the direction of former president Herbert Hoover, came out in a series of reports from April through June 1955. Both studies sought to enhance military readiness and reduce costs through greater utilization of commercial contracts to move routine military traffic. The Murray Report recommended that "the government should, to the greatest extent practicable [sic] use [the] existing unutilized capacity of United States air carriers." But the report but did not explain whether "greatest extent practicable" meant that MATS planes would fly empty on their training missions or if they would be able to utilize their "training by-product" to move routine traffic and then contract out what was left.[35] The Hoover reports also ended vaguely, though with harsh words for the existing management of MATS.[36] Although acknowledging that "there must be a strong . . . military air transport operated and staffed by military personnel," they went on to direct the military to maximize its use of commercial contracting and to paint MATS as a bloated organization that flew too many training hours and used the resulting capacity irresponsibly to move things like concrete to Bermuda and dog food to Okinawa.[37] Observing that "the role of military air transportation for mobilization purposes must be clearly delineated . . . before the status of MATS can be satisfactorily resolved," the commission told the Air Force to blueprint its airlift program by assigning as much of its peacetime and wartime traffic to the airlines as possible and then building a small military air transport arm to carry the rest. "Failure to accomplish this," the commission declared, "means a continuing and expanding military socialism extending down into other forms of commercial transportation."[38] These were strong words indeed in the age of McCarthyism.

Coming, as they did, on top of intensifying army and airline complaints, the Murray and Hoover Reports prompted Senator Stuart Symington (D-MO) to add airlift to the docket of his general hearings on American air power in the spring and summer of 1956 and thereby initiate what would become a nine-year-long series of hearings into the issue. What Symington learned was that the Army didn't have enough airlift, and no one could say authoritatively who was supposed to provide it. The Army's director of operations, General Earle G. Wheeler, started things off by saying that while he wanted the ability to move two divisions anywhere in the world, the Air Force probably could not lift one. Then the commander of TAC, General Otto P. Weyland, said that he agreed with the Army's pessimistic assessment, but the job really belonged to MATS. This was a stunner for the committee, since General Smith was on record as having said that TAC had the job. Focused as it was on nuclear capabilities, Symington's committee did not press the airlift issue to any conclusion, but it did recommend that the Air Force work harder to satisfy the Army's mobility needs.[39]

Congressman Daniel J. Flood (D-PA) was the real agent of change in the airlift policy debate. A onetime vaudeville actor, he was flamboyant, sported a Simon Legree handlebar moustache, loved the Army (in which he had served in World War II), and counterbalanced that with a strong dislike for the Air Force. He eventually would be driven out of Congress for influence peddling.[40]

But in 1956 he was on a crusade to make the Air Force step up to its army airlift obligations, and as chair of the House Subcommittee on Army Appropriations, he had a lot of power. After hearing Major General Hamilton Howze, the director of Army Aviation, complain that "a sort of vacuum" had appeared in the Air Force's support of the Army, Flood invaded the Air Force Subcommittee's hearings to charge the Air Service with violating congressional intent by using the money allocated for utilitarian C-124s to buy "plushed up" C-118s for passenger operations.[41] Thundering and posturing as if on the stage, Flood badgered air force witnesses unmercifully, particularly Undersecretary of the Air Force James H. Douglas. As the former chief of staff of the Air Transport Command in World War II, Douglas was the Department of Defense's point man to "ride herd" on MATS and deal with the flood (pun intended) of theatrics before him.[42]

The showdown between the Air Force and "Dapper Dan" Flood was not pleasant for either side. Flood knew nothing about the statutory foundations of MATS or Troop Carrier Aviation, and he didn't care. He wanted planes for the Army, and he choked with bluster and fury at Secretary Douglas's patient explanation that "the highest priority airlift requirement in the event of war is asserted by SAC." Flood didn't get any happier when General Smith appeared to back up Douglas's defense of his command's four-hours-per-plane daily operating rate, the resulting limitations in commercial contracting, and the ideal characteristics of the C-118 for the bomber-support mission.[43] Though always in control of his emotions, unpretentious Joe Smith despised Flood for his grandstanding flamboyance and assessed him as a "crook in the pay of the Air Transport Association."[44] If duels had been legal, Smith and Flood probably would have drawn swords and hacked away in the Capitol rotunda.

The confrontation, however, did add more heat to the airlift policy debate. Editorializing on the implications of the Symington and Flood hearings, the staff of *Army Magazine* pointed out that since no one expected MATS to be available to the Army at the start of a war, the solution lay in the Air Force's buying several hundred additional long-range air transports reserved for the Army's use.[45] The Army's chief of staff, General Earle Wheeler, some months afterward, suggested that the right number of aircraft needed might be around 300 C-124 equivalents.[46] The Symington and Flood reports made less specific recommendations than Wheeler's, though Flood did endorse the Department of Defense's plan to begin managing MATS operations through an industrial fund. The planned industrial fund was to be no more than a revolving account into which MATS users would "pay as they went" for their airlift support and out of which MATS would then cover its operating costs. Such a fund, the Department of Defense hoped, would discipline the use of MATS aircraft by forcing airlift users to justify their airlift support requirements in the annual budget process.[47] Finally, and probably most important, the 1956 hearings, for the first time, placed all the elements of the national airlift system—MATS, Troop Carrier Aviation, Army Aviation, other organic users, and the civil carriers—under the congressional microscope at the same time. The confusion revealed in that spectacle guaranteed that Congress would come back to airlift in the near future.

Struck by a Gale: Congress Examines Airlift in Depth

As expected, the 1958 congressional legislative season included several hearings on airlift affairs. Though these hearings did not result in legislation or other congressional edicts, they did heighten awareness of airlift's strategic importance and operational and institutional complexities. Air force leaders maintained their defense of the airlift status quo—one that preserved the separate existence of MATS (reserved for the Air Force) the 18th Air Force (reserved mainly for TAC), and that left the Army cringing around the table looking for scraps. The Army and a growing cohort of congressmen pressed simply for more airlift capacity dedicated to its use.

Representative Chet Holifield (D-CA), chairman of the Military Subcommittee of the House Committee on Government Operations, opened the congressional inquiry in January with hearings designed to give the Army and the airlines their say regarding MATS. After the Air Force gave a single classified briefing on its plans, they got the floor for the rest of the hearings.[48] Army witnesses took the opportunity to rehash their grievances with established airlift policies. The airlines complained again that the four-hour daily utilization rate flown by MATS exceeded legitimate training needs and artificially increased the amount of training by-product passenger and cargo airlift flown by the command instead of by commercial contractors. In the end, Holifield's subcommittee suggested that all MATS, navy, and troop carrier long-range air transports be consolidated into a single command and then largely replaced by civil contractors. Purely military airlift forces would be retained only to move air force and army combat units and, perhaps, "outsized or exceptionally heavy cargo."[49]

In May, Senator A. S. Mike Monroney (D-OK), chairman of the Committee on Interstate and Foreign Commerce's ad hoc subcommittee on airlift, shined an even brighter light on airline concerns. Describing MATS as "one of the largest airlines in the world," he set out to determine "whether or not MATS is functioning within the scope intended by Congress . . . [or] impeding the expansion and services of the commercial air carriers." Replicating Holifield's docket, Monroney gave air force witnesses just two hours to outline the size and operational tempo of MATS.[50] Monroney then criticized the Air Force for its recent decision to cancel development of the C-132. "We have failed," he protested, "to put anything on the drawing boards . . . that could transport a division ready to fight. . . . We go merrily on our way buying Pullman cars when we should have purchased freight cars for M-Day [mobilization day]."[51] Monroney then gave the airlines two hearing days to detail their readiness and ability to absorb most of the MATS mission. The report on these hearings actually made no specific recommendations for airlift policy, perhaps because potentially more decisive hearings were under way already over in the House.

In the realm of congressional military affairs, L. Mendel Rivers (D-SC) was the pit bull to Mike Monroney's porch dog. Rivers was a powerful member of the House Armed Services Committee, the right arm of the very powerful Carl Vinson (D-GA), a peppery proponent of military preparedness who, at the moment, was very interested in airlift. Tasked by Vinson to look into the matter, Rivers began hearings in April 1958, intending in particular to give the Air Force a fuller opportunity to present its case than Flood, Holifield, and Monroney had allowed. Assistant Secretary of the Air Force Dudley Sharp opened the hearings with a defense of the four-hour utilization rate of MATS transports and the Air Force's use of the resulting training by-product to move actual passengers and cargo. Next, and no longer willing "to take this [airline] lobbying for MATS contracts lying down," General Smith shed his usual reticence and added confident testimony on the importance of the MATS fleet and its need for an injection of 144 C-133s and 96 new cargo jets (C-Jets) to replace his piston-engine aircraft. General Tunner also was at the hearings, speaking as the Air Force's deputy chief of staff for plans. He repeated Smith's call for C-Jets, describing them as an "immediate requirement."[52] The call for cargo jets was a particularly sensitive issue, everyone knew. Their ability to shuttle rapidly back and forth across the oceans would be of great value to the Army, with its massive movement requirements. But SAC war plans called only for a single sortie from each MATS aircraft, so for air force purposes, C-Jets appeared to be something of an expensive luxury.[53]

Senior air force leaders made it clear that they remained satisfied with the existing state of affairs in airlift. Asked by Rivers if, based on Smith's and Tunner's testimony, the Air Force might buy an initial batch of jet transports, the vice chief of staff, General Curtis LeMay, declared, "If you gave us money now for jet airplanes, I would buy tankers, not airplanes for MATS." Given the single-sortie airlift requirements of SAC, LeMay saw no military difference between 350-mph and 600-mph transports.[54] LeMay spoke with the full authority of his boss, General Nathan Twining, who told a Senate committee at about the same time that he had plenty of airlift and would buy no more, even if his budget were increased by $2.5 billion.[55] Twining, on his part, was repeating the recent findings of secret air force and JCS studies that found MATS was adequately equipped for its nuclear war mission and that commercial carriers could pick up the slack for limited war requirements.[56]

The standoff between the Air Force and other airlift advocates might have stymied progress beyond 1958 but for several developments. The first was the critical and effective role played by MATS during the Lebanon and Quemoy-Matsu crises that summer that provided irrefutable evidence of its importance and flexibility as a strategic mobility asset for the Army, as well as SAC. In that context, the Air Force's stubborn and at times high-handed rejection of change hardened the determination of Mendel Rivers, other powerful legislators, William Tunner, and a handful of his fellow global airlift believers to make something happen anyway. Observing the ruckus, President Eisenhower directed Secretary of Defense Neil H. McElroy to "see that careful consideration is given to worldwide combat mobility, with due regard to the . . . economical use in peacetime of airlift necessarily generated by a ready D-day force."[57] Last, and this was really important, Tunner must have stunned a lot of his colleagues by rising from the ashes of his airlift career to take over MATS at this critical moment. By whoever's string pulling or political orchestration he got there, he got there at a critical juncture of airlift's destiny. Things were about to change.

14. The National Military Airlift Hearings

AS HE RECALLED a few years later, L. Mendel Rivers, Democratic congress-man from Charleston, South Carolina, had had enough of the enemies of the Military Air Transport Service (MATS), whose objective, he charged, was to serve the "so-called patriots" in the airline industry.[1] Following years of wran-gling between the Army, the Air Force, the airline industry, and Congress over the size, equipage, and operations of MATS, he scheduled hearings in the spring of 1960 to settle the issue. He promised to conduct comprehensive hearings solely in the interest of the national defense. But, from the start, the organiza-tion and witness list of the hearings indicated his predetermination to preserve MATS institutionally, modernize its fleet, and tighten its linkage to the mobil-ity requirements of the Army.[2] Under Rivers's leadership, the National Military Airlift Hearings resulted in regulatory and budgetary actions that set the orga-nizational, matériel, and doctrinal foundations of global airlift, the ability to move battle-ready ground and air combat forces to anyplace on the planet by air. In so doing, the hearings would influence the ways in which the United States and its enemies fought wars for decades into the future.

Background to the Hearings

Several background elements shaped the conduct and outcome of the National Military Airlift Hearings. Most important, the future of American airlift forces, particularly of MATS, had become an issue of Byzantine complexity and great importance to American defense. Every major group and interest involved was unhappy with the state of affairs and uncertainty over the direction of airlift policy. National interest in the issue heightened as it became clear that the com-position of the airlift force was linked to the outcome of the broader debate over national strategy. Critically also, the balance of power within the Ameri-can government shifted in favor of modernizing and expanding MATS to improve its ability to move ground and air forces overseas. When all of these elements came together in the spring of 1960, airlift concepts that theretofore had found little traction in the halls of power suddenly became national policy.

As discussed in the preceding chapters, a lot of people and interest groups were involved in airlift policy by 1959, and few of them liked the way things were going. Although the general mission of MATS was to provide common-user transportation to the whole Department of Defense, the Air Force was resisting all pressure to expand the command beyond what was needed to move the Strategic Air Command (SAC) in the early days of war. Most of that pressure was coming from the Army and its supporters. They wanted the Air Force to expand MATS and/or Troop Carrier Aviation and equip them with long-range transports capable of moving ground units and all of their heavy vehicles over transoceanic distances. For the Air Force, the costs of developing such aircraft were staggering in their financial and strategic implications. Compared to the movement requirements of SAC, the Army's costs were at least an order of magnitude greater. Moreover, building a fleet for the Army would divert resources away from what air force generals considered the all-important buildup of nuclear strike and air defense forces. From their perspective, the airliner and airliner-derived aircraft currently composing the MATS fleet had the virtues of being inexpensive and adequate to the needs of SAC. It was on this point— equipping MATS with airliners—that the actual airlines got involved. If MATS could perform its missions with the same aircraft that their companies flew, reasoned the leaders of the commercial industry and many congressmen, then so could the airlines under contract and probably at less cost. So by 1959 MATS was under strong attack from the Army, which wanted more from it, and the airline industry, which wanted less.

By the late 1950s, the debate over the future of airlift was proceeding against a changing strategic backdrop. Since 1954 the template for American defense strategy had been New Look, which was anchored to the unstoppable nuclear striking power of SAC. But by 1958 Army Chief of Staff Maxwell D. Taylor and others were arguing that the emergence of Soviet nuclear parity undermined the credibility of New Look's reliance on nuclear weapons in response to even minor regional aggressions by the Soviets. Since neither country was likely to risk a nuclear Armageddon to achieve its aims, they reasoned, future Soviet aggressions would be below the nuclear threshold. Rather than attack the American homeland, they could be expected to undermine the West's strength by sponsoring limited wars and insurgencies in troubled areas of the world. To deal with such actions, the United States would need a balance of land, sea, and air forces to respond flexibly, proportionately, and quickly wherever they occurred. Taylor dubbed this new strategy Flexible Response.

The linkage between airlift and Flexible Response was obvious. General Taylor wrote, "Our [defense] program must provide for mobile, ready forces pre-pared for rapid movement to areas of strategic importance overseas."[3] Henry Kissinger, a defense and security studies scholar at Harvard and future secretary of state, agreed, saying, "The tactics for limited nuclear war should be based on small, highly mobile, self-contained units, relying on air transport, even within the combat zone."[4] B. H. Liddell Hart, a British military scholar linked to mobile warfare theories since the 1920s, described a concept of quick response and "controlled dispersion" on the battlefield, in which strategic and tactical airlift would play a vital role.[5] From the perspectives of these writers and others, then, the efficacy of Flexible Response would hinge on "the swift transport of finely trained troops and tactical air forces" by MATS and the Army working in concert.[6] For that reason air force generals, who liked massive retaliation, just as adamantly argued against Flexible Response and seemed even more determined to defend the status quo in the mission and equipage of MATS.

Then, in July 1958, there appeared a crack in the wall of air force resistance to airlift expansion. Lieutenant General William H. Tunner returned to MATS, this time as the commander. "Mr. Airlift," the man who had led the final months of the Hump Airlift to China and most of the Berlin Airlift, was back in the cockpit of airlift policy. Given his fame and his reputation as a grandstander who loved publicity, no one could doubt that Tunner's arrival at Scott AFB, Illinois, the new location of MATS headquarters, portended an intensification of the airlift policy debate. Indeed, Tunner's passion for big airlift was so well-known, his elevation to such an important role could only have reflected some sort of change of heart at air force headquarters. Characteristically, Tunner griped in his memoirs about being passed over for command of MATS in 1952 and then "exiled" by his enemies to a series of assignments away from his beloved world of airlift. But the assignments he went to included vice commander of the Air Materiel Command, commander of United States Air Forces in Europe, and then as the deputy chief of staff for plans at air force headquarters. These were not the assignments of an exile. They were assignments indicating that the Air Force was seeing to it that he gained the breadth of experience and credibility for senior command. Far from being the crusading outsider he depicted in his memoirs, Tunner may not have been an insider at the highest levels of command, but he was treated well and with respect. Some senior leaders, such as Lieutenant General Devol Brett, viewed Tunner as a maverick and disloyal to his comrades. Fortunately for Tunner, though, the most senior officers in the

Air Force, including the acerbic general Curtis LeMay, valued his skills and considered him suitable for important duties.[7] In reasonable likelihood, they sent him to MATS because he was the smartest person in the universe on airlift matters, and he had the fame and connections to catalyze a settlement of all of the uncertainty and political turmoil surrounding airlift affairs.

Background: Tunner Sets the Stage

Tunner charged into MATS with a Templar's zeal. MATS was his Holy Land, modernization his Grail. There was something else: Tunner had suffered a heart attack, so he was in his final act as an air force leader, and he wanted a legacy. Before he could build that legacy, he first had to purify influences unfriendly to his vision of global airlift. He took pains to diminish the reputation of his predecessor, Lieutenant General Joseph Smith. By unspoken agreement, there was no formal change of command ceremony between the two, as neither wanted to be in the presence of the other. Smith left Scott; Tunner showed up the next day. That was it. Next, Tunner sponsored an "independent" study that painted him as the rescuer of MATS, who took "characteristically bold" steps to advocate MATS's interests. Smith, the report went on, had given up on defending the command from outside critics, "apparently [from] resentment . . . against unfair and unjustified attacks and his feeling of futility."[8] In other words, Smith was a weakling and Tunner the knight-errant returned to save the command. Tunner also turned over the MATS staff, filling it with officers more to his liking than those left behind by Smith. Most important for the long run, he drew John Shea back into his inner circle. A staff officer in Air Transport Command and MATS since 1943, Shea had been Tunner's "stay behind" during the years that the general was away at Air Materiel Command and in Germany. Shea was an unstinting advocate of global airlift and had of necessity become an astute bureaucratic politician as he worked under General Smith, who was not receptive to such ideas. Now, with Tunner at the yoke, Shea quickly rose to a level of prominence as a global airlift thinker and policy strategist well beyond his formal position as a minor civil servant on a military staff.

With his staff reorganized and vengeance served, Tunner shifted his attention to laying the foundations for a successful policy coup. Knowing that his advocacy of global airlift would take him into confrontation with some higher Department of Defense and air force leaders, Tunner turned to the Army for an alliance. He began by contacting army leaders in November 1958 to propose the largest-ever peacetime airlift of ground combat forces to an offshore location. With army backing, Tunner coaxed the Air Force out of $10.5 million to fund the exercise. With money in hand, Tunner's staff sat down with their army counterparts and planned the details of the exercise, which they named Big Slam/Puerto Pine. Seeking a show, Tunner asked the Army for 21,000 troops. The Army countered with a more affordable 6,000. Tunner then asked the army generals if they thought the Marine Corps might like to get involved. Perhaps to spare the marines the trouble, the generals suddenly located 18,500 troops and 11,800 tons of cargo for MATS to move around. Finally, the planners chose Puerto Rico as the exercise site mainly because it was within productive range of piston-engine transports.[9]

While pulling the Army into his camp, Tunner also nurtured his links to Congress. His ideas already enjoyed the powerful support of Representative Carl Vinson (D-GA) and Representative L. Mendel Rivers (D-SC), both of whom believed that airlift was important to the national defense and who also had significant airlift interests in their home districts. Rivers had a MATS wing at Charleston AFB, while Vinson had the Lockheed Aircraft C-130 assembly plant in Marietta, Georgia. The emerging linkage between airlift moderniza-tion and Flexible Response drew the attention of other important politicians as well. These included Senator Dennis Chavez (D-NM), Chairman of the Sen-ate Appropriations Committee Strom Thurmond (D-SC), Senator Howard Can-non (D-NV), and Senator Mike Monroney (D-OK); the latter were two former critics of MATS who turned advocates. Of great future significance, Senator John F. Kennedy (D-MA) and Senator Lyndon B. Johnson (D-TX) were airlift supporters. Kennedy's interest went back to the late 1940s, when he sponsored several bills related to the establishment of an air merchant marine. Most of these congressmen were members of the so-called Congressional Reform Move-ment, a group of mostly Democratic congressmen advocating increased gov-ernment spending on defense, particularly for nonnuclear, limited war forces.[10]

Even as Tunner and Shea worked Congress, the military bureaucratic balance of power shifted in favor of airlift expansion. Of critical importance, James H. Douglas, who had served as the Air Transport Command's chief of staff during World War II, had become the secretary of the Air Force. He revealed his con-tinued loyalty and enthusiasm to airlift in several congressional hearings dur-ing 1959.[11] Hardly less significant, General Thomas D. White had become the Air Force's chief of staff. Noted for being more open on doctrinal issues than his predecessors were, White had given Tunner freedom to articulate his views before Congress and also told the House Appropriations Committee, "We are accused of not providing airlift . . . there are even suggestions that the airlift functions should go to some other service. . . . I say we want it and cannot get it. . . . If there is to be more airlift, the only question is to establish a requirement for it and provide the funds."[12] Almost before anyone was aware, it seemed, the Air Force's rock-solid resistance to airlift modernization had begun to crumble.

As resistance to airlift change went down, pressure for it went up. In mid-1958 President Eisenhower tasked his staff to study MATS and the overall airlift program. Recognizing the likely influence of the report, Tunner offered up John Shea as a technical adviser for the study team. Once inside the tent, Shea employed all his persuasive wiles to shape a report that embodied most of the global airlift vision.[13] Shea's success was evident when the president released "The Role of MATS in Peace and War" in February 1960. The report culminated in nine "presidentially approved courses of action," which, taken together, composed a manifesto of the global airlift vision. Most important, these courses of action included authorization to equip MATS for both general and limited war requirements, which in practical terms meant preparing to move the Army and the Air Force. Thus, when "The Role of MATS in Peace and War" hit the streets, receptive military leaders were on notice to expand the long-range airlift fleet. The tasks left to Mendel Rivers and his pending airlift hearings were to clarify the actual requirement and to gain funding to develop and buy new aircraft.[14]

The Hearings

From the moment he started the hearings on March 8, 1960, Congressman Rivers made it clear that they would be comprehensive and decisive and emphasize military over commercial requirements. The hearings themselves would be organized into three phases. Phase 1 would be an appraisal of the overall airlift problem, including testimonies by senior officials in the Air Force, Army, and Department of Defense. Big Slam/Puerto Pine would occur between phases 1 and 2. Phase 2 would let airline officials make their cases for increased commercial contracting and consequent reductions in the scale of the MATS fleet and operations. Phase 3 would give military witnesses opportunities to restate their airlift concerns and requirements and rebut the testimonies of the airlines. "I trust," Rivers said of his hearing plan, "that all will now agree that we propose to consider all pertinent aspects of the national airlift."[15]

Well, Rivers could trust whatever he wanted, but the hearings were not balanced. They were, instead, a carefully orchestrated presentation of global airlift ideas leading to foregone conclusions. Acting as the bureaucratic insurgents they were, John Shea and Robert Smart, general counsel of the Armed Services Committee, met every night to assess the day's testimony and plan the presentations and questioning of the next session to help Rivers "prepare the testimony . . . to develop the record to support the conclusions he felt were appropriate."[16] Shea and General Tunner also provided army witnesses with the technical information and air force planning information they needed to strengthen their testimony. Shea thought the army witnesses were the most "outspoken, dedicated and persuasive" airlift advocates at the hearing, while Tunner later praised them for working "closely and faithfully with us."[17] James Douglas, just elevated to undersecretary of defense, was the highest-ranking civilian official to testify, and he promised Rivers that MATS and the services had "worked together to make a comprehensive presentation of airlift requirements, capabilities and operations."[18] Douglas's team included General Tunner, Army Chief of Staff General Lyman Lemnitzer, Air Force Secretary Dudley C. Sharp, and Army Secretary Wilbur M. Brucker. All were outspoken advocates of airlift expansion and modernization. Probably in keeping with his promise to give Tunner a free hand at the hearings, Air Force Chief of Staff General White did not make an appearance until the very end of the hearings.[19] After a decade of suffering short dealings at the hands of the Air Force, airlift progressives were about to get their day in the sun.

The only note of tension in phase 1 of the hearings came when the Army revealed the scale of its airlift needs. General Lemnitzer must have caused a gasp in some quarters of the hearing room when he announced his desire for enough airlift to move two airborne or infantry divisions by air to anyplace on the planet within four weeks. This was a huge requirement! General Tunner had just pointed out that the SAC reconstitution mission required only 354 aircraft sorties, or about one for each aircraft in the fleet. The Army's new requirement equated to moving something like 25,000 troops and 50,000 tons of cargo. Considering the cruise speeds and capacities of the aircraft available, the Air Force Deputy Chief of Staff for Plans Major General Hewitt T. Wheless admitted that the mission was impossible. He also could not have been happy at the potential costs of building the fleet needed to make such a move.[20]

As the representative of air force headquarters, General Wheless further undermined the subcommittee's confidence, first, by blaming delays in new aircraft purchases on the debate over the utilization of MATS and, then, by his frequent use of the term "consistent with military requirements" when he spoke of air force modernization plans for MATS. Since Congress was at the center of the airlift debate, one wonders how the subcommittee members felt about Wheless's assertion, in essence, that they were to blame for the stagnation of the airlift fleet. His frequent references to "military requirements" prompted Representative Melvin Price (D-IL), whose district included MATS headquarters at Scott AFB, to doubt the sincerity of the Air Force's commitment to airlift expansion and modernization. The subcommittee's doubts were reinforced further by the absence of any funding for new air transports in the Air Force's budget for the next year.[21] Thus, phase 1 closed on a skeptical note, when the subcommittee recessed to view and assess exercise Big Slam/Puerto Pine.

Big Slam/Puerto Pine stretched American airlift capabilities to the limit. Starting up on March 14, 1960, the exercise involved virtually every transport aircraft MATS could muster, 477 in all. The entire command worked 84-hour weeks to support the surge. From fourteen on-load bases, old C-54s still dripping Berlin coal dust, lumbering C-124s, and a few new C-133s groaned heavily into the air and turned through stormy skies toward Puerto Rico. Crews were pounded, nauseated, and sometimes frightened by some of the most violent weather they could remember. No one fell out of the sky, but they took a beating from thunderstorms, hail, ice, and turbulence. Working 35 hours at a stretch, MATS crews flew 50,496 hours and 1,263 individual missions to lift over 29,000 troops and nearly 11,000 tons of cargo to Puerto Rico. Later flights in the stream of aircraft going into Puerto Rico began lifting out the initial echelons of troops and equipment. This reduced the overall cost of the exercise by limiting the number of empty trips and allowed the army units to complete their training at their home posts.[22]

Impressive as the exercise was, Tunner made sure that the appropriate people got the message he and Rivers wanted them to get: Big Slam/Puerto Pine was as good as MATS could do, but the effort still fell well short of army needs. Tunner organized planeloads of senior commanders, congressmen, business leaders, and a total of 352 reporters to fly out to exercises bases to see what was going on. His staff officers briefed them on the way down to on-load bases and then on to Puerto Rico. They made sure they saw the tired crews and obsolescent planes and understood that MATS could not make the same move over the Atlantic, let alone the Pacific. Chortling over the success of these efforts, Tunner's longtime publicity officer, Lieutenant Colonel Raymond Towne, calculated that the exercise garnered 33,000 column inches of newspaper coverage and declared it "the most spectacularly successful failure in the history of military training."[23]

Back at the hearings, while John Shea and Jacob Smart worked on the Big Slam/Puerto Pine after-action report, Mendel Rivers let the airlines present their views on MATS's operating rates and peacetime contracting. In contrast to the more aggressive demands they had made during earlier hearings, airline spokesmen appeared meek before the decidedly unsympathetic Mendel Rivers, who did not mince words, lecturing them on patriotism and voicing his doubts about the willingness of contract pilots to fly into danger.[24] Correctly assessing their position, the major carriers dropped their earlier calls for the dissolution of MATS. Instead, the representatives of the large, scheduled airlines satisfied themselves by asking for more contract work and for the Civil Aeronautics Board to set the rates for those contracts and block small charter carriers for bidding on them.[25] In the face of Rivers's malevolence, the airline pride had broken its charge and turned on itself, bickering over scraps.

Following the airline testimonies, Congressman Rivers opened phase 3 of the hearings by letting military witnesses summarize the implications of Big Slam/Puerto Pine and to recapitulate their airlift objectives. Regarding Big Slam/Puerto Pine, Major General Ben Harrell, the Continental Army Command's deputy chief of staff for operations, pointed out that troops and cargoes were delivered to secure bases and without their full complements of equipment and supplies. Harrell noted that even ammunition and gas masks were left behind to lighten the load. General Tunner pointed out that even this fractional movement obliged MATS to surge its operational tempo from a routine rate of 4.3 hours/per aircraft/per day to 7.8 hours. By the end of the exercise, he noted, "the trend was definitely downward" in the conditions of his planes and people. In sum Tunner estimated that MATS needed 332 modern transport aircraft to satisfy the Army's needs. This estimate included 200 copies of a new turbofan-powered jet transport described in a recent Air Force Statement of Operational Requirements 157 (SOR 157).[26]

The final air force witness, Chief of Staff White, did try to sound a note of restraint but without success. Though he had just signed an agreement with General Lemnitzer to provide more airlift to the Army, White balked at expanding the transport fleet in the near term.[27] When Congressman Rivers offered to request $335 million for new aircraft, White suggested that the money would be spent better on the floundering B-70 bomber program. He further irritated Rivers by brushing off his suggestion that MATS should become a specified, or single-service, combatant command under a four-star general, like SAC. Convinced that such a command would do much to clarify airlift responsibilities and protect its interests, Rivers rebutted White with a vow to set up the command himself and "make a man have a little responsibility."

The final recommendations of the airlift hearings were a triumph for global airlift. On April 30, Rivers requested $335 million for fifty interim civil-type jet transports and fifty C-130Es, a long-range version of that design. Rivers liked the Hercules, because it was built in the home district of his boss, Carl Vinson, and it was the only new military-type transport immediately available with transoceanic range. After the usual wrangling, Congress appropriated $310 million for MATS's modernization, including $50 million for development of the SOR 157 aircraft, $170 million to buy the fifty C-130Es, and the rest to buy a couple of dozen interim, commercial-type jets.[28] Then in June the subcommittee issued a report calling for improvements in the capabilities, flexibility, and effectiveness of air force airlift forces. In relation to the size and equipage of the strategic airlift fleet, the report directed development and purchase of "an uncompromised turbine powered cargo aircraft," transfer of redundant C-97s and C-124s to the Air National Guard and Air Force Reserve, and expansion of MATS's peacetime flight hours and training activities. The subcommittee also asked the Air Force to rename MATS as the Military Airlift Command in reflection of its strategic importance and expanded combat mobility role.

Aftermath

Even a bare outline of the subsequent course of airlift affairs reveals the importance of the National Military Airlift Hearings. Funding for the "uncompromised cargo aircraft" produced the C-141 Starlifter, which became the mainstay of the Air Force's long-range airlift fleet through the 1990s. Follow-on hearings in 1963 produced funding for the C-5 Galaxy, the giant hold of which finally allowed the United States to deploy even heavy armored equipment by air. Following more hearings in 1965, the Air Force renamed MATS as the Military Airlift Command (MAC), a move that imparted coequal institutional status with SAC and TAC and elevated the rank of the airlift commander to four stars. This new status and the performance of MAC forces during the Vietnam War led the Air Force in 1974 to consolidate all theater and long-range airlift forces under MAC, and in 1977 the Department of Defense designated MAC a specified combatant command. With that, all the essential elements of the global airlift vision were in place: a centralized command, managed as a defense-wide asset, operating a truly global fleet of modern aircraft.

The record of these hearings also provides insight into the relationship of doctrine, interest, and power in the military policy process. Although General Tunner and others had advocated the doctrinal elements of global airlift for years, they got nowhere in the face of the Air Force's resistance to any proposal that reduced its control over or increased the costs of airlift forces beyond the needs of SAC. Only when the Army and Congress protested the strategic liabilities of this limited airlift program did the Air Force open serious discussions, mainly by putting General Tunner back into the airlift limelight. The success of Tunner's and Rivers's advocacy, in turn, stemmed more from the alignment of a continuous chain of airlift supporters above them than to their doctrinal brilliance. Resistance from any bureaucratic level could have derailed their efforts. But all the key decision makers—Rivers, General White, Secretary Douglas, the president, and defense reformers throughout Congress—supported modernization. This happy constellation of support didn't last long, but it was critical at the moment, and it provided a case study in the workings of policy: doctrine set the terms of debate and the boundaries of acceptable outcomes, interests attracted the participants, and power determined the outcome.

15. Inventing the Civil Reserve Airlift Fleet

THE VITAL CONTRIBUTIONS of the U.S. airline industry during World War II implied the need for some sort of mobilization policy for it after the war. There were many precedents for such a policy, particularly in the merchant marines or navies organized by most major powers. Throughout history, militaries have always contracted, called up, impressed, or simply commandeered civil transportation assets in wartime. Beginning in the nineteenth century, maritime powers, including the United States, established programs to organize and finance the expansion and modernization of their merchant fleets as on-call military reserves. So not long after the end of the war, interested and/ or responsible individuals began looking for an organization and mobilization model suitable to the U.S. airline industry.

As might be expected in a policy realm blending military and civilian interests so closely, a complicated interaction of many considerations influenced the ultimate shape of the American civil airlift reserve. These considerations included national strategy, budget priorities, technology, political philosophies, military culture, shareholder interests, and individual personalities and perspectives. Of these considerations, national strategy exerted decisive influence. Just as U.S. national security strategy went through two distinct phases in the 1950s— New Look and Flexible Response—airlift planners developed Civil Reserve Airlift Fleet (CRAF) programs for each one. The first CRAF program reflected the strategic and operational expectations of military leaders anticipating nuclear war with the Soviet Union in the early 1950s. The second program addressed potential American commitments to a wider range of conflicts. Each of these CRAF iterations answered the questions of need, composition, and method in ways that made sense to contemporary policymakers and provided the country with a civil reserve appropriate to evolving military requirements.

First Thoughts

Immediately after World War II, two mobilization models existed to guide the establishment of a civil airline reserve. The first was based on the Merchant Marine Act of 1936. Under that act, most officers on U.S.-flagged merchant ships held commissions in the Naval Reserve, and all merchant seamen were required to be U.S. citizens or immigrants in the process of naturalization. These requirements, along with others designed to modernize the fleet, created a merchant navy "capable of serving as a naval and military auxiliary in time of war or national emergency." In the event of war or national emergency, therefore, the Navy and/or the Army would have authority either to direct the movements and loading of civilian ships or to bring them and their crews directly into military service.[1] The first chairman of the Maritime Commission, Joseph P. Kennedy, immediately saw the connection between ships and planes. In 1937 the father of the future president encouraged shipping companies to create "air auxiliaries" of seaplanes and airships. By implication, these auxiliaries would have fallen under the provisions of the Merchant Marine Act as well, including those regarding mobilization.[2]

The second mobilization model available was the one actually utilized during World War II and might best be described as "voluntary impressment." Operationally, voluntary impressment looked like the merchant marine model, in that the government left much of the airline industry in civilian hands while bringing the rest into military service. Those aircraft and personnel left in civil livery flew routes and passengers in accordance with plans and priorities set by the military. The others were painted green or put in uniform and followed orders or suffered the consequences. The only real difference between the two models was that, under voluntary impressment, airline executives met and chose among themselves who would serve in uniform and then determined which of their employees would fill the allocation for uniformed military service. Much of this allocation was found through volunteerism, while calls to local draft boards could take care of the rest.[3]

The success of voluntary impressment left some military leaders with the impression that a more formal setup was not required. The wartime commander of the Air Transport Command (ATC), Major General Harold George, extolled the value of "the experience, men, and equipment which the airlines threw into the struggle" and made no effort establish a more authoritative process.[4] Instead, George and his successor after September 1946, Major General Robert M. Webster, endorsed an indirect approach: the "maximum encouragement of the development of private competitive enterprise in United States international air transport operations."[5] They did this in several ways, including pressing the federal government's interdepartmental Air Coordinating Committee to encourage the growth of American international air commerce and by taking a role in the organization and activation of the International Civil Aviation Organization.[6] They sought, in other words, to help maximize the size and modernity of the American civil fleet and presumed that it would come forward again when the nation called.

ATC also encouraged commercial development through the award of contracts to commercial carriers to move military passengers and cargo. The need for such augmentation airlift grew rapidly; ATC's postwar fleet shrank from 3,000 to 500 transport aircraft while the demand for military airlift remained high.[7] With U.S. occupation forces settling into Germany and Japan and dozens of other overseas bases remaining active, ATC and the Naval Air Transport Service (NATS) moved tens of thousands of military personnel and their dependents, along with unprecedented amounts of cargo, back and forth across the oceans. Turning to the airlines for help, ATC expanded the share of its traffic moved by contractors from 581,000 of 3.3 million flight hours in 1945 (17.6 percent) to 139,000 of 320,000 hours (43 percent) in 1947.[8]

Much of this increasing share of business went to a new class of charter carriers rather than to large airlines, like American and United. Immediately after the war, demobilizing veterans purchased around 5,500 small and large war surplus transport aircraft and established 2,700 air charter companies.[9] These companies did not possess the coveted certificates of common carriage issued by the Civil Aeronautics Board (CAB) that authorized established airlines to conduct scheduled operations. Consequently, the would-be airlines initially could not advertise or provide scheduled, cargo, or individually ticketed passenger services. In 1948 CAB did authorize some of the better-financed and managed nonskeds—Slick, Flying Tiger, Seaboard, and others—to provide scheduled cargo and charter passenger services on a limited basis. Less-favored carriers sometimes conducted so-called fly-by-night passenger services until caught and shut down by CAB.[10] Most of the rest scrambled for whatever cargo and passenger charters they could find. Called a variety of names indicating their status or operating patterns—non-certs, irregulars, tramps, and most commonly nonskeds—most went out of business in short order. A few survived by making lowball bids for ATC passenger and cargo contracts, which were not subject to CAB supervision.[11] ATC traffic managers found these nonskeds an economical way to fill both unexpected requirements and "call-contracts" that retained a carrier to pick up whatever short-notice assignments ATC might require of it.[12] The ones that got these contracts became a sort of beggar's band, banging their drums around ATC's back door for handouts.

Knowing that the nonskeds generally were unstable financially, ATC would have preferred to contract the major airlines for augmentation airlift. But the majors were too busy reestablishing postwar markets to worry much about military contracts.[13] Furthermore, under the provisions of the 1938 Air Commerce Act, their certificates of common carriage prevented them from bidding below minimum rate schedules set by CAB. These schedules protected certificated carriers from cutthroat rate wars that would jeopardize their financial health and ability to modernize their fleets and conduct safe operations. But, over time, CAB's protectionism also encouraged the carriers to build up overstuffed staffs and raise the salaries of their personnel to the point that they simply couldn't compete with the leaner nonskeds in open bidding. Even if the scheduled carriers had wanted government business at the time, which they didn't, the military's insistence on lowball bidding kept them away.[14]

The growth of the contract airlift effort raised an even bigger issue for ATC commanders: it called the mission and even the institutional survival of the command into question. By regulation, ATC's mission was to operate "air transport services (except transport service specifically assigned to other commands by the Commanding General, AAF, and intra-theater services required by overseas commanders) for all War Department agencies supplementary to United States civil air carriers."[15] The "supplementary" clause was worrisome enough for ATC leaders, since it implied that their command existed only to do what commercial carriers would not or could not do. But in combination with the absence of any mention of a combat role in the mission statement, it opened the way for a complete takeover of the mission by the airlines. Putting the issue succinctly, General Webster advised his boss, Chief of Staff General Carl A. Spaatz, that "the Air Transport Command must have a fundamental mission that states clearly its primary responsibility in a war emergency. Its continued existence . . . as a convenience for military activities, is questionable since such transportation service can eventually be provided . . . by the civil air transport industry."[16] No combat mission, no command—simple as that.

General Spaatz did see a combat mission for MATS, but it was not one that required the establishment of a large military airlift fleet equipped with state-of-the-art aircraft. In 1947 he wrote,

> It [ATC] must be in being . . . for the long-range striking force will not be effective and will not be able to move unless it has the Air Transport Command to carry its mechanics, its bombs and ammunition, spare parts, and

all needed equipment until the land and sea lines of communication are established. Thereafter it will continue to carry emergency spares and replacement combat crews.[17]

However, moving bomber support or reconstitution teams to forward bases did not require more than a couple hundred military transports, so long as they were all available to the Strategic Air Command (SAC) on short notice.[18] In reflection of their boss's vision, Air Staff planners called for the reduction of ATC's fleet to the "maximum consistent with sound military planning . . . and the policy of minimum competition with commercial airlines."[19] Once the needs of SAC were taken care of, then, senior air leaders presumed that the commercial carriers would and should pick up the rest of the military mission.

Pressure to shrink ATC increased when the economic recession of 1947 pushed the major carriers into demanding access to government business.[20] General Webster protested that increasing contract business further would force him to either leave military aircraft on the ground and/or waste public funds by not utilizing the by-product airlift they created during training missions to move actual traffic. But airline politicking won out over military logic, and by the end of 1947, a government directive prohibited ATC from carrying "anything but military traffic on routes where commercial services are available."[21] Pushing to break down another barrier to expanded contract operations, freshman senator John F. Kennedy introduced legislation in 1947 to create an air merchant marine along the lines previewed by his father prior to the war. Kennedy also proposed developing a civil-military transport aircraft to be operated by the airlines and ATC. Despite the efforts of Kennedy and others on its behalf, however, the civil-military aircraft concept faded away in 1948 from lack of funding and airline–air force disagreements over its operational characteristics. The airlines wanted a plane capable of cruising at 260 knots while carrying 15 tons for 2,000 miles, while the military wanted one cruising at only about 220 knots but able to carry 25 tons for 2,600 miles.[22]

Civil-military air transport policy went dormant for the remainder of the 1940s. Civil contracting was a fact of life, and MATS had too few aircraft to do anything about it. Furthermore, neither General Webster nor his successor, Major General Robert W. Harper, had the time or political force to address the civil reserve issue, though both liked the air merchant marine concept. Harper, in particular, simply was too busy with the contentious process of joining ATC and NATS into the new Military Air Transport Service (MATS) in 1948 to worry about airline mobilization. His successor, Lieutenant General Laurence S. Kuter, had his hands full supporting the Berlin Airlift and refining the new command's ability to support SAC. In any case, airline lobbying kept the mobilization issue tied up in government studies and inquiries.[23]

The First Civil Reserve Airlift Fleet Plan

The outbreak of the Korean War in June 1950 reminded everyone that the civil airlift reserve needed some sort of organization. Most important, the major airlines balked at ATC's call for help. It was, after all, the start of the tourist season, and there were profits to be made. Not in a position to ask the North Koreans to cease further offensives until American children went back to school, ATC turned to the nonskeds for augmentation. They jumped at the windfall and put sixty ex-military C-54s on the Pacific routes in a matter of days. Not long afterward, Pan Am and other scheduled carriers did offer aircraft to MATS, but the damage was done, and planning for an authoritative mobilization plan began only a month after the start of hostilities.[24]

Knowing that a political bloodbath would serve no good purpose, the military and civilian planners came together in July 1950 ostensibly in a spirit of compromise. Leadership for the planning process fell to James H. Douglas, who had credibility in both camps. He was a prominent aviation lawyer and had served as ATC's chief of staff during World War II. He would go on in the next decade to serve as the secretary of the Air Force and then undersecretary of defense. Despite the experiences of the previous month, the military, or at least General Kuter at MATS, was willing to consider a plan based on volunteerism and contracts, as long as it received authoritative control over "maintenance, pilots, security of communications, traffic functions, [and] inspection."[25]

Despite the appearance of cooperation, however, the airlines feared an air force takeover and so worked successfully behind the scenes to put the program into friendlier hands.[26] On March 2, 1951, President Eisenhower handed the program to the Department of Commerce, with directions to provide for "the transfer or assignment of aircraft from the civil air carriers to the Department of Defense, when . . . approved by the Director of Defense Mobilization."[27] Under Douglas's deft leadership, the coup did not derail the planning effort, and in November the Department of Commerce established the Defense Air Transportation Administration (DATA) to manage the new CRAF and its counterpart for civil services in wartime, the War Air Service Plan.[28] In the next month, the National Security Resources Board released Douglas's final plan for administering CRAF. The Douglas plan called for a reserve fleet capable of producing 450 C-54 equivalents of lift, approximately equal to what MATS could produce on its own. To provide flexibility and buffer the airlines from the effects of mobilization, the plan allowed the government to call up the first tier of 350 C-54 equivalents in forty-eight hours but delayed second-tier mobilization of the remaining 100 equivalents for two weeks.[29] With this seemingly equitable plan in hand, the Department of Commerce activated CRAF on December 15.

Thereafter, the CRAF program languished from disinterest and neglect. Few senior air force leaders saw its value. Almost to a man, they believed that American atomic bombers would settle future major wars well before the airlines could be mobilized and their crews and planes put to use. General Kuter's replacement in November 1951, Lieutenant General Joseph Smith, did not share his predecessor's enthusiasm for the airlines. His focus was on the buildup of the active duty fleet of C-118s and C-124s, which he would need in the first days of a nuclear conflict to support the movement of SAC units to overseas bases. He also began increasing the command's utilization of its training by-product airlift. MATS continued to award augmentation contracts on the basis of minimum bids, which excluded the big carriers once again. But the economy was back on a roll and their planes were full again, so the majors flew away with hardly a look back. CRAF, consequently, existed on paper, but no carrier joined it, and MATS gave it little attention beyond establishing a squadron of reserve navigators to guide mobilized airliners across the oceans and conducting a few command post exercises.[30]

Even on paper, the final details of the new CRAF program made it an awkward, almost unusable instrument of war. Participation was voluntary. The major carriers had no incentive to volunteer, since there was no linkage between the privilege of bidding for peacetime contracts and CRAF membership. Worse, MATS continued to let peacetime contracts to lowest bidders, leaving the big carriers out. The nonskeds didn't need to join, since they were getting peacetime contracts already, and their experience in the early days of the Korean War implied they would get wartime contracts as well. MATS couldn't afford to have airlines join anyway, since DATA set CRAF reimbursement rates well above what it was paying the nonskeds.[31] DATA also guaranteed that CRAF carriers could not be mobilized for training and that their planes and crews would fly in civil livery in wartime.[32] Almost as if to build a wall around CRAF, DATA replaced James Douglas's two-tier mobilization plan with a single-tier, all-or-nothing concept.[33] This concept ensured that CRAF would not be used in conflicts or missions short of general and/or nuclear wars, since a complete mobilization of the industry would unhinge the national economy. So not a single air carrier joined CRAF until 1959. From the start, Secretary of the Air Force Thomas K. Finletter and General Smith recognized that call-ups would happen only when authorized by the "highest authority, in cases of demonstrable necessity."[34]

Ironically, Congress and the president became involved in civil-military airlift policy in response to airline complaints about their declining shares of MATS's contract business, rather than the stillbirth of CRAF. By late 1953 the Air Transport Association and its congressional allies were demanding that MATS open more of its traffic to civil contractors.[35] In response, President Eisenhower and Congress chartered separate commissions to study whether civil contractors could move more military traffic and whether MATS was engaged in illegal competition with commercial carriers when it moved cargo on its training flights. Robert B. Murray, chairman of the National Air Coordinating Committee, directed President Eisenhower's study, which was released in May 1954. Congress's study group, under the leadership of former president Herbert Hoover, issued its report in mid-1955. Both reports supported the contention of airline industry leaders that they could and should take over larger shares of government air transport business. Declaring that "the Department of Defense . . . should continue its policy not to engage in competition with private industry," the Murray Report recommended that "the government should, to the greatest extent practicable, adjust its use of air transport so as to use existing unutilized capacity of United States air carriers."[36] The Hoover Commission recommended an even more drastic curtailment of the military air transport arm. Assessing that MATS had more aircraft than needed and flew too many training hours, the commission recommended that it be reduced in size and operations to carry only the traffic that the airlines could not.[37] "Failure to accomplish this," the report later declared, "means a continuing and expanding military socialism extending down into other forms of commercial transportation."[38] Suddenly, it seemed, something akin to treason had become an element in the discussion of airlift policy.

As discussed previously in the chapter on air transport in the 1950s, the findings of the Murray and Hoover Commissions provided grist for several congressional hearings friendly to airline interests from 1956 through 1959. Most led to proposals to reduce MATS in order to increase peacetime contracting. Congressman Daniel Flood (D-PA) opened the airlift hearing cycle in 1956.

But after indulging his theatrical proclivities by baiting air force witnesses and fuming that MATS was no more than a plushed-up government airline, he faded out of the airlift debate.[39] Representative Chet Holifield (D-CA) and Senator A. S. Mike Monroney (D-OK) conducted more substantive hearings in 1958. After listening to airline complaints at length, Holifield's Committee on Government Operations recommended putting all transports in MATS, Navy Fleet Logistics Groups, and Troop Carrier Aviation into a single command and then reducing it to the minimum strength needed to move combat units and "outsized or exceptionally heavy cargo."[40] Of a like mind, Monroney's Committee on Interstate and Foreign Commerce's ad hoc subcommittee on airlift questioned "whether or not MATS is functioning within the scope intended by Congress . . . [or] impeding the expansion and services of the commercial air carriers." Monroney did not issue any policy recommendations, but he did voice concern that "we go merrily on our way buying Pullman cars when we should have purchased freight cars for M-Day."[41]

Holifield's second round of hearings, held in 1959, did preview a number of recommendations that, if acted on together, would have fundamentally changed CRAF and civil contracting programs. Air force witnesses opened the talks by announcing that some carriers were ready to enter into CRAF contracts.[42] One committee staffer asked an air force witness if the right to bid for peacetime airlift contracts could be reserved for airlines in CRAF.[43] In a related recommendation, the vice chairman of CAB, Chan Gurney, prodded the committee to eliminate lowball bidding from CRAF contracting and replace it with the same sort of fixed-rate structures CAB imposed on commercial airlines. Gurney asserted that fixed rates would attract the most modern carriers by protecting their financial stability and guaranteeing profits.[44] Following Gurney, the head of the Federal Aviation Administration, retired air force Lieutenant General Elwood (Pete) Quesada, proposed creating a civilian air cargo fleet able to fulfill most of the military's air transport needs in peace and war.[45] In sum these witnesses were proposing a new CRAF plan, one based on first-line air carriers flying at rates of reimbursement appropriate to their business characteristics and enjoying exclusive access to peacetime contracts as a reward for membership.

The Second Civil Reserve Airlift Fleet Plan

By early 1960 the Air Force and the Department of Defense had several reasons to consider an overhaul of the CRAF program. Perhaps most important, the impending adoption of the strategy of Flexible Response would greatly expand the military's demand for airlift. If army and air force tactical units were going to be racing to global trouble spots and limited wars, MATS would need augmentation by the major airlines, not just the little nonskeds. But given the lowball bidding process, General William H. Tunner noted during the 1958 Quemoy-Matsu crisis, "Some of the airlines were loath to release to us on a low-bid basis planes which could be used for the lucrative passenger business."[46] The nonskeds remained insistently available, of course, but their cutthroat competitive habits were leaving them financially unstable and unable to replace their rapidly aging fleets of C-46s and C-54s with newer aircraft. Thus, although the Air Force remained uncomfortable with the legal issues involved in reserving contracts for CRAF carriers, expanding the contract airlift program had become a "requirement and trend" by the middle of 1959.[47]

In February 1960 the Department of Defense committed itself to a new CRAF program. Tasked by President Eisenhower to study the whole span of airlift policy, the Department of Defense released its report "The Role of MATS in Peace and War" just on the eve of major airlift hearings in Congress. Twenty-one pages in length, the report contained numerous recommendations, but its core was composed of nine "presidentially approved courses of action." The president's directives included modernizing MATS "in an orderly manner" to meet its military, or "hard-core," requirements. The president also directed MATS to reduce its carriage of routine, or "channel," traffic "on an orderly basis." While everyone was being "orderly," President Eisenhower also believed, "as commercial carriers make available modern, economical long-range aircraft . . . use should be made of the services of such carriers." Additional courses of action endorsed by the president included awarding airlift contracts "at tariff rates filed with the [CAB]," awarding them only to carriers "effectively" committed to CRAF, and "insuring optimum effectiveness and responsiveness of commercial airlift . . . under all conditions."[48] Taken together, these courses of action and other provisions of the report composed the nation's first comprehensive airlift policy statement and promised to give a reborn CRAF attributes lacked by the old one, members and flexibility being chief among them.

Close on the heels of the president's report, Congressman L. Mendel Rivers (D-SC) convened the first of what would become a multiyear series of National Military Airlift Hearings. Rivers made it clear at the beginning of the 1960 hearings that the airlines were no longer working in a friendly venue. The purpose of his hearings, Rivers announced, was "to give the military the best thing they can get . . . that is simply and solely what it is." Clearly disdainful of the motives of the airline industry executives giving testimony, Rivers at several points lectured them on patriotism and questioned their willingness to actually fly into combat. Also, in reference to the civil-military transport concept raised earlier by General Quesada and others, the congressman declared that there would be no defense purpose served by financing aircraft for the airlines to carry government traffic if that meant that MATS transports would sit idle or fly empty on training sorties.[49] A few years after the hearings, the fiery proponent of military preparedness scorned pro-airline witnesses as so-called patriots working against the national interests.[50]

Getting the message, the airline witnesses approached their testimonies cautiously. The president of the Air Transport Association, Stuart Tipton, took an indirect approach to gaining more airline business. He tried to convince Rivers that MATS needed to fly each of its aircraft only one hour per day to train its crews and that any additional flying to move traffic was a waste of public money given the ability of the airlines to move it more cheaply. He and other airline spokesmen also pressed the Air Force to let contracts at CAB rates and to prevent noncertificated carriers from bidding for them. In return for these actions, the big carriers promised to provide augmentation airlift during limited conflicts and to provide the Air Force the modern civil airlift reserve it wanted. Seeing fixed-rate floors as the lever that would let the big carriers push the nonskeds aside, the president of the Independent Airline Association spoke against Tipton's proposals. But the writing was on the wall: the military wanted the big carriers in CRAF, and the price for their cooperation was a CAB fee schedule that guaranteed their profits.[51]

As expected, the final report of the airlift hearings addressed a wide range of issues and set MATS on a path to modernization and recognition as a major operational element of modern war. The report was no less revolutionary for the CRAF program. Consistent with the presidential report released earlier that year, the report directed MATS to maintain a peacetime daily utilization rate equal to one-half of its planned wartime rate, which MATS had set as eight hours per day for planning. MATS and the Department of Defense could utilize any by-product airlift produced by this training, but they also were to expand their use of civil contractors. The Rivers committee also called for a restructuring of CRAF to allow for partial mobilizations "in periods of national emergency short of war." Finally, in the future, the Air Force was to allow only CRAF member airlines to bid for peacetime contracts. In addition, those contracts would be let at "fair and reasonable rates" over three-year periods to encourage CRAF carriers to purchase modern aircraft and make them available to the military.[52]

By the time the Rivers committee reported out, senior air force leaders had seen the light and were well into preparations to modernize MATS and CRAF. Even as the National Military Airlift Hearings were under way, the secretary of the Air Force released a report in April that, perhaps not surprisingly, made eight recommendations that largely encapsulated the ones released earlier by the president in the "Role of MATS in Peace and War."[53] Next, the Air Force and CAB jointly announced that carriers bidding for MATS's international contracts henceforth would do so at the same published rates imposed on commercial carriers.[54] Then in May the Air Force released its "Program of Implementation of the Presidentially Approved Courses of Action," which contained point-by-point plans to give reality to the president's directives. In addition to purchasing and developing new aircraft for the military fleet, the Air Force also promised to comply with the president's directives regarding MATS's peacetime operations, letting contracts at peacetime rates, and recasting CRAF for greater capability and flexibility in limited war situations.[55]

Moving CRAF from policy declarations to actual capabilities was a case study in interdepartmental coordination. President John F. Kennedy energized the effort in February 1962 with Executive Order 10999, which reaffirmed the Department of Commerce's control of the program but also directed it to work with the Department of Defense and CAB to "develop plans for a national program to utilize the air carrier civil air transportation capacity and equipment . . . in a national emergency."[56] The resulting plan gave the Department of Commerce final say on CRAF membership but assigned to MATS responsibility for aircraft inspections, operational planning, and the negotiation of specific contracts. Naturally, in keeping with what it did already for the scheduled airlines, CAB set Department of Defense contract rates but also reduced them several times to ease the burden on military commands not used to paying or funded to pay for their airlift at market rates.[57] MATS and CAB involved airlines in the process from the start. By making arrangements to involve airline personnel in the equitable call-up and management of mobilized carriers, they got the major certificated carriers and the smaller certificated supplemental airlines on board.[58]

MATS staffers worked out the details. With joint training with the Army now added to its existing load of SAC exercises and routine air transport operations, MATS was obliged to significantly increase its contract airlift account.

From $89.8 million in 1960 (15 percent of the MATS's operational load), civil contracting increased to $186.8 million in 1964 (31 percent).[59] The MATS staff also developed a new set of CRAF contract templates for on-call operations, preplanned domestic and overseas peacetime missions, and wartime activation. MATS began letting these contracts in proportion to the relative contributions that specific CRAF members committed to the wartime mobilization fleet. Under this concept, CRAF planners on the MATS staff assigned productivity values for the aircraft identified by the carriers for mobilization: 1.0 for DC-6s, more for larger piston-engine aircraft, and all the way up to 3.39 for Boeing 707s and Douglas DC-8s. A carrier's total productivity values as a percentage of the whole program would determine the approximate share of the long-term, fixed-buy contracts it would receive in peacetime. Contributing 15 percent of the planned wartime fleet, in other words, would bring a carrier about 15 percent of MAT's available peacetime contract business.[60]

These provisions, along with new regulations preventing them from bidding for MATS contracts, put the nonskeds out of the picture. Even if they had been allowed to bid, most could not provide the modern aircraft and quality of service now demanded by the military. The Army continued to charter a few non-certificated carriers to move recruits and other trainees between assignments. Even this business ended, after an Imperial Airlines plane crashed in November 1961, killing eighty soldiers and crewmen. Both the Department of Defense and then Congress restricted further government air transport contracting to major or supplemental airlines holding certificates of common carriage. Some nonskeds still survived, hauling car parts, flowers, medicines, and other cargoes, but they were out of the business of MATS. A few others obtained CAB operating certificates, found money to buy new planes, and continued as mainstays of MATS's contracting operations. Useful as the nonskeds had been, their old planes and cutthroat ways had made them a long-term liability, and several senior air force officials told Congress that their passing was not mourned.[61]

The major carriers and certificated supplemental airlines composed CRAF after 1961. Protected financially by CAB's iron grip on ticket prices and competition, the big carriers—American, United, TWA, Pan American, and so on—were in good shape and in the process of transitioning their long-range fleets to jets. The charter carriers were more problematic. A number were having difficulty upgrading their fleets. Some, such as Flying Tiger, Slick, and Southern Air Transport, drew most of their peacetime business from MATS. Their high dependence on MATS's peacetime traffic, however, raised questions about how much "expansion airlift" they could provide in war.[62] Convinced by CAB that there were too many supplemental airlines in the market, in July 1961 Congress passed Public Law 87-528, which allowed CAB to pull the certificates of carriers it determined to be financially unstable and/or operating unsafely. As a sop to the major carriers, who were feeling the competitive sting of those supplementals able to modernize their fleets, PL 87-528 also allowed CAB to prescribe the operating routes of each supplemental airline and to block all of them from individually ticketed passenger operations after 1965.[63] These actions, which reduced the industry from twenty-two to fifteen supplemental airlines, created political fireworks, but they also improved the quality of the aircraft associated with CRAF.[64]

By 1965 CRAF had evolved into a crisis reserve of substantial capacity, flexibility, and economy. From a largely paper fleet of just one enrolled carrier and a list of 171 piston-powered and 58 turbine-powered aircraft in 1960, the program grew to 20 member companies committing 62 piston-powered and 198 turbine-powered aircraft. Most of the turbine aircraft were DC-8s and Boeing 707s, with plenty of range for transoceanic operations and three to five times the ton-mile productivity of a DC-7.[65] Under arrangements developed after the 1960 National Military Airlift Hearings, the military could call up this fleet in three increments, depending on the level of emergency and whether authorization came from the secretary of defense, the president, or a declared state of war.[66] Upon activation of any CRAF increment, MATS also would open an Airlift Schedule Center in its headquarters command post at Scott AFB to coordinate directly with mobilized airlines. At overseas air terminals during such times, selected carriers would provide "senior lodger" services to coordinate aircraft servicing, cargo handling, crew support, scheduling, and security for any CRAF aircraft passing through, regardless of its livery.[67] These rationalizations of CRAF's fleet, membership, and contracting procedures profoundly reduced the cost to the government of maintaining reserve airlift capacity. In 1960 MATS spent $3 million for equipment and other costs to maintain a program capable of producing 50 million ton miles of lift per year. By 1965 the cost was $250,000 for a reserve capacity of 200 million ton miles.[68]

This evolution of CRAF reflected a rational linkage of national strategy and subordinate policy. Embracing presumptions in the early 1950s that most future wars involving the United States directly would involve the use of nuclear weapons, the community of airlift planners wrote the first CRAF plan to serve a country facing the possibility of nuclear devastation. These military planners, airline executives, interested academics, and congressmen set up CRAF as a blunt instrument, capable of being swung in total or not at all. This all-or-nothing mobilization plan conformed to the scale and desperation of a postnuclear military and civil-recovery environment. It had the additional political advantages of reflecting what everyone knew the country would do in such circumstances anyway and avoiding a fight with the airlines over partial mobilizations. Then when the nation began to dabble with the notion of fighting limited, nonnuclear conflicts in the far reaches of the Soviet periphery, the second CRAF plan provided an appropriately flexible instrument. By linking CRAF membership to the privilege of bidding for peacetime contracts at negotiated rates, the program drew in the big carriers and their modern fleets and organized them into mobilization increments tailored to the demands of specific levels of conflict. Apart from the impotent grumblings of the non-certificated carriers, this second CRAF plan also went into place with broad support from all other relevant quarters. Perhaps if the evolution of the CRAF program had required major investments in specialized hardware or had threatened institutional boundaries, as did other areas of airlift policy, the political fight would have been tougher. But it wasn't, and the second CRAF program settled out just in time, for the United States was entering a war in which movement by air would be a defining strategic and tactical characteristic, not just a peripheral and/or episodic feature.

16. Vietnam

The Air Mobility War

IN THE YEARS just prior to and during the Vietnam War, air mobility became a central element of the American way of warfare. A sudden conjunction of technology developments, exercise results, and then the experience of the war itself changed the way U.S. military forces utilized airlift *quantitatively* and *qualitatively*. Modern turbine-powered aircraft, new cargo-handling systems, command-and-control arrangements, and operational doctrines increased the quantity of airlift available severalfold just before American ground combat units entered the war in 1965. A series of exercises and then practical experience in Vietnam revealed that the enhanced capacity of the system had pushed it over a qualitative threshold between airlift as a valuable adjunct to war and airlift as a central element of war. For the first time in war, the great majority of personnel traveling between the homeland and Vietnam did so by air and so did an increased percentage of supply and matériel. Airlift also became another primary means of movement around the battlefield—the other was the booted foot—for all line soldiers, not just a few elite airborne units. Taken together, these technological and doctrinal changes created an interconnected fort-to-foxhole mobility system that increased the flexibility, pace, and security of American combat operations. The American military had become an air mobility culture, and that would change warfare for it and its enemies.

Getting Ready: Engines, Planes, and Doctrine

Turbine engines were at the heart of the airlift revolution. For transoceanic transports, bypass turbofans greatly reduced the cost of air movements and made possible cargo aircraft able to carry almost any piece of military equipment. The Pratt & Whitney JT-3D ushered in the new era in airlift efficiency. Designated the TF-33 by the Air Force, this engine essentially was a JT-3C turbojet modified with the addition of a bypass fan at the front. The result was an engine that produced 21,000 pounds of thrust from a fuel flow of about 600 gallons per hour versus the 13,750 pounds of thrust produced from about the same fuel flow by the 3C engine. Similarly, the 4,050-horsepower Allison T-56 turboprop gave the C-130 transport greatly increased performance, reliability, and lift capacity in comparison to its theater airlift predecessor, the C-119. Finally, the Lycoming T-53 linked a small turbine to a helicopter rotor to expand the operational envelope and reduce the maintenance requirements of tactical helicopters. Powering thousands of UH-1 assault helicopters during the war, the T-53 weighed just 600 pounds and produced up to 1,400 horsepower, compared to the 1,400 pounds and 1,425 horsepower of the Wright R-1820 used in the H-34. With both engines consuming about 100 gallons of fuel per hour, the difference in weight translated into greater payloads, more range, and greater maneuverability in flight.

For strategic airlift, the Military Air Transport Service (MATS) entered the new war with a fleet in transition. In 1965 its core fleet consisted of about 350 C-124s, 40 C-133s, and 40 new C-135s, which were military versions of the Boeing 707. The command also operated seven squadrons of C-130Es on an interim basis, pending replacement by incoming C-141s.[1] C-141s were just coming into the inventory, and the command would have a fleet of 276 by 1972. The successor of MATS, the Military Airlift Command (MAC), would begin receiving a fleet of 77 C-5s in 1969.[2] In addition, MATS and MAC were augmented by six squadrons of C-97s from the Air National Guard and several reserve groups of C-124s. Commercial contract airlines, most of them members of the Civil Reserve Airlift Fleet (CRAF), completed the list of American long-range capabilities. They too were in the process of modernization, trading last-generation piston-engine transports, mainly DC-7s and Lockheed Constellations, for turbofan-powered Boeing 707s and Douglas DC-8s.

Air force theater airlift forces underwent little change in aircraft technology during the war. Capable of carrying up to nineteen tons of cargo, the C-130 anchored the theater fleet throughout the war. Depending on the version, the big planes cruised at 260 to 280 knots and, more important, could operate into airfields as short as 2,500 feet in length and on surfaces such as gravel, clay, or even just firm soil. The smaller cousin of the Hercules (Herc) was the Fairchild C-123 Provider. These planes came with two 2,400-horsepower piston engines and, later in the war, two 2,850-pound thrust J-85 auxiliary turbojets. Thus powered, the Provider could lift about eight tons and get in and out of airfields as short as 1,500 feet in length. The C-7 Caribou completed the theater airlift triumvirate in Vietnam. The Army introduced the "Bou" into the theater in 1962 as the CV-2 and then handed six companies of them (96 aircraft) to the Air Force in 1967. Redesignated as the C-7, the plane came with two 1,450-horsepower radial piston engines, carried about three tons, and could get into rough airfields as short as 1,000 feet long. Like the C-123, the C-7 cruised at around 140 knots. At its peak in 1968, the Air Force's theater airlift fleet consisted of six C-7, one C-118, five C-123, one C-124, and fifteen C-130 squadrons, or about 400 aircraft in total. The C-7s and C-123s were based in Vietnam. The C-130 wings were based permanently in the Philippines, Taiwan, and Japan, but those wings kept as many as 100 Hercs at in-country bases on temporary rotations.

The Army began deploying airlift units to Vietnam in 1961, beginning with a single Caribou on a test basis in August, followed by two companies of sixteen CH-21 Shawnees each on a permanent basis in December. Their role was to support American Special Forces' camps and provide limited logistics and air assault lift to Vietnamese forces. By the middle of 1962, three more Choctaw companies were in country, along with a marine CH-34 company and small numbers of other aircraft. Helicopter deployments increased drastically after mid-1965, when the United States began sending regular combat forces to the theater. By that time, most of the helicopters sent by the Army were turbine powered. The UH-1D Iroquois (more affectionately called the Huey) became the mainstay of the fleet. This aircraft initially came with an 1,100-horsepower engine, cruised at 110 knots, and could carry a maximum useful load of 4,650 pounds. Its theoretical mission radius with ten assault troops on board was about 90 nautical miles, though most combat lifts were only a fraction of that distance. CH-47s provided logistics lift. CH-47As came to the theater in 1965, powered by two 2,850-horsepower engines, while CH-47Cs began arriving in 1969 with 3,750-horsepower engines. Both aircraft cruised at about 140 knots and carried nine to ten tons in ideal conditions, though a more typical load was three to four tons in the hot and high conditions of the Vietnamese highlands. For specialized heavy airlift operations, the Army initially deployed CH-37s but then replaced them with the CH-54. The CH-54 "flying crane" was able to lift up to ten tons of damaged helicopters, modular hospitals, artillery pieces, and other awkward loads.

The expanding operational capabilities of Army Aviation, particularly where they overlapped with those of air force C-123s, obliged Secretary of Defense Robert S. McNamara in April 1962 to call for a "fresh and perhaps unorthodox" reexamination of the service's tactical mobility requirements.[3] Stuck with supervising what could become a major interservice donnybrook, the U.S. Strike Command (STRICOM) hedged its exposure by declaring, "The job at hand . . . is not to attempt to prove Army and Air Force doctrine, etc., right or wrong, but to develop better ways and means for the two to fight a common enemy."[4] To begin that process, STRICOM and the Department of Defense freed both services to conduct unilateral conceptual studies and exercises in preparation for a series of joint maneuvers in 1964: one to deploy an air assault division (AAD) up to 175 nautical miles, another to move an air assault brigade to an intermediate staging area, and then another to move a battalion of that brigade within the battle zone.[5]

Lieutenant General Hamilton H. Howze directed the Army's conceptual study. Howze was the commander of the Strategic Army Corps and former director of Army Aviation. After several months of study supported by small-scale field experiments, Howze's ad hoc Tactical Mobility Requirements Board reported out in August 1962. Predictably, the board proposed a transformational program calling for the establishment of five airmobile divisions, three air cavalry combat brigades, and five air transport brigades, all supported by a vastly expanded aviation arm to provide tactical mobility and logistics support. In the realm of logistics, the Howze report proposed a coordinated "air line of communication" (ALOC) concept, in which air force transports would bring troops, equipment, and supplies to secure, rear area bases from which army aircraft would complete their movements through intermediate bases and on to frontline positions. The board estimated that the number of army pilots on strength would have to grow from 8,900 in 1963 to 20,600 by 1968 to handle all the new aircraft required under the proposed concept.[6]

Also in August, the Air Force's Tactical Air-Support Evaluation Board issued its report in defense of the status quo. The board's director, TAC Deputy Commander Gabriel P. Disosway, argued that the Air Force should retain responsibility for moving personnel and matériel to the forward-most airstrips in division and even brigade combat areas. Pointing out that C-123s and even C-130s could operate into fields "not materially greater than [required] for the *Caribou*," Disosway suggested that the Army's only proper airlift role was to make "retail" distributions from forward strips to tactical combat positions, probably by helicopters.[7] Implicitly, then, Disosway and the Air Force accepted the Army's possession of a large aviation arm but not one that infringed on the existing responsibilities of Troop Carrier Aviation.

To move from the Howze report to actual service tests, the Army activated the 11th Air Assault Division and the supporting 10th Air Transport Brigade at Fort Bragg, North Carolina, in February 1963. While still in the process of organizing and manning itself, the division began a series of company-size and then battalion-size tests, from May through the end of the year, under the general title of "Air Assault I." During this period, the aviation units assigned to the 11th AAD developed battlefield mobility tactics, techniques, and procedures, while the 10th Brigade provided short-distance ALOC support. By the end of 1964, the 11th controlled 176 UH-1s and 45 CH-47s, plus supporting observation and fire-support aircraft, and the 10th operated 8 UH-1s, 22 CH-37s, 13 CH-47s, 69 CV-2s, and 4 CH-54s. This total force of 470 aircraft dwarfed the normal allotment of about 120 aircraft to a standard division. The Air Assault II test series ran through 1964 and culminated in a brigade-size exercise in October and November. Kicking off in the teeth of Hurricane Isbell's onshore effects, this exercise began with a formation of 120 helicopters flying tree-skimming "nap-of-the-earth" tactics for a hundred miles to put the combat elements of an entire brigade into forward landing zones. Despite frequently stormy weather and toad-strangling rains, the 11th AAD and 10th Air Transport Brigade spent the next month hurtling around a seven-million-acre test area, honing their skills at launching aerial attacks, reinforcing and withdrawing troops in contested areas, moving artillery into firing areas, defending themselves from air attack, and performing a host of other drills.[8] Taken together, it was a vision of a new style of ground war.

The Air Force's service tests ran parallel to the Army's. While the Air Assault I tests were under way, Colonel William G. (Bill) Moore, commander of the 314th Troop Carrier Wing, directed Project Close Look, an exploration of new aerial delivery techniques and tactics designed to exploit the capabilities of the C-130. Acutely unpretentious by nature, Moore nevertheless had come into troop carrier in 1961 from an exceptional background as a bomb unit commander in World War II and Korea and as a successful staff officer. Thorough to a fault, his preparations for his new responsibilities included learning to fly the Herc, going down to Fort Benning to earn army paratrooper wings, and observing the air assault exercises closely. Back at Stewart AFB, Tennessee, the 314th's home, his program of experimentation included refining assault landing procedures, developing new formation flying techniques, and exploiting the enhanced cargo-handling and delivery capabilities of the C-130.

Facilitating these experiments, Moore's C-130s were equipped with the floor rollers and guide rails of the Air Force's new 463L cargo-handling system. These components maintained secure control of aluminum cargo pallets, even if they were being yanked out of the aircraft at high speeds by parachutes or arresting cables. This security of control, in turn, allowed Moore's test group to experiment with the low-altitude parachute extraction system (LAPES) and the ground proximity extraction system (GPES). LAPES employed drogue chutes to pull heavy, palletized loads from a C-130 flying only feet above the ground. The chutes then slowed the sliding pallet to a stop in just a few hundred feet. The GPES used an anchored arrestor cable to pull them out and stop their slides within a hundred feet. To improve drop accuracies, Moore's study resulted in troop carrier largely abandoning the time-honored Vs-of-Vs formation with serial formations of individual Hercs releasing their loads at precisely computed air release points (CARPs).[9]

Moore and the Air Force applied the technologies and tactics refined in Close Look to the Gold Fire I exercise in November 1964. Conducted simultaneously with the final phase of Air Assault II, Gold Fire tested the Air Force's notion of an ALOC. C-130s, C-123s, and CH-3s delivered and supported the maneuvers of the 1st Infantry Division in the Ozark hills of southern Missouri. In the course of the exercise, MATS moved 8,300 soldiers and 17,000 tons of cargo into the exercise area and then sustained them with airland missions into forward strips and a variety of airdrop techniques for thirty days. In reality, apart from its employment of the new formation and aerial delivery techniques, Gold Fire only "tested" concepts, command-and-control arrangements, and missions already well established in troop carrier doctrines and organization. Thus its success was predictable, as were the Air Force's assessments of its significance.[10]

In the end, STRICOM's prediction that the airlift exercises would not settle any doctrinal disputes proved correct. Regarding theater air mobility, the service chiefs rejected or outright sneered at the results of the others' exercises. During the exercises, the air force chief of staff, General Curtis LeMay, "blasted" the Army's aviation plans as "wasteful duplication" of costs and capabilities.[11] Following the exercises, the army chief of staff, General Harold K. Johnson, told Congress that the Air Force's concept had its merits but that the standard army division supported by an air force ALOC was an "elephant" compared to the "gazelle" of the air assault division supported by organic aviation.[12] The analogy probably wasn't apt, since elephants do useful work while gazelles just flit about until something eats them. But everyone got the point: the Army and the Air Force were too wedded institutionally to their respective airlift concepts to change their plans on the basis of exercise results. So with increasing commitments to Vietnam at hand, the Department of Defense called off STRICOM's schedule of concluding joint tests, Air Assault III and Gold Fire II. The Army, meanwhile, accepted the Air Assault II test director's recommendation to put air assault on a permanent basis by disbanding the 11th and assigning many of its experienced soldiers to the 1st Air Cavalry Division, activated on July 1, 1965.[13]

While the Army and the troop carrier community tested their visions of airlift, Lieutenant General Joseph W. Kelly Jr., who replaced the ailing Lieutenant General William H. Tunner as commander of MATS in June 1960, led the technical and operational development of global airlift. Since Tunner and Congressman Mendel Rivers had settled the major doctrinal battles of strategic airlift during the 1960 National Military Airlift Hearings, Kelly largely was free to focus on operational matters during his tenure. Kelly came to MATS from a background as a successful bomber unit commander and staff officer, but he had no experience in airlift. He took his job and airlift seriously, however, and listened well to the experts on his staff, particularly John Shea. Shea, the ever-present airlift zealot, had risen to MATS's deputy director of plans just before Kelly arrived. Working together, they came up with the term "globility," which Kelly used to describe the command's rapidly emerging ability to move combat forces of all types to global trouble spots.[14]

Real-world contingencies gave MATS leaders and personnel plenty of opportunities to hone doctrines and techniques and to realize the critical importance of modernizing the airlift fleet. During Kelly's tenure as commander (1961–1964), MATS was called on to move large forces to Europe in response to the 1961 Berlin Crisis and around the United States during the Cuban Missile Crisis of 1962. Internationally, the United States moved supplies to India during a confrontation with China and to the Congo in support of UN peace-keeping forces.

Called New Tape, the Congo operation ran from 1961 to 1964 and ultimately involved movements of 63,798 passengers and 18,593 tons of cargo in 2,128 missions. As did the Berlin and China contingencies, New Tape illustrated the greatly expanded capabilities and operational flexibility offered by turbofan-powered aircraft. C-124s made most of the early movements. Pounding along at 180 knots, they typically took about forty-eight flight hours and five to six days of travel time for a given crew to make the round-trip between Europe and the Congo. Later, C-135s took fifteen flight hours to make the round-trip, sparing their crews the necessity of spending nights in sometimes unpleasant and/or unsafe places along the way.[15]

Exercise Big Lift taught much the same lessons. MATS conducted the exercise in October and November 1963 to address shortfalls discovered during the prolonged "emergency" lift during the Berlin Crisis and to broadcast American determination to reinforce Germany in the event of a future confrontation. Big Lift marked a profound step forward in American global airlift capabilities in that it was the first movement of a combat division—more correctly, the personnel of a division—overseas by air. After months of planning, a mixed fleet of MATS C-124s, C-130s, and C-135s lifted 15,377 soldiers, 307 air force airmen, and 444 tons of equipment over the 5,000 miles between Texas and Europe in just 63 hours and 229 sorties. On arrival, the soldiers fell in on prepositioned combat equipment, including 319 M48 tanks, 76 howitzers, and 429 armored personnel carriers. The need to preposition heavy equipment reinforced everyone's realization that if global airlift was in the future of MATS, it needed new, specialized transports to replace its existing fleet and quickly. C-135s had made the trip from Texas to Germany in ten hours, but their airliner fuselages were too small for anything but troops and baggage. C-124s had larger cargo decks, but they took thirty-two hours to make the trip, carried passengers in unpressurized discomfort, and could carry only about 20 tons over the Atlantic. By way of comparison, and as an obvious effort to sell more planes, the Lockheed Aircraft Corporation calculated that the seventy-seven C-141s presently on order, augmented by four C-133s, could have made the same lift in just 158 sorties.[16] Missing from all of this was an aircraft capable of lifting tanks and other heavy equipment so that MATS could move an actual combat-ready division to somewhere other than a preexisting base structure stocked with prepositioned equipment. That plane would be the C-5, ordered into development in large part as a consequence of Big Lift.

So to an unprecedented degree, American airlift forces were ready for the Vietnam War. Troop carrier and army aviators had not settled any of their core doctrinal disputes. But the service exercises of 1963 and 1964 had been opportunities for both to refine their knowledge and equipment. MATS and its military reserve and civil components already possessed robust transoceanic logistics capabilities. Moreover, the command's contingency operations and exercises between 1961 and 1965 had clarified the procedures and technical requirements of global combat unit movements. It remained only for C-141s and C-5s to enter the fleet to make such movements practical.

Strategic Airlift in the Vietnam War

As the American war effort expanded, MATS and then MAC focused on increasing their speed of movement and total throughput of people and matériel back and forth across the Pacific. As an initial step, in early 1965 MATS initiated the Fast Fly program, which involved expanding the crew force, supply stocks, and support units along the Pacific routes.[17] At the same time, the command activated a Red Ball Express service from Travis AFB, California, to Southeast Asia that reduced transit time for Category 1 cargo from supply depots in the continental United States (CONUS) to units on the front lines to as little as five days. MAC streamlined maintenance procedures in late 1966 by replacing its phased inspection program, based on hard-to-predict accumulations of flying hours, with isochronal inspections, which occurred at fixed calendar dates and allowed maintenance units to plan their workloads and keep aircraft moving more predictably. As the Air Force deactivated B-47 bomber and KC-97 tanker units, MAC grabbed the released crewmen and put hundreds of them into the new C-141 squadrons and other units.[18] C-141s began flying to Vietnam in August 1965, even as the Air Force increased the order book for that aircraft from 150 to 184 and placed the giant C-5 on order. Meanwhile, the Air National Guard and Air Force Reserve activated four-engine transport units to participate in long-range lift operations. Choosing not to mobilize CRAF airlines outright, the Department of Defense instead contracted for as much lift as it could make available, to the tune of $192 million in fiscal year 1964 and over $500 million in fiscal year 1966.[19]

The effort was a success. Overall throughput to Southeast Asia increased from a monthly 34,000 passengers and 9,000 tons of cargo in 1965 to 65,000 passengers and 42,000 tons in 1967.[20] By that time the Air Force's air reserve components—the Air National Guard and the Air Force Reserve—were flying 8 percent of the worldwide airlift effort, including about seventy-five to ninety missions per month to the war zone.[21] The year 1968 was a watershed in reserve operations, when five C-124 groups went on active duty to alleviate growing pressures on the Air Force's airlift forces, and the Air Force activated the first reserve associate wings at C-141 bases. The purpose of the associate units was (and is) to get more productivity from the most capable aircraft available by partnering active and reserve wings to fly common pools of C-141s and, later, C-5s.[22] Contract airlift also became increasingly important. Between 1966 and 1970, civil airlines and charter companies carried over 90 percent of the passengers and 25 percent of the bulk air cargoes moved in support of the war.[23] Combined with the 240 long-range jets in the CRAF, MAC had the capability to produce 34 million ton miles per day (MTMD) of lift in 1970, a tenfold increase in a decade.[24]

Building on skills gained during Big Lift and other prewar exercises, trans-oceanic air movements of large, combat-ready units became a routine feature of American operations. One of the earliest was Operation Blue Light, the movement of most of the 3rd Brigade of the 25th Infantry Division—2,952 troops and 4,749 tons—from Hawaii directly to Pleiku, Vietnam, between December 23, 1965, and January 23, 1966. By flying the participating C-124s past their normal off-load terminals at Saigon, Da Nang, and Cam Rahn Bay to off-load at Pleiku, which was vulnerable to enemy attack at any time, MAC cut days off the movement, minimized risks, and got soldiers into combat sooner. Indeed, early arriving 3rd Brigade soldiers were in combat before the movement was complete. Eagle Thrust, which came in November 1967, involved the movement of 10,024 troops and 5,357 tons of vehicles and helicopters of the 101st Airborne Division from Fort Campbell, Kentucky, to Bien Hoa Air Base, South Vietnam. As in the case of Blue Light, MATS spread the 391 C-133 and C-141 sorties of Eagle Thrust over a monthlong period, beginning on November 17, 1967, to minimize disruptions of other operations in Southeast Asia and worldwide. But had a military emergency required faster movement, MAC planners estimated that a fully mobilized effort could have moved the division in as little as three days.[25] Of course, these were movements of units between developed air bases well stocked with munitions, food, fuel, and other supplies. Had these units been required to bring along their own supplies, deployments would have taken much longer.

Theater Airlift

It is no overstatement to say that the United States committed a huge theater airlift force to Southeast Asia in comparison to previous conflicts. Compared to the three troop carrier wings and average of 140 transports that supported operations during the Korean War, the Air Force's Common Service Airlift System (CSAS) in Vietnam in 1968 included twenty-eight squadrons of aircraft, an aerial port group, and dozens of airlift control elements assigned permanently or as needed to any base handling more than an occasional airlift flight. A host of other units and organizations complemented these air force units, including several Vietnamese Air Force (VNAF) squadrons; small squadrons from Australia, South Korea, and Thailand; covert airlift organizations equivalent to four or five squadrons and operating mainly in Laos and Cambodia; and some civil contractors operating charter and scheduled flights within Vietnam. After October 1966, all CSAS operations were under the centralized control of the 7th Air

Force's 834th Air Division based at Saigon's Tan Son Nhut Air Base. Fresh from his successes in Close Look and Gold Fire I, and with a little politicking, Brigadier General William G. Moore became the 834th's first commander. It was a big operation: during 1968, the peak year for just about everything in the war, the CSAS alone moved a monthly average of 83,500 tons of cargo and 375,000 passengers. Counting the passengers as cargo, this equated to 4,000 tons per day, compared to peak efforts of 2,200 tons and 1,050 tons per day over the Hump in World War II and during the Korean War, respectively.[26]

Continuing the trend started in World War II, the mission of theater airlift was almost exclusively logistical. Vietnam is a tropical country, characterized by terrain not easily traversed by large military units or their supply convoys. Most of what wasn't lowland swamps or rice paddies was hilly or mountainous. If the land surface was above the water table, its natural vegetation cover usually was jungle. Most roads moved from ports directly inland. The only developed north–south road was Highway 1 on the coast. The enemy frequently interdicted main transportation units by ambushing, erecting roadblocks, or just blowing up things. So most supplies and people moved by sea or air for any significant distances. In 1967, for example, trains and U.S. military trucks traveling more than 50 miles carried 2,741,000 tons of cargo, while coastal sealift carried 1,823,000 tons, the CSAS carried 984,000 tons, and army and marine helicopters carried 827,000 tons.[27] Most of theater airlift's tonnages were lifted only short distances in a small country; 100 to 200 miles was typical. Most cargo and passenger loads were delivered to their destinations through simple airland operations, loading and unloading from a parked aircraft on the ground. A significant percentage of cargo items arrived at their destinations via parachute or by being yanked out the rear cargo doors of their aircraft by parachutes or cables. On numerous occasions, fixed-wing transports did airland troops into combat, sometimes under direct fire. But these operations were always reinforcements of units already engaged in or trying to extract themselves from combat. As such, they only reinforced the reality that theater airlift was a critical and highly dangerous business in Vietnam, but its signature role was logistics.

Virtually absent from the theater airlift picture in Vietnam were airborne assaults. In 1961 and 1962 USAF and VNAF C-47 and C-123 squadrons conducted company- and battalion-size airborne assaults on several occasions, usually in reaction to local Vietnamese communist (Vietcong) attacks. None of these operations produced more than minimal results. The hours or days of planning involved in preparing an assault gave the Vietcong warning and plenty of time to move away from likely drop zones. Even if the communists were in the vicinity of landing paratroops, they had the option of fighting or melting back into the jungle. They were on foot, but so were the Army of the Republic of Vietnam (ARVN) paratroopers. Later, the United States put the 82nd and 101st Airborne Divisions in the theater, along with the 173rd Airborne Brigade. They never jumped, except for a single battalion group of 845 paratroopers during Operation Junction City on February 22, 1967. The drop was made as part of a blocking operation in which eight other battalions went in by helicopter to intercept North Vietnamese Army (NVA) and Vietcong units fleeing from an American advance.[28] After Junction City, Army Green Beret teams led at least four other company/battalion parachute assaults by "indigenous paratroopers."[29] Unmistakably, the helicopter had rendered large-unit parachute assaults over short distances largely obsolete.

Sensitive to the doctrinal dispute going on in the States, air force and army commanders in Vietnam initially did not welcome the predominant role of logistics for troop carrier forces. The early deployments of troop carrier advisers, individual pilots (the "Dirty Thirty"), and C-123 squadrons (Operation Mule Train) aimed at improving VNAF assault capabilities, not supply operations. Even Pacific Air Forces commander General Emmett O'Donnell warned that failure to create a "market" for air assault operations would encourage the Army to bring more of its aircraft to the job instead.[30] Out of opposite doctrinal concerns, army commanders planned to use their organic lift for air assault and to maintain their ALOCs from the Air Force's main bases to forward positions.

The Army's intent to operate more or less independently from air force airlift in the forward areas was clear in the early operations of the 1st Air Cavalry (Cav) Division. The Cav arrived in central South Vietnam in September 1965, under the command of Major General Harry W. O. Kinnard. With 470 aircraft under his command, including 18 CV-2s and 50 CH-47s, Kinnard and his planners presumed they had enough lift to maintain their own ALOC over the seventy miles between Qui Nhon and the Cav's main base at Pleiku. While the Caribou and Chinook had only about 3-ton payloads, the Cav's officers believed that they could generate enough sorties each day to carry most, if not all, of the division's 800-ton daily supply requirements. Accordingly, division planners were slow to request air force airlift support during their initial operations into Pleiku and then on into the Ia Drang Valley in September through December.

It did not take long for theater commanders to realize that both sides were beating dead doctrinal horses and needed to come to a more sensible method of operations. The failure of ARVN parachute assaults were too obvious to gloss over, and once sufficient helicopters became available in the theater, they just disappeared from allied operations. The Cav's sanguine expectation of supplying itself also didn't last long in the face of trying to move a lot of supplies with small aircraft. Once the division was engaged in heavy fighting in the Ia Drang Valley, the strain of operations overwhelmed its air transports, supply levels declined, and aircraft began to experience maintenance problems. On October 27, the Air Force finally received an army request to bring fuel to Pleiku. Within a few hours C-130s began arriving, each delivering up to ten 500-gallon fuel bladders. Soon C-130s and C-123s were delivering about 190 tons of supplies per day to forward fields, while the Army brought in another 80 tons by air and 40 tons or so by truck.[31] This ad hoc integration of theater and battlefield airlift, in the words of airlift historian Ray Bowers, was "a pragmatic and sensible accommodation . . . to the . . . airmobile doctrines of the early sixties."[32] From that point on, air force theater airlift forces focused on providing high-volume logistics support and on the airlanding of combat forces into forward areas of operation, while Army Aviation units perfected the complex choreography of helicopter air assault operations and performed bulk logistics missions only over short distances. As often happens in actual operations, pragmatic accommodations to reality trumped official doctrines and Pentagon bureaucratic politics.

No single operation revealed the importance and complexity of theater airlift support more than the aerial sustainment of a marine brigade at Khe Sanh from January through March 1968. Six thousand marines, air force airmen, and South Vietnamese Rangers defended this outpost and outlying defensive positions against nearly 20,000 NVA soldiers for seventy days. During that time, airlift was the only conduit for their supplies, reinforcements, and evacuation. C-123s and C-130s brought 12,430 tons of cargo and 2,676 passengers into the besieged base and took 1,574 passengers out, including many wounded. Marine helicopters staging out of Dong Ha, twenty-five nautical miles from Khe Sanh, carried 14,562 passengers into and out of the area and brought 4,661 tons in. Enemy antiaircraft fire was heavy. Three C-123s—one in the air and two on the ground—were lost, and many transports suffered battle damage. Helicopter losses reached as high as three per day, until the U.S. Marines instituted "super gaggles," which were convoys of CH-46s heavily escorted by UH-1 gunships and A-4 fighter bombers.[33]

To keep the airlift flow moving in the face of the enemy and weather characterized by fog and rain, air force airlift crews employed every trick in their bag. Airland operations continued throughout the battle. C-123 crews benefited from the plane's ability to roll to a stop in less than 1,500 feet, for it allowed them to pull directly into Khe Sanh's cargo area, unload and load passengers, and get back into the air in as little as three harrowing minutes under almost constant mortar and sniper fire. Landing C-130s usually overshot the cargo ramp, had to turn around at the exposed end of the runway, and taxi back to the ramp. Their ground times typically were fifteen minutes or more. The Air Force also extensively employed aerial delivery techniques. Parachuting one-ton supply bundles, the so-called container delivery system, and snatching heavy loads out of the rear of low-flying C-130s with the GPES were the most successful techniques. The LAPES also was useful. But the big sliding steel sleds delivered by the system tore up the runway and sometimes malfunctioned, with fatal results to marines on the ground.

There was a human side to the theater airlift story, and it was that the mission remained a combat mission and demanded brave men to accomplish it. The Air Force lost 175 aircraft to all causes while performing airlift missions from 1962 through 1975, along with a lot of crewmen and ground support personnel.[34] Probably most theater transports suffered some degree of damage; maybe a couple of bullet holes or perhaps gaping wounds bleeding jet fuel caused by heavy antiaircraft weapons. The author, who entered the crew force just after the war ended, flew numerous C-130Es with repaired battle damage and met few veteran squadron mates who did not have tales of taking hits, having comrades wounded or killed, and limping home in dying aircraft.

Perhaps no one epitomized the tactical airlift spirit more than Lieutenant Colonel Joe Madison Jackson, an ex-fighter and U-2 pilot who volunteered to fly C-123s and wound up winning the Medal of Honor during the evacuation of Kham Duc in 1972. His Medal of Honor citation sums it up:

> Lt. Col. Jackson volunteered to attempt the rescue of a 3-man USAF Combat Control Team from the Special Forces camp at Kham Duc. Hostile forces had overrun the forward outpost and established gun positions on the airstrip. They were raking the camp with small arms, mortars, light and heavy automatic weapons, and recoilless rifle fire. . . . In addition, 8 aircraft had been destroyed by the intense enemy fire and 1 aircraft remained on the runway reducing its usable length to only 2,200 feet. . . . Although

fully aware of the extreme danger and likely failure of such an attempt, Lt. Col. Jackson elected to land his aircraft and attempt a rescue.

With three fellow airmen trapped on the ground and facing certain death, Jackson did what he called "the right thing" and put his aircraft on the ground, literally skidding past NVA soldiers firing at him from yards away. He stopped exactly in front of the three combat controllers hiding in a ditch, got them on board, and then took off through a crosshatch of tracers, with mortar explosions seeming to chase him down the strip. Amazingly, his aircraft did not suffer a single hit. God sometimes smiles on the foolish and/or the brave. Said one of the rescued controllers, "We were dead, and then we were alive."[35]

Battlefield Airlift

I heard them call "Orange Four, we're hit!" Then they dropped back out of sight. They had taken a burst through the cockpit, and the debris from the shot had temporarily blinded Sherman. Leese tried to stay away from the villages, but there was no way to do that. . . . Tricky flying was to no avail here. I could stare at muzzle flashes for long moments as we flew straight at them. . . . Low-level flying was supposed to minimize exposure time, but it wasn't working here . . . up ahead a VC jumped out of a hidden hole and charged Connor's ship . . . his wing man's door gunner . . . shot him in the back.[36]

In truth, few army aviators would be comfortable with the term "battlefield airlift." They probably would prefer to describe what they did in Vietnam simply as "aviation," to emphasize their close integration into the combined arms team, or "air assault," to indicate their primary mission of inserting infantry and artillery units directly into forward positions. Unquestionably, what Army Aviation did was unique in the world of airlift. In contrast to theater airlift, which was centrally controlled and provided common-user support throughout the theater, Army Aviation units operated as integrated, or organic, elements of the brigades and divisions to which they were assigned. Everything battlefield airlift did—air assaults, positioning units for future operations, quick-reaction reinforcements or extractions of embattled units, medical evacuations, and so on—involved close, flexible, and often minute-by-minute integration with other combat and combat-support elements. Aviators lived with the soldiers they carried into battle, sharing the same hardships of vermin-ridden hooches, endless C rations, bucket latrines, and unmitigated exposure to a harsh climate. Aviators, consequently, knew intimately how army soldiers, weapons, and units performed and how their own aerial operations fit into the overall picture. But for all the choreography of aviation and nonaviation units, and their mutual trust and understanding, when helicopters moved people and things around the battlefield, they were performing *airlift*. So for the purposes of this book, which aims to describe American air mobility as a continuum of capabilities and doctrines, "battlefield airlift" seems like a good way to indicate both the uniqueness of what the Army did in Vietnam and its linkage to a broader story.

Frequent and close fighting also distinguished battlefield airlift from other airlift organizations. Air force strategic airlift crews rarely even heard gunfire during their short stops in country. Theater airlift crews came under fire regularly but usually from a distance. Only in heroic circumstances, such as those few moments of Joe Jackson's brakes-locked slide down the runway at Kham Duc, did they actually see their assailants. But army helicopter pilots and their crews expected close combat, even eyeball-to-eyeball shoot-outs, as a matter of routine. After preparatory artillery fires stopped, air force fighters broke off their strafing runs, and while the shrapnel of helicopter gunship rockets was still falling back to earth, it remained for the troop-carrying "slicks" to actually set down in possibly "hot" landing zones. Knowing the odds, the Army equipped each UH-1 with two door gunners and M-60 machine guns to defend the crew and to provide last-second fire support for the soldiers scrambling out of the doors. Hundreds of accounts of these desperate moments exist in the historical literature and oral records. But perhaps none capture their hazard and the courage of the crews more than the 2002 film *We Were Soldiers*. There was a similarity between the experience of the helicopter crews sliding into the firestorm on Landing Zone X-Ray and those of World War II glidermen sailing into places like Normandy and Weser. But few glidermen went into more than two, maybe three assaults. Vietnam helicopter crews might face the same minutes of fear, anger, determination, heartbreak, and emotional bounce back *a dozen times in a day*. Again, they might have been performing a kind of airlift, but their experiences and powerful group identities were not those of a typical fixed-wing airlifter crew.

The assignment of aviation units directly to corps, divisions, and brigades, and the existence of some "independent" units, meant that Army Aviation in Vietnam became a very large and complex force. At the end of 1962, the Army had one U-6, one CV-2, and five H-21 companies deployed in country to provide mobility support for the ARVN, plus a company of armed UH-1Bs for escort, for a total of about 150 aircraft. By mid-1964, only a few months before American ground combat units entered the fray, Army Aviation strength included ten companies of UH-1 transports and a number of gunship and other companies, for a total of about 400 aircraft. Thereafter, aviation strength grew rapidly, and in March 1966 the Army established the 1st Aviation Brigade to manage personnel and logistics at the theater level. In 1968 the brigade supervised 641 fixed-wing aircraft, 311 CH-47s, and 2,202 UH-1s, along with 441 AH-1Gs and 635 OH-6As.[37] "Supervised" is the appropriate word, since the 1st Brigade's principal roles were to oversee the distribution of Army Aviation units within the theater, conduct standardized training programs, develop doctrine manuals, manage supply depots, and operate heavy maintenance facilities. In contrast to the 834th Airlift Division's tight control of theater airlift operations, the 1st only seldom commanded aviation units operationally. Corps, division, and brigade commanders did that.[38]

As the war progressed, the scale of aviation capabilities reached the point that division- and corps-size operations were planned routinely around its capabilities, augmented by air force airlift and tactical support from all the services. Operation Pegasus, the relief of Khe Sanh, was a representative example among many from the war. Planning and execution responsibilities went to General John J. Tolson and the 1st Air Cavalry, with support from two attached marine regiments and an ARVN Ranger battalion. As the marines held fast in the surrounded garrison, Tolson and his staff spent the weeks of January through late March planning the operation and preparing the battlefield. As he shifted his brigades from the central to the northeastern part of the country, military engineers constructed a huge forward operating base, Landing Zone Stud, just ten kilometers east of Khe Sanh. Meanwhile, the Cav's reconnaissance aircraft and intelligence branch scrutinized the future battlefield closely and identified targets that subsequently were attacked by nearly 700 tactical fighter strikes and a dozen B-52 "Arc Light" pattern bombing raids.

The operation began on April 1 with an advance by marine ground units on the highway to Khe Sanh and air assaults by three 1st Cavalry battalions to separate landing zones about 1.5 nautical miles from Stud. It was only a short distance, but it leapfrogged the forward NVA defensive units and put them between the 1st Cavalry units and the advancing marines—not a good place to stay. On subsequent days, cavalry battalions and the ARVN Rangers made other assaults in response to the changing tactical situation. Beset unpredictably from all sides, the NVA forces in the area abandoned their prepared defensive positions and disintegrated quickly into retreat. Thus, a cavalry battalion air assaulted into Khe Sanh on April 6, and advancing marines came down the road to the base on the 8th. In a week, the siege was lifted without the necessity of any relief units having to make frontal assaults against the large, dug-in enemy units that had been waiting for them. Tolson summarized the operation as a "classic example of . . . the speed and effectiveness with which a large force can be employed."[39]

A New Kind of War

Well before the American heavy combat phase of the Vietnam War ended in 1970, then, the United States had developed something new: a continuum of airlift capabilities that stretched from the concrete parking ramps of homeland airfields to muddy landing zones directly under enemy fire. Indeed, the fort-to-foxhole integration of the supply system reached the point that a helicopter mechanic at Pleiku, Vietnam, could request a key part and not be surprised to have it arrive directly from the Bell Helicopter plant at Hurst, Texas, via air shipment within the week. Airlift thus had closed the gap between homeland and battle theater, peace and war, to a degree never before seen in intercontinental warfare.

The consequences of this truly global airlift capability were many. Strategically, the new ability of the United States to move large combat forces so quickly had implications for its military commitments elsewhere in the world. In terms of operations in Vietnam, airlift minimized the costs and lost time involved in moving personnel and high-value cargo. It also permitted rapid reinforcement during crisis periods, such as in the aftermath of the 1968 Tet Offensive and the 1972 Easter Offensive. Tactically, the airlift system almost guaranteed that field units, large and small, would stay connected to their bases, reinforcements, supplies, and evacuation capabilities. This had a profound effect on the flexibility of operations and even the mind-sets of field commanders and soldiers.

There also was a social impact of air mobility, though not one understood well at the time. In earlier Pacific wars, soldiers returning from war might have weeks of emotional decompression during their sea voyages back to the States. The endless conversations with their peers, ample sleep time, and decent food on the ships amounted to a rough sort of postcombat therapy, but it was therapy nevertheless. Soldiers leaving Vietnam might walk away from their fighting holes one morning, catch a "freedom bird" the next afternoon, arrive in the States the following evening, and be demobilized and on the street a day later. The stress of such abrupt transitions was not mitigated later in the war, when the new civilians, with their obvious military haircuts, often were subject to verbal and even physical abuse from fellow citizens opposed to the war. At the human level, there was at least one back side to the shiny new "coin" of global airlift.[40]

17. Nickel Grass

IT WOULD BE an overstatement to say that General Paul K. Carlton saved the world all by himself during the Arab-Israeli War of 1973. He had some help. Most important, the Israeli military fought its way back from the verge of defeat and retook the territories lost in the first days of the war and then some. Those victories were the indispensable backdrop of the brilliant public and private diplomacy of U.S. secretary of state Henry Kissinger, to end the fighting, avoid a direct military confrontation with the Soviet Union, and set the stage for a long-term peace. But it was Carlton and the people and planes of the Military Airlift Command (MAC) he commanded that enabled both Israeli military and American diplomatic successes. When unexpectedly skillful and determined Arab offensives forced the Israeli Army and Air Force to consume their supplies and equipment at unprecedented rates, MAC provided the means to replenish their stocks and sustain their counteroffensive. In the process, Carlton emerged both as an exceptionally effective operational commander and as a military statesman who could orchestrate all the other pieces of the American defense establishment participating in the airlift. MAC's operational success, therefore, made the United States the power broker of Middle East affairs. So even if "P. K." Carlton did not save the world alone, he did lead events that changed it significantly.

P. K. Carlton Discovers Airlift

General Carlton received command of MAC in September 1972. As was normal for MAC commanders at the time, he came to Scott AFB with no direct operational experience in airlift. He was a "LeMay Kid," an acolyte of the great bomber leader, General Curtis LeMay, former commander of the Strategic Air Command (SAC) and ultimately chief of staff of the Air Force. From an assignment as LeMay's aide-de-camp from 1949 to 1953, Carlton's career vaulted through a series of assignments in command of bomb wings and an air division (the 15th Air Force) and as supervisor of the Single Integrated Operational Plan, SAC's blueprint for nuclear war. So if the "bomber mafia" in charge of the Air Force in those days did not consider airlift generals qualified to lead MAC, they at least sent their best to do the job.

A study in contrasts, Carlton was genteel and good humored by nature but ferocious in his dedication to his duties and expectation that all around him were as well. Those who knew him away from work saw his unpretentiousness and appreciation of a joke. Those in whom he sensed a lack of diligence in their conduct of operations and staff duties saw a different person. Carlton's anger came out in a roaring blast that rocked colonels in their shoes and left junior officers stunned. An eyebrow singeing from Carlton was not to be forgotten, ever. And God help an officer who gave into the temptation to smirk in the frequent event that Carlton pushed his voice to the point that it cracked and squeaked. The consequences of that temerity were too awesome to contemplate but presumably involved a lingering professional death in some of the more unpleasant places from which the Air Force conducted its business.[1]

By his account, General Carlton gave himself a year to learn the airlift business before trying to change anything. To his surprise, John Shea emerged as his guide into the mysteries of MAC operations, doctrines, and policies.[2] Shea had been a civil servant in the Air Transport Command, the Military Air Transport Service, and MAC since 1946 and had been the assistant deputy chief of staff for plans since 1961. Besides knowing every nook and cranny of MAC's history and plans, Shea's work had built respectful and powerful connections for him in Congress and the Department of Defense. So as the oracle of the history and visions of global airlift, Shea was neither inclined by personality nor obliged professionally to fear a confrontation with the new boss from SAC. The showdown came quickly. In an early staff meeting, Carlton found himself contradicted by Shea and blasted out, "Why should I listen to all of this from a goddamn civilian?" Shea thundered back, "Because I know more about airlift than anyone else in this goddamn room, so you had better listen to me!" It was the start of a professional and personal friendship. The two big, loud, silver-haired Irishmen took an instant liking to the dedication and personality they saw in each other. They sparred frequently, but their mutual respect and admiration endured even after they both had left government service. Before Carlton's year of listening was over, Shea had the pleasure of hearing him say one day, "Those SAC guys, they don't know anything about airlift!"[3] Airlift was back in the hands of another believer tutored by John Shea.

Even as he learned the ways of airlift, Carlton had plenty of activities to direct in his new command. The United States was pulling the last of its forces out of Vietnam. A steady flow of C-5s and C-141s, consequently, was moving thousands of tons of high-value matériel from there to depots in the continental

United States (CONUS) and overseas. This flow was in addition to the usual schedule of routine air transport, exercises, humanitarian relief operations, and other missions. With the MAC fleet largely composed of new C-141s and C-5s, Carlton and his staff faced few major aircraft woes to distract them from other initiatives, such as improving MAC's global control and communications capabilities. The general's insistence on unbroken communications with MAC aircraft extended to telling U.S. ambassadors to expect no airlift support in countries that did not permit his planes to use their long-range radios while on the ground. He also pushed to strengthen the ability of MAC intelligence to warn traveling crews of local threats and to gather and process the vast amount of information that they collected during their global travels.[4]

During his year of learning, Carlton became concerned about his limited ability to tap the airlift resources of other commands, particularly the hundreds of C-130s assigned to the Tactical Air Command (TAC) or the theater air forces of joint combatant commands. Even TAC's C-130s were assigned to the U.S. Readiness Command (REDCOM) for combat operations. Carlton's status as the commander of a mere air force major command (MAJCOM) gave him no stature to demand assistance from the powerful commanders in chief (CINCs) of REDCOM and the Pacific and European commands. Doctrinally, CINCs were the nation's war fighters, and they vigorously guarded their prerogatives and assigned forces. They were always on alert for threats in their own areas, and Carlton realized that they would be loath to let MAC use their aircraft to augment operations on behalf of other CINCs. The problem of augmentation had General Carlton's attention by mid-1973, but he was not ready to press for organizational or procedural changes to ensure his access to the airlift units of other commands.[5]

Nickel Grass

The twin attacks of Egypt and Syria on October 6, 1973, caught Israel flat-footed and immediately put it in desperate straits militarily. Displaying unprecedented competency and determination, the Egyptians destroyed all but one Israeli fortified outpost along the Suez Canal and poured hundreds of tanks and thousands of troops into the Sinai Desert beyond. The Syrians had less success on the Golan Heights, but they still threatened a breakout into Israel proper. Things went from bad to terrible for the Israelis when their counterattacking air and armored forces suffered heavy casualties in the face of hard-fighting Arab troops armed with an array of antitank rockets and missiles. By October 9 Israel was short of ammunition, had lost large numbers of tanks and aircraft, and was taking heavy casualties. Defeat at the hands of states that had threatened its total destruction was a real possibility. Early that morning in Washington, the Israeli ambassador, Simcha Dinitz, called Secretary of State Henry Kissinger and pleaded for an airlift of munitions and other matériel thus far consumed or lost in the fighting.[6]

Despite the danger of an Israeli defeat, American leaders contemplated the possibility of an airlift only reluctantly. An airlift would run a real risk of putting the United States in direct confrontation with the Soviet Union, which already had large numbers of advisers and technicians in Egypt and Syria. The Soviets had confirmed their intent to support their Arab allies on October 8 by announcing the start of an airlift of their own. Fearing that the Arab states would make good on their threats to impose an oil embargo, America's North Atlantic Treaty Organization (NATO) allies were cowed into refusing to allow cargo planes bound for Israel to fly through their airspace or refuel at bases in their territories. Only Lajes AFB in the Azores remained as a potential staging base, but Portugal was seeking weapons for its colonial wars in Angola and Mozambique in return for its use.[7] Lajes would be critical, since C-5s would be able to carry only twenty to thirty tons nonstop over the 6,450 miles between the United States and Israel, while C-141s had no cargo capacity at all over that distance.[8] In the face of these difficulties, Kissinger and Secretary of Defense James Schlesinger stalled during the first three days of the war, hoping that Israel would pull off a military miracle and defeat the Arab offensives without direct U.S. involvement.

At the same time, U.S. officials knew they could not allow Israel to suffer even a partial defeat. An Arab victory, on the heels of America's retreat from Vietnam, would force even friendly regional states, like Saudi Arabia and Jordan, closer to the Soviets.[9] Also, Israel had "The Bomb"—the 800-pound gorilla in the cockpit of Middle East politics. All American diplomatic and military leaders involved knew or at least presumed that Israel had nuclear weapons and the means to deliver them. But no one, most particularly the Israelis, discussed them or even admitted their existence in public. To do so would change the face of Middle East affairs, most disturbingly by legitimizing the acquisition of nuclear weapons by Arab states. More immediately, no one wanted to see what Israeli leaders would do with those weapons if they feared being overrun.[10]

So after Dinitz convinced Kissinger that Israel's forces were running out of ammunition, President Richard Nixon agreed to provide munitions and electronic warfare equipment and replace Israel's aircraft and tank losses. If necessary, Kissinger told the ambassador, the United States would deliver their supplies in "American planes."[11] Still hoping to minimize U.S. risks, Secretary Schlesinger first tried to have El Al Airlines jets and or commercial contract airlines pick up the necessary cargoes in the United States or at Lajes, if it opened. But El Al's passenger planes, though converted into "plywood transports" with protective wooden sheeting in their cabins, were too few and too difficult to load to carry all that Israel needed. Worse, not a single commercial carrier was willing to risk Arab retaliation by picking up the load. So with no other options at hand, President Nixon ordered MAC on the afternoon of October 13 to carry supplies all the way to Israel. At the same time, U.S. diplomats had talked the Portuguese government into opening Lajes to MAC transports. So the way to Israel was clear, and there was no time to lose.

MAC was ready. General Carlton had initiated preparations for a lift to Lajes or Israel on October 7. He started by directing his wing commanders to prepare their aircraft and crews for a sustained operation. Undaunted by his supposedly limited authority as a MAJCOM commander to work in joint channels, Carlton went directly to Major General Maurice F. Moe Casey, the Joint Chiefs of Staff deputy director for logistics, to organize the supplies to be lifted and to preposition them at MAC bases. Next, once his planners had worked out the air routes to Israel, General Carlton coordinated recognition codes, communications, and aerial escort procedures directly with the U.S. Navy's 6th Fleet commander, Admiral David J. Murphy. Murphy, a subordinate commander of the U.S. European Command, responded by positioning his carriers and guided missile ships down the Mediterranean to provide continuous coverage to within 150 miles of Lod Airport, outside of Tel Aviv. From that point, Israeli fighters would escort the big planes. Carlton also asked U.S. Readiness Command to make some of its C-130s available to pick up MAC missions in CONUS and thereby free more MAC jets for the long lift to Israel. Finally, MAC quietly sent out Airlift Control Elements (ALCEs) to Lajes and Lod on October 12 to organize ground support for the transport stream.[12]

The airlift, considering the urgency of the moment and the distances involved, was an operational and statistical wonder. The first C-5 landed at Lod Airport at 2200 on Sunday, October 14, carrying 97 tons of 105mm tank ammunition. In less than four hours, Israeli volunteers manhandled the shells onto waiting trucks and sent them to the fronts. By October 20, MAC had flown 100 missions into Lod and, just four days later, passed the 200-mission milestone. Logistical coordination was tight, as the Americans filled their planes according to Israeli priorities, crews met their new tanks as they drove off C-5s, and A-4 Skyhawks stood ready to receive aft fuselage sections as they arrived from America. In total, the American airlift involved 566 sorties delivering 22,395 tons of cargo over an average distance of 6,450 nautical miles. This equated to a total lift of 144 million ton miles in 33 days, or 4.4 million ton miles per day. On average, the Berlin Airlift had produced only 1.7 million ton miles per day.

By comparison, the Soviet lift was paltry. Flying an average distance of only 1,700 miles, Soviet Air Force and Aeroflot airliners moved only 15,000 tons in 935 missions, for a total effort of 25 million ton miles over a period of 37 days.[13] Moreover, the Soviets managed their lift poorly. Apparently grabbing whatever war supplies came to hand, their loads arriving at Cairo included tanks that weren't battle ready and low-priority matériel that "was lost track of as it was trundled in warehouses."[14] Though a useful propaganda statement, the Soviet airlift was too disorganized and poorly coordinated with its Arab recipients to have a concrete effect on operations. They had transport aircraft, but they clearly didn't know much about airlift.

In truth, apart from the diplomatic tensions and military drama of its start, Operation Nickel Grass, the code name for the airlift, quickly settled down to a matter of routine for MAC and its personnel. Once the flow was scheduled, fuel supplies were stabilized at Lajes, and ALCE movement support personnel were deployed (425 at Lajes and 55 at Lod), the initial sense of rush faded quickly. Indeed, Nickel Grass never engaged more than 24 percent of the operational fleet. The smallness of the effort allowed MAC to meet all of its other scheduled commitments. Several major exercises, including REFORGER (REturn of FORces to GERmany) V and Absalom Express (Norway), continued as planned. There were even C-141 sorties available to carry Air Force Academy cadets to football games and choir events. On average during the airlift, seven C-5s and forty-six C-141s sat on parking ramps, operable but without missions to fly.[15] As General Carlton later reported, "The entire operation was accomplished without degrading other worldwide commitments . . . mobilizing the reserves, or activating the [CRAF]."[16] So while there was importance and diplomatic tension in the background of the airlift, operationally it was just part of the daily grist of a command that truly knew its job.

At the individual level, the experience of the airlift was similarly ordinary. Probably only the ALCE personnel at Lod experienced Nickel Grass at an intensely emotional level. Working exhausting hours beside Israelis struggling to save their country, the ALCE commander, Colonel Don Strobaugh, and other team members remembered the experience as a highlight of their professional careers.[17] For aircrews, in contrast, the Nickel Grass experience was less intense and generally more pleasant. Their flights out and back were the usual routine of watching autopilots fly their planes, monitoring instruments, tracking courses, and checking cargo restraints. Lod, for the crews, was a gratifying experience of contributing to the war effort and enjoying the snacks and beverages brought out to their planes or served in a special lounge by El Al stewardesses. Back at headquarters and on home base flight lines, most MAC personnel understood the importance of the mission. But it also was just another item on their menu of ongoing operations to plan and planes to service. Professionals, not amateurs, they did their jobs well and would keep the transport stream flowing to Lod until they got orders to direct it somewhere else. In an age when transoceanic flight was a matter of safe routine, the excitement and romance of air transport rested more in the diplomatic, military, and humanitarian importance of its missions than in their actual conduct.

Walter J. Boyne wrote in his history of Nickel Grass that the "airlift was decisive before it started."[18] His point was that the promise of resupply freed the Israelis to pour fire and steel onto their attackers without worrying about depleting their munitions' reserves. Knowing that intensified Israeli operations likely would reverse Arab gains and undermine Soviet influence in the region, the Russians asked the Americans to help them broker a cease-fire. The Soviets' effort went nowhere, however, since their terms of a cease-fire in place and ultimate Israeli withdrawal from occupied territories were unacceptable to both Washington and Tel Aviv. So fighting continued unabated, and the 750 tons or so of supplies coming into Lod every day allowed the Israelis to launch counteroffensives on the Golan and Sinai fronts on October 16. With Israeli forces crossing the Suez Canal and threatening even Cairo, the Soviets spent the 16th to the 19th trying to persuade the Egyptians to accept a cease-fire before they suffered another major defeat. When that effort failed, they asked Kissinger to come to Moscow on the 20th to negotiate with Premier Leonid Brezhnev. Kissinger and the premier worked out an agreement, and following a visit by the secretary to Israel to explain the terms, the cease-fire went into effect on the 22nd. As Secretary Kissinger briefed his staff the next day, Israeli military successes, the airlift, and careful diplomacy had put the United States in the preeminent position as the broker of peace in the region, while Soviet influence and even interest in Middle East affairs were diminished severely.[19]

Then, in a way that no one outside of the Israeli government could have anticipated, the airlift proved almost too successful. Well supplied and full of vengeance, Israel gave lip service to the cease-fire, while it continued offensive operations in Syria and Egypt. By October 23, the Israeli Army had all but surrounded Egypt's III Corps and was in a position to destroy it and take the city of Suez. By the afternoon of the 24th, President Anwar Sadat was begging for a joint U.S.-Soviet peacekeeping force to separate the two armies. Later that evening, the Soviets threatened "to consider the question of taking appropriate steps unilaterally" if the United States did not join with them in forcing the Israelis to stop fighting and return to the positions they held at the start of the war.[20] Not sure if the Soviets were serious or just posturing for diplomatic and domestic political effects, the U.S. government put its nuclear forces and the 82nd Airborne Division on DEFCON III alert, which equated to "cocking" them for immediate action. Fortunately, cooler actions prevailed the next day. President Nixon promised to "take every effective step to guarantee the implementation of the ceasefire" and the Soviets limited their "unilateral action" to sending a contingent of observers to Cairo.[21] But for a few days and some particularly acute hours, the success of the American airlift had empowered Israel to pursue its own course, unhinge American diplomatic objectives, and put the world at risk of a wider conflict.

Things Learned

As one might expect, Nickel Grass received a lot of analytical attention. MAC and the General Accounting Office issued reports, and Congress conducted hearings on the performance of the C-5 during the airlift. These studies provided important insights into the strategic characteristics of global airlift, its operational maturity, and some shortfalls needing correction. Taken together, these studies affirmed the emergence of MAC and global airlift as essential and reliable components of America's ability to influence global events.

Strategically, airlift revealed itself as a two-sided coin during Nickel Grass. On the face of it, global airlift allowed the United States to engage the conflict quickly and decisively, without provoking an armed confrontation with the Soviets. On the back of the airlift coin, commitment to an airlift operation proved as entangling diplomatically as perhaps would have been a commitment to armed intervention. Given Israel's instant dependence on the flow of supplies through Lod, an interruption of that flow could have endangered the whole balance of power in the region. Thus, the United States found itself trapped by the airlift, even when its continuation also encouraged the Israelis to flirt dangerously with further conquest beyond the Suez and Golan Heights. Airlift made it easier to get involved in the October War, but it did not put the United States in complete control of events.

MAC's operational maturity, following a decade of modernization and gaining operational experience, was manifest in its conduct of Nickel Grass. With only a few days' notice to plan and initiate the operation, MAC and its unstoppable commander pulled together the aircraft, crews, plans, schedules, support structures, control facilities, cargoes, interagency and interservice coordination, and diplomatic agreements to start a flow of 750 to 1,000 tons of cargo per day down a 6,400-mile route that substantially did not exist the week before. No other nation on earth, not even the Soviet Union, could replicate more than a shadow of that capability. MAC had debuted as a force that put America's enemies at risk and offered reassurance to its friends.

There were some things that needed fixing, of course. Materially, all reports recognized the irreplaceable value of the C-5 while also lamenting the fleet's persistent maintenance difficulties and the shortage of trained crews available to utilize its air-refueling capabilities. At times, over half of MAC's C-5s were not operational as a result of spare part shortages or delayed maintenance. Recognizing the risk, General Carlton and others pressed the Air Force and Department of Defense afterward for funding to add refueling receptacles to all C-141s and to train all C-141 and C-5 crews in those operations.[22] Procedurally, Carlton's earlier concerns over access to the C-130 fleet were accentuated by the refusal of the European and Readiness Commands to make them available at the peak of tensions in the last days of the conflict. United States Air Forces in Europe and TAC C-130s had relieved MAC jets of a number of missions during the early days of Nickel Grass. But those commands withdrew their planes when American forces went on alert on October 24. Carlton was vexed in particular by REDCOM's decision to hold its Hercs on the ground in readiness to support a deployment of the 82nd Airborne Division to the Middle East.[23] Not only did he need their immediate help, but he also knew that it would be his planes that moved the 82nd overseas and not the relatively short-legged C-130s.

All things considered, Nickel Grass was the operational watershed of global airlift. Before 1973 the U.S. Air Force's long-range airlift arm performed air transport functions between developed bases. Even its movements of army brigades during the Vietnam War proceeded as administrative airlifts stretched out over weeks. After Nickel Grass, every friend or enemy of the United States knew that MAC was a force with which to reckon. In an amazingly short amount of time, it could shift the operational and strategic balance in a combat theater or even on a global scale. As in the case of Nickel Grass, it also could spare the United States the risk and culpable irresponsibility of rattling its nuclear arsenal to force concessions from enemies in minor conflicts. MAC, in summary, had become a war-fighting organization and "a substantial pillar of realistic deterrence."[24] Now the challenge was to bring its organizational and doctrinal arrangements in line with its new identity.

18. Airlift Consolidation in the 1970s

BEFORE DISCUSSING THE course of airlift consolidation, we must understand its organizational context. After the establishment of the Department of Defense (DOD) in 1948, the operational, or war-fighting chain of command of the United States ran from the president through the secretary of defense to the commanders in chief (CINCs) of the specified and unified combatant commands. CINCs were enormously powerful individuals, since they were assigned distinct war-fighting missions and responsibilities. To accomplish their missions, the commanders of specified commands directed forces drawn primarily from a single military service. The commanders of unified commands directed forces drawn from all of the services and oversaw military operations in specific geographic areas. The Strategic Air Command (SAC) was an example of a specified command, while the U.S. Pacific Command exemplified a unified command. The role of the military departments of the Air Force, Navy, and Army was to train, organize, and equip forces for assignment to combatant commanders. Neither the individual service chiefs nor the Joint Chiefs of Staff (JCS) organization over which they presided had war-fighting responsibilities. This is not to say that individual service chiefs did not involve themselves in combat operations, but generally they were not supposed to. Within the Air Force, major commands (MAJCOMs), like SAC and the Military Air Transport Service (MATS), handled specialized parts of its "service" functions of training, organizing, and equipping forces. SAC and MATS were somewhat anomalous in that they both were MAJCOMs but also had global operational responsibilities that made them like combatant commands. Indeed, SAC was a specified command, but MATS had never received that recognition of its operational responsibilities.

Getting Almost Nowhere:
Airlift Consolidation Prior to the Vietnam War

Now to the main point: the idea of airlift consolidation went virtually nowhere between the end of World War II and the end of the Vietnam War because none of the giants commanding the combatant commands and the services paid any attention to it, or if they did they generally saw it as untimely and/or a threat to their missions and prerogatives. When they found time to ponder the notion (which wasn't often), they easily grasped that consolidation could offer logistically efficient and operationally flexible use of available airlift assets in support of *national* priorities. But they also saw that it might undermine the timely availability of airlift forces to *them*. It did not help the prospects of consolidation that there were significant technical barriers to its practicality prior to the late 1960s and that some believed that a consolidated global airlift command would become a jack-of-all-trades, unable to do vital missions as well as smaller, specialized organizations could. Simply put, the piston-engine propeller aircraft and the command-and-control systems of the time precluded the conduct of coordinated airlift operations on a global basis. The planes were too slow, unreliable, and specialized in their designs to move quickly from mission to mission, and global requirements could not be gathered, assessed, and acted on in a timely manner. Thus, advocacy of airlift consolidation was limited to a very small, sometimes noisome group of officers and a few like-minded civilian leaders centered on MATS and Military Airlift Command (MAC). Until the early 1970s they were voices in the wilderness, either not taken seriously or viewed as out-of-step zealots by everyone else in authority.

At the end of World War II, the distribution of American airlift forces and capacity was anything but consolidated. The Army Air Force's Air Transport Command (ATC) stood unique for its size and its establishment as a common-user service in accordance with JCS priorities and guidance. All other airlift organizations and units were attached directly, or organically, to their primary users. Most theater air forces had troop carrier commands of various sizes that they sometimes utilized in their primary airborne assault mission but mostly to provide air transport support as directed by their theater commanders. The Materiel Command chartered most of its air transport needs from civilian companies in the United States, while theater service commands operated military squadrons to link their supply depots and maintenance facilities to operational squadrons in the field. Medical commands had their squadrons to move the sick, wounded, and psychologically injured. The Navy had the Naval Air Transport Service (NATS) operating long-distance routes in areas of naval activities. The U.S. Marines had their own transport squadrons. Even the Army attached a few two- and three-seat light aircraft to every field army, corps, and division to provide small-scale air transportation of commanders, staff officers, dispatches, and pieces of high-value cargo. In addition to these larger units, there literally were thousands of transport aircraft scattered around the U.S. military as the dedicated transports of senior commanders and were attached to bases and combat units as on-call taxis and for other specialized uses. These organically assigned units and planes were everywhere, then, all owned by commanders who liked having them at their beck and call and who operated them according to different sets of priorities and utilization rates.

The potential and reality of misapplication and wastage in this fractionated airlift system during World War II prompted several experiments in coordinated, but not consolidated, operations of theater airlift and long-range transport organizations. Under conditions of extreme scarcity in 1942, the Army and the Marine Corps submitted a few squadrons to the combined scheduling authority of the Southwest Pacific Combat Air Transport System.[1] Later, in Europe, the Combined Air Transport Operations Room functioned as a central planning and operational control node for Troop Carrier Command, Royal Air Force, and Air Support Command transport units operating in the theater after the Normandy invasion in June 1944.[2] Since they operated the same types of aircraft on routes that often overlapped, ATC and NATS seemed to some to be likely candidates for coordination, perhaps even outright consolidation. L. Welch Pogue, chairman of the Civil Aeronautics Board, proposed absorption of the two commands in 1942 into a War Transport Command.[3] Pogue's recommendation never got traction in the hurly-burly of wartime events. But the commanders of ATC and NATS did establish the Joint Army-Navy Air Transport Committee in September 1942 to meet regularly and coordinate on commercial contracting, allocation of new-production aircraft, route overlaps, movement priorities, and other matters of mutual interest.[4] Thus, at war's end the principle of mutual augmentation between airlift operating commands was an established practice, while the idea of commands actually transferring control of their organic assets to consolidated commands didn't have many supporters.

In the two decades after World War II, the Air Force made mutual augmentation a successful practice. MATS C-54s conducted the Berlin Airlift under a theater air force, the United States Air Forces in Europe (USAFE), in 1948 and 1949. In May 1950 MATS and troop carrier units cooperated to establish and supply a division-size airhead during Operation Swarmer. Beginning in 1956 TAC C-130 troop carrier wings provided transoceanic deployment lift for Composite Air Strike Forces, usually with significant support from MATS. After the Cuban Missile Crisis of 1961, all MATS C-124 units began training in tactical formation flying and airdrop procedures. During Exercise Big Lift in 1963, MAC, TAC, and USAFE air transport and logistics planners worked jointly to move a division of troops from Texas to Germany in sixty hours. Meanwhile, MATS C-124s and C-135s flying under USAFE's control supported UN peacekeepers in the Congo during Operation New Tape from 1961 to 1964. Whether reflected in the organizational setup or not, integrated operations of theater and strategic airlift organizations were the norm by the early 1960s.

Meanwhile, and despite the success of mutual augmentation, a small group of airlift practitioners continued to press for consolidation of airlift forces under a single command. All of the commanders of ATC—Major General Hal George, Major General Robert Harper, Major General Robert Webster, and Lieutenant General Laurence Kuter—pressed the issue. Kuter and his staff submitted several consolidation plans to the Air Staff in 1949 and 1950, calling for establishment of a Strategic Air Support Command that would operate the global air transport system and provide troop carrier elements to the theaters.[5] Singing from the same sheet of music, and flush from his success in command of consolidated theater airlift forces in Korea, Major General William H. Tunner advised air force commanders in 1950 that "much greater airlift can be developed with available resources by placing . . . [it] in one organization and making it available to theater commanders as required by them."[6]

The debate over airlift consolidation went dormant in late 1951, when the Air Force replaced Kuter with a commander more to its doctrinal liking, Lieutenant General Joseph Smith. Smith, the man who had set up the Berlin Airlift, was an accomplished commander who cared not a fig for changing the existing organizational or doctrinal setup of airlift. So fixed was he on the Air Force's vision of MATS as the peacetime provider of common-user air transport and wartime mobility for SAC, Smith and the staff he built at MATS avoided any discussion of the organization of airlift forces, even those contained in draft doctrine manuals.[7]

Only when Congress began to look more closely into airlift affairs in the latter 1950s did consolidation reemerge as an issue.[8] Even then, it did not become an active discussion within the Air Force until Tunner returned to MATS as commander in 1959. Ever the outspoken proponents of consolidation, Tunner and Mendel Rivers, chairman of the House Committee on Armed Services, made sure that studies emerging from the president's office and the National Military Airlift Hearings of 1960 contained recommendations for consolidation and possible elevation of MATS to combatant status.

The military services did make minor adjustments to the organizational structure of airlift during this period. When Secretary of Defense James Forrestal needed a quick example of the supposed advantages of the newly unified defense establishment, he turned to ATC and NATS as low-hanging fruit and blended them into MATS. Indicative of the weakness of the arrangement, the Navy gave up only some of its transport squadrons, and, for that small contribution, the Navy gained an admiral's billet to fill the vice commander position at MATS headquarters. The Far East Command made the next noteworthy effort at consolidation when it allowed General Tunner to bring all *air force* transport units in the theater under his control.[9] In an effort to placate congressional complaints that the mission of MATS was not clear, the Air Force named it the single manager for four-engine *transport* aircraft. "Transport" was the operative word, since it restricted MATS's purview to aircraft performing its assigned peacetime and wartime missions, not those of troop carrier or the other services.

None of these adjustments, therefore, significantly changed the airlift organizational status quo. In the cases of the establishment of MATS and assignment of single manager responsibilities, they also weren't much more than expedient eyewash. No command was ever obliged to give up assets that it was not willing to release. The Navy gave MATS aircraft that were surplus to its postwar needs and air reservist crewmen for which it did not have billets. The theater air commander in the Far East did not give up a single aircraft; he merely let Tunner reshuffle them a little. The substantive impact of single managership was that SAC and TAC sent their already decrepit C-124 squadrons to MATS. They kept their brand-new turbine-powered KC-135 jets and C-130 turboprops for their own use. *They*, not MATS, would introduce the Air Force to the world of turbine-powered air transport operations. In the division of resources, the Air Force and the other services unmistakably favored their organic airlift arms and took little interest in the one organization that had common-user responsibilities.

Though never more than a minor issue to most senior military commanders, airlift organization did produce a small literature of journal articles, reports, and official letters. Many of these are discussed in previous chapters. But the unusual couplet of articles appearing in 1950 issues of the *Air University Quarterly Review* are worth revisiting, because they encapsulated both sides of the debate. A MATS staff officer, Lieutenant Colonel George E. Stover, opened in the summer issue by telling his readers that separating the troop carrier and air transport arms was unnecessary and harmful, since crews could be trained to perform both missions, and a unified command would be better at "furnishing air transportation of all kinds for the Joint Chiefs of Staff."[10] Responding to Colonel Stover's article, Lieutenant Colonel Leroy M. Stanton, a TAC staff officer, wrote that the practice of cross-command augmentation was as far as airlift consolidation could or should go. "The tasks involved," he wrote, "are so different that standardization would jeopardize one or the other's mission."[11] So while Stover focused on strategic concerns, Stanton fell back on a belief that individual pilots generally could not embrace the skills of both the air transport and the troop carrier missions.

Given the technological realities of the time, neither Stover's nor Stanton's arguments had much credibility. In his enthusiasm for consolidation, Stover overlooked the inconvenient truths that no aircraft powered by piston engines could meet both SAC's and the Army's requirements optimally. SAC needed small and fast aircraft to move the people and equipment of its reconstitution teams in time to meet bombers returning to overseas recovery bases following initial strikes against the Soviet Union. The Army needed big planes capable of carrying troops, vehicles, artillery, and even tanks. SAC liked the C-118, a derivative of the DC-6 airliners. The best planes the Air Force could provide the Army were the C-119, C-123, and C-124. Even when operated in concert, these aircraft could not provide a continuum of airlift for ground forces between the United States and forward fields. Moreover, in an age when teletypes, high-frequency radios, and mail were the core of the military's communications capabilities, any notion that a command based in the United States could make timely operational decisions for another theater was far fetched. Stanton's argument, in contrast, was just silly. To say that no single crewman could embrace the skills of both air transport and tactical airborne operations was to ignore the fact that troop carrier units and crews did both of those things already.

Reenergizing the Debate

From the mid-1960s several developments strengthened the logic of consolidating theater and intertheater airlift forces in the views of an increasing number of influential leaders. A new generation of turbine-powered aircraft caused the capabilities of both airlift arms to overlap substantially. Operations during the Vietnam War provided ample opportunities to observe these overlaps in action. Improvements in the command-and-control capabilities at MATS and its successor organization after 1967, MAC, enhanced their abilities to monitor and influence events in overseas theaters of operations. Perhaps most important, certain leaders in the theater airlift community began to see a better operational and professional future in a consolidated airlift command. There remained substantial resistance to overcome, but these developments set the stage for the sudden shift of the policy balance in favor of consolidation and specification in the early 1970s. The new generation of turbine-powered transport aircraft created an existential crisis for Troop Carrier Aviation. Since troop carrier's beginning in World War II, its distinctions from ATC and MATS were its responsibilities for airborne operations and operations into the short and often poorly developed airfields found in combat theaters. In the 1950s this distinction was manifested in the fleets operated by troop carrier and MATS. Troop carrier flew a family of rugged, specialized, medium-size transports—namely, the C-119, C-123, and C-130. MATS flew airliners or aircraft derived from airliner concepts—most important, the C-118 and C-124. The entry of the C-141 blurred this technological distinction, since it not only had long range but also could air-drop anything a C-130 could. Worse, for troop carrier advocates, while the C-141 encroached on the "upper" end of their mission, the Army's expanding helicopter fleet trespassed its "lower" end, assault airlift. Assault airlift was the airlanding of combat forces and supplies at the shortest and least developed airfields possible. Utilizing C-123s, troop carrier could push, maybe, an aircraft every ten minutes through an airfield 2,000 feet long and with limited parking space. Ten army CH-47s or fifteen UH-1s could land on that same runway simultaneously, unload, and fly clear in half that time or less.

The organizational implications were troubling, as even Secretary of Defense Robert S. McNamara recognized that the lines dividing MATS and troop carrier forces were blurred.[12]

The Air Force's efforts to sharpen the operational and organizational lines between troop carrier and MATS contradicted themselves. In 1962 General Curtis LeMay, the air force chief of staff, declared that all future official documents would emphasize that troop carrier performed "assault airlift."[13] But when it became clear that the Army had taken over at least the short-range assault airlift mission, the Air Force changed the designation of all troop carrier units to tactical airlift in 1967. But while this new designation may have emphasized the difference between theater airlift and Army Aviation, it also pointed to the similarities between what C-130s did in the theaters and what C-141s did globally— namely, airlift.

Airlift operations during the Vietnam War were integrated to an unprecedented degree. By early 1966, C-119s and C-130s from the TAC and Air National Guard were flying about 3,800 hours per month on MAC routes in the United States to free jets for the Pacific routes.[14] Some of those freed jets, in turn, picked up missions normally flown by Pacific Air Forces' C-130s to free them up for operations in Southeast Asia. MAC transports routinely delivered their cargoes directly to airfields in the interior of Vietnam to speed operations and ease the operational load on the theater transport fleet.[15] In an unprecedented arrangement, MAC commander General Paul K. Carlton gave the 834th Airlift Division permission to divert inbound C-141s to interior fields to expedite deliveries or carry cargoes that wouldn't fit into C-130s.[16]

Integrated operations drove organizational adjustments and doctrinal ruminations. The 834th Airlift Division in Saigon, for example, was obliged to draw staff personnel from both MAC and TAC to control operations in Vietnam. Indeed, Brigadier General William G. Moore, the first 834th Airlift Division commander, came from troop carrier, while his successor, Brigadier General Hugh E. Wild, was from MAC.[17] Wild's successor was Brigadier General Burl W. McLaughlin. Like Moore, McLaughlin was a SAC man who had entered Troop Carrier Aviation as a wing commander only in 1962. Whether acknowledged in official doctrines or not, the Air Force's two primary airlift arms had become interlinked for planning and operations on a daily basis. Even TAC headquarters was obliged to admit in 1966 that although the two airlift systems were different, "MAC personnel must be trained to be responsive . . . to aspects of tactical operations . . . [and] tactical airlift forces must train for strategic operations."[18]

Away from TAC headquarters, mid-level tactical airlift leaders were considering the implications of the daily interaction of tactical and strategic airlift forces. General Moore used his end-of-tour report as 834th Air Division commander to advocate continuing the separation of the theater's airlift and combat airpower command-and-control systems established in Vietnam. Official doctrine called for an airlift division within the theater's Tactical Air Control Center to run airlift operations. Standing up a separate Tactical Airlift Center was to be done only when airlift operations were on a large scale. Moore argued in contrast that the differences in procedures and command channels between airlift and combat airpower justified the separate arrangement as the norm.[19] Back in the States, Moore found an opportunity to voice his full opinion on airlift organization during his interviews for the Air Force's official CoRONA

HaRVEST reports on the Vietnam War. He minced no words in assessing TAC as a "fighter-oriented command" and that tactical airlift belonged under MAC. His only caveat was that theater-assigned airlift forces must remain under the authority of theater air commanders responding to the directives of their commanders in chief.[20] In his interview with the CoRONA HaRVEST airlift study director, Colonel Louis P. Lindsay, Major General Burl McLaughlin, now the vice commander of the 15th Air Force, endorsed Moore's call for consolidating airlift forces "as soon as possible."[21]

Quite frankly, many and perhaps most senior tactical airlift officers were itching to leave TAC. Major General James I. Baginski, who had a long and storied career in tactical and strategic airlift, put it succinctly: "We were the bastard child [of the fighter community] who wanted to keep us for their own use . . . to carry their bags, personal items, motorcycles, and scooters." The career prospects of tactical airlift officers were so poor in TAC, Baginski said, they needed to go to overseas commands to improve their likelihood of promotion.[22] In truth, few troop carrier officers made it to colonel, and most troop carrier general officers earned their spurs in other realms of air force operations, usually in bombers. Bill Moore and Burl McLaughlin were cases in point. Flying transports around the world and in combat was exciting and romantic stuff. But if aspiring officers also wanted to make colonel or higher, it was time to leave TAC and go to a command where airlift was its core business.

Obstacle to Change

There were a lot of people in the Air Force who did not like the way things were going in the tactical airlift community, but the one who counted was General William W. (Spike) Momyer. As a storied combat leader, an influential writer of early air force doctrines, and now the commander of TAC, General Momyer was inclined by conviction and position to stop the insurrection in his tracks. If he had a mantra, it was that the authority of the theater air commander over all air force assets and operations in his theater must be total.[23] The idea, to him, of an airlift commander operating independently of the theater air commander was anathema, and he did his best to make sure that such a thing did not come to pass. He succeeded in the short run, but his efforts to make that happen also helped drive the tactical airlift community into the arms of MAC later on.

Momyer attacked the notion of separating tactical airlift from TAC at every level. In his end-of-tour report as the theater air commander in Vietnam, he

1. The 1st Aero Squadron arrives at Columbus, New Mexico, May 13, 1916, to take part in the Punitive Expedition and begin the history of U.S. military airlift. (U.S. Army Signal Corps)

2. The Douglas C-1 was the first "C" aircraft acquired by the U.S. Army. (U.S. Army Air Service)

3. During the Great Flood of 1927, the 154th Observation Squadron, Arkansas National Guard flew over twenty thousand miles to locate survivors and deliver supplies. (Painting by Gil Cohen, National Guard Image Gallery)

4. Lieutenant Colonel Henry H. Arnold was an early thinker on air transport operations and later, as the chief of the Army Air Forces in World War II, would influence airlift affairs greatly. (U.S. Army Air Corps)

5. The Air Corps' purchase of the all-metal XC-32 and its derivatives marked the beginning of modern airlift and sparked an internal debate over whether they should go to field units or a central airlift organization. (U.S. Army Air Corps)

6. Nancy Harkness Love played a pivotal role in creating the Women's Auxiliary Ferrying Squadron and, later, Women Airforce Service Pilots program. (U.S. Army Air Forces)

7. Major General Paul L. Williams commanded troop carrier forces throughout the war in North Africa, Sicily, Italy, France, and Germany. (U.S. Army Air Forces)

8. Flight Nurse Lieutenant Mae Olson records the identification of a soldier being loaded on her C-47 for evacuation from Guadalcanal in 1943. (U.S. Army Air Forces)

9. In the iconic photo of the Berlin Airlift, German children wait eagerly in the hope that a Troop Carrier C-54 will drop candy to them as it passes over on its final approach to land at Tempelhof Air Base. (USAF)

10. C-119 loading a truck in Korea in late 1950. While the plane had valuable features, particularly the rear cargo door, its drawbacks included having just two engines and a weak structure. (USAF)

11. Infantrymen in Korea board an H-19 for transportation to the front lines in late 1953. (U.S. Army)

12. YC-130A prototypes of what became the first modern military airlift aircraft possessing transoceanic range and modern cargo-handling features, and able to take off and land fully loaded from a three-thousand-foot runway. (USAF)

13. Brilliant and forceful, General Laurence Kuter led the Military Air Transport Service through its initial organization and the Berlin Airlift and pressed hard for the consolidation of theater and global airlift forces. (USAF)

14. The birth of global strike; a KC-135A refuels a B-52D in the late 1950s. (USAF)

15. Lieutenant General William H. Tunner, "Mr. Airlift," at the peak of his career as the commander of the Military Air Transport Service. (USAF)

16. Deceptively quiet in demeanor, General William G. Moore was a tough commander who modernized airlift tactics and led theater airlift operations in Vietnam and finally became the commander in chief of the Military Airlift Command. (USAF)

17. Lieutenant Colonel Joe Jackson upon receiving his Medal of Honor for his actions at Kham Duc. (USAF)

18. C-17 departing Aviano Air Base, Italy; out of a complex political battle and troubled development program, the Globemaster III has emerged as the Air Force's highly regarded core airlifter. (USAF)

19. Battlefield airlift in 2010; the CH-47 entered service during the Vietnam War, and its much upgraded variants will remain the U.S. Army's principal airlifter for years to come. (U.S. Army)

20. If the KC-135's longevity in service is indicative, KC-46s could be serving at the dawn of the twenty-second century. (USAF)

wrote, "Tactical airlift . . . operates in an environment which demands association and integration with other tactical forces and it must be directed and controlled by the theater air commander."[24] After Momyer took command of TAC in 1968, his main focus was on preparing forces for the war in Southeast Asia. But as he became aware of the findings of the CoRONA HaRVEST reports and sentiments in the tactical airlift community, he turned some of his always decisive attention to that corner of his command. In March 1971 he disbanded the independent Tactical Airlift Center at Pope AFB, North Carolina, and handed its research and development responsibilities to the more generalized Tactical Air Warfare Center at Eglin AFB, Florida.[25] In the next year, he issued a doctrinal pamphlet directing "all TAC personnel [to] speak with one voice" on issues and include its statement that "TAC fully supports the HQ USAF [1968] position to maintain a distinction between the strategic and tactical airlift systems."[26] In one particularly stark instance, he surprised a group of officers at the Tactical Airlift Center that he had learned were discussing the issue. Momyer bitterly excoriated the group, which included General McLaughlin, Colonel Lindsay, and center commander Brigadier General William A. Dietrich, for spending TAC travel funds to plot its dismemberment. He then ordered the plotters back to their bases, and he left. Recalled Lindsay later, Momyer's effort at repression strengthened their determination to get out of TAC.[27] They could not break out on their own. But if anyone asked for their expert opinion, they now had their own mantra, and it was not Spike Momyer's.

Breaking the Stalemate

Even as General Momyer fought to keep his command in line on the issue, events beyond his control were shifting the policy balance of power in favor of airlift consolidation and specification of MAC. A perfect storm of reports, circumstances, and a serendipitous coalescence of powerful advocates overwhelmed the proponents of the status quo. Almost before separation proponents could remarshal their arguments, the Air Force in 1974 directed the consolidation of virtually all of its airlift capabilities under MAC, and the DOD designated MAC as a specified combatant command in 1977.

Colonel Lindsay's final CoRONA HaRVEST report focused the process. Its core recommendation was to establish a single organization for airlift (SOFA) that would manage all airlift forces, operate the global system, and "provide airlift resources to theater commanders under current concepts and doctrine."[28] By alluding to "current concepts and doctrine," Lindsay opened the door for compromise by implying that MAC would take over responsibility for training, organizing, and equipping theater airlift forces, but theater air commanders would retain operational control over them. Thus, Lindsay's proposal preserved the operational prerogatives of theater commanders and thereby sidestepped the kind of doctrinal and turf fight that heretofore had stymied progress. Others had made similar proposals in the past. But Lindsay's iteration had the advantages of appearing amid "growing concern . . . [for] some type of merger" and enjoying broad support among tactical airlift leaders.[29]

These reports fell on fertile political ground. Operating under the Nixon Doctrine since July 1969, the DOD and the services were struggling to reduce military spending and enhance their ability to rush aid to threatened allies. Under this doctrine, the United States pledged to keep its treaty commitments and shield allies from nuclear coercion. But in the event of lesser conflicts, the doctrine also stated that the United States would "look to the nation directly threatened to assume the primary responsibility of providing the manpower for its defense."[30] Though not really a new policy (it closely resembled the principles articulated by National Security Council Paper 162-2 in 1953), the Nixon Doctrine did reaffirm the DOD's goals of minimizing the number of American troops based overseas and of developing the means to get them back overseas quickly in times of crisis. The implications for airlift were obvious—expansion with emphasis on economy of effort. Accordingly, in early 1974 Secretary of Defense James Schlesinger tasked General Carlton to estimate the airlift force enhancements necessary to move a division per day from the United States to reinforce the North Atlantic Treaty Organization in the event of an attack by the Warsaw Pact.

General Carlton's response revealed a linkage between expansion, efficiency, and consolidation. He presented Secretary Schlesinger with two options. For $3.5 billion, he said MAC could finance upgrades to its existing fleet that would enable it to move a division to Europe every two days. For $10 billion in investments, Carlton said that MAC would enhance the existing fleet and buy 100 new C-5s to meet the division-a-day goal.[31] Polling his congressional contacts on the matter, Schlesinger quickly learned that no money would be available until the DOD took actions to ensure that the nation was getting the most out of the dollars going into airlift already. This put the spotlight squarely on the hundreds of old transports still operating in penny packets for various commands, a recent navy request to recapitalize its organic transport fleet, and the organizational division between MAC and tactical airlift.[32] Getting the message, Schlesinger directed his staff to prepare a program decision memorandum (PDM) calling for the consolidation of all air force airlift forces under MAC's control.

The resulting PDM proposed to change the airlift world.[33] In addition to "the consolidation of all DOD airlift forces under a single manager," it directed that MAC become a specified command. The only airlift forces to be left out of the consolidation were those that were essential and absolutely unique to the operations of the other services. These included navy carrier onboard delivery aircraft and marine KC-130 tanker transports. Army Aviation was not mentioned in the document.[34]

At no other time in the history of airlift could Schlesinger's memo have fallen to an air force leadership more willing to put it in effect. Seasoned by his experiences during the Nickel Grass airlift, P. K. Carlton had become a firm advocate of some arrangement to give MAC more reliable access to augmentation airlift, even if that meant that he had to "own it."[35] Carlton's boss, General George S. Brown, was the first air force chief of staff to have airlift command experience having led a troop carrier group during the Korean War and the Eastern Transport Air Force of MATS later on.[36] When General Brown rose to the chairmanship of the JCS in July 1974, he was replaced by General David C. Jones. Jones supported putting most airlift forces into MAC, but he feared that specification would shift direct control of airlift forces from the Air Force to the DOD.[37] Also supporting consolidation and specification were Lieutenant General Robert E. Huyser, the air force deputy director for operations, and Major General Richard L. Lawson, who preceded Huyser as deputy director for operations and then became the military assistant to the president in August 1973. Both were fans of Carlton's and were convinced by the Nickel Grass experience that airlift needed a strong organization to minimize its misuse and maximize its responsiveness.[38] According to John Shea, the global airlift cause never had a stronger "offensive line" on its side.[39]

Once Secretary Schlesinger released the consolidation PDM, the first order of business for MAC and TAC was to develop the necessary implementation plan. Planning began in August 1974, and MAC staff officers were pleasantly surprised to discover that many of their TAC counterparts were eager to make the change.[40] General Carlton and General Momyer's replacement as commander of TAC, General Robert J. Dixon, signed the plan in September, and General Jones directed complete transfer of all TAC airlift assets to MAC by December 1. The two commands continued to work out the remaining details, and by March 31, 1975, MAC had gained administrative, logistics, and training responsibility over an additional 29,300 personnel and 370 aircraft from TAC, the Air Force Reserve, and the Air National Guard.[41]

Making progress in the overseas theaters, where consolidation impinged directly on local command authorities not subordinate to the air force chief of staff, required more time and compromise than was required when the Air Force merely moved forces between its own commands. Acceding to the undeniable ability of theater CINCs to derail the whole process, MAC proposed a setup consistent with Colonel Lindsay's plan and that, consequently, preserved the status quo. In the proposal, MAC general officers would serve as "theater single managers" (TSM) for airlift and would direct MAC operations in response to MAC guidance and theater forces in response to the orders of theater commanders.[42] Thus, the two lines of command remained distinct, except that they passed through a single MAC officer responding to orders from two four-star commanders. The Air Staff essentially proposed the same setup, except that its plan replaced the TSM concept with theater airlift managers (TAMs). In keeping with General Jones's concerns about specification, the Air Staff also proposed maintaining MAC as a MAJCOM.[43] This move served mainly to undermine General Carlton's negotiating position vis-à-vis the theaters and obliged him to accept agreements based on distinct strategic and theater airlift command lines passing through dual-hat commanders wearing MAC patches.[44]

The Navy and Marine Corps exploited the weakness of Schlesinger's and Carlton's position by demanding reinstatement of their airlift programs in return for their acquiescence to the general plan. Their most energetic supporter in Congress was the chairman of the House Armed Services Committee, F. Edward Herbert (D-LA). Herbert loved the Navy and routinely pressed Secretary Schlesinger to reinstate the Navy's request for new C-9 and CT-39 logistics and administrative transports.[45] Under Herbert's cover, the Department of the Navy actually went ahead and funded the purchase of eleven new transports in late 1974, despite Secretary Schlesinger's ban.[46] Under continued pressure from Herbert, Schlesinger eventually gave in and, in April 1975, allowed the allocation of $191 million to buy even more navy transports, a move that Herbert's committee promptly endorsed.[47]

While Schlesinger placated the Navy, General Carlton concentrated on breaking down the Air Force's resistance to full airlift reform. He promised General Jones in late 1974 that MAC would preserve the "image of tactical airlift after the consolidation."[48] One of Carlton's most important proposals along these lines was to disestablish two *MAC* air divisions—one each in Europe and the Pacific—and replace them with *theater* airlift divisions.[49] Carlton also tried to smooth things over with General Dixon. In January 1975 he somewhat awkwardly told Dixon that if TAC planners would declare their requirements a year in advance, "MAC can satisfy TAC's airlift requirements cheaper than your guys can." Dixon wasn't amused, replying, "We fully appreciate that personnel and cargo can be moved cheaper on MAC aircraft if we help you plan for it. Whenever MAC service is available, TAC will use it."[50]

If, despite Secretary Schlesinger's directive, consolidation was meeting stiff resistance, the prospects for specified command status seemed hopeless in late 1975. When General Brown submitted the Air Force's plan in December to the new secretary of defense, Donald H. Rumsfeld, he had no support for specification from any CINC or service commander. Brown told Rumsfeld, nevertheless, that specified command status would strengthen the operational command of MAC and the JCS's ability to apportion its capacity among the various joint commands.[51] While his plan underwent prolonged review in the Pentagon, Brown attempted to sway his four-star peers to support specification, but he met with little success. The most decisive centers of resistance to his arguments were in the DOD staff. Assistant Secretary of Defense for Installations and Logistics Frank A. Schrontz endorsed consolidation, but he argued strongly that granting specified command status to MAC would not improve the allocation and management of airlift forces.[52] Apparently agreeing with Schrontz, the DOD general counsel, Richard A. Wiley, impressed some specification proponents as being determined to kill the move through prolonged and repetitious legal reviews.[53]

Fortunately, for its proponents, specification had champions elsewhere in the defense staff. Assistant Secretary of Defense for Programs and Analysis Leonard Sullivan Jr. was first among them. It was he who conceded to let the Navy buy new transports in return for their acceptance of airlift consolidation.[54] Acting Assistant Secretary of Defense (Program Analysis and Evaluation) Edward C. Aldridge Jr. shared Sullivan's enthusiasm for specification of MAC, believing that it would put the United States "in a better position to provide prompt airlift support for either a minor contingency or a full-scale conflict."[55] Undersecretary of Defense William P. Clements also endorsed specification but would not take the issue to Rumsfeld for final decision unless it had broader support.[56]

Building that support base required broad and continual advocacy on a wide front. General Huyser and General Carlton conducted an aggressive telephone campaign to sell specification to other senior commanders worldwide. General Brown worked the Pentagon, particularly Secretary Schrontz, promising him in April 1976 that specification actually would strengthen the ability of the DOD and the JCS to allocate and control airlift operations.[57] Brown also had air force chief of staff General Jones assure combatant commanders that consolidation would not undermine the flexibility and responsiveness of their theater-assigned C-130 units during crises.[58] Finally, when Schrontz and his staff continued to logroll on the JCS's implementation plan for airlift consolidation and specification, Brown decided to go around the assistant secretary to Secretary Clements.[59] At Brown's urging, Clements signed a memorandum on May 5 directing the JCS to prepare the necessary documents and plans to stand up MAC as a specified combatant command. The memo also directed Schrontz and his staff to "assist as necessary in the expeditious completion of these tasks."[60] The Air Force and MAC began writing an implementation plan that day, expecting to begin coordinating it for approval in July.

Of course, the fight wasn't over. Criticisms and challenges to his memo led Secretary Clements to issue another memorandum in June, reaffirming his conviction "that our interests can best be served by establishing MAC as a specified command, with the . . . Air Force retaining responsibility for administrative and logistic support."[61] He had reason to push. The chief of naval operations was linking his acceptance of specification to increased funding for more new navy air transports.[62] Secretary Schrontz and the DOD general counsel collaborated to delay coordination on MAC's implementation plan by demanding detailed clarifications of its strategic and tactical functions in wartime and raising questions about its acceptability to Congress.[63] But determined to get the implementer up to the secretary of defense and then on to the president for their signatures, Brown and Clements brushed those obstacles aside and just kept the process moving.[64] They succeeded in getting the secretary of defense's approval of the implementation plan on September 20, with his direction that no navy or marine assets would move to MAC.[65] The president authorized specified command status for MAC on December 13, and General Carlton became the first airlift commander in chief on February 1, 1977.

Implications

In the history of airlift policy, no battles were ever more complex and prolonged than those over consolidation and specification. The roots of these issues went back to the mid-1930s, when the Air Materiel Division and General Headquarters Air Force disputed the assignment of new Douglas transports. Later proposals and efforts to consolidate airlift forces met with no success, mainly because there was no case to be made for doing so. Despite the theoretical possibilities of consolidating forces and enhancing the combatant status of airlift, the technologies of the time rendered the issue moot. Then, when new technologies and experiences suggested the need for stronger airlift organization, its ubiquitous importance to so many commanders made consolidation and particularly specification major policy battles across the DOD. Only the new strategic context and the astute and determined bureaucratic maneuvering of a powerful cohort of advocates kept airlift reform moving.

The irony was that nothing really changed. Consolidation and specification in the 1970s did not change the basic lay down of airlift command relations and did not rob a single service commander or CINC of airlift assets he wanted to keep. As had been the case since World War II, the TAM concept of 1974 left command of theater airlift forces under theater commanders and command of intertheater forces under the JCS's airlift arm, or in this case, MAC. There would be later iterations of the TAM concept, notably the commander of airlift forces (COMALF) concept of the later 1970s and the director of mobility forces (DIRMOBFOR) position established in the early 1990s. In these positions dual-hat airlift officers also were beholden to both their theater boss and their strategic airlift boss. The persistence of this division of command authority suggests both its wisdom and, probably, the unyielding determination of CINCs and theater air commanders to own what goes on in their areas of responsibility.

The linkage of airlift policy change to changing context does not diminish the importance of the doctrinal thought and policy advocacy of earlier airlift gadflies like Generals Kuter and Tunner. While they were prophets before their time, they also created and kept alive a line of thought that proved invaluable when the time came for airlift reform. For thirty years they and like-minded individuals articulated the global airlift model of a modernized and consolidated national airlift arm operating with the authority of a combatant command. Basically, it was their model that the defense community took up, when it felt the time was right.

And this all says something about the nature of dissent within the U.S. military. The happy conjunction of doctrine and events was accidental; no one planned it, let alone could have controlled it. But it would not have happened, at least not quickly, if it had not been possible for good officers to articulate unpopular ideas without repercussion. No one lost his career by being an airlift advocate. Kuter left MATS to a fourth star. Tunner rose to three-star rank and got command of his beloved MATS. William Moore rose quickly to general and became the commander in chief of MAC. Somehow every great organization must make that happen: protect the ones who can think and express their thoughts in constructive ways, whether they are timely ideas or not, for it is in the available body of thinkers and ideas that organizations find the wherewithal to respond to unexpected changes more quickly than their opponents and competitors do. In the case of air force airlift, it may have taken four decades for airlift policy to catch up with doctrine, but the result was going to be another four decades, and more, of opportunities for global airlift to show its value as a bulwark of American security and influence.

19. Airlift in the 1980s

THE LAST DECADE of the Cold War was as close to a golden time for American military airlift practitioners as they would ever get. They worked hard. The myriad tasks involved in moving and linking the forces and global network of bases facing down the Soviet Union placed heavy demands on people and aircraft. Small-scale military contingencies, natural disasters, routine training, and nuclear alert duties added to the burden. But American air mobility forces also were never stronger in relation to the demands placed on them than they were in the 1980s. Apart from short-duration surges to handle contingencies and other emergencies, the pace was brisk but bearable. There was time for people to rest and planes to be refurbished. The airlift fleet was new and state of the art, and newer aircraft and support systems were in design or production. Professionally, airlift personnel benefited from the creation of a consolidated, global airlift command increasingly recognized for its strategic importance and the competency of its people. A Military Airlift Command (MAC) uniform patch garnered respect, and airlift experts could rise to senior ranks. Apart from the possibility that the Russians might grow desperate in their waning power and do something ugly, it was a good time to be in airlift.

REFORGER 78

For the crewmen gathered in the briefing room of the 37th Tactical Airlift Squadron at Rhein-Main Air Base, the man before them represented the generally happy state of their airlift world in 1978. Speaking with quiet confidence of his plans for MAC, General William G. Moore held their attention. Tall and slightly weathered in appearance, he left no doubt that he knew his stuff, cared deeply and purposefully for his responsibilities, and could be trusted. Those were good things to get across, because Bill Moore was the commander in chief of MAC. Beyond that, he was one of them, the first four-star general ever to command the U.S. Air Force's airlift arm from a background in both theater and strategic airlift operations. Though Moore started out in bombers, his rise through the general officer ranks was built on assignments in command of a C-130 wing, airlift operations in Vietnam, and the 21st Air Force, which oversaw MAC's global operations stretching westward from the Mississippi River to Africa. His presence in Germany that morning sent a clear message to the C-130 pilots, navigators, loadmasters, and flight engineers that the Air Force had placed its recently consolidated airlift forces in good hands. It also implied that officers making their careers in transport operations could aspire to great rank and responsibilities. Those messages and the knowledge that General Moore would fly with them in the ongoing REFORGER 78 exercise made for a pretty good meeting.[1]

REFORGER 78 (REturn of FOrces to GERmany) was an indication of the power and strategic importance of American airlift capabilities. The REFORGER exercise series began in 1969 to show America's resolve and ability to reinforce the North Atlantic Treaty Organization in the event of a Soviet bloc attack. In most years the exercise involved the movement of the personnel of an armored division to Germany, where they fell in on prepositioned equipment and supplies. The movements also involved deployments of several air force fighter squadrons and of enough army heavy equipment to prove that MAC could lift whole combat units, not just personnel. During REFORGER 78, MAC planes lifted 14,000 troops, including two brigades of the 1st Infantry Division and a brigade from the 1st Cavalry Division.

The exercise revealed an airlift community capable of organizing a huge and complex operation as a matter of routine. After a year of planning, the REFORGER operational guide had "the thickness of a phone directory for a good-sized city."[2] It included complex scheduling for over 300 aircraft missions in a two-week period. Planning each individual mission involved coordinating cargo and passenger pickup points and loading times, food and rest facilities for crews and passengers at planned and even unplanned stops, linkages to theater airlift at off-load bases, prepositioning maintenance personnel and spare parts at en route stops, and so on. On average during the exercise, a C-141 passed through Goose Bay, Labrador, about every hour. Once entering European airspace, MAC transports flew to their off-load bases under radio silence, using traffic procedures coordinated with a dozen control agencies. Theater airlift forces were also busy. MAC C-130s, C-123s, and C-7s shuttled troops and supplies throughout the theater and conducted several airborne assaults. General Moore made the first landing on a newly completed stretch of autobahn near Stuttgart on September 27 to test the feasibility of operating transports into auxiliary landing strips designed primarily for fighters. C-130s established shuttles from airfields at Koksijde, Belgium, and Ypenburg, the Netherlands, to hustle cargoes arriving by ships to forward airfields. It was a display of operational sophistication and power that no other country on earth could hope to emulate.[3]

MAC went into REFORGER with a robust fleet of aircraft already in hand. Within the active Air Force in the continental United States (CONUS) and overseas, General Moore commanded 77 C-5s, 271 C-141s, and 276 C-130s. These were reasonably new aircraft: the C-5s averaged about eight years old, the C-141s about twelve, and the C-130s about twelve as well. Between them, the Air National Guard and the Air Force Reserve could reinforce MAC with three squadrons of C-7s, four squadrons of C-123s, and twenty-nine squadrons of C-130s, for about 360 aircraft. The Air Force Reserve also fielded four associate wings, which provided additional crews to fly C-5s and C-141s in partnership with active wings. Last, the Civil Reserve Airlift Fleet (CRAF) listed some 300 aircraft, mostly four-engine jets, for call-up in an emergency. As an incentive for making themselves available in wartime, CRAF carriers were receiving about $200 million in routine passenger and cargo transportation contracts per year and moved about 90 percent of all military passenger traffic.[4]

MAC also was in the midst of a well-funded modernization program. Most important, the command was two years into a program to repair structural cracks discovered in the wings and fuselages of the C-5 fleet. These repairs would allow MAC to preserve the operational life of these aircraft and remove payload restrictions placed on them after the cracks were discovered.[5] As a consequence of lessons learned during the Nickel Grass airlift to Israel in 1973, the Air Force funded a program to stretch the fuselages of its C-141As by twenty-three feet, install air-refueling receptacles in them, and return them to service as C-141Bs. The stretch modification alone amounted to the addition of ninety C-141As to the fleet.[6] In a new kind of venture, MAC and the Strategic Air Command (SAC) were cooperating in the acquisition of twenty KC-10A Extender tanker transports, which were modified Douglas DC-10-30 freighters. Though SAC would operate these aircraft primarily as tankers, they could be available to MAC as freighters. Last, MAC had initiated a so-called CRAF enhancement program in 1974 to finance the installation of heavy cargo features in new passenger aircraft of member airlines. Eventually, most CRAF airlines volunteered aircraft for the modifications and the lucrative reimbursements associated with them. But Congress balked at the apparent generosity of the program and its complex mobilization provisions. So in 1978 CRAF enhancement remained an idea with promise, but no modified aircraft actually were in service.[7]

MAC also was on the verge of a revolutionary modernization of its theater airlift fleet. When MAC took over all of the Tactical Air Command's C-130s in 1974, it also gained responsibility for the Advanced Medium Short-Takeoff-and-Landing Transport (AMST) program. The AMST program aimed at producing an aircraft capable of operating into and out of airfields of less than 3,000 feet in length, carrying a 32-ton payload for 1,000 nautical miles, and getting into a 2,000-foot runway with a 13.5-ton payload.[8] Testing of two competing prototypes, the two-engine Boeing YC-14 and the four-engine McDonnell Douglas YC-15, had been completed in the summer of 1977. Both aircraft had been successful in head-to-head testing, and both represented substantial improvements in payload, speed, and short-field capabilities over the C-130. In 1978 General Moore was looking forward to completion of the selection process, mainly because "ground forces are simply outgrowing the C-130."[9]

A New Baseline

For all of the unequaled capabilities of the American airlift fleet in 1978, events would soon reveal the need for further expansion and modernization. Since the early 1970s, MAC commanders had asserted repeatedly that they needed an additional 100 C-5s to meet the division-a-day movement requirements called for in NATO defense plans. But MAC had yet to receive funding for aircraft beyond the 50 C-5As already in the fleet.[10] The urgency of airlift expansion heightened, however, when Islamic militants overthrew the shah of Iran in January 1979 and the Soviets invaded Afghanistan in the following December. The strategic importance of Iran and the speed of the Soviet invasion, which relied heavily on airlift, threatened U.S. interests in the region and shortened the timelines of making effective responses to future crises. An effective American military posture in the region, therefore, would demand more airlift support than was then available.

One thing became clear immediately: the new emphasis on long-range airlift doomed the AMST. The immediate requirement was for an aircraft with greater range and payload capabilities. President Jimmy Carter actually stopped work on the program in December 1977, since the aircraft involved could not contribute significantly to transoceanic lifts. Finding the AMST an inadequate platform for augmenting long-range operations, MAC and the Air Force defined and sought proposals for a C-X aircraft capable of carrying up to 200 tons for 3,500 miles and of operating into 10,000-foot runways.[11] Recognizing that such an aircraft offered capabilities only marginally different from those provided by the C-5, MAC later added a requirement for operation into "austere" airfields. That addition duplicated a key parameter of the AMST aircraft and prompted the Department of Defense to cancel the theater transport program outright in December 1979.[12] Later, in October 1980, the Air Force refined its requirements to place greater emphasis on range. McDonnell Douglas won the ensuing design competition on August 28, 1981, with an aircraft based broadly on the C-15 but larger and designated as the C-17.

Recognizing the importance of airlift expansion and its likely costs, Congress directed the Department of Defense to study future airlift requirements comprehensively. The resulting Congressionally Mandated Mobility Study (CMMS) came out in May 1981. The CMMS was groundbreaking in a number of ways, not the least of which was its simultaneous examination of the airlift elements of four major contingencies. These contingencies included a war in Europe, a Soviet invasion of Iran, a regional conflict within the Arabian Gulf region, and a simultaneous deployment of forces to Europe and the Gulf.[13] In gross tonnage, the European requirement was the largest, since it involved airlifting 478,000 tons of matériel and troops to Europe in fifteen days, compared to 200,000 tons in the same amount of time to the Gulf region. When Department of Defense planners factored in the distances involved, a European conflict called for 125 million ton miles per day (MTMD) of lift, while a Gulf war would call for 73 MTMD.[14] However, the report recommended that the airlift fleet be built up to only 66 MTMD plus an ability to move 9,000 tons per day in the theaters. While acknowledging that the 66 MTMD bogey did not meet any wartime requirements, the Department of Defense asserted that it was fiscally prudent and all the country could afford.[15]

In response to the CMMS, the Air Force directed MAC to develop an airlift master plan (AMP) to detail the steps needed to reach the congressional study's goals. Even as MAC staff officers worked on the new plan, the Air Force announced in January 1982 that it intended to add 50 Lockheed C-5Bs and 44 KC-10s to the existing MAC and SAC fleets.[16] When it hit the streets in September 1983, the AMP fleshed out the modernization program. By 1998 the plan called for the acquisition of 180 C-17s, 44 C-5Bs, and 41 KC-10s and the retirement of 54 C-141s and 180 older C-130s. These actions would bring the MAC fleet to 66 MTMD in capacity. To maintain that level over time, the AMP also called for the acquisition of 40 more C-17s and modification of 19 widebody CRAF passenger aircraft for conversion to cargo operations during wartime to offset the retirement of the rest of the C-141 fleet by 2015.[17]

Some elements of the airlift modernization program progressed smoothly. As a proven design already in service, the KC-10 faced no serious competition, and the Air Force quickly let a contract for forty more. The CRAF enhancement program also fared well. With the major airlines strongly behind the program, Congress authorized initial funding for the necessary modifications in June 1983. By 1990 the Air Force had modified twenty-three jumbo passenger jets for wartime cargo operations at a cost of $582 million. These modifications included the installation of reinforced cabin floors, floor fittings for cargo pallet rollers, and, on some Boeing 747s, "visor" nose doors. In peacetime, the airlines owning these aircraft operated them in passenger operations and received a subsidy for the payload capacity lost to the added cargo-handling features. If the aircraft were mobilized, the airlines would refit them as cargo haulers.[18]

In contrast, the C-5 acquisition and the C-17 development programs ran headlong into each other. As part of the Department of Defense's assessment of the C-17, the deputy secretary of defense asserted that its expected short-field capabilities probably did not justify its greater cost per ton mile of capacity in comparison to that of the C-5 and Boeing 747.[19] Similarly, the General Accounting Office argued that the Air Force's design sacrificed long-range capabilities to operate on small, austere airfields.[20] Meanwhile, the C-5 came under criticism as "a disservice to the taxpayer and the nation" for its inefficiency, compared to the Boeing 747, and its lack of short-field capabilities, compared to the C-17.[21] Politics also hindered progress on either aircraft. Congressman Norman D. Dicks (D-WA), whose district included Boeing's headquarters and main production facilities, emerged as a ferocious opponent of the C-17 and the C-5. His equally ferocious opponent was Congressman George (Buddy) Darden (D-GA), who served as the paladin of the Lockheed plant in Marietta, Georgia.[22] In the end, these criticisms slowed the C-5B program only slightly— it went into quantity production in January 1986—but substantially slowed the C-17 program, which did not begin limited production until mid-1988.

Concerned that the increased focus on long-range airlift would undermine progress in theater airlift developments, the commanders of MAC and the Army Training and Doctrine Command—General Thomas M. Ryan Jr., General William R. Richardson, respectively—established the Airlift Concepts and Requirements Agency (ACRA) in 1984. The tasks of the new organization included doctrine development and "coordination of airlift requirements to meet battlefield mobility and sustainment needs."[23] In reflection of advice from the General Accounting Office and a Lockheed Aircraft Corporation study calling for more army–air force coordination in the development of requirements and aircraft specifications, ACRA's first task was to develop a comprehensive study of theater airlift concepts and requirements.[24] ACRA released its initial report the Qualitative Intratheater Airlift Requirements Study (QUITARS), in 1985. The QUITARS called for an overhaul of the theater airlift fleet to include acquisition of a "small-to-medium-load, vertical or short takeoff and landing (V/STOL) aircraft . . . to support operations in . . . contingency theaters" and another aircraft "capable of delivering outsized cargo to small, austere airfields . . . 3000 feet long."[25] Not wasting time, MAC released an initial concept paper detailing a new advanced theater transport (ATT) in November 1985.[26]

The ATT project struggled for support from the beginning. Looking at the short operational distances of Europe and the Korean Peninsula and the strength of Army Aviation, air force headquarters reported that it had "not identified any requirement . . . to commit resources" to service missions covered already by the Army's C-47 helicopter fleet.[27] Even MAC leaders found it difficult to assign a high priority to the ATT, given the competing demands of the C-17 program for financial and political capital. The study and coordination demands of the project were such that MAC was not able to release a draft statement of operation need (SON) until October 1989. Even as the MAC SON emerged from headquarters, Senator Samuel A. Nunn (D-GA) was pressing the Air Force to modernize theater airlift with new Lockheed C-130Js built in his home state. For MAC, the aircraft and the timing of the proposal were wrong. As a modification of an almost forty-year-old design, the Js offered only marginal improvement over existing C-130 capabilities. Also, MAC wanted to buy a more capable aircraft after the C-17 production run ended in a decade or so. But Nunn was the chairman of the Committee on Armed Services and was "expecting the AF to request C-130s . . . and MAC may be asked to oblige him."[28] With a big buy of new C-130Js in the offing, the need for a second new C-130 replacement aircraft could become redundant, no matter what its operational capabilities.

Grenada

As a military operation, the U.S. invasion of the Caribbean island nation of Grenada on October 25 was a small-scale affair. Only about 7,000 U.S. troops and about 600 from other Caribbean states went onto the island. Their target, the unstable Marxist-military dictatorship that had just taken over the government, mustered only about 1,500 lightly equipped troops, buttressed by a few hundred Cuban special forces troops posing as construction personnel. With victory for the invaders a foregone conclusion, fighting lasted only a few days, with the Americans suffering nineteen killed and the Grenada-Cuba coalition losing about seventy. In support of the invasion, code-named UrGENT FuRY, MAC C-130s air-dropped two battalions of Army Rangers under fire onto Salines Airport at the southern tip of the island and later flew in 82nd Airborne Division paratroopers as reinforcements. In all, MAC aircraft supported early operations with 496 missions carrying 11,389 passengers and 7,709 tons of cargo.[29]

But limited as it was in scope, this first major U.S. military action since the Vietnam War gave the airlift community an opportunity to showcase its ability to plan, organize, and execute a complex operation on short notice. MAC planners only had five days to put the operation together. But they benefited from extensive planning and exercise experience with the principal organizations involved: the U.S. Atlantic Command, the Air Force Special Operations Command (AFSOC), the XVIII Airborne Corps, and MAC operating units.[30] Brigadier General Robert B. Patterson, deputy commander of MAC's 21st Air Force (21AF), orchestrated much of these planning efforts. With the clout of a combatant command behind him, direct experience in air force special operations, and the command of two C-130 wings, he had the breadth of knowledge to aid in developing the general concept of operations and then coordinating MAC's part in it. In the first days of planning, he shuttled between the various units and headquarters involved. He flew down to Barbados to set up a tactical headquarters and support base. From there, Patterson coordinated with local authorities and military units and supervised the transfer of cargo from arriving C-5s to C-130s bound for the small airfields on Grenada.[31] The MAC and 21AF command posts directed operations overall, but Patterson and his airmen in Barbados completed the airlift chain of command and control in the operational area. Reflecting on the agility and smoothness of MAC's planning and operations, Lieutenant General Duane H. Cassidy, who commanded 21AF at the time, believed that the MAC-Army-AFSOC team members "were the only people ready" in an operation otherwise characterized by communications breakdowns and planning errors.[32]

The U.S. Transportation Command

For MAC, the policy consequences of UrGENT FuRY were somewhat ironic. The command's performance during the operation vindicated its status as a specified combatant command with centralized control of the Air Force's airlift assets. But problems in the planning and interservice coordination of the operation overall led to legislative actions that would withdraw MAC's specified command status and subordinate it to a new joint, unified command, U.S. Transportation Command (TRANSCOM). TRANSCOM would have land, sea, and air components, the latter of which would be MAC. In reflection of the much larger operational scope and size of MAC compared to the other components, the MAC commander would be dual hatted as the commander in chief of TRANSCOM (CINCTRANS).

The engines of such radical change in the organization of U.S. military transportation were a host of planning and coordination failures during the operation. These failures manifested in intelligence breakdowns, radios working on different frequencies, units going astray, friendly fire incidents, and so on.[33] Concerned that these failures reflected shortfalls in joint operational command arrangements, President Ronald Reagan chartered a blue ribbon commission to study the issue under the chairmanship of industrialist David M. Packard. Among many recommendations, the Packard Commission pushed for the establishment of a joint transportation command.[34] On April 1, 1986, President Reagan directed the Department of Defense to act on the Packard Commission's recommendations. Meanwhile Senator Barry M. Goldwater (R-AZ) and Representative William F. Nichols (D-AL) championed the necessary legislation, which included "creation of a unified combatant command for transportation missions which would combine . . . the Military Traffic Management Command (MTMC), the Military Sealift Command (MSC), and the Military Airlift Command."[35] Congress approved the Goldwater-Nichols Act on October 1, 1986, and thereafter Secretary of Defense Caspar Weinberger directed activation of TRANSCOM in October 1987. General Cassidy, then serving as the commander in chief of MAC, became the first dual-hat commander of MAC and commander in chief of TRANSCOM. The headquarters of the two commands were situated adjacent to each other at Scott AFB, Illinois.

Panama

Even as the Rangers began parachuting onto the airfields at Rio Hato and Torrijos-Toc-umen, a second wave of paratroopers was literally minutes away. A third wave of light infantry was boarding aircraft in distant California, bound for the Isthmus of Panama.[36]

The army historian thus summarizing the airlift part of Operation Just Cause was painting only part of the air mobility picture of the U.S. invasion of Panama in December 1989. Launched to overthrow Manuel Noriega, the country's dictator, the operation depended on air mobility. As tensions rose between the United States and Noriega over his criminal activities, repressive governance, and increasingly aggressive assaults on U.S. citizens, American plans and preparations for an invasion depended on rapid movement by air. Even before hostilities began, MAC transports made clandestine deliveries of Sheridan light tanks, light armored vehicles, attack helicopters, and other matériel to U.S. forces stationed in the Canal Zone. To overawe Panamanian resistance and prevent Noriega from escaping, the operational plan called for airborne assaults to capture major airports in Panama City and at Rio Hato and quick takedowns of some twenty-five other military objectives. Paratroopers from the 75th Infantry Regiment (Ranger) and 82nd Airborne Division would make the parachute assaults, while troops based in Panama already would make simultaneous ground and heliborne attacks against the other targets. Waves of MAC transports would bring in more supplies and reinforcements, including two brigades of the 7th Infantry Division (Light) from Fort Ord, California. SAC air-refueling aircraft also would be present over the Caribbean to provide support as needed.

The planning and execution of the airlift portion of Just Cause revealed the confidence, competence, and capabilities of the airlift community at the end of a decade of modernization and institutional reform. Fully engaged in the Army's planning for the looming operation, MAC's director of operations, Major General James D. Kellim, promised that he could begin operations within sixty hours of receiving a "go" order.[37] When the order came on December 16, MAC aircraft began moving army units to their jump-off points, even as headquarters and tactical unit planners worked the final details of the big drops. Fulfilling its roles as a joint combatant command, TRANSCOM coordinated air and surface transportation requests coming from all directions, notified some preexisting "customers" that their planned missions would be delayed, and prepared intelligence briefs for units and crews. Operating under the authoritative umbrella of TRANSCOM, MAC units were pleased to find that their "intelligence, charts, and targeting data were complete . . . and they could talk to all the major Air Force commands, as well as to the Army."[38]

> Red tracers began raking the single-file train of C-130s. . . . Even more dangerous was the unseen fire from scores of hand held automatic weapons wielded by Panamanian troops. . . . The aircraft began to vibrate with a "chink, chink" from small arms fire hitting it . . . a paratrooper went down with a bullet in one leg.[39]

Actual operations reflected the depth and competence of airlifters from head-quarters all the way down to individual crews pressing into their drop zones. When ice storms and a shortage of deicing equipment at Pope AFB, North Carolina, threatened the 82nd Airborne's flow plan, MAC and the Army coordinated a road march of its heavy equipment and supply bundles to Charleston AFB, South Carolina. In an unusual tactic, two formations of C-141s flew parallel tracks to drop heavy equipment and 900 paratroopers simultaneously on the adjacent runways of the Torrijos-Tocumen civil-military airport complex just after midnight on December 20. The heavy equipment landed on and closed the Tocumen civil runway, while the Rangers secured the adjacent military runway at Torrijos.[40] Shortly after, fifteen C-130s bored through antiaircraft fire to drop 500 Rangers on Rio Hato Airport with set-piece precision and timing, despite hits on almost every plane. When two C-141s bound for Torrijos experienced malfunctions in their airdrop equipment, MAC and SAC coordinated a linkup with tankers to give the transport crews time to fix their problems and drop their loads of paratroopers into the battle.[41] In all, MAC flew 775 missions in support of Just Cause and follow-up operations. Those aircraft put almost 14,000 troops into Panama in the first five days of the operation and in total moved 39,994 passengers and 20,675 tons of cargo into and out of the country by mid-February 1990.[42]

On the Threshold of a New Strategic Era

Even as U.S. paratroopers were demonstrating the global reach of MAC, events elsewhere were about to change its strategic context. As those parachutes blossomed in Panama's night sky, the Cold War was racing to its conclusion. Only six weeks before Just Cause, the communist government of East Germany had opened the gates between East and West Berlin and set the stage for the reunification of Germany in the next year. By the time American paratroopers descended into Panama, most of the communist governments in Eastern Europe were losing or had lost their formerly iron grips on their citizens. At the center, the Soviet Union was crumbling, beset by failed political and economic reforms, looming economic collapse, and nationalist movements in most of its "republics." In 1991 it would disintegrate into fifteen independent states and enter the pages of history.

The implications of all this for airlift policy were profound though not yet understood. Since the end of World War II, the Cold War had shaped airlift planning, operations, and force structure. ATC C-54s rumbling into Berlin,

MATS C-124s plodding to Germany in Big Lift, and MAC C-5s carrying tanks for REFORGER all did so because the goal of the United States was to contain the Soviet Union and its client states. MAC's size and power in 1990 were the culmination of almost five decades of development with that goal in mind. While its fleet of large, specialized, turbine-powered aircraft still fell short of planning requirements, it still could move fully equipped divisions and air wings quickly to most parts of the world.

Now with the Soviet Union crumbling, there was reason to question whether such a powerful airlift arm would be needed in the future. As events would soon demonstrate, the answer to that question turned out to be "yes, and even more so." The world after the Cold War turned out to be one beset by numerous local and regional tensions and conflicts. As the only superpower left standing, the United States found itself in the role of global hegemon. Its position and power compelled it to orchestrate effective international diplomatic, economic, and military responses to a seemingly constant stream of conflicts, genocidal civil wars in Europe and Africa, and natural disasters. The price of this hegemonic role would prove to be expensive and tiring for the airlift community as much as for any other part of the U.S. military.

20. Acquisition of the C-17

*The C-17's birthing took place amidst heated
competition and the excesses of political influence.*
Betty Raab Kennedy

IN THE HISTORY of American military aviation, the list would be short of aircraft development programs that were as protracted and publicly contentious
as that of the C-17. The viability and strategic impact of some other aircraft were
controversial, of course. But in comparison to the C-17's experience, the con-
troversies over such aircraft as the B-36 and FB-111 and air-launched cruise missiles were short and fought out in large part behind *classified* doors. The C-17,
in contrast, was the focus of a bitter and very public political fight before an
engineer's pen ever touched a drafting pad. As aviation historian Betty Kennedy
described in her definitive history of the C-17 Globemaster III's development,
a phalanx of competing corporations, politicians, scholars, military commanders, pundits, and quacks fought over the plane for more than two decades.[1] Several times, its opponents brought it to the verge of cancellation.

Given the protracted and contentious nature of the policy confrontation over
the C-17, it's worth asking if it helped or hindered the national defense. Did it
produce a fleet of well-designed aircraft in a timely manner, or did it merely
delay the program and increase its costs? In addition, was it a productive example of democracy at work or no more than a distracting squabble incited by
competing manufacturers and allied politicians trying to sell aircraft they knew
the U.S. Air Force did not want or need?

As it turns out, the answers will be as complex as the questions. First, the
historical record suggests that prolonged debate did not produce a better aircraft. Debate did oblige hard thinking about and more careful testing of the
plane. But it also delayed the program and destabilized its early funding, which
in turn accentuated its developmental challenges and costs. So in this case, the
really valuable outcomes of the prolonged debate were clarity and acceptance.
By the time C-17 production stabilized in the latter 1990s, everyone had had a
say, the plane's necessity and virtues generally were understood and accepted,

and the Air Force largely was free to focus on developing and exploiting it operationally. Open debate in this case may have been as much about the health of the American public policy process as it was about refining the plane itself.

Origins: Filling the NATO Strategic Airlift Gap

The C-17 was a product of the "Second Cold War," a period of increasing military competition and instability between the United States and the Soviet Union following the years of détente, roughly 1972 to 1978. Even during détente the Soviets had pursued a wide program of technological modernization, including introductions of new tanks, aircraft, and mobile and multiwarhead ballistic missiles and the development of a "blue-water" navy. Of particular concern to American strategists in the mid-1970s, the improvements in Soviet and Warsaw Pact (WP) military forces and surface transportation networks in Eastern Europe suggested that they could mobilize for war more quickly than before.[2] Until then, the U.S. and North Atlantic Treaty Organization (NATO) military plans presumed that any WP mobilization would become obvious at least thirty days prior to the start of hostilities (D-day). They next assumed that NATO political leaders would discuss the issue for a week and then authorize countermobilizations with at least twenty-three days to get ready for a war. In contrast to this "30/23" mobilization profile, Western planners began to fear by the mid-1970s that the WP had gained the ability to mobilize and move to combat in as little as fourteen days.[3] Given the expectation that NATO political leaders would still dither a week or so before authorizing countermobilization, this profile would leave the allies with only seven days to get ready. In 1976 the Congressional Budget Office (CBO) estimated that this "14/7" profile could permit the WP to launch major attacks into the heart of Germany while pinning down NATO forces elsewhere.[4] These perceptions of growing Soviet bloc military competency and foreshortened mobilization profiles triggered new American and NATO efforts to restore the military balance, partly by improving American transoceanic airlift capacity.

Shorter mobilization profiles carried serious implications for American airlift planning. Under the 30/23 profile, the principal role of the airlift fleet was to augment sealift in the reinforcement of the European theater. The thirty-day window between the start of mobilization and the anticipated peak imbalance between WP and NATO strengths on D+7 provided just enough time for American sealift to move reinforcing army divisions and most replenishment supplies from the United States to Europe. While the sealift effort was getting under way, plans called on the Military Airlift Command (MAC) to lift replacement weaponry and supplies to Europe in the early days of combat. MAC's small fleet of 77 C-5s would move tanks, self-propelled artillery, and other "outsize" replacement equipment, while its 234 C-141s and some C-130s would rush "oversize" vehicles, towed artillery, palletized munitions, and similar loads to the theater. Meanwhile, the airlines of the Civil Reserve Airlift Fleet (CRAF) would carry almost all passengers and much of the bulk cargo to Europe. Even MAC's ongoing airlift enhancement program reflected this supplementary role. Since most of the cargo bound for Europe in the early days of a conflict would be oversize or bulk, the command was lengthening the fuselages of the C-141 fleet, adding cargo features to CRAF passenger aircraft, and planning to acquire limited numbers of an airliner-based advanced tanker-cargo aircraft. Increasing supply stocks and repairing structural problems for the existing C-5 fleet were the only initiatives under way to improve outsize airlift capabilities.[5]

Addressing a 14/7 mobilization profile mandated a profound change of direction for airlift modernization. With so little time available, airlift replaced sealift as the means for moving combat units to Europe in the first weeks of a war. Such movements would create a demand for outsize airlift that far exceeded the capabilities of MAC's C-5 fleet; no other aircraft available could do the job. In 1976 Secretary of Defense Donald H. Rumsfeld warned Congress that the Air Force could not move the required divisions to Europe, because "C-5A wing fatigue problems and flying hour limits reduce our capacity to move outsized cargo."[6] A year later, the RAND Corporation advised the Air Force that the only way to shorten air deployment times significantly would be to increase the efficiency of the existing C-5 fleet and to double MAC's outsize capacity by acquiring "some major modification derivative of the [Boeing] 747 or C-5."[7] Simultaneously, an air force study estimated that the fleet required to handle a 14/7 mobilization scenario was unattainable. Such a scenario would demand a fleet of 1,100 "C-5-equivalent" transports to lift 479,082 troops, 725,300 tons of equipment, and 165,000 tons of supplies to Europe in fourteen days. Recognizing that such a multifold expansion of the airlift fleet was unaffordable, the study suggested instead that the United States position two additional divisions in Europe, buy fifty C-5-equivalent aircraft, and stretch the fuselage design of whichever aircraft won the Advanced Medium Short-Takeoff-and-Landing Transport (AMST) theater air transport program. Even with those actions in place, the study estimated that deployment times would be reduced by only a week.[8]

In the face of such dire warnings, the AMST died in favor of a program to produce an aircraft with better range and outsize capacity. President Jimmy Carter took the first action in December 1977 by deleting funding for the theater transport. In rear guard actions to harvest the benefits of this tactical airlift program, air force headquarters and MAC conducted design studies over the next several months to "increase the range/payload characteristics of the AMST without degrading its short-field landing performance." MAC also conceptualized the so-called C-XX, an aircraft that its planners hoped would carry 200 tons of outsize cargo for 3,500 nautical miles but that also would require 10,000-foot runways to operate.[9] Unconvinced by the resulting design proposals, and unwilling to initiate two new airlift designs at the same time, Secretary of Defense Harold Brown canceled the AMST program outright on October 31, 1979, and directed studies for a new "C-X" transport that was probably smaller than the C-XX and able to operate into shorter runways.[10]

During 1979 events in the Middle East reinforced the need for a new transport aircraft that could lift outsize loads overseas and also get into and out of short and minimally developed airfields. In January a popular revolution overthrew the shah of Iran, a staunch ally of the United States who had made his country a bulwark against Soviet aspirations in the Middle East. In December the Soviet blitzkrieg invasion of Afghanistan heightened U.S. fears that the Soviets planned further aggression in the oil-rich region. Moreover, the speed of the Soviet conquest of Afghanistan, the distance of the Middle East from the United States, and the scarcity of large airfields in the region pointed to the need for a big plane with modest runway requirements. The challenge was that the design characteristics of range (highly swept wings and long fuselages) were not those of a short-field-capable aircraft (less wing sweep, robust construction, shorter fuselage, and the like). Addressing Congress on the issue in early 1980, Secretary Brown affirmed that the new C-X would have to carry "outsize materiel . . . to contingencies outside of Europe." But beyond that, he was prepared only to say that its design would be "optimized for inter-theater, not intra-theater missions."[11]

Acquiring the C-17: Requirements + Interests = Politics + Delay

The C-X Task Force, a team of experts from the Air Force, Army, and Marine Corps convened to define the operational requirements of the C-X, worked out the trade-off between range and airfield requirements. Under the leadership of USAF Major General Emil Block Jr., an experienced airlift commander, the task force settled on an aircraft significantly smaller than the C-XX concept but also able to operate into drastically shorter airfields. Specifically, it proposed a plane capable of carrying around 65 tons (roughly the weight of an M1 battle tank) over 2,400 nautical miles into a 3,000-foot runway. Furthermore, the task force wanted an aircraft capable of operating on unpaved surfaces, narrow taxiways, and small parking ramps. Such an aircraft, the task force described, would be flexible tactically and maximize cargo throughput in a given ramp space. As an example, the task force assessed that C-Xs operating into an airfield with a 500,000-square-foot parking ramp could achieve a throughput of 5,760 tons per day, while C-5As could deliver only 1,728 tons.[12] As a later MAC analyst pointed out, "The conclusion was obvious; the Air Force needed the C-X in order to best meet modern combat needs."[13]

Although the secretary of defense and the service chiefs endorsed the task force's recommendations, others questioned their validity. Some defense officials, such as Assistant Secretary of Defense for Program Analysis and Evaluation Russell Murray II, questioned the technical risks and likely development costs of an aircraft designed for such a complex mission profile.[14] A number of congressmen raised similar concerns, though some with mixed motives. Most outspoken were Senator Sam Nunn (D-GA) and Representative Norm Dicks (D-WA), who represented districts containing the Lockheed and Boeing Aircraft Corporations, respectively. Both companies had alternative aircraft to sell, neither of which could meet the 3,000-foot runway requirement. Made cautious by the widespread skepticism that greeted the C-X design proposal, Congress restricted fiscal year 1982 development funding to $35 million and tied further allocations to completion of a definitive Department of Defense (DOD) airlift requirements study in the spring of 1981.[15] Barely a year after its initial conception, then, the C-X teetered on the brink of extinction.

The ensuing corporate battle to make a winning proposal was complex and fast paced. The Air Force released its request for proposals in October 1980. Boeing and McDonnell Douglas proposed enlarged versions of their AMST designs. Lockheed offered a version of the C-141 with a larger-diameter fuselage. Boeing and Lockheed also maneuvered to have their Model 747 and C-5 aircraft considered, respectively.[16] As the design competition proceeded through the spring of 1981, the DOD released the Congressionally Mandated Mobility Study (CMMS) in the preceding fall. Among its findings, the CMMS demonstrated that American airlift capabilities fell short of war plan requirements for Europe, Korea, and the Middle East and that acquiring an outsize aircraft possessing serious short-field capabilities was a necessity.[17] Having thus recertified the C-X requirement, the air force chief of staff in August 1981 selected McDonnell Douglas to develop an enlarged derivative of its YC-15 AMST, designated as the C-17. Rejecting the decisions, Boeing, Lockheed, and their supporters in Congress made unsolicited and cut-rate offers of 747s and C-5s. Lockheed actually argued that the C-5 could operate on small fields just as well as the C-17, an assertion that MAC leaders considered "inaccurate, and misleading."[18] In an effort to get additional capability into the airlift fleet in the near term and to moderate the political heat, the Air Force in February 1982 announced a plan to acquire an interim fleet of fifty new Lockheed C-5s and forty-four McDonnell Douglas KC-10s while continuing to develop the C-17. Left out of the deal, Boeing and Congressman Dicks redoubled their efforts to sell freighter versions of the 747.[19] Despite some improvements in its cargo-handling equipment, the plane remained awkward to load at forward locations and still needed nearly two *miles* of runway for safe operations.[20]

And that is pretty much the way it went from then on. Legitimate doubts about the need for the aircraft, the soundness of its design, and the political maneuverings of the other manufacturers and their friends obliged the Air Force and the DOD to conduct ever more rigorous studies of future requirements and the C-17's suitability to fill them. These studies included the CMMS (1981), the Mobility Requirements Study (1992), the Mobility Requirements Study—Bottom-Up Review Update (1995), and a host of design reviews, program milestone decisions, cost certifications, airlift force mix analyses, and more. In general, all of these assessments validated the need for an aircraft of the C-17's characteristics. They all also had little or no impact on the determination of Lockheed and Boeing to debunk the C-17 and to sell their planes as alternatives.

Austere airfield requirements remained both the justification for the new design and the main avenue through which its opponents attacked it. Defense analyst Jeffrey Record, for example, wrote that the plane was a "hybrid design that maximizes the preferred values neither of a strategic lifter nor a tactical lifter." Record, a former legislative assistant to Senator Nunn and consultant to Lockheed, went on to extol the virtues of both the C-5 and the C-130 as a team of aircraft better able than the C-17 to fill the Air Force's air mobility needs.[21] With more objectivity, the CBO at about the same time found that Congress could save $3.7 billion by buying an aircraft other than the C-17 to achieve the 66 million ton miles per day (MTMD) goal set in the CMMS. But, the CBO cautioned, Congress "would have to weigh this earlier gain in capability against the qualitative improvements expected with the C-17."[22] To airlift practitioners, "qualitative improvements" were what the C-17 was all about, particularly where they added up to getting the most through a given airfield infrastructure. Writing as part of a broad-based effort to retain congressional and DOD support for the design, the new commander in chief of MAC, General Duane H. Cassidy, wrote, "Our solution . . . for providing the airlift that will be useful in the fluid battlefields of the future is the C-17." The key to that usefulness, Cassidy asserted, was the plane's ability to "pick up forces and equipment at the main operating base in the US and deliver them directly to the battlefield locations."[23]

Fortunately for the proponents of the C-17, the aircraft really wasn't much more expensive than its alternatives in terms of overall life-cycle costs. MAC cost estimates in 1984 placed the cost for a ready-to-fly C-17 at around $100.3 million each and C-5Bs at $141.0 million.[24] Even on the basis of gross lift capacity, the C-5's 41 percent greater cost was hard to justify, since it offered only a 28 percent increase over the C-17, or 222,000 versus 172,000 pounds of payload. In a milestone report, the CBO declared that a fleet of C-17s would be more flexible operationally than one of C-5s and would cost $17.9 billion less over a thirty-year life cycle and require 16,500 fewer personnel to operate.[25] The C-5 could not match the C-17's "direct delivery" ability to move military forces from their main bases to forward airfields. Furthermore, its higher maintenance and personnel costs and lower expected daily flying rate would more than offset the initially greater acquisition cost of the C-17.

Through the 1980s, fumbling McDonnell Douglas managers were the real Achilles' heel of the C-17 program. During the decade, the company's senior managers were overloaded with development and marketing problems in their commercial aircraft line, growing debt, a shrinking pool of engineers and skilled production personnel, and a series of lawsuits. In such a context, the insistent pressure from air force acquisition managers for progress on the C-17 program drove a wedge between military and corporate project managers. Civil-military coordination reached a nadir in the latter 1980s, just as C-17 designers ran into a host of challenges with the plane's avionics, flight control, defensive features, and other subelements. Resulting production delays and the ongoing political battles steadily drove up the plane's costs, while its weight increased and performance went down. Faced by these management and performance flaws, the DOD in January 1989 limited initial production to just ten planes. Further production authorizations would be contingent on McDonnell Douglas getting the program back on track and on the outcome of pending tests and reviews of the aircraft.[26] When things did not get better at McDonnell Douglas and congressional support of the C-17 "nose-dived" in 1993, the DOD told McDonnell Douglas leaders that production would stop at forty aircraft unless they got the program and the delivery schedule under control.[27]

The wobbling state of the C-17 program reopened the quest to replace it with existing aircraft. Recognizing in 1993 that the C-17 might not make it into quantity production, the new commander of MAC, General Ronald R. Fogleman, directed his staff to look into buying a nondevelopmental airlift aircraft (NDAA) to pick up the slack, at least in terms of gross lift capacity. Fogleman needed the NDAA fallback on hand not only to offset the possible failure of the C-17 program but also in light of the accelerating technical decline of the C-141 fleet.[28] Predictably, Boeing and Lockheed put forward 747s and C-5s. Recognizing that a recovery of the C-17 might bring their window of opportunity to a close at any time, both companies and their home court politicians engaged in high-pressure sales and lobbying campaigns. Reviewing the free-for-all, one reporter said, "The debates . . . now raging over the C-17 are dominated by lawmakers who . . . see hometown jobs at stake . . . [and] questions as to what the military's genuine needs are and how to meet them often are treated as afterthoughts."[29] The frenzy came to an end, mostly, when McDonnell Douglas's improving management and delivery success led the DOD to announce in February 1995 that the "C-17 Globemaster III will continue to be acquired as the Defense Department's core airlifter."[30]

Shifting strategic circumstances added to the instability of C-17 development in the early 1990s. For some, the collapse of the Soviet Union in 1989 removed much of the logic for purchasing such a specialized aircraft. Most important, in April 1990 Secretary of Defense Richard Cheney announced that the program would be capped at 120 aircraft.[31] In all likelihood, this announcement was more about ameliorating political pressure on the program than a firm statement of its declining importance. After all, the C-17 had been designed to provide a capability needed in every major scenario considered in the CMMS and other studies thereafter. Indeed, the original plan to buy 180 C-17s was predicated on 180 C-141s remaining in the reserve components until either more C-17s or a follow-on aircraft went into production. By the early 1990s, however, the Air Force calculated that the C-141 fleet would wear out sooner than planned. So under the circumstances, the first 120 planes would be a start but almost certainly not the end of C-17 production.

In reality, the need for the C-17 was too obvious and becoming too pressing for the program to die. Even in the midst of McDonnell Douglas's management woes and delivery delays, Congress authorized $1.7 billion in 1987 to begin production. When workers started on the first test aircraft in August 1988, the program was three years behind the initial schedule. By the time the first production aircraft arrived at Charleston AFB, South Carolina, on June 14, 1993, the program was another two years late. Even when the poor conditions of arriving aircraft delayed the first squadron from reaching initial operational capability until December 1994, seven years behind schedule, deliveries continued, and the Defense Acquisition Board in the following November endorsed an initial production run of 120 aircraft, with more likely to come later.[32] By that time, the program was secure, with only the final number of aircraft to be produced really in question.

If any one factor saved the C-17, it was the unwavering requirement for an aircraft of its characteristics. The 1995 Mobility Requirements Study—Bottom-Up Review Update accepted the DOD's reduction in the total airlift goal from the 66 MTMD of the CMMS to 49.4–51.8 MTMD. But it also reaffirmed the need for 120 to 140 "C-17-equivalent" aircraft. Since only the C-17 was "equivalent" to the C-17 in operational flexibility, the report essentially was an endorsement of that plane over the C-5 and Boeing 747 NDAA. A derivative Strategic Airlift Force Mix Analysis hammered the point home, declaring, "There is no existing substitute for the C-17 . . . [and] no combinations of C-5Ds and/or C-33s [Boeing 747 NDAAs] that can provide the equivalent of 120 C-17s."[33] A contemporary RAND analysis added to the total number of C-17s needed by assessing that each combat theater engaged in a "major regional contingency" would require the support of around 12 C-17s over and above those required for the strategic effort.[34] As had been the case for over a decade, experienced airlift planners and analysts usually found the C-17's operational flexibility and direct delivery capabilities essential.

Sheer willpower and persistence on the part of the aircraft's supporters also contributed to its success. Within the military, every commander of MAC and the Air Mobility Command (AMC) supported and advocated the aircraft tirelessly. Their ranks included initial skeptics, like General Fogleman, who initiated the NDAA program in 1993 but in 1995 said of the C-17, "This is an airplane the nation needs to move its surface forces forward to fight. And we need them now."[35] Many mid-career airlift officers tied their professional destinies to the aircraft. Thomas R. Mikolajcik, for example, was involved in the design competition for the C-17 as a major and went on to command the first C-17 wing, the 437th at Charleston, South Carolina, as a brigadier general.[36] One of his contemporaries, Duncan J. McNabb, served as the C-17 action officer on the MAC commander's personal staff as a major; commanded the second wing of C-17s, the 62nd at McChord AFB, Washington; and finished his career as the commander of AMC. In the mid-1990s, this author wrote a pair of articles to explain that the NDAA concept violated the basic organizational doctrines of the airlift system, while the C-17 was exactly the right aircraft to fill the military's role in that system.[37]

In the civil realm, CRAF member airlines supported the C-17 indirectly by arguing that a military purchase would violate the new 1987 National Airlift Policy document. This document, signed by the president, replaced the 1960 Presidentially Approved Courses of Action. Among other things, it reaffirmed that the military would acquire aircraft only to cover lift requirements that the airlines were not equipped or available to handle in a timely manner. By acquiring a civil-based transport, then, AMC would violate the national objectives of giving the airlines as much business as possible to incentivize their membership in CRAF.[38] The C-17 had many enemies, but it also had numerous friends inside and outside of the military.

Last, the plane was saved by the successful efforts of McDonnell Douglas program managers and air force acquisition officers to improve the quality of the C-17s delivered to the Air Force and, eventually, to get deliveries ahead of schedule.[39] By the end of 1995, a year that began with the fate of the aircraft still in doubt, AMC commander General Robert L. Rutherford reported that the plane had performed "much better than we had hoped" in a recent reliability, maintainability, and availability evaluation.[40] McDonnell Douglas's close coordination and support in that process contributed to the success of the participating C-17s, which achieved a 99.2 percent departure reliability rate in 513 sorties flown over a period of thirty days. By then many government and military leaders, including former opponents, were singing the praises of the plane and McDonnell Douglas, which had "visibly turned the program around."[41]

Implications

In the messiness of policymaking in a democracy, where every interest has a voice, the contentiousness and prolongation of the C-17's development should not be surprising. The money involved in modernizing airlift drew in every manufacturer of large aircraft in the country that saw it as a ripe plum or, in the case of McDonnell Douglas, a lifeboat in the storm of its economic woes. What distinguished the struggle for airlift dollars in the 1980s and early 1990s was the unwillingness of Lockheed, Boeing, and their supporters to accept the Air Force's selection of the C-17 to fill the C-X requirement. Their resulting political maneuverings and propaganda efforts reflected their narrow visions of the airlift mission and their simple business imperative of capturing the market. Ignoring such a lucrative market opportunity would have raised the ire of their stockholders and constituents, so the leaders of Lockheed and Boeing and their vest-pocket politicians just kept coming back, regardless of the logic or lack of logic of their sales strategies.

Whether the persistence of these companies was a good thing is a matter of perspective. Reflecting a pretty common view of those trying to get the C-17 into the fleet, General Duane Cassidy chaffed at the "arrogance" of corporate personnel and other outsiders presuming to tell the military what it needed.[42] He also might have added that the resulting delays substantially increased the cost of the program. But besides being an inevitable element of military procurement in a democracy, the repeated assaults of the C-17's critics did force the military to think very hard about it. While the Air Force's and DOD's many studies of the aircraft resulted in few if any fundamental design changes, they did refine the military's understanding of how the plane actually could be used and with what impact on theater campaigns. Beginning with the simple idea of designing an aircraft that could generate more throughput at austere airfields, the Air Force came to understand it as a revolutionary "direct delivery" platform that could lift heavy combat units to the very edges of future battles. Many at the time questioned the logic of risking such an expensive aircraft so far forward. But airlift planners took the idea seriously, as later events would prove. Last, the hard fight over the C-17 seasoned the future leaders of the airlift forces and increased their connection and credibility with other senior service leaders and the overseas combatant commands. The successful coordination of so many organizations in support of a troubled aircraft program laid the foundations for a successful introduction of the new aircraft into operations.

21. The First Gulf War

IT WAS AN AIRLIFT characterized by superlatives. In terms of daily effort and ton miles flown, the airlift of American combat forces during Desert Shield and Desert Storm, the defensive and offensive phases of the 1990–1991 Gulf War, respectively, was by far the largest and fastest in history. More raw tonnage was moved during the Berlin Airlift of 1948–1949 but only over a distance of about 250 miles. So the Berlin effort amounted to an average of 1.7 million ton miles per day (MTMD), while that of Desert Shield produced 13.6 MTMD.[1] Beyond that, Desert Shield was the first time battle-ready divisions were moved over intercontinental distances by air. Within the Gulf War area of operations (AOR) U.S. Central Command (CENTCOM's), American and other nation's theater airlift forces produced similarly impressive results, moving thousands of tons of matériel and tens of thousands of personnel.

But the Gulf War also revealed troubling shortfalls in American air mobility capabilities. A variety of shortfalls in planning, training, organization, and technology prevented the strategic fleet from producing more than a fraction of its 49 MTMD capacity.[2] The theater fleet, composed almost exclusively of C-130s, did better in terms of meeting general expectations, but it too suffered from limitations in its ability to meet all of the demands placed on it. So a post-conflict analysis of Desert Shield and Desert Storm suggests that the American airlift fleet was stronger than it ever had been but still needed significant overhaul to fulfill future missions.

Strategic Airlift

The strategic circumstances of the Gulf War placed a premium on intercontinental airlift. When Iraq's dictator, Saddam Hussein, sent his army into Kuwait on August 2, 1990, he posed an immediate threat to the rest of the Arabian Gulf oil-producing states. His most important reasons for going into Kuwait had been to negate Iraq's debts to the emirate and to gain control of its oil fields. Next in line was Saudi Arabia, to which Iraq also owed a lot of money, and the oil fields of which were just south of the Iraqi divisions now lining up on its northeastern border. Faced by Saddam's ability and possible intent to advance down the western shores of the Gulf and take control of most of the world's oil supplies, the U.S. government conferred with local leaders and on August 8 committed military forces to the region. The imminence of the threat made an airlift of combat-ready forces essential. Only airlift could get blocking forces to the region in time to forestall any Iraqi thrust south.

But time and distance also constrained CENTCOM's use of the airlift force. Typically, transports would take two to four days to make the 14,000- to 19,000-mile round-trips between Southwest Asia (SWA) and the continental United States (CONUS). The actual throughput of the airlift fleet, the amount of people and matériel it could deliver in a given amount of time, went down accordingly. Adjusting to reality, CENTCOM optimized the airlift flow by moving only light forces by air in the first weeks of Desert Shield. During the month of August, those movements included about fifteen fighter squadrons, four bomber squadrons, numerous air support units, the entire 82nd Airborne Division, much of the 101st Airborne Division, the personnel of two Marine Expeditionary Brigades (MEBs), and a host of ground support units and organizations. There was not enough airlift capacity in the world to move heavy armored and mechanized divisions to the region by air in a useful span of time. The heavy equipment of those units and the MEBs—tanks, self-propelled artillery, large trucks, and so on—traveled to the theater by sea.

Fortunately, the Military Airlift Command (MAC) and its military and civil components had never been so ready to conduct large-scale intercontinental operations. Nearly a decade after the 1981 Congressionally Mandated Mobility Study had decreed an airlift system capable of 66 MTMD, MAC's fleet in 1990 could produce 49 MTMD, at least on paper. At its core, the command's long-range fleet consisted of 83 C-5s and 250 C-141s, and a crew–aircraft ratio of 4.0: 2 crews from air force reserve associate wings and 2 from active air force wings. The Civil Reserve Airlift Fleet (CRAF) was also available through either contract or outright mobilization. If all three of its long-range international stages were mobilized, CRAF could reinforce the military with 252 passenger jets and 150 cargo jets, each also with four crews available to keep them flying.[3] In addition, MAC had access to some of the 59 KC-10 tanker transports operated by Strategic Air Command (SAC).

Organizationally, the command also was as ready as it ever had been. After decades of deployment exercises and contingencies, the community of MAC planners and operators knew how to lay down robust air lines of communications to unexpected destinations. They had an extensive body of histories, doctrines, ingrained expertise, computerized planning systems, global communications, and organizations from which to draw for vision, guidance, and capacity. Even before official orders came on August 7 to start the airlift, MAC commander General Hansford T. Johnson activated his crisis action team to prepare the command for whatever came next. By the time the first C-141 took off from Charleston AFB bound for Riyadh at 10:54 a.m. local time on the 7th, MAC staffers and operators in the field were deep into preparations to move air force combat wings and the 82nd Airborne to the Arabian Peninsula. Their task was eased by the fact that the MAC fleet was in motion already when the balloon went up in Kuwait. As always, the command was flying hundreds of sorties every day in support of the routine needs of America's global military power. So once told to start a lift to SWA, MAC commanders had only to redirect the airlift stream in a new direction, not start it up cold. Finally, as part of its global responsibilities, MAC possessed a set of air bases in Germany (mainly Rhein-Main and Ramstein) and Spain (Torrejon, Morón, and Rota) about midway on the routes to the Middle East. When augmented with additional personnel and equipment, they proved capable of servicing and refueling large numbers of transient aircraft.[4] MAC may not have been "thinking" about the Middle East on August 1. But on August 2, it was ready to ramp up for a big airlift anywhere, and that made all the difference.

Just as fortunate, the airlift of American forces into SWA was part of a larger logistics effort that, in total, made the movement of truly combat-ready forces possible. In the decade prior to the war, Saudi Arabia and other potential allies in the region, often with American funding, had built a number of first-class civil and military airfields capable of serving as major aerial ports of debarkation (APODs) and of bedding down tactical air units. In concert with this buildup of infrastructure, the U.S. military had positioned large quantities of matériel and supplies in or near the theater. Out in the middle of the Indian Ocean, anchored at the island of Diego Garcia, the five ships of Maritime Prepositioning Squadron 2 (MPS 2) stood by with enough equipment and supplies to outfit the 16,500 marines in an MEB and then supply it in combat for thirty days. Two other MPSs were available in the Pacific and Mediterranean to reinforce the supply effort. Twelve afloat prepositioning ships also were anchored at Diego and were loaded with 117,000 tons of vehicles, supplies, and ordinance earmarked largely for the Army and the Air Force. The Air Force also had large quantities of Harvest Falcon equipment and supplies located in or near the AOR to support the bed downs of ten operational wings and 55,000 personnel at "bare bases" in the theater—that is, bases offering only runways, parking ramps, and water to arriving units. These prepositioned supplies would not support the entire movement of forces into the theater during Desert Shield, but their early availability allowed American commanders and airlift planners to focus on moving combat forces, rather than basic supplies, in the early weeks of the deployment.

Sealift also went a long way to making the airlift effort effective. As the naval component of the U.S. Transportation Command (TRANSCOM), the Military Sealift Command (MSC) transported the bulk of unit equipment and supplies to the theater. Most of MSC's capacity for supporting Desert Shield resided in several reserve fleets of cargo ships and tankers. The ships in the prepositioning fleets were available almost immediately. Fully crewed and preloaded, they could get under way within hours of notification. All of the maritime prepositioning ships in MPS-2 (Diego Garcia) and MPS-3 (Saipan) got under way on August 8 and arrived at Al Jubayl, Saudi Arabia, between August 15–30 to deliver 105,000 tons for the 1st and 7th MEBs.[5] Next to get under way were TRANSCOM's eight fast sealift ships, which were berthed in several U.S. ports and generally ready to sail on ninety-six-hours' notice. At 50,000 tons displacement, these very large roll-on-roll-off (RORO) ships were designed to carry trucks, armored vehicles, helicopters, and other types of vehicles. The *Capella*, the first to arrive in Saudi Arabia after an eighteen-day voyage, carried 20,000 tons of cargo, including 135 armored vehicles. Capable of making thirty-three knots, fast sealift ships made thirty-two trips to the Gulf during Desert Shield. They unloaded 360,000 tons of unit equipment and other cargoes. By comparison, the entire airlift fleet delivered 334,000 tons during the same period, and the *Capella*'s first run alone would have required a fleet of approximately 130 C-5s to replicate in the same amount of time.[6] Progressively during Desert Shield, TRANSCOM also activated seventy-two ships in the Maritime Administration's Ready Reserve Fleet. In all, these ships and MSC's partial- and whole-ship charters of U.S. and non-U.S. cargo vessels accounted for 496 shiploads of cargo arriving in the theater and carried 95 percent of all unit equipment, dry bulk cargo, and liquid products delivered to CENTCOM forces. Absent sealift, then, the main product of the airlift effort would have been large numbers of unequipped and undersupplied soldiers and airmen standing around in the desert without offensive and very little defensive power.

Once kicked off, Desert Shield proceeded in two phases. Phase 1 ran from August 7 through November 7. By the end of that phase, American transportation elements had delivered 235,000 personnel, about 170,000 tons of dry cargo, 565 air force combat aircraft, and the infantry, armor, aviation, air defense, combat support, and services elements of four divisions and two aviation brigades making up the XVIII Airborne Corps. A marine expeditionary force of 42,000 troops was also in place, complete with vehicles, tanks, and almost 200 aircraft. Virtually all of the personnel of these units had arrived on MAC transports or commercial charters. Planes also brought in the lighter equipment and helicopters of the 82nd and 101st Airborne Divisions. But the bulk of everything else came by sea.[7] Phase 2 commenced on November 8 with President George H. W. Bush's announcement that the allies would double the force present in the Gulf to give it the offensive power needed to defeat the Iraqi Army and liberate Kuwait. This reinforcement required the movement of the three mechanized divisions of III Corps to Saudi Arabia. Once again, MAC moved passengers, light equipment and vehicles, some helicopters, and supplies. Sealift moved the Corps' M1 tanks, M3 armored fighting vehicles, engineer equipment, and the like. The flow continued through the execution of Desert Storm, January 16 to February 24, 1991. During Phase 2, MAC carried another 316,261 passengers and at least 345,468 tons of matériel and supplies into the conflict area.[8]

Because the visible parts of airlift streams are the takeoffs and landings of big jets at various airfields, it is easy for lay observers to miss the gigantic complexity of such operations. But by the time the first C-141 from Charleston landed at Riyadh at 10:00 a.m. local time on August 8, there was a chain of C-141s and C-5s airborne already behind it. Many of them carried personnel and equipment to flesh out MAC service and support units at bases along the route to SWA. A few carried advanced parties to prepare the way for the flood of units and supplies soon to arrive. More carried the first echelons of combat units. First to arrive were the personnel and twenty-five F-15Cs of the 71st Tactical Fighter Squadron that same day. Between August 8 and 12, 106 MAC flights deposited over 4,000 soldiers—mostly members of the 2nd Brigade of the 82nd Airborne Division—along with fifteen AH-64 Apaches, eighteen Sheridan light tanks, and twelve 105mm howitzers.[9] Soon 100 or more U.S. transport aircraft were landing in the AOR every day, carrying an average of about 2,000 passengers and 2,200 tons of cargo. The airlift flow would slacken during October and November, when most of the XVIII Airborne Corps was in place, but it would pick up again to as many as 127 aircraft per day, when the Phase 2 buildup began.[10] With big planes stretched out about every ten minutes over the Atlantic, MAC planners coined a new term, "aluminum bridge," to capture the meaning of what they were doing. Almost 8,000 miles long, the bridge could be seen only in the mind's eye. But it took little imagination to realize what an amazing creation of planning, coordination, discipline, and innovation it was—a mechanism acutely dependent on the smooth workings and interconnections of its many parts.

To reach this pace, MAC strained every fiber of its bodies of expertise and capability. In a series of call-ups, the command activated 7,600 personnel from virtually every one of its units of the Air Force Reserve and Air National Guard. As an example of the value of these activations, reserve augmenters allowed the 625th Consolidated Aircraft Maintenance Squadron at Torrejon AB, Spain, to handle a traffic flow eight times larger than its normal peacetime levels.[11] MAC also activated the first two stages of CRAF. Stage 1 activated on August 17, bringing a total of thirty-eight long-range passenger and cargo aircraft into service; Stage 2 came on line on January 17, 1991, placing seventy-eight more aircraft under MAC's direct control. During the course of the buildup and the end of active hostilities, civil carriers under contract and in CRAF flew some 3,606 missions for MAC, carrying 171,100 tons of cargo and 405,448 personnel.[12] In a practice harkening back to earlier wars, MAC and TRANSCOM also established a "Desert Express" service on October 30, 1990, to expedite the movement of "war-stopper" repair parts and supplies to the AOR. At its initiation, the service consisted of a C-141 leaving Charleston AFB, South Carolina, every day at 12:30 p.m. En route, the plane received priority servicing at its intermediate stop of Torrejon AB, Spain, and priority unloading and distribution services at its destinations, Dhahran and Riyadh. The value of the service was such that many army and air force units hand delivered urgent packages to Charleston to ensure that they got to the AOR the next morning. During the Phase 2 buildup, MAC also established a "European Express" out of Germany and increased the Desert Express mission to two flights per day.[13]

Help came from several outside sources, most important from the fleet of sixty KC-10 Extenders operated by SAC but managed in a dual-role status with MAC. By agreement, SAC had priority claim to the big aircraft. Their primary role as tankers was to support unit moves, during which they would refuel the aircraft of deploying squadrons in flight while simultaneously carrying their people and equipment. SAC moved its own bomber and tanker squadrons in this way.[14] In all, SAC tankers lifted around 14,200 personnel and 4,800 tons of the command's own cargo. The rest, presumably, went forward in the common-user system. Finally, SAC made a handful of KC-10s available to MAC schedulers during Desert Shield and released twenty to them once fighting began on January 16. In total, MAC estimated that KC-10s lifted 4,185 passengers and 25,100 tons in the common-user transport role, plus more during fighter drags and moving SAC personnel outside of CENTCOM's control.[15] MAC operators appreciated the help, of course. But they also found that their high cargo decks made KC-10s difficult to load, and their curved cabin walls made it necessary to re-contour pallets built up for C-5s and C-141s.[16] But as the first sustained use of tanker aircraft in a "swing" transport role, Desert Shield provided proof of the general wisdom of the dual-ownership arrangement.

More help came on a smaller scale from the U.S. Navy and other nations. In late December 1990, as the Phase 2 airlift was hitting its peak, four navy C-9 squadrons (VR-55, 57, 58, and 59) each sent three planes and about 245 personnel to augment TRANSCOM operations. Three VRs were based in Germany and one at Naples, Italy. Initially, they moved passengers to the AOR during the Phase 2 surge. In February the Germany-based VRs also shuttled bombs and fuses from Germany to Morón AB, Spain, to support B-52 operations. In all, these twelve aircraft carried about 18,000 passengers and 3,750 tons of cargo between January and March.[17] Korea and Japan also participated, the former by chartering Korean Air Lines aircraft and the latter by chartering American flag aircraft to carry cargoes to the Gulf region.

Overall, foreign augmentation was marked more by its absence than contribution to the allied cause. Almost all non-U.S. civil carriers and their crews simply refused to participate. European countries—Germany, notably—further restricted U.S. operations during airport "quiet hours," even during the height of Desert Storm, when U.S. bases and Israeli cities were under attack by Iraqi ScUD missiles. Rather than participate in the war effort, European carriers much preferred keeping their planes on the winter tourist routes and capturing international market shares abandoned by mobilized U.S. carriers.

When all was said and done, the Gulf War airlift effort was impressive in scale and strategic impact. In all, the United States and the thirty-three other nations involved sent over and took home more than 600,000 troops; 508,000 of these were American, and 99 percent of them traveled by air. About 540,000 tons of unit equipment and cargo went into the theater by air, representing about 5 percent of the 9.7 million tons of cargo and fuels delivered to the AOR.[18] Despite its relatively small share of the total lift effort, airlift nevertheless exerted great strategic effect. The American air and infantry forces it rushed to the front unhinged any plans the Iraqi Army may have had for moving farther south.

Rather than pick a fight with the United States and the organizing coalition of allied states ranged against him, Saddam Hussein ordered his army to dig in. At that point, his ultimate defeat became only a matter of time.

Theater Airlift

CENTCOM commanders, particularly Commander in Chief H. Norman Schwarzkopf, knew from the start that air force theater airlift capabilities would be important in the unfolding contingency. The only real questions were what missions would they perform and how many C-130s would be needed. These uncertainties were unavoidable, of course, since no one knew at the beginning how big the conflict would become. So theater airlift commanders brought in two increments of C-130 squadrons and a handful of Lear C-21s. The first increment was sized to support defensive operations, and the second was sized to round out lift capabilities for the coming offensive. As events transpired, their judgment of how many planes they would need turned out to be very accurate.

Brigadier General Fredric N. Buckingham led the first increment of C-130 squadrons into the theater. He was one of the most experienced tactical airlift commanders in MAC, having flown C-130s for his entire career and commanded two airlift wings and then rising to vice commander of the 21st Air Force at McGuire AFB, New Jersey. The 40th Tactical Airlift Squadron, from Pope AFB, North Carolina, brought the first sixteen C-130s into the theater on August 11. By early October, Buckingham had ninety-six C-130s on hand, the original strength requested by CENTCOM.[19] Consistent with established practices, Buckingham became the commander of airlift forces (COMALF) responsible for facilitating the inbound strategic airlift flow and directing theater airlift forces for the CENTCOM Air Force Component (CENTAF). Accordingly, he set up an airlift control center in CENTAF headquarters at Riyadh to plan and coordinate operations in theater. Immediately on arrival, these units began distributing cargoes arriving by air and sea to deployed units.[20]

Brigadier General Edwin E. Tenoso replaced Buckingham in mid-October as the COMALF. Buckingham had fractured a foot, and, besides, his boss at the 21st Air Force, Major General Paul E. Landers Jr., needed his deputy back to run the air bridge to Saudi Arabia. In contrast to Buckingham's résumé, Tenoso's background was a more eclectic mix of assignments in radar picket aircraft (EC-121), forward air control in Vietnam (O-1s), C-141 units, and staff assignments. He had little direct C-130 experience. But he had served as the aide to General William G. Moore when he commanded the MAC's 22nd Air

Force at Travis AFB, California, and then the 13th Air Force at Clark AFB, the Philippines. These assignments, Tenoso felt, gave him a good understanding of both strategic and tactical airlift from the senior commander level.[21] Later, Tenoso commanded the 62nd Military Airlift Wing at McChord AFB, Washington, and was serving as vice commander of the 22nd Air Force when sent to Saudi Arabia. Tenoso continued Buckingham's efforts to increase the productivity and efficiency of C-130 operations. In November he tightened up the management and support of his widely dispersed squadrons by activating the 1610th Airlift Division to direct operations and three provisional wings to oversee the squadrons directly. He also began pressing for additional aircraft, being convinced that demand for theater airlift support would mushroom once hostilities began. In January 1991 Tenoso won approval to bring his force up to 144 C-130s, including 5 provided by the Republic of Korea Air Force, and 8 C-21s.

For the most part, the C-130 force flew routine training and logistics missions. But once the air war began, a significant portion of it helped move the XVIII Airborne Corps from positions near the Arabian Gulf to flanking positions opposite the extreme western end of the Iraqi lines. In support of the westward shift, army logisticians used 4,000 heavy trucks to transport the Corps' bulk logistics—mostly rations, fuels, and munitions.[22] But to save time, minimize vehicle wear, preserve secrecy, and avoid exposing personnel to the hazardous roads in the region, most of the Corps' people and light vehicles made the trip in air force C-130s. Most flew about 400 nautical miles from King Fahd Air Base near Jubayl to a stretch of highway near the town of Rahfa. While the road was paved, it was only thirty-eight feet wide, compared to the sixty feet normally required for C-130 assault landings. Nevertheless, 1,175 C-130 missions landed at the strip between January 16 and 28.[23] Flying day and night in radio silence, the Hercs arrived at intervals as short as seven minutes (the Army's truck flow past the same spot equaled eighteen per minute) to deliver 13,843 passengers and 9,396 short tons of cargo. During the short, four-day ground war that followed, the Air Division was called on only twice to air deliver emergency supplies. In all, the C-130 fleet flew 13,900 missions during Desert Shield and Desert Storm to move a total of about 159,000 tons of cargo and 184,000 passengers.[24]

In addition to the Air Force, the Army, Navy, and Marine Corps all contributed to the theater airlift effort, though on a much smaller scale and almost exclusively in support of their organic needs. The Army brought in 163 CH-47 helicopters. These helicopters and smaller ones, mainly UH-60s, moved plenty of people and matériel. The Chinooks alone flew 16,955 hours. But with useful radii of action in the 100-nautical-mile range, they simply didn't have the legs to contribute more than short-range logistical lifts within division and corps boundaries and administrative lifts of personnel and high-priority cargo between bases and headquarters. Once the ground war began on August 24, they expended most of their sorties moving supplies forward in support of deep air assaults and to resupply maneuver and artillery units that had outstripped ground lines of communication.[25] The Navy and U.S. Marines also established a squadron of twenty-five C-130s in the theater (five from the Navy and twenty from the latter). But, once again, these aircraft operated independently from the air force theater airlift effort and almost exclusively in support of their own services.[26]

Shortfalls

For all of the accomplishments of the various components of the national airlift system, there was no doubt after the war that they had not performed up to general expectations. In all cases, their productivity fell short of their theoretical capacity. Several post-conflict civil and military studies identified and quantified the causes of these shortfalls. These included organizational, communications, technological, infrastructure, and supply problems. Undisciplined estimates and prioritization of transportation requirements by supported units were major problems in the early days of the conflict. In aggregate these issues significantly degraded the throughput of people and matériel into the theater and, consequently, highlighted the need for a broad overhaul of the airlift system.

Shortfalls in the airlift system emerged from the start of Desert Shield and generally persisted throughout the conflict. CENTCOM's planning for a major intervention in SWA was undeveloped in August 1990. Thus, there was no time-phased force deployment list (TPFDL) available as a common reference for who would move, with what supplies, from where to where, when, and who would move them.[27] So planners built the TPFDL on the fly, with units already in motion and with predictable consequences for the cohesion and efficiency of the airlift. Most important, the marry-ups of transports and major units seldom went well in the first few weeks of Desert Shield. A great deal of time and potential lift went to waste as airplanes showed up on ramps with no one around, loads improperly configured, and incomplete or improper documentation. Poor coordination, in fact, contributed to at least 1,031 of the 3,120 mission delays during the war. On average C-5 missions experienced eight to thirteen hours of delay while C-141s were held up about six hours. Just as wasteful, C-5s capable of lifting 100 tons went out with an average of 61 tons while 45-ton capacity C-141s averaged only 19 tons.[28] Fortunately, the Iraqis had decided to sit and merely bluster about the deployment of American forces, so no casualties resulted from the routine delays and wastage in the system.

Disciplining the airlift priorities system was a major challenge. In their determination to get to the theater ready to fight, many units took to inflating their movement priorities and to assigning the highest priority to their supply requests. Some individual items and even whole cONEX containers were marked mysteriously with recipient addresses like "TOP SECRET, rush, Riyadh." Air traffic specialists at the APODs did their best to move such loads, but the glut soon overwhelmed their marshaling yards. The Desert Express service addressed this problem simply by allocating so many pallet positions in the C-141s to each service and leaving it to their logisticians to decide what their rush cargoes really were. MAC traffic personnel also quit accepting cargoes that were not properly addressed or had not been prioritized by proper authorities.

Relative to the performance of the strategic airlift fleet, the C-130s operating in the AOR came closer to meeting expectations but not without raising questions about the expectations themselves. Theater airlift units were manned at a ratio of 1.5 complete crews per aircraft, as compared to 4.0 crews per C-5 and C-141. Consequently, plans called for a daily utilization rate of 4.0 hours per day per aircraft. In practice that's just about what the units produced. During Desert Storm, the daily utilization rate averaged 3.7 hours. What operations revealed, however, was that the Hercules' design was getting a little long in the tooth for modern war. The planes were small and slow in relation to strategic airlifters. These attributes restricted their ability to distribute the glut of troops and equipment arriving at theater debarkation points and their ability to support in-theater movements such as the westward shift of the XVIII Airborne Corps. So while the tactical utility and the ability of the Hercs to get into and out of short, dirt airstrips drew praise from all quadrants, they were not a panacea for all of the logistics and mobility requirements of modern armies and air forces operating in expansive theaters.[29]

General Tenoso and his command faced a host of other challenges. As the CENTCOM COMALF he was responsible for the theater airlift effort and for directing the reception and onward air shipment of cargoes coming in by strategic airlift. But he often felt like the "red-haired stepchild" of CENTAF. Sym-

bolic of the relationship, his airlift control center was located in tents in the parking lot of the Saudi Air Force headquarters building, where all other CENTAF
staff elements resided in air-conditioned comfort. Although Tenoso never felt
isolated or taken for granted by the CENTAF commander, Lieutenant General
Charles (Chuck) Horner, the physical separation from the rest of headquarters
did undermine coordination. As an example, the CENTAF staff failed to coordinate the airlift routes into and out of Rahfa during the XVIII Airborne Corps'
movement. As a consequence, Tenoso was stunned to find out at the start of
operations that his crews were expected to fly in and out of the forward field at
the same altitude along a narrow corridor with inadequate navigation facilities
or ground references. When Tenoso threatened to "stop the airlift" unless he was
given two altitudes, CENTAF made the necessary airspace allocation.[30]

On the strategic front, Tenoso and his staff struggled with a number of little
problems that in aggregate significantly undermined the efficiency of the inbound
airlift flow. The K-loader cargo pallet transfer vehicles coming off the prepositioning ships were in poor repair. With only half of them in operation, Tenoso
demanded that MAC send him "every goddamn K-loader available," including
those in war reserve stocks. A critical shortage developed in aluminum cargo
pallets and cargo netting, as air force and army field units took to keeping them
as tent floors, bunker roofs, and sunshades. Airlift teams solved the problem,
at least partially, by driving out into the field and gathering them up wherever
they found them. The challenge of efficiently interfacing arriving strategic aircraft and theater C-130s was never solved to Tenoso's satisfaction. But the Desert Express service made it easier for him to have C-130s standing ready to load
the highest priority cargoes and distribute them to their destinations with minimum delay. Greater priorities discipline at the APODs began to reduce the
amount of cONEX containers sitting at Riyadh and Dhahran with incomplete
addresses and manifests. At one time, though, Tenoso had over a thousand
containers sitting in a yard of "frustrated cargo" with addresses like "Top Secret"
and "Desert Storm" and nothing more.[31]

CRAF came closest to meeting expectations during the conflict. Member
airlines volunteered planes and crews from the first day of the conflict and
responded willingly and on time when the military activated Phase 1 and 2 of
the long-range international segment. But once mobilized, many CRAF flights
suffered delays or lost missions due to the same planning and coordination
shortfalls affecting the military components. CRAF also had more passenger
aircraft than the military needed but not enough cargo transports. The result

was a steady backlog of sustainment cargo at major aerial ports of embarkation (APOEs). More troubling for the future were several unanticipated problems with the mobilization process. The immediate concerns were over wartime insurance and support for civil crews flying into a war zone. Initially, the government insurance pool was capitalized at only $50 million, about half the cost of a single modern jumbo jet. Provisions for providing civil crews with current intelligence on threats, theater communication procedures, and chemical defense clothing and equipment were just as inadequate. Sheer patriotism motivated the airlines and their crews to go in anyway, despite the possibility that the former were not insured for losses and the latter might face attacks by Iraqi ScUD missiles, impacting forward airfields with chemical warheads.

The war was difficult financially for many of the carriers. They lost market shares to unmobilized airlines in the United States and particularly to foreign carriers that took the war as an opportunity to expand into American market shares. Already weakened by the hypercompetition that afflicted the airline industry as a consequence of the 1978 Airline Deregulation Act, several carriers went under. Pan American Airways declared bankruptcy during the war, while TWA and Continental went under several years later. Pan Am's bankruptcy also resulted in MAC losing access to the company's eighteen Boeing 747s modified under the CRAF enhancement program at a cost of over $500 million in the 1980s. Thus, while CRAF jets transported 62 percent of the passengers and 27 percent of the cargo that moved into the theater by air, its operational robustness belied an underlying fragility that troubled airlift planners and other proponents of the program for the next decade.[32]

Implications

The successes and revealed shortfalls of the American airlift system carried implications for almost every nook and cranny of the national military airlift system and related policies. Above all else, the inability of the system to perform at its notional capacity needed correction. Correcting that deficiency would involve many actions, since it had been the consequence of problems in so many areas, including planning, the rapid creation and disciplined modification of TPFDL plans, requirements discipline, computer and communications capabilities, tracking cargoes, shortfalls in materials-handling equipment, and the condition of the aircraft fleet. Airlift leaders had particular reason to be worried about the airlift fleet, since the intense pace and heavy loads of the Gulf War effort had accelerated the aging of the C-141 fleet to the point that it would need replacement by the end of the decade. The general configuration of the airlift fleet was also a concern, given the inability of C-141s and C-130s to move large vehicles and other cargo items and their generally limited carrying capacity in relation to the demands placed on them. Last, the CRAF program clearly was in trouble, as several carriers went under and others considered leaving a program that had left them vulnerable financially and harmed competitively. If the United States was going to undertake something like Desert Shield again, then the Department of Defense would have to match the ongoing modernization of the MAC aircraft fleet with equally intense investment in a range of organizational and matériel programs.

The logic for such a broad-based modernization was compelling. In the realm of military operations, the United States had become an air mobility nation. Just as commercial aviation had replaced ocean liners, trains, and buses as the mode of mass transportation for people and high-value cargo in the civil world, air transports had become central to the way the military thought about and conducted war. Studies shortly after the war asserted the "time value" of airlift as a reducer of risks and casualties in future deployments. Military thinkers in all of the services recognized rapid global and theater mobility as essential to future war-fighting concepts.[33] In the future, then, the modernization of air mobility forces would be a compelling matter for the American defense community. But its costs and importance to so many different potential users also would make it a contentious matter. It would not simplify things that the decade of the 1990s also would prove to be one of the most active in American military history, particularly for the airlift arms.

22. Messing with Success

The Reorganization of Air Mobility Forces after the Gulf War

HAVING ASCENDED TO the position of chief of staff in October 1990, General Merrill A. McPeak disassembled the U.S. Air Force and put it back together in unfamiliar ways. To be sure, he was not acting on a whim. The ongoing dissolution of the Soviet Union had created expectations of major changes in U.S. defense policies. The current *National Security Strategy of the United States* (March 1990) and an air force white paper *Global Reach—Global Power* (June 1990) set the stage for significant changes in strategy and force structure in response to unfolding events.[1] But General McPeak came to his new position with strong views on how air force reorganization should proceed.[2] So following discussions with senior air force commanders, he deactivated the Air Force's core commands—the Strategic Air Command (SAC), the Tactical Air Command (TAC), and the Military Airlift Command (MAC)—on June 1, 1992. He redistributed their people and resources between two new organizations, the Air Combat Command (ACC) and the Air Mobility Command (AMC). ACC got everything that fired or directly supported the firing of weapons: fighters, bombers, ballistic missiles, warning and control aircraft, and the like. AMC got mobility aircraft: long-range transports and all but a few of the Air Force's tankers. In a reversal of decisions made in the 1970s, C-130s based in the continental United States (CONUS) went into ACC, while those assigned to overseas theaters fell under the theater air forces (TAFs).

To say that McPeak's reforms were controversial would be an understatement. The chief and his supporters saw these changes as logical responses to changing strategic circumstances, tightening budgets, and a matured understanding of airpower.[3] For many others, the chief's action seemed a drastic treatment of an air force structure that had held the Soviet empire at bay for forty years and that had performed so brilliantly during the Gulf War. Some saw the chief's actions as "messing with success" or maybe just a bald power grab on behalf of the "fighter mafia." In a pointed and lengthy spoof of McPeak's vision, an anonymous document circulated the halls of the Pentagon in the summer of 1991 that argued that the whole thing was a plot to increase the promotion opportunities of the "meat eaters" (fighter pilots) at the expense of the "herbivores" (everyone else).[4] By 1993 the perceptions of many in the Air Force that the new setup disproportionately favored fighter pilots had gained national attention.[5] In a vein much more supportive of McPeak, General Russell Dougherty, a former SAC commander, nevertheless captured the tension of the moment in a speech in which he simultaneously advised his air force listeners, "Don't be grit in the Chief's machinery" and recounted the bravura of his recently promoted fighter pilot son. On hearing his dad's advice to learn a little humility, the new lieutenant colonel Dougherty responded, "Dad, you were a bomber and tanker pilot all your life . . . *so you've got an awful lot to be modest about!* But sitting here where I am . . . at the top rung of the fighter pilot ladder . . . it's hard to be modest when you're at the top of the world!"[6] But whether it was the product of megalomania or a reasoned accommodation of changing realities, McPeak's plan would be the basis of air force policy, operations, and debate for years to come.

Smoke and Mirrors

In the realm of air mobility, particularly of airlift, there was little substantive innovation in the reorganization of the Air Force in 1992. Moving tankers from SAC to AMC amounted to shifting their logistics, training, and scheduling from one "big-aircraft" command to another. Even the assignment of tanker squadrons directly to overseas TAFs, like United States Air Forces in Europe (USAFE) and Pacific Air Forces (PACAF), merely changed the chain of command of units that were present in those theaters already. Similarly, giving direct control of theater-assigned airlift squadrons back to the TAFs was little more than returning to patterns of command and control in place before the consolidation of airlift forces in the mid-1970s. In those years, the Air Force and its precursors had assigned theater airlift to tactical air forces and strategic airlift to commands providing common-user air transport services.

But the circumstances of global airlift had changed in ways that made a return to old patterns questionable. Divided command arrangements had made some sense in the age of piston-engine-powered transports. Their slow speeds and design limitations made it difficult for the theater and strategic airlift arms to augment one another. So, in that case, divided command reflected operational reality. But the arrival of turbine-powered transports in the early 1960s changed all this. As revealed during the Vietnam War and the 1973 Nickel Grass airlift to Israel, their greater speeds, ranges, and carrying capacities enhanced the ability of tactical and strategic airlift units to influence and/or augment one another's missions. This continuity and the obvious economic advantages of centralized management are what compelled the Air Force to consolidate its airlift forces in 1975.

Still, placing theater and strategic airlift forces under separate chains of command was a significant step. Prior to airlift consolidation, intercommand coordination of airlift was handled by theater airlift commanders and senior Military Air Transport Service officers or, later, MAC officers also stationed in the theaters. Given the minimal overlap of their operations, these arrangements worked well enough. One of the key features of consolidation, however, was that it placed all matters of airlift in the theaters under commanders of airlift forces (COMALFs). COMALFs were dual hatted, meaning they had two bosses. They operated theater-assigned forces in accordance with the priorities of their theater commanders in chief and facilitated strategic operations in accordance with directions from MAC. This was a sensible arrangement in the jet age, since the overlapping capabilities and operating profiles of the C-5s, C-141s, and C-130s in the MAC fleet made it possible and necessary to manage them as a unified whole. So when General McPeak swept all of that away to return to an earlier day, the seam between theater and strategic airlift management and operations reappeared. Once again, coordination and cooperation required consultation between two entities: the TAF commander and AMC's replacement for the COMALF, the director of mobility forces (DIRMOBFOR). As did preconsolidation MAC theater liaison officers, DIRMOBFORs coordinated inbound strategic airlift flows with their theater counterparts and provided advice to theater commanders as requested. In biblical terms, therefore, McPeak had retrieved the old "skin" of divided airlift command and control to contain the new "wine" of airlift operations in the jet age. Whether the old skin would hold or burst was a matter for time to tell.

Old Wine in New Skin

Realization came quickly that the new setup for theater airlift would not work without serious modification. Even before the Air Force's reorganization was completed, senior commanders recognized that the combat air forces (CAF) community (ACC and the TAFs) was not prepared to handle its new logistics and management responsibilities. Then, unfolding military events revealed the folly of expecting TAF headquarters to conduct effective airlift operations as part of a global system. It did not and likely could not develop the robust body of staff expertise needed to run major airlift operations. So probably to the relief of all parties involved, in 1997 the theater system returned to all the essentials of the consolidated model, except that personnel in overseas squadrons wore the chest patches of the TAFs rather than that of AMC.

Logistics realities drove the first major modification to theater airlift reorganization. The commander of MAC, General Hansford T. Johnson, had resisted McPeak's initiative on the bases of operational and logistics common sense. Johnson's background largely was in SAC and as a senior staff planner. But he flew C-130s in his early assignments and had been around theater operations and issues at various times in his planning career. From those perspectives, he believed that eliminating the COMALFs and their robust staffs would break the critical connection between theater and strategic airlift operations and create a "catastrophic problem" in the future.[7] In the face of McPeak's determination to have his way, however, Johnson's protests only succeeded in marginalizing him from the decision process, while his boss waited for him to retire. McPeak picked General Ronald R. Fogleman to replace Johnson in August 1992. Fogleman was perhaps the most experienced fighter pilot and leader in the Air Force. He had been McPeak's squadron mate during the Vietnam War and fully endorsed his boss's visions for air mobility forces. He wasted no time sweeping aside residual resistance to those visions at AMC headquarters and transferred all CONUS-based C-130s (106 from the Air Force and 276 from the Air National Guard and Air Force Reserve) to ACC in October 1993.[8] But in a mutually agreed concession to ACC's limited experience and capabilities in the management and logistics support of airlift aircraft operating away from their home bases, AMC kept those responsibilities for CONUS-based C-130 units.[9]

Air mobility operations during the Bosnian conflict (1992–1995) provided the first sustained opportunity to test the reorganized air mobility system. Acting as a member of NATO and in concert with the United Nations, the United States conducted continual air operations into and over Bosnia for almost this entire period. During Operation Provide Promise (July 1992–January 1996), the U.S. Air Force flew 4,597 of 12,895 humanitarian relief missions into Sarajevo and over 2,200 additional sorties to air-drop food to other areas of the country. Simultaneously, the United States participated in Operation Deny Flight (April 1993–December 1995) to suppress the use of aircraft for military purposes by the combatants in the conflict. NATO conducted sporadic ground attacks against Bosnian Serb forces during Deny Flight to enforce UN mandates protecting Bosnian Muslim cities. These culminated in Deliberate Force

(August 1995–September 1995), a bombing campaign that punished the Serbs for repeated violations of the UN mandates and that helped to force them to sign a peace agreement in November 1995. Following that, air force transports flew over 3,000 airlift missions to deliver 15,600 peacekeepers and 30,100 tons of cargo into Bosnia during the first three months of Operation Joint Endeavor. Since most of these missions went into the small airfield of Tuzla, Bosnia, the airlift stream consisted mainly of C-130s and, for the first time in a major operation, C-17s.

The conduct of these operations, particularly Joint Endeavor, said much about the global interconnectedness of airlift operations. The capabilities of USAFE's one squadron of sixteen C-130s at Ramstein and one squadron of KC-135 tankers at RAF Mildenhall, England, fell well short of requirements. Help came from outside of the European theater. AMC and then ACC rotated C-130 units to Ramstein on temporary assignments, generally keeping the force available at around thirty aircraft. AMC sent expeditionary tanker units as needed. Meanwhile, AMC staff officers augmented the NATO Combined Air Operations Center at Vicenza, Italy that controlled air operations over Bosnia. Under the direction of an AMC-provided director of mobility forces, Brigadier General Charles H. Coolidge, they manned the Combined Air Operations Center's tanker cell and a new organization, the Regional Air Movement Control Center (RAMCC, pronounced "ramsee"). RAMCC's role was to meter the flow of air transports into the crowded and dangerous airspace of Bosnia, particularly into Sarajevo Airport. When the heavy demands of Joint Endeavor loomed on the planning horizon, USAFE and AMC took the unprecedented step of deploying an expeditionary force of strategic transports to Ramstein but leaving them under an AMC commander Brigadier General Richard C. Marr. USAFE would have preferred to control the operations of Marr's unit directly. But AMC commander, General Robert L. Rutherford and others realized that the USAFE staff did not have the expertise and facilities needed to direct the expanded force, so they retained direct control of General Marr's unit.[10] As it turned out, the arrangement worked well; the lift capacity of the twelve C-17s, ten C-141s, and two C-5s sent to Ramstein dwarfed that of USAFE's C-130s. The C-17s alone flew 20 percent of the sorties into Tuzla but moved over 50 percent of the cargo.[11]

Despite the successful augmentation of USAFE, a number of problems emerged during Bosnia operations that could be attributed directly to the new disconnect between theater and strategic airlift. Neither USAFE nor ACC had the staff or logistics resources to coordinate and support enlarged airlift operations.

Consequently, AMC units deployed to Europe routinely went around USAFE to request replacement personnel and supplies directly from AMC. AMC and USAFE coordinated flight clearances with EUROCONTROL through separate offices, sometimes to the confusion of European air traffic controllers. Shipment priorities also were not well coordinated between the strategic and theater airlift flows. In the early months of Provide Promise and Deny Flight, cargo items rushed to Germany sometimes sat for weeks in USAFE cargo yards waiting for onward shipment.[12] Even more troubling, the practice of unloading AMC cargoes at Ramstein for onward shipment by C-130s increased risks to U.S. aircrews. "Direct delivery" sorties by Globemaster IIIs into Sarajevo would have reduced the number of C-130 sorties going into that dangerous place by a ratio of about 1:5. This would have been obvious to a command staff responsible for all phases of the airlift operation. But the idea of trading C-17s or even C-141s for C-130s didn't seem to catch on until well into Provide Promise.[13]

The implications of these problems were obvious to most experienced airlift planners and leaders. Full of concern and zeal, Lieutenant Colonel Chris J. Krisinger and I wrote a pair of articles in the fall of 1995 challenging the presumptions of airlift fractionation. My article, "The Airlift System: A Primer," argued that fractionation flew in the face of the global nature of airlift operations and was "artificial and prone to produce unnecessary redundancies between the planning, acquisition, and training programs of the two commands."[14] Krisinger's article, "Towards a Seamless Mobility System: The C-130 and Air Force Reorganization," zeroed in on the planning and operational disconnects revealed during recent operations in Europe. Juxtaposing what happened in Europe with what should have happened under a consolidated system, Krisinger declared, "The seamless, single-manager airlift system increased US combat capability . . . [while] the present format . . . is an invitation for future operational failure at a key juncture."[15] Well written and focused on a specific issue, Krisinger's article was the more influential of the two and even prompted a direct exchange between him and General Fogleman, now the air force chief of staff.[16] These articles served to clarify the airlift policy debate for many. But as the musings of two relatively junior officers, they could have only an indirect effect on air force policy.

But even as Chris and I wrote, senior AMC commanders were having a direct effect on General McPeak's airlift vision. General Rutherford, who took over command of AMC in October 1994, set the stage in late 1995 with his adamant refusal to give USAFE tactical control of General Marr's airlift force during

Joint Endeavor and by pressing for further reviews of the new setup. Later, Rutherford said he was willing to consider an arrangement whereby the theaters gained the capability to run major airlifts. But down deep he really believed that Transportation Command and AMC should provide the airlift expertise needed by the theaters. "My bottom line," he later said, "is we have to get the C-130 force and the strategic airlift force back together in some way, shape, or form."[17] His successor, General Walter J. Kross, took over AMC in July 1996 and wasted little time picking up the consolidated airlift banner. Backed up by recent experience in Europe and elsewhere, he convened a mini summit of the involved commands in August. By then, General Fogleman had shifted his position to full support of consolidation and worked with Kross to get the other four-star commanders on board. In announcing his decision to move the Hercs back to AMC, Fogleman revealed the influence of Colonel Krisinger's article by declaring, "When we split the CONUS-based theater forces, we created seams in our training and deployment capabilities by spreading aerial port, tanker airlift control elements, and operations among two commands."[18]

In 1997 General Kross and the new chief, General Michael E. Ryan, released the "USAF Concept Paper on Theater Air Mobility," which solidified the general retrenchment of airlift policy. DIRMOBFORs gained responsibility for planning and supervising, but not commanding, theater airlift operations and for linking them to the strategic flow. Theater air commanders retained command authority over their theater-assigned airlift forces, but their planes, people, doctrines, and logistic support came from AMC. All this equated to greater coordination and accountability for the use of airlift assets on a global basis. Capturing the moment, AMC's historian gloried at the "repatriation" of the C-130 fleet, as if they were hostages returning home—which was pretty much what was happening.[19]

There was an irony in this quick return to the consolidated airlift organizational model. Fogleman and Rutherford were fighter commanders, the former with virtually no direct experience in airlift operations or doctrines and the latter with an earlier assignment as the AMC vice commander (AMC/VC). Kross was a highly experienced airlift commander, whom McPeak had handpicked to set up AMC, break out the C-130s, and otherwise get the airlift community in line with his vision. But within the bounds of following his orders from McPeak, he had pushed to keep global airlift forces intact. McPeak overrode him on every count and replaced General Hansford Johnson with a fighter commander, Fogleman, instead of Kross or another airlift expert. But as did the SAC generals sent to command the Military Air Transport Service and MAC in earlier years, Rutherford and Fogleman came to understand the importance of consolidation. With a stint as the AMC/CV, Rutherford probably returned to AMC a global airlift believer. Working from a cold start, Fogleman took longer. He didn't really become an advocate for reconsolidation until after he became the chief of staff.

So far in the history of American military affairs, it seemed ordained that the airlift arm would be commanded only occasionally by experts. But, with no exceptions, the outsiders who came to the commander's office were men of intelligence and integrity who responded well to the teachings of experience and those who knew the business. Thus the dabblings of senior bomber and fighter leaders in the workings of airlift, and their refusals to listen to experts carrying news they didn't want to hear, were only temporary nuisances for American airlift operations and policy. No matter which fellow-believers senior commanders sent out to put a lid on things, the logic of global airlift always converted them into acolytes. That said a lot about the general quality of air force leadership and its ability to adapt and change.

23. The 1990s

Years of Steady-State Surge

AT FIRST GLANCE, "steady-state surge" reads as an oxymoron. But by the end of the 1990s, the term had specific meaning for the Air Mobility Command (AMC) and for the U.S. Air Force in general. Basically, "surge" meant a pace of operations that precluded adequate rest for the command's personnel and the proper maintenance or replacement of its aircraft and other resources.[1] Like an athlete in training, AMC needed rest between periods of intense activity to accomplish the "housekeeping" activities needed to maintain readiness in relation to its overarching obligation to support American forces during major conflicts. But following the First Gulf War, AMC entered a seemingly endless series of crises and conflicts that gave it and its people too few opportunities for rest and recovery. By the end of the decade, the debilitating effects of this condition of steady-state surge on training, personnel retention, staff manning, aircraft, and supporting units were matters of daily concern for AMC and the Air Force. After a decade of the national airlift system being ridden hard and put away wet, its capabilities in relation to the demands it faced had deteriorated—not by much but noticeably.

Obligations and Capabilities at Decade's Start

Riding on the crest of modernization programs started in the 1980s and the experience of the First Gulf War, AMC's predecessor organization, the Military Airlift Command (MAC), was in good shape in 1991. Against the 66 million ton miles per day (MTMD) capacity goal set by the 1981 Congressionally Mandated Mobility Study, AMC's theoretical capacity had reached 54 MTMD. The command was well exercised and had just delivered a sterling performance during the Gulf War. Its commander, General Hansford T. Johnson, was both commander of MAC and the commander in chief of the U.S. Transportation Command (TRANSCOM). The Department of Defense (DOD) had just given him full combatant authority over TRANSCOM's three "modal" commands: MAC, the Military Traffic Management Command, and the Military Sealift Command. His dual-hat responsibilities also gave MAC access to the highest

halls of defense policy and reason to expect steady funding in a time of budgetary retrenchment.[2] In terms of matériel, the C-5, C-130, and C-141 fleets
were showing signs of age but generally were in good condition and reliable.[3]
The KC-135 fleet was definitely showing signs of age, but MAC's main focus
would be on airlift programs during the decade.

There were reasons, however, for worry. As discussed in chapter 20, the C-17
program was lagging and in danger of cancellation if the McDonnell Douglas
Corporation did not clean up the program's financial and technical problems.
The possibility of further delays in the C-17 program raised the specter of the
C-141 fleet wearing out before its replacement came on line. Hard use over three
decades had aged the Starlifters ahead of expectations, and they were becoming increasingly costly to maintain. Even if McDonnell Douglas worked a miracle, there was no doubt that the Starlifters would be in the boneyard well before
enough C-17s came on line to replace their lost capacity. Worse, the 120 C-17s
currently on the Air Force's purchase list would replace only the C-141 fleet's
existing capacity, without moving AMC closer to the 66 MTMD bogey.[4] Meanwhile, the Civil Reserve Airlift Fleet (CRAF) program was staggering from the
liquidation of Pan American Airways and the looming departure of other major
airlines, like American and United. Then there was the problem of finding
money to replace the hundreds of Vietnam-era forklifts and "K-loaders" in the
materials-handling equipment inventory. Their poor condition had disrupted
and even jeopardized the airlift flow during the Gulf War. All things considered, then, AMC was in good operating form at the start of the 1990s, but its
long-term condition would depend in large part on the demands placed on it
and the availability of money to modernize its equipment.

The Surge That Would Not Stop

To understand what was about to happen to the airlift command, one needs to
appreciate that it did not have a lot of surplus airlift capacity sitting around on
the parking ramps of its bases. Day in and day out, the airlift fleet was engaged
fully. A percentage of aircraft were away from their home stations performing
prescheduled, special assignment airlift missions (SAAMs) to move people and
cargo and for Joint Army–Air Force Training (JAAT) and other exercise activities. C-130s also carried SAAM and JAAT missions, both in support of training
activities in the continental United States (CONUS) and in support of theater
air forces (TAFs) overseas. Theater airlifters also covered steady-state deployments in places like the Middle East, Europe, and Latin America. In addition,

MAC and the TAFs would "fence" 30 percent or more of their transports from operations so they could undergo maintenance and inspections. Training "fences" kept other aircraft at their home stations to cover aircrew-training requirements. Thus, on a typical day an airlift wing would have only a small percentage of its planes on hand to answer unexpected calls for airlift support. More could be provided by lowering the maintenance and training fences or calling aircraft in from other missions. But these actions degraded the long-term readiness of the unit and/or had adverse impacts on other users.[5] A rough measure of surge, therefore, was when the airlift command and local units began calling in aircraft, dropping fences, and canceling personal leaves. If continued over time, these actions unavoidably degraded readiness and morale.

A crisis in Somalia kicked off the era of surge for AMC. Violent factional fighting and growing famine in the impoverished country galvanized a UN relief operation in early 1991. In August 1992 the United States began a food airlift from Kenya called Operation Provide Relief. In six months, ten air force C-130s and 400 support personnel based at Mombasa transferred 32,000 tons of food, cooking oil, medicines, and other supplies that MAC transports had brought in from the States. When Somali militias began to threaten the lift, MAC flew over 30,000 U.S. troops and tens of thousands of tons of equipment and supplies directly into Somalia as part of Operation Restore Hope between December 1992 and March 1994.[6] These often were arduous missions for airlift crews. After flying a nonstop leg from the United States to Mogadishu, they would continue immediately to Egypt for rest, having covered a distance of over 10,000 miles. To make these thirty-hour marathons possible, AMC augmented crews with additional pilots and set up the first "tanker-bridge" solely to accelerate an airlift flow. AMC also used some of its newly acquired KC-10s to move cargo. Compared to type-designed airlifters, the Extenders were balky to load, but they also were fast and efficient movers of palletized cargoes, such as rations, tentage, ammunition, and the like.

In still another first, AMC sent two brigadier generals, Thomas R. Mikolajcik and then George "Nick" Williams, to Mogadishu as directors of mobility forces (DIRMOBFORs). Doctrine was still being written on these new positions, which had only just replaced the earlier commander of airlift force (COMAFOR) concept during the reorganization of airlift forces in 1993. Despite the uncertain nature of their new responsibilities, Mikolajcik and Williams professionally filled their roles as air mobility advisers to more senior commanders and kept cargo operations at Mogadishu and elsewhere running as smoothly as possible. They and the Tanker-Airlift Control Element (TALCE) working for them under miserable conditions of heat and dust worked wonders and validated the DIRMOBFOR concept.[7]

Even as Provide Relief and Restore Hope were under way, intensifying conflict in the Balkans region increased the load on airlift forces. Chapter 22 of this volume dealing with the reorganization of air force airlift forces lays out the operational details and doctrinal implications of the various UN and North Atlantic Treaty Organization (NATO) operations in Bosnia. So it is necessary only to point out that all of those operations—Provide Promise, Deny Flight, Deliberate Force, and Joint Endeavor—consumed a lot of air mobility support. During Provide Promise (July 1992–January 1996) transports from AMC and United States Air Forces in Europe (USAFE) flew almost 6,800 relief missions into Bosnia, including 2,200 missions to air-drop food to isolated areas of the county. The airdrops were controversial, since they involved free-fall (no parachute) drops of heavy bundles and showers of ration packets from altitudes as high as 10,000 feet through clouds and at night. However, despite expectations that they would be inaccurate and injure people on the ground, the aircrews making the drops learned to get their loads to within forty yards of their aim points and caused little collateral damage. By the end of 1993, over 345,000 Bosnians depended on air-dropped supplies for their survival.[8] Deny Flight also consumed about a half dozen AMC airlift sorties per day and the sustained deployment of around twenty tankers to the theater. Finally, Joint Endeavor involved over 3,000 airlift missions to move peacekeepers into Bosnia starting in early December 1995.[9]

The aftershocks of the First Gulf War kept up the pressure on MAC and AMC. As its contribution to the aerial occupation of Iraq (Operations Southern Watch and Northern Watch), the commands kept about a squadron each of tankers and C-130s and about 2,000 personnel in the theater.[10] Later in the decade, AMC surged its commitment to the region in response to Iraqi provocations. AMC designated the airlift portions of these operations as Phoenix Scorpions (PSs). PS 1 (November 19–25, 1997), PS 3 (November 12–15, 1998), and PS 4 (December 16–19, 1998) were modest deployments of a few dozen aircraft and about 1,500–2,500 passengers to confront the Iraqis or, in the case of PS 3, actually launch punitive strikes. PS 2 (February 8–March 4, 1998) was the largest air deployment, involving some 16,000 passengers and 16,000 tons of equipment.

In a companion operation to PS 4, AMC and USAFE innovated once again to facilitate the movement of Patriot air defense missile units to Israel (Operation Nobel Shirley). AMC's new commander, General Charles "Tony" T. Robertson, gave USAFE direct tactical control (TACON) of a provisional squadron of seven C-17s based temporarily at Ramstein. In compliance with DOD regulations, Robertson actually made the TACON grant, which was the first of its kind, under his authority as the commander in chief of TRANSCOM. To ensure that these new and specialized aircraft were used with maximum effect, Robertson and the USAFE commander, General John P. Jumper, agreed that the unit would be commanded by Brigadier General Robert D. (Rod) Bishop. Bishop was the commander of the 437th Airlift Wing, from which the C-17s would be drawn, and he had commanded Globemaster operations from Ramstein before, though under AMC control. A skilled commander and well versed in the doctrinal details and sensitivities of intercommand relations, Bishop was an excellent ambassador between the various commands involved. In the end, he pulled off Noble Shirley smoothly and, in so doing, reinforced the doctrinal truth that astute and knowledgeable individuals can make almost any command structure work, given freedom of action, open communications, and support from their chains of command.[11]

Throughout the decade, presidential airlift missions, called Phoenix Banners, and vice presidential lifts, Phoenix Silvers, increased significantly as an element of AMC's operating tempo. During the presidency of William Jefferson Clinton, the logistics of moving the vehicles, helicopters, communications equipment, secure food supplies, support and security personnel, members of the press, and invited guests of the presidential entourage approached the scale of small wars. During the president's trip to Africa in 1998, for example, AMC had to choreograph the movement of two full complements of equipment and support teams—one serving the president at the moment, another standing by for his next whirlwind arrival—and a substantial front team working the next stop after that. To support this entourage of over 800 people, AMC activated a crisis action team at headquarters; committed virtually the entire C-5 fleet to the mission for six weeks; deployed maintenance teams to Ascension Island, Cape Verde Island, and Johannesburg; and sent out Phoenix Raven security teams to protect the big aircraft at less-secure stops. AMC tankers also flew over a hundred missions to top off Galaxies bound for airfields without adequate refueling facilities. Unsurprisingly, Banner and Silver missions consumed 40 percent of all AMC SAAMs in 1999, flying 1,252 missions to move 26,481 passengers and 20,314 tons of cargo.[12]

Just to keep things hopping for the air mobility world, the decade that started with a major war in the Gulf ended with a major conflict in the Balkans region. In response to Serbia's brutal repression of insurgents and unarmed citizens in its province of Kosovo, the United States and NATO conducted a war of four air campaigns against the government of Slobodan Milosevic. NATO's Operation Allied Force (March 24–June 9, 1999), the main effort, began with attacks against Serbian field forces and, beginning May 3, added attacks against strategic power, communications, economic, and military targets. On April 4 NATO initiated Operation Shining Hope to move relief supplies to the Kosovar people through Rinas Airport near Tirana, the capital of Albania. Next, to increase pressure on the Serbs, the United States airlifted a composite, mechanized/air cavalry brigade, Task Force Hawk, into Rinas for a possible thrust into Kosovo. Finally, following the capitulation of Serbia on June 3, 1999, NATO deployed a force of nearly 30,000 peacekeepers into Kosovo. AMC and USAFE air mobility forces, naturally, were engaged heavily in all of these efforts, flying around 11,742 sorties to move 55,802 passengers and 99,243 tons of cargo during all phases of the conflict. USAFE flew 3,810 of those sorties with its C-130s and C-17s on loan from AMC.[13] In addition, AMC tankers supported the transoceanic deployments of over 500 aircraft to the theater and transferred some 18,000 tons of fuel in the air during deployment, combat, and redeployment missions.[14]

Once again, innovation and cooperation were the essentials of success. AMC placed another provisional squadron of twelve C-17s under USAFE's TACON to move the helicopters, armored vehicles, and rocket artillery of Task Force Hawk into Rinas. This time they operated under the direct command of Colonel Ronald Richardson, another AMC officer. AMC also sent eight reserve component (Air National Guard or Air Force Reserve) C-130s to Ramstein to augment the ten already present in "Delta" squadron, a rotational unit augmenting the sixteen C-130Es in USAFE's permanently assigned 37th Airlift Squadron (AS). Together, the new Hercs and those already in Delta squadron became the 38th Expeditionary Airlift Squadron (AES)—another first. The 37th AS and 38th EAS integrated their staff processes and operations fully, planning missions and preparing crews for flights together and picking up extra missions when another part of the team became overloaded. Similarly, USAFE and AMC ground support units worked together closely, particularly at Rinas. On April 4, USAFE sent thirty-six members and a few light vehicles of its just-activated 86th Contingency Response Group (CRG) to Rinas to conduct and secure the unloading of humanitarian supplies. AMC came in later with a sixty-person TALCE to support the

Task Force Hawk movement. Both organizations, the "lean" CRG and the more robust TALCE, pooled and coordinated their efforts and helped each other whenever their primary missions allowed.[15] Once again, dedicated service members transcended doctrinal and institutional seams to get the job done.

As had become the norm, General Bishop was the glue that bound the USAFE and AMC airlift efforts together. Now acting as the USAFE DIRMOB-FOR, he worked through AMC's Tanker-Airlift Control Center at Scott Air Force Base, USAFE's Air Mobility Operations Center, and about two dozen other military headquarters and civil air traffic organizations to keep the air mobility effort running, coordinated, and legal. The presence of Lieutenant General William J. Begert as the vice commander of USAFE was a boon to Bishop's efforts. Begert was a career airlifter and the first one to hold a senior command position in USAFE since General Tunner left in 1957. Besides being the poster boy for the Air Force's growing respect for the air mobility community and its ability to rear up senior commanders, Begert ensured that USAFE's air mobility planning and operations ran well, and he made Bishop's world as simple as possible.

Coordination did not go so smoothly at the headquarters of NATO's 5th Allied Tactical Air Force in Vicenza, Italy, from where USAF Lieutenant General Michael C. Short commanded air operations over the Balkans. Throughout the conflict, Short's staff controlled access to the theater by air transport aircraft through the unique organization RAMCC. With no direct authority over airlift units, the RAMCC only *modulated* the airlift flow into regional airfields through assignment of landing slot times. Under the circumstances, the RAMCC concept worked well enough, though outside observers noted that it was redundant to the Air Mobility Operations Center's capabilities and created an unnecessary coordination node. Short's provisions for tanker operations were even more awkward. Anticipating a short war, he first attempted to direct the operations of over 150 tankers with a small planning cell of junior officers within his Combined Air Operations Center (CAOC) at Vicenza. When concerns arose elsewhere in the Air Force regarding the number of tankers going into the theater, and with the tanker cell's management of them, the general reluctantly accepted augmentation by AMC experts. Colonel Tom Stickford, one of AMC's best tanker operators, led the contingent.[16] Despite Stickford's expertise, Short limited his responsibilities to planning and coordinating tanker operations and logistics support. He otherwise left their oversight and direction to his AOC director and the junior officers in the tanker cell. It was a clumsy setup, but it did provide adequate support for the NATO jets engaged in the virtually one-sided air battle in the skies of Serbia and Kosovo.[17]

In the end, the Allied Force experience rang alarm bells throughout the system. To meet demands, General Robertson had been forced to lower the training and maintenance fences for all of his tanker and airlift units. He knew full well that the continued high tempo of events after the conflict likely would make it impossible to mitigate the material and human costs of that action without drastic measures. Furthermore, the combination of lowering the fences and deploying—perhaps overdeploying—so many tankers to Europe had put other theaters at risk. If a military emergency had broken out in the Korean theater, for instance, it would have taken days longer to swing planned tanker support from Europe, instead of stateside bases, to the western Pacific. In the event of a full-scale attack by North Korea, such a delay could have resulted in thousands of additional allied casualties.[18] General Robertson had put everything on the table, and it had not been enough to cover all of America's strategic bets.[19] Worse, the eminent departure of the C-141s from the fleet, deteriorating reliability of the C-5 fleet, and declining personnel retention rates indicated that the level of risk was going to go up, not down.[20] So USAFE and AMC leaders were missing the point when they quibbled over getting "more robust tanker planning in the AOC and the CAOC," the importance of DIRMOBFORs, and managing mobility forces on a "continuous and global basis."[21] The really sobering implication of the recent war was that AMC was wearing down and was not capable of serving the mobility requirements of two major theater wars (MTWs), as called for in national strategy.

Mitigating the Effects of Steady-State Surge: Equipment

AMC and air force leaders worked numerous programs and actions to keep the airlift fleet efficient and modern. Expanding the C-17 fleet was their top priority. But the command also pursued vigorous upgrade programs for existing aircraft and key ground support elements. In net, these programs and actions kept the airlift fleet effective through the end of the decade. But it was less clear that these efforts maintained the full readiness of the fleet to meet daily demands and stay ready for major war.

Strategic airlift modernization programs continued at a steady pace throughout the 1990s. Despite constant attacks, the C-17 program kept moving forward. By 1999 the DOD had authorized production of 135 of the planes, and plans were afoot to buy at least 60 more. After some years of dithering over the plane's future, AMC began a major modernization of the C-5s in the latter 1990s. Aiming to keep the huge cargo decks of these planes available through at least 2040, AMC began the modernization program in 1997 with a contract to upgrade the high-pressure turbines of the Galaxy fleet's engines. This contract was followed in 1999 with another one to modernize the plane's avionics. Finally, in early 2000 Congress began funding a multibillion-dollar Reliability Enhancement and Reengining Program (RERP) to raise the aircraft's departure reliability rate up to 91 percent and to reduce its life-cycle costs by as much as $1.6 billion.[22] This expensive project carried some technical risks. But it was still far cheaper than replacing the C-5 fleet with additional C-17s of similar net capacity.

AMC found itself in the odd position of resisting modernization of the C-130 fleet. Although air leaders sought to keep the command's political and financial capital focused on the C-17, Congress foisted some 251 unrequested C-130s on the Air Force between 1978 and 1998.[23] Seeking to buttress the futures of Air National Guard and Air Force Reserve units in their home districts, waves of congressmen budgeted year in and year out for C-130s that the Air Force said weren't needed, at least not yet. In 1998, for example, the Joint Chiefs of Staff complained that Congress had ordered them to purchase another twenty unwanted C-130s, which would be built in the home district of House Speaker Newt Gingrich and with some deployed to Mississippi, the home state of Senate majority leader Trent Lott.[24] C-130Js, upgraded versions of the venerable design, entered the mix in 1994. The first squadron of the Air National Guard received Js that year, the Air Force Reserve started getting them in 1999, and the 50th Airlift Squadron became the first active component airlift unit to get them in 2004. The result was that the reserve components had a significantly newer fleet of C-130s than the active fleet, providing a prime example of the power of pork politics over military planning criteria.[25]

AMC pursued several support programs with much the same fervor it gave to the C-17. On the basis of lessons learned from the Gulf War, AMC set out to modernize its inventory of materials-handling equipment, mainly the forklifts, loaders, and other vehicles used to get cargo on and off aircraft. The heart of the program was the development of the Tunner and Halvorsen flat-deck loaders, which could raise 60,000 or 25,000 pounds of palletized cargo and/or vehicles, respectively, to the cargo decks of almost any aircraft. The Air Force acquired 318 Tunners between 1997 and 2005. The Halvorsens entered service in 2000, and AMC had over 400 on hand by 2011. These were expensive vehicles—about $1.5 million for each Tunner and around $1 million for the smaller vehicles. After experiencing difficulties in getting the Tunners into the Air Force's budget, AMC named the vehicle as its highest-priority program, second only to C-17 acquisition.

Through some astute financial moves, AMC incentivized the CRAF program back to health. Even as the Gulf War had been under way, MAC announced a program of five initiatives to improve the "business case" of CRAF participation. The most important of these initiatives were improvements in the War Risk Insurance program and a plan to maximize the use of CRAF carriers by all government agencies.[26] As a result of the latter initiative, the total amount of government cargo and passenger business going to CRAF carriers rose from about $1.4 billion in 1994 to $1.8 billion in 1998, enough to entice major carriers, like American and United Airlines, back into the program. The effect of these incentives was such that by late 1996 AMC Commander General Robert L. Rutherford wondered if "we have too much CRAF" as the number of airlines joining was on the verge of exceeding requirements.[27] Later studies encouraged further development of the program, which was the cheapest source of wartime reserve airlift capacity.[28]

Mitigating the Effects of Steady-State Surge: People

While the planes were wearing out, the people were wearing down. MAC and AMC commanders took actions at the individual and institutional levels to mitigate the hardships on the personnel working in the air mobility system. Unit commanders did their best to give personnel opportunities to take leave, train at home stations, and otherwise get breaks from the grinding pressure of the surge. As the pressure mounted, General Fogleman began the Phoenix Pace program in 1995, in which individual wings would stand down for two-week periods each year and give their people predictable opportunities to take their leaves. Fogleman had wanted to give the wings more time off from the away-from-station schedule, but the pace of operations made longer breaks impossible.[29] Finally, at the end of the decade, the Air Force provided AMC with opportunities to systemically manage the operational load.

Chief of Staff General Michael E. Ryan's Air Expeditionary Force (AEF) plan provided the first opportunity to ease the strain on AMC personnel systemically. Extrapolating a concept developed by the Air Combat Command to manage deployments, Ryan announced in 1998 that the Air Force was about to divide its deployable forces more or less equally between ten AEFs. Normally, only two AEFs would be available at any one time to cover so-called steady-state contingencies in Southwest Asia and elsewhere. Twenty percent of the Air Force was all that Ryan believed could be deployed or kept immediately ready for deployment on a continual basis without undermining readiness for major conflicts. The AEF construct, he said, would use "all of our capabilities" to meet requirements and mitigate strain on personnel.[30] General Walter J. Kross, who commanded AMC from July 1996 to August 1998, was an early cheerleader for the concept, which he considered critical to increasing the Air Force's strategic effectiveness and reducing the operational strain on AMC.[31]

Tasked by General Kross's successor, General Charles "Tony" T. Robertson, to develop the role of the mobility air forces (MAFs) in the AEF plan, Colonels Gary Phipps and Robert Owen hosted a MAF-CAF conference at AMC headquarters in early September 1998. The most important outcome of the conference and subsequent discussions in the fall was the realization that not only the MAFs but also cross sections of pretty much all of the people in the Air Force had to be allotted to or at least aligned to the AEF "buckets" to maximize steady-state deployment levels and to fairly share the load. In large part due to MAF leadership, the AEF project had grown in a few months from an effort to mitigate strain on fighter forces into a program intended to draw virtually every member of the Air Force into a rotational deployment schedule.[32]

Getting the AEF program off the ground proved a massive undertaking. An initial challenge was developing personnel management procedures that assigned more and more airmen to specific unit type codes (UTCs), which were deployable operational and support elements that might range from single individuals to whole squadrons in size. They were the building blocks of AEFs. Soon, thousands of air force educators, trainers, staffers, medical workers, engineers, logisticians, and so on were dragooned into UTCs. Many of these individuals, or at least their positions, had been fenced from deployments in the past. But, suddenly, everyone was going into a bucket and would share the overseas deployment load. Hardly was the UTC process under way, however, when the Kosovo conflict confirmed the real devil in the details of the concept: no two contingencies are alike, and sometimes their force requirements exceeded 20 percent of what the Air Force had on hand. Thus, by the time the bombs stopped falling, the cumulative exhaustion of AMC's people and degradation of its equipment had reached crisis proportions, and the AEF plan was destabilized.

So General Ryan did something even more radical than the AEFs to give AMC and the rest of the Air Force a new context for managing its readiness.

In May 1999 he announced that the entire service was going to take a pause to "reconstitute" from the Kosovo surge. Only by standing down units long enough to catch up on training, maintenance, and rest, Ryan knew, could the Air Force get itself back on track to handle the steady-state load and be ready for any big wars that might come along. AMC assessed the chief's reconstitution guidelines and then "stopped a few hearts" at the Pentagon with a report that no C-130 or KC-135 squadron would be available for AEF deployments until mid-spring 2000.[33] That projection was unacceptable, of course. So AMC set out to reconstitute on the fly, giving units time to do so, while making sure that all AEF commitments were met. The task of monitoring the process fell to Colonel Owen and a small team of planners called the R-Team.[34]

Owen's team, led by his deputy Lieutenant Colonel Christopher Bence, reported the results weekly in a grand 300-plus slide briefing to the command staff. After giving a brief overview of the command's general status, Colonel Owen would field questions about specific units. If someone asked about the 40th Airlift Squadron, for example, Bence might call out, "Left screen, slide number 115," and his boss would brief coolly from a slide that he likely had not seen before that moment. Seldom in the history of modern war were the meanings of "PowerPoint Warriors" and "Death-by-PowerPoint" clearer. Somehow, largely unaware of the weekly dog and pony show at headquarters, the field units reconstituted themselves and allowed AMC to meet all of its AEF and other obligations. People were still tired, but not so tired, and things were holding together.

Mitigating the Effects of Steady-State Surge: Analysis

Airlift studies became a cottage industry in the 1990s. Everyone—including Congress, the Joint Chiefs of Staff, the Air Force, AMC, the other services, aircraft manufacturers, academics, journalists, and private citizens—had something to say about the future and composition of the national air mobility system. Given the drastically changed strategic situation following the dissolution of the Soviet empire and the great costs of the C-17 program, the magnified interest in airlift was natural. The resulting official studies broadly fell into two categories: those that proposed fleets in relation to anticipated requirements and those that proposed fleets in keeping with anticipated budgets. Most major official studies tried to do both, with mixed results. Internal MAC/AMC and air force studies did result in specific fleet plans. But restrained by budget concerns, DOD studies produced few original concepts or goals and largely rationalized the preservation and/or modernization of existing gross capabilities.

Secretary of Defense Richard Cheney set the pattern. Seeking a "strategically prudent force that is fiscally responsible," he notified Congress in 1991 that he was reducing the airlift-planning baseline from 66 MTMD to 48 MTMD. The lower target, he said, would satisfy the requirements of future MTWs at a "moderate" level of military risk. Predictably, the DOD's 1992 Mobility Requirements Study (MRS) endorsed the secretary's goals and acceptance of a moderate risk of military failure in one MTW and a "high" risk for a "simultaneous" MTW elsewhere.[35] While the MRS did not clarify the meaning of "high" risk, it took no leap of military imagination to understand that it equated to possible defeat and a certain increase in the butcher's bill for the second MTW. Backlash to such notions compelled Cheney's successor, Les Aspin, to release a "bottom-up review" of military requirements in 1993. The resulting review dealt with airlift force structure only in general terms. But it did further cloud the airlift planning regime by simultaneously sidestepping the "risk" issue and asserting that the United States would "maintain sufficient military power to be able to win two major regional conflicts that occur nearly simultaneously."[36]

Airlift practitioners weren't long in putting out countervailing studies. Even as the bottom-up review was under way, a RAND study found that existing airlift and tanker fleet limitations would preclude effective response to a second MTW if it broke out less than three weeks after the first.[37] In 1994 AMC issued the first of what became an annual series of air mobility master plans, largely to express the command's future needs and concerns that its rapidly aging aircraft inventory was undermining its ability to handle two "near-simultaneous" MTWs. Although implicitly accepting the 48 MTMD bogey, the Air Force's 1995 New World Vistas study recommended acquisition of modernized cargo-handling and tracking systems, development of precision airdrop capabilities, and possible development of a "million-pound airlifter."[38] In the next year, the Air Force's 2025 study linked airlift and air-refueling capabilities to the future effectiveness of airpower and called for a new transport capable of flying 12,500 miles unrefueled, of detecting and surviving threats, and of operating into austere airfields.[39]

The DOD's response to all the pushback over airlift reinforced the gap between airlift bill payers in the DOD and airlift users in the field. The response was the 1995 Mobility Requirements Study—Bottom-Up Review Update (MRS-BURU), an iteration of the original study informed by the guidelines of the bottom-up review. Although the report team included AMC planners and involved detailed analysis of near-simultaneous movements to the Southwest Asian and Korean theaters, its final recommendations adhered to DOD priorities. Moderate risk—whatever that was—and affordability remained the main planning constraints. The planning baseline went up a little, to 51.8 MTMD, but remained well below actual requirements. The new bogey left AMC planners concerned over what they perceived as the update's too-sanguine presumptions about operational issues, like attrition, airfield capacities, warning times, CRAF mobilizations, and so on.[40] Drawn to the noise, the Congressional Budget Office found that such disputes were natural results of conflicting perspectives and the "large number of assumptions about how major deployments will take place." In classic understatement, the office concluded, "Those uncertainties are so fundamental that there will always be room for debate over how much lift is enough."[41]

Implications

It would be easy to assess the 1990s as a period of decline for the American national air mobility system. Other than being used hard, tanker forces underwent only modest upgrades of existing systems and no replacement of the doddering fleet of KC-135s. Airlift modernization programs (AMPs) were far more robust. They included acquiring the C-17, contracting the C-5's AMP and RERP, replacing the materials-handling fleet with Tunners and Halvorsens, and even reluctantly upgrading the C-130 fleet. But there was no escaping the fact that these programs were barely maintaining gross capabilities, albeit with improvements in operational flexibility. More disturbing, the gross capabilities of the fleet clearly fell below planning requirements for major theater wars, to the extent that they guaranteed higher American casualties and possible defeats. DOD studies of the problem merely glossed over the danger with clerkish pronouncements about fiscal responsibility and risk levels. The simple fact was that by decade's end, American major war plans were beyond the capabilities of the air mobility fleet to support at a reasonably acceptable risk, and the fleet's equipment and people were pretty tired.

But beyond material issues, there were some really good things happening to the community of air mobility practitioners. Most important, its operational and planning communities were growing up professionally. The challenges of constant operations and of defending their visions and programs against all comers for over a decade had increased their intellectual sophistication and gravitas in the halls of power and debate. Moreover, their growing credibility opened unprecedented opportunities for leadership. General William Begert's departure from USAFE in 1999 to become the air force assistant vice chief of staff and then to take over the Pacific Air Forces in 2001 was the bellwether of air mobility's rise in status and integration into the broader Air Force. But other events marked the new era as well. These included General Rod Bishop's eventual rise to vice commander of USAFE and commander of the 3rd Air Force, the close integration of CAF and MAF planning in the AEF and reconstitution initiatives, and a host of other officers going into positions previously dominated or even reserved for CAF officers. So by the end of the decade, MAF people may have been a little stretched, but they also held the respect of the Air Force at large, their programs were taken more seriously, and they had unheard-of opportunities for professional advancement and influence. This was all good, since the next decade was going to be still tougher on them, their command, and the U.S. military as a whole: they were about to transition from a steady state of surge to a steady state of war.

24. The 2000s

Years of Steady-State War

IT IS A testament to the American military system that its national air mobility system came out of the first decade of the twenty-first century stronger than it went in. When al Qaeda attacked on September 11, 2001, America's mobility fleets were robust and modernizing, and their personnel were seasoned though slightly worn by the previous decade's high operating tempos. Together they would be strained but not broken by the coming years of continual war, routine logistics missions, training, humanitarian responses, and other operations that would press their limits of capability and endurance. The air mobility practitioners of the Army and the Air Force would rise to these challenges and learn to operate their aircraft and support systems with unprecedented effectiveness. In their support, the military logistics system generally kept the mobility fleet maintained and modernizing. Interest politics and rare cases of outright corruption would undermine the integrity and progress of some mobility programs, particularly modernization of the air-refueling and theater airlift fleets. But tankers aside, the national air mobility system was better equipped in 2011 than in 2001 and in the hands of experts who were unequaled masters in the art and science of moving things by air in war.

A Time of Wars

The ruins of the World Trade Center still smoldered when the United States began the war in Afghanistan. On October 7, 2001, it opened Operation Enduring Freedom with the insertion of small special operations teams into the country. Their role was to coordinate air support and resupply of the mujahidin insurgents already fighting the country's Taliban government. But within weeks, U.S. Marines and Army Rangers and infantry arrived to control the airfields at Kabul and Kandahar. Then, when the Taliban initiated an insurgency in 2003, America became the predominant member of a UN-NATO coalition of combat forces spread throughout the country. American troop numbers grew steadily, from about 4,000 at the end of 2001 to a peak of 97,000 in 2011. Other NATO troops throughout this period equaled about 20,000 to 30,000, while Afghan army strength grew to 300,000.

Given the remoteness and landlocked nature of Afghanistan, air mobility was an indispensable foundation of the American and allied war efforts. In the first months of the conflict, everything and everyone went into the country via airlift and/or behind a chain of aerial refuelers that stretched back to the homeland. Over time, trucks from Pakistan or Uzbekistan delivered most of the fuel, food, and construction materials. But these landlines of communication were long, slow, and subject to insurgent attacks and mine warfare. So throughout the war, the United States transported virtually all personnel, ammunition, weapons, vehicles, and other high-value supplies by air. In just the first year, over 11,000 airlift missions, or the bulk of the productive efforts of Air Mobility Command's (AMC), carried around 158,000 passengers and 222,000 tons of cargo into and out of Afghanistan.[1]

Then, following years of confrontation with Iraq, the United States and another coalition of allied partners opened the Second Gulf War on March 19, 2003. The campaign, Operation Iraqi Freedom, began with air attacks followed a day later by an invasion across Iraq's southern border with Kuwait. An airborne assault on Bashur Airport, near the town of Harir, by 954 American paratroopers of the 173rd Airborne Brigade opened a northern front on March 26. C-17s airlanded 1,200 more soldiers, five M1A1 tanks, five Bradley fighting vehicles, fifteen armored personnel carriers, and forty-one Humvees at Bashur over the next several days.[2] Baghdad fell to coalition troops on April 5. Thereafter, much of the airlift effort shifted to bringing in relief supplies for the Iraqi people. After an all-too-brief period of quiet, fighting between Islamic denominations broke out and grew rapidly in scale and ferocity. Also, by early 2004 politically and religiously motivated insurgents were attacking coalition units in wide areas of the country and held sway over suburbs of Baghdad and outlying towns. Fighting escalated during the next two years, prompting the United States to send a surge force of 30,000 troops to the country in early 2007. U.S. troop strength in the country rose to 218,500 during this period and declined to about 80,000 at the end of 2010 and just a few thousand by the end of 2011.

As could be expected, air mobility was a crucial element of Operation Iraqi Freedom. Virtually all of the 424,000 U.S. personnel deployed for the initial invasion went in by air, as did thousands of tons of supplies. AMC flew 7,413 airlift and 6,193 tanker missions in support of these movements, at times launching a transport every twelve minutes from bases in the United States. In addition, the Air Force deployed some 255 tankers and 140 C-130s to the theater. The U.S. Central Command's Air Force (CENTAF) flew 2,203 C-130 and C-17 missions during the campaign to move 9,662 passengers and 12,444 tons of matériel in support of the advance.[3] AMC Tanker-Airlift Control Elements (TALCEs) moved into forward bases on the heels of advancing infantry to open them for air transport operations. By 2004, with about 200,000 American troops in Iraq, AMC was moving as many as 5,000 personnel and hundreds of tons of cargo into or out of the region each day just to support ordinary administrative and troop rotational requirements. At the same time, CENTAF-assigned C-130s and C-17s were moving hundreds of passengers and 350–450 tons of cargo each day into and around Iraq. As in Afghanistan, this theater airlift effort reduced the exposure of military and civilian personnel to ambushes and mines along the dangerous roads of the country.[4]

Beyond the wars in Afghanistan and Iraq, AMC supported many routine and crisis operations. AMC transports and civil contract carriers linked the United States and its global network of military bases with scheduled passenger and cargo flights. Crisis operations included flying single-mission requests to evacuate ailing American citizens from foreign lands, dozens of sorties in support of military exercises, and sometimes hundreds of sorties in response to a humanitarian crisis. In 2005 alone AMC flew 375 sorties to alleviate suffering following a tsunami off the coast of Indonesia in February, 881 sorties in the aftermath of Hurricane Katrina in August, and another 551 sorties to Pakistan following a major earthquake.[5] These were not atypical numbers for other years and represented only a small fraction of AMC's total effort.

Rediscovering Some Old Issues

Wars and the general press of events highlighted some old lessons about air mobility operations and exacerbated troubling shortfalls in the tanker and theater airlift fleets. These revelations would form the backdrop of numerous air mobility studies and mitigating actions during the decade of the 2000s.

Lesson One of the early phases of Operation Enduring Freedom and Operation Iraqi Freedom was that AMC was a one-war organization. Regardless of the presumptions of national planning documents, the command had the capacity to deploy forces for one conflict at a time, not two near-simultaneous ones. The initial deployment to Afghanistan used up AMC, because it was so remote. Iraq did the same, because it involved such a large deployment. Indeed, the real-world shortfall in airlift capacity sharply constrained the deployment and battle plans of the U.S. Central Command in both conflicts.

Lesson Two was that large-scale counterinsurgencies consumed huge amounts of air mobility support. AMC's mission load, for example, grew from about 200 per day prior to the 9/11 attacks to over 400 afterward, mostly in support of Middle East operations.[6] Theater airlift requirements also grew rapidly as American and coalition forces spread out to secure populations and protect governmental activities. In Iraq and rugged Afghanistan, many units operated well beyond practical resupply and evacuation along landlines of communication. So heliborne air assaults became a common means to reduce transit times and risk and to maximize tactical surprise.[7] Aerial resupply kept maneuvering units effective and confident in the availability of quick support. To provide the necessary lift, the Air Force rotated squadrons of C-130s in and out of the region, and the Army committed hundreds of airlift and attack helicopters. Since the early 1940s, American doctrine had admonished commanders to bring lots of airlift into counterinsurgency operations. The new wars in the Middle East reminded everyone of just how much "lots" could mean.[8]

Seeking to enhance its ability to support small units in remote locations, the Air Force expanded and modernized its airdrop systems. In the first years of both wars, theater airlift units relied on the Vietnam-era container delivery system (CDS) to parachute small increments of supplies—a few hundred pounds to a ton in each CDS container—into small drop zones. But the fabric parachutes of the CDS were expensive, prone to damage, expensive to recover for repacking, and lacked the accuracy to put bundles onto mountain drop zones reliably. To improve drop accuracy, theater transport units began using the joint precision airdrop system (JPAD) in 2006. This system used global positioning system guidance to put 80- to 500-pound loads almost into the laps of waiting soldiers. To reduce costs further, AMC teamed the JPADs with the low-cost aerial delivery system (LCADS). LCADS consisted of single-use polypropylene parachutes and cargo containers that did not require expensive efforts to recover them for repacking. By 2010 theater airlift units were dropping almost 130 tons of supplies per day in Afghanistan, a tenfold increase since 2006, and virtually all via the JPADS-LCADS combination.[9]

Lesson Three was the need to enhance the amount and responsiveness of fixed-wing theater airlift support available to army units in the field. In Iraq and Afghanistan, army commanders identified almost bottomless requirements for fixed-wing airlift. They particularly wanted transports to supplant as many dangerous road convoys as possible, to accelerate the pace of operations, and to respond to time-critical requests to move mission-essential cargo and personnel. The Army covered as many of these "direct support" missions as possible with helicopters. But the UH-60 Black Hawk and CH-47 Chinook helicopters available lacked the range for many missions and could be as much as ten times more expensive per ton mile of lift produced than fixed-wing aircraft. To get more fixed-wing airlift, army commanders pressed the Air Force for additional C-130s, and they deployed handfuls of their own C-12 Huron and C-23 Sherpa aircraft to the region. But there never seemed to be enough C-130s available, and army commanders chaffed at the time required to coordinate airlift support through normal channels, even for time-critical loads. Also, while Hurons and Sherpas provided useful, on-call direct support, they were slow and relatively short ranged and carried maximum loads of only one or three tons, respectively.[10]

Asserting a right to address their direct support airlift needs in any way necessary, senior army commanders set out to acquire a theater airlift fleet of their own. On the basis of his own field experiences, the commander of the 101st Airborne Division, and future vice chief of staff of the Army, Major General Richard A. Cody led the charge in 2002, saying, "We must have an intra-theater, fixed-wing resupply capability."[11] The Army National Guard echoed Cody's call for a new aircraft, seeing it as an opportunity to replace the aging C-12s, C-23s, and C-26s in its inventory.[12] Hopes for a new transport received a boost in early February 2004, when the Army's cancellation of the Comanche helicopter program suddenly freed $14 billion for other aviation modernization efforts.[13] The Army's plans for spending this windfall included acquisition of an off-the-shelf future cargo aircraft (FCA). The plane wanted by the Army and the guard would be of modest size but more capable and efficient than the cargo airplanes currently on hand. The front-runner candidates were the Lockheed-Aeritalia C-27J and the CASA 295. Of the two, the Army leaned toward the CASA design, which was smaller and cheaper and had cargo deck dimensions compatible with those of the CH-47. The Air Force, which took an early interest in the Army's intended excursion into theater airlift, preferred the C-27, which was the larger and faster of the two aircraft. By 2005 the Army National Guard was eagerly awaiting selection of an FCA design.[14]

Important for future developments, the two aircraft under consideration for the FCA requirement were more alike than different from the C-130 in key operational characteristics. Both aircraft were twin-engine turboprops with the normal military loading features of aft ramps and doors, reinforced floors, rollers, and tie-down points. The CASA 295 carried a maximum payload of ten tons and could lift five tons for 2,300 nautical miles. The significantly larger and more expensive C-27 Spartan carried about twelve tons maximum and seven tons for 2,300 miles. Like the C-130, both aircraft were capable of operations onto austere runways of soil, gravel, or other unpaved surfaces. They could operate onto more narrow runways than the Herc, but they still needed them to be 2,000 to 2,500 feet in length for routine operations. In short, the two smaller planes were modern and capable. But operationally they were hard to differentiate from the C-130s already in the Air Force's inventory, and that would weaken the Army's argument that it needed a new aircraft to do much the same mission.

Studies: Balancing Affordability and Sufficiency

Continuing the trend established in the 1990s, Department of Defense (DOD) air mobility studies remained inconclusive and contentious after 2000 for two reasons. First, since no one really knew what the future would bring, the scenarios on which mobility estimates were based lacked credibility and authority. The guesswork of one group of planners was no better than that of another. Second, all DOD studies done during this time, like those in the 1990s, resulted in force structure proposals that were "fiscally prudent" but fell short of real-world requirements. The inability of the DOD to produce air mobility plans that were both prudent and sufficient for actual requirements left the mobility policy debate unsettled and divisive.

The Mobility Requirements Study 2005 (MRS 05) was the first major mobility assessment of the new millennium. Released as an unclassified summary in December 2001, MRS 05 examined mobility in the context of overall national strategic objectives. These objectives called for military forces able to win two major theater wars (MTWs) while conducting smaller-scale contingencies and other high-priority missions. From their detailed modeling of American movements in the early days of such conflicts, the drafters of the report suggested a reduction in the gross airlift capacity target from the 66 MTMD of the Congressionally Mandated Mobility Study to 54.5 MTMD. In addition, MRS-05 called for acquisition of 126 to 176 C-17s.[15] General Charles "Tony" T. Robertson Jr., the commander of both USTRANSCOM and AMC, and most other senior combatant commanders endorsed the study's findings only reluctantly. They knew that an inadequate mobility fleet would delay wartime deployments, which, in turn, would produce increased casualties.[16] The air force chief of staff, General Michael E. Ryan, however, endorsed the study's restrained recommendations, saying publicly, "The service will never have enough lift to support the conduct of two simultaneous major theater wars . . . we can't afford to go there."[17] As the man charged with paying the bills for *all* of the Air Force's development and operating costs, Ryan knew what he was talking about.

The debate over MRS 05 didn't get very far before the events of September 11, 2001, mooted its relevance. The airlift and air-refueling demands of heightened homeland defense operations, two overseas wars, and numerous lesser contingencies quickly invalidated the study's planning assumptions and recommendations. Initially, AMC defended MRS 05's 54.5 MTMD benchmark.[18] But by October 2004 General Robertson's successor, General John W. Handy, reported that AMC airlift operations had hit 67 MTMD. This, Handy said, "adds up to an airlift fleet that is too small to carry the load and personnel who cannot maintain a breakneck pace forever."[19] As Handy spoke, the DOD had begun a new study, which it released in late 2005 as the Mobility Capabilities Study (MCS).

As did its predecessors, the new MCS assessed the mobility requirements of several planning scenarios. These included those involved in "two overlapping war fights . . . homeland defense/civil support, lesser contingency operations, and sustainment of forward deployed forces." What set it apart from its predecessors was its level of detail. Earlier reports had assessed movements over average distances between the United States and the appropriate theaters of operations. The MCS developed and used detailed movement plans that tracked units from their actual departure points to their tactical assembly areas. Despite all the detail and complexity, however, the report's findings merely endorsed existing air mobility force structure. The current strategic airlift program of buying 180 C-17s and modernizing 112 C-5s, its authors found, could cover all requirements with "acceptable risks." In a similar vein, the study team found that intratheater lift capacity was in good shape and sufficient to address the scenarios considered. Tankers were a potential problem, they conceded, since the Air Force had 545 on the line, while various war plans called for 520 to 640.[20]

Also like the preceding reports, the MCS immediately came under fire from all directions. Months before the report even saw the light of day, General Handy publicly revealed that he was "uneasy" about its conduct and conclusions. Handy specifically worried that the report would be too sanguine in its expectations of early mobilization of the Civil Reserve Airlift Fleet (CRAF) and components of the Air Force Reserve and in its assessments of the condition of the KC-135 and C-130 fleets.[21] After completion of the study, the Government Accountability Office cast doubts on its assumptions, analytical discipline, completeness, and documentation. In conclusion, it advised "Congress and other decision makers [to] exercise caution in using the MCS to make programmatic investment decisions."[22] The Defense Science Board reiterated concerns over the utility of the report and urged the DOD to keep the C-17 available for production pending further studies.[23] Given all the political heat, the DOD keep a tight hold on the study, releasing only an executive summary of its basic findings to the public. With its credibility thoroughly undermined, the DOD's magnum opus on mobility requirements became a mere point of departure for discussion, not a definitive road map.

In March 2010 the DOD released still another mobility update, the Mobility Capabilities and Requirements Study 2016 (MCRS-16). In this study, DOD and USTRANSCOM planners worked together to produce the clearest and most realistic snapshot of mobility needs to date. For planning baselines, the planners focused on three complex cases, each involving multiple simultaneous engagements in combinations of theater wars, major air-sea campaigns, prolonged asymmetric conflicts, irregular wars, homeland defense, and/or other activities. After assessing these cases, the study team determined that the capacity of the strategic airlift fleet planned for that time—111 C-5s and 223 C-17s—"exceeds the peak demand in each of the three MCRS cases." This fleet was capable of lifting 35.9 MTMD, compared to a peak demand for 30.7 MTMD. So, the study found, the Air Force needed only 304 of the 334 strategic airlifters planned and just 335 of the 401 active-duty and reserve component C-130s on hand. The only really ominous note was an anticipated shortage of nearly 90 tankers needed in the worst case.[24]

This time, though MCRS-16 was subject to the usual scrutiny and accountability, the discourse over mobility lacked rancor. To minimize criticisms of the study's planning assumptions and analytical discipline, the DOD embedded a "Verification, Validation and Accreditation" team within the actual study group.[25] This step seemed to defuse strong criticisms of the study. The director of the Air National Guard, Lieutenant General Harry M. Wyatt III, did protest that MCRS-16 did not reflect an "unfulfilled requirement" for seventy-eight new C-27s for army direct support. But when pressed on the matter in the House Armed Services Committee, he said only that the correct combination of C-130s and C-27s to cover the direct support mission was under study.[26]

Beyond that, MCRS-16 seems to have become the first baseline air mobility study that implied a reduction of the fleet and that did not elicit strong reactions from all sides.

Although less controversial and costly than AMC programs, Army Aviation attracted numerous internal and external studies as well. These studies generally followed two themes. One was a visionary program to acquire a vertical-takeoff-and-landing (VTOL) aircraft capable of carrying twenty or more tons over theater distances. Studies for such an aircraft went back for decades. But the Army War College began war-gaming a modern version, the Air Maneuver Transport (AMT), in the late 1990s. The Army saw this aircraft as a linchpin of the Future Objective Army. Composed principally of air-portable mechanized brigades equipped with twenty-ton "future combat systems," the Future Objective Army would depend on "mounted vertical maneuver" for its effectiveness.[27] In early 2005 the Army contracted the National Aeronautics and Space Administration to conduct a concept design analysis for a joint heavy lift (JHL) VTOL aircraft. Replacing the AMT and reflecting weight growth in the future combat system design, the JHL was to be capable of lifting twenty-seven tons over an operational radius of a thousand kilometers. The other theme of Army Aviation studies was to maintain and selectively modernize its existing fleet as a bridge to the next generation of aviation aircraft. The 2001 Army Aviation Modernization Program articulated both of these goals. While aimed at "posturing" Army Aviation for transition to the Objective Force, its main foci were on modernizing the existing helicopter fleets of CH-47s, UH-60s, and AH-64s and acquiring the Comanche armed reconnaissance helicopter and unmanned aerial vehicles.[28] Subsequent modernization plans appeared in 2004 and 2010 but generally presented iterations of this basic theme: keep existing systems working while searching for the money and political support to pursue future concepts.

Actions: Keeping Things Working

Despite the general inconclusiveness of the DOD's major mobility studies, the Air Force and Army worked steadily to modernize and exploit the capabilities of their fleets. Their experiences with specific modernization programs varied in relation to the amount of money involved and the possibility of competition. The difficulty of achieving a joint service agreement also hampered army efforts to acquire a fixed-wing transport aircraft and to pursue more revolutionary modernization of aviation overall.

By the late 1990s C-17 acquisition had transitioned from a program in constant jeopardy to a program with a life of its own.[29] In 1997, when the DOD's commitment, or "program of record," was for 120 copies, AMC's commander, General Walter J. Kross, and others were pressing for more to cover theater and special operations requirements.[30] After a period of debate, the Air Force raised the program of record to 180 aircraft in 2002. This number did not satisfy General John W. Handy, who commanded AMC from 2002 to 2005. Arguing that airlift shortages were "beginning to limit military options," he proposed C-17 fleet goals of 222 to 300 aircraft.[31] Most other senior air force and defense leaders, however, accepted the 180 number as about right. Despite the military's satisfaction with 180 C-17s, the plane's congressional sponsors began to add unrequested aircraft to the budget in 2006. Their motivations included preservation of C-17 production as an economic engine and as a hedge against the still uncertain outcome of the C-5 modernization program.[32] Since these add-ons came on top of approved defense budget ceilings, some suspected that the DOD was playing a coy game of "leaving the program to survive on congressional plus-ups" rather than drawing funds from other programs to pay for it. Whatever the DOD's strategy, the Air Force's C-17 program of record in 2011 was for 223 aircraft.[33]

The story of the C-130J acquisition program was much the same as that for the C-17: the Air Force got more than it wanted but wasn't really unhappy once it had it.[34] The year 2005 was a pivotal one in the program. First, Congress blocked yet another attempt by Secretary of Defense Donald M. Rumsfeld to halt further purchases of the aircraft. Rumsfeld was acting on studies showing that the existing fleet had years of useful life ahead of it. Congress was acting to continue the upgrade of the wings of the Air Force Reserve and Air National Guard and thereby ensure their continued existence. Second, the secretary of defense's whole case was invalidated when AMC permanently grounded 37 of its older C-130Es for unrepairable structural failures and when it became clear that the penalty costs of canceling the ongoing program to acquire 62 C-130Js would exceed its completion costs.[35] Thereafter, C-130J production became a foundation of AMC's future. By mid-2011 the Air Force had over 90 on strength and planned to acquire as many as 134. This influx of Js would be accompanied by modernization of all older C-130s remaining in the fleet.[36] By that time the new plane and its advanced systems were proven performers in Iraq, Afghanistan, and anywhere else air force C-130s went.

Meanwhile, AMC pursued the modernization of the C-5 fleet steadily, albeit slowly and with sporadic concerns over funding. Even as C-17s were coming into the fleet, AMC leaders recognized that the big plane's substantially larger carrying capacity and cargo deck dimensions remained indispensable for many operations.[37] Accordingly, AMC initiated engine and avionics upgrade programs in the late 1990s, and in 2000 Congress began funding the Reliability Enhancement and Re-engining Program (RERP).[38] Estimates were that "RERPed" C-5s would cost about $148 million, compared to about $250 million for a new C-17. But their operational costs would be reduced compared to earlier models, and their performance characteristics would improve significantly. The first fully modernized C-5M Super Galaxy rolled out of Lockheed's Marietta, Georgia, plant in May 2006, with the final one expected around 2016. Immediately on the C-5M's entry into service, its higher climb rate, better range/payload characteristics, navigational performance, reliability, and quieter engines dazzled crews.[39] In this case, stretching out the life of an older system appeared to be remunerative.

During the course of two decades of steady-state surge and war operations, managing CRAF became something of an art form at AMC headquarters. The challenge, as always, was to finesse the need to utilize CRAF to the maximum extent possible day to day while preserving its availability and viability for emergency mobilizations. The sustained war-level operational tempo in the 2000s made this challenge acute. A founding concept of the program was that mobilizations would be infrequent and of short duration. Historically, this was the case. The only two call-ups of CRAF involved just fractions of the available fleet and were short: eight months for the First Gulf War and four months for the Second Gulf War. Following 9/11, however, CRAF surged operationally as if it were on a war footing. On an average day CRAF aircraft flew a third of AMC's 400–500 missions, carrying 90 percent of its passengers and around 40 percent of its cargo. To minimize the impact of this load on their daily commercial operations, most major CRAF carriers subcontracted their missions to a half dozen smaller carriers. To minimize future business shocks to CRAF carriers, AMC commanders sought to limit the number of C-17s coming into the fleet, since they would suck up potential contract traffic in peacetime. Likewise, they sought to reduce expectations in transportation plans that CRAF would be available for early mobilization and sustained use. Such expectations could either drive carriers out of the program and/or cause it to grow beyond a size that could be incentivized through peacetime contracting.[40] The success of AMC's walk along this fine line between overutilization and long-term viability was indicated at the end of the decade by the general health of the program and its membership.

The years of surge and war also pushed AMC, as part of the DOD's Future Total Force (FTF) program, to seek ways to extract more from its reserve components. Under the earlier Total Force program, the reserve and active components generally trained and operated separately. Actual integration of reserve and active units was unusual. Exceptions were the Air National Guard's "round-out" brigades attached to active divisions and the Air Force Reserve's associate wings paired with MAC and, later, AMC strategic airlift wings. *Future* Total Force, in contrast, sought to blend active and reserve elements within actual units at or below the wing level. AMC began its FTF effort in 1999, with studies and small-scale efforts to blend reserve flights and squadrons into active units.[41] Soon the command was putting active personnel into reserve and guard units, where they could help increase operational tempos while also being seasoned under the tutelage of more experienced reservists. In 2007 the RAND Corporation recommended expanding the integration program into AMC's operational center, the Tanker-Airlift Control Center, and the Air Mobility Divisions of theater Air Operations Centers.[42] That same year, the Air Force exchanged the "future" in FTF in favor of *Integrated* Total Force (ITF), indicating that integration had become a comprehensive reality and no longer just a future goal.

By 2008 the new reality of ITF was shaping AMC at all levels. In January, the Air Force issued a "major weapon systems road map" that, among many ITF provisions, assigned the first fifty new C-27s to the Air National Guard and promised to allocate more incoming KC-X tankers to the reserve components.[43] At the end of that same month, the congressionally chartered Commission on the National Guard and Reserves raised the ITF bar by recommending full integration of all military components into a centrally budgeted, trained, and directed "operational force."[44] By 2011 AMC literally had hundreds of ITF initiatives in place or under way to improve its ability to get the most service possible from its shrinking pool of active and reserve resources.

Barriers to Action: Interest Politics and Corruption

Interest politics and outright corruption slowed the progress of several air mobility modernization programs during the 2000s. These included the Air Force's tanker program and the Army's efforts to upgrade its fixed-wing direct support fleet. From a historical perspective, the play of interest politics and even a mild degree of corruption had been a normal feature of most, perhaps all, airlift programs since World War II. The amount of money involved in producing and then basing these aircraft made for pork battles that grew in complexity and fervor as the costs of individual mobility programs grew. Nevertheless, the travails of the tanker replacement and army airlift programs were troubling. These programs were vitally important to the immediate needs of airmen and soldiers at war, and their outcomes would shape service identities and capabilities in future wars. So the serious delays and retrenchments forced on them by selfish interests were sad evidences that human foibles could trump reason in the air mobility policy process, at least in the short run.

By 2000 no knowledgeable person could doubt the urgency of initiating an expeditious replacement program for the KC-135 fleet. The planes were old; all had entered service by the early 1960s. By 2000 their age was showing as routine maintenance overhauls began to reveal structural cracks, skin wrinkles, corrosion, and other major problems. By 2002, despite the pressing demands of Afghanistan and homeland defense operations, nearly a quarter of the Stratotanker fleet was in depot-level heavy maintenance at any one time. Their average stay in depot was 400 days. By 2003 General Handy worried that the Air Force might not be able to keep the KC-135 fleet "alive" until the replacements arrived. As evidence of the poor reliability and corrosion problems of AMC's older 133 KC-135Es, Handy had had to withhold them from overseas deployment during the Second Gulf War.[45] If there was any component of the national air mobility system that was approaching a showstopper crisis, it was the tanker fleet.

By the time of the Second Gulf War, AMC was in the midst of a worsening crisis in the management of its program to replace its KC-135s with KC-Xs. At the turn of the millennium, AMC planners were deep into a series of studies to assess the condition of the existing fleet and future requirements. The outcome of these studies, they hoped, would lead to an industrial competition to begin producing KC-Xs by 2012. The Air Force unhinged this orderly process in early 2002 by announcing that it intended to lease 100 tanker versions of the Boeing 767 airliner, the so-called KC-767. The deal stunk from the beginning. Normally, the DOD could not make such a huge commitment without open competition. In the absence of any completed studies showing the urgency or options for buying a new tanker, Senator John McCain (R-AZ) and the Government Accounting Office raised objections to the lease deal.[46] Senator Norman Dicks (D-WA) reinforced perceptions of a sweetheart deal for Boeing when he excoriated the director of the Office of Management and Budget, Mitch

Daniels, for criticizing the program to McCain. "Mitch Daniels," Dicks declared, "is a major concern. . . . Trying to make calls and teaming up with McCain, who only seems to care about Airbus, and doesn't have anything to do with the United States, is just flat-out wrong."[47] Clearly Dicks, "the senator from Boeing," was going to fight for a program of such obvious benefit to his home state.

A year later, the story was out. Seeking to ingratiate herself to Boeing, Assistant Secretary of the Air Force Darleen A. Druyun had engineered the tanker lease in collusion with at least one senior company official. Then she passed proprietary Airbus Industry information to Boeing to help it negotiate the terms of the lease. Druyun did succeed in securing a position for herself at Boeing and protecting the job held there already by her daughter. But investigations by several government agencies caught up with her, and after confessing her crimes, she was sentenced to nine months in prison on October 1, 2010. Druyun's revelations effectively killed the tanker lease deal, though the Air Force flirted for a few months with a reduced lease/buy arrangement. Otherwise, AMC and other government agencies restarted the interrupted process of analyzing tanker requirements and modernization options.[48]

Things went from bad to worse. The Air Force published a request for proposals for a new tanker design in April 2006. The new request came under fire immediately as favoring the Boeing-767-derived KC-45 design by placing primary emphasis on the cost of individual aircraft rather than on the overall costs of satisfying the Air Force's requirements.[49] Airbus Industries refused to submit its tanker version of the larger Airbus 330, the KC-46, until the Air Force adjusted the selection criteria. The Air Force complied, with criteria that assigned equal weight to individual aircraft performance and total fleet costs and thereby favored the KC-46. The favoritism of the new criteria exposed the Air Force's selection of the KC-46 in February 2008 to harsh and telling criticism from the Boeing camp and its supporters. In June 2008 the Government Accountabitily Office upheld many of these charges, reporting that the "Air Force had made a number of significant errors that could have affected the outcome of what was a close competition . . . [and] conducted misleading and unequal discussions with Boeing."[50] This second mishandling of such an important and high-visibility program undermined the confidence of Secretary of Defense Robert M. Gates in the Air Force's managerial competence. He, therefore, transferred control of tanker acquisition from the Air Force to the Defense Acquisitions office. When even this drastic move did not defuse the political uproar, he put the whole program into a cooling-off period of indefinite duration in December 2008.

Given the deteriorating condition of the tanker fleet, however, the competition for a replacement could not be put off for long. In 2008 AMC began to retire the KC-135E fleet. The planes simply had become too expensive and risky to maintain. Seeking to get a replacement program under way, a coalition of congressmen in 2009 pressed the DOD and Air Force to split the first buy of new tankers between both the KC-45 and the KC-46. A leader of the coalition, Representative John Murtha of Pennsylvania, declared, "The days of lawmakers fighting for one of the two airplanes, based on jobs each would generate in home districts, are now over."[51] Citing the logistics support costs of buying two different aircraft, the DOD demurred and countered with a new plan. That plan involved buying 179 KC-Xs from a single company. These would be followed by another increment of similar but not necessarily the same KC-Ys and finally by KC-Zs around mid-century to replace the KC-10s in the fleet. On the basis of that plan, the Air Force reopened the tanker competition in September 2009. This time, the Air Force managed the competition between Boeing and Airbus with greater care. Despite complaints from Senator McCain and others about the competition's selection criteria, the DOD inspector general in December 2010 upheld the Air Force's selection of the KC-45. Finally, the Air Force was on its way to purchasing a fleet of tankers that, if it remained in service as long as the KC-135, would be in operation beyond the year 2100.

In contrast to the KC-X program, the Army's advocacy of a new theater airlift aircraft made little progress. Having contracted NASA in 2005 to explore design options, the Army worked hard to build support for its mounted vertical maneuver concept and the aircraft needed to make it a reality. Although astounded at the technological challenges of such a large VTOL aircraft, the Air Force had little choice but to cooperate. In May 2008 it joined the Army to study the attributes of a joint future theater lift (JFTL) aircraft. Knowing full well that the Air Force's main intent was to gain some control over the program, the Army acknowledged only that its sister service had "administrative lead" of the JFTL program. Regardless of where the JFTL program went, ground warriors intended to keep their focus on developing a VTOL-capable aircraft tailored to their battlefield mobility needs rather than one optimized for the Air Force's joint logistics mission.[52] In keeping with their long experience in failing to agree on theater airlift needs, the two services never came up with a common vision. Analysts throughout this period recognized that "the Army needs VTOL to enable mounted vertical maneuver . . . but the USAF has a wider range of airlift missions to perform and wants to combine extreme STOL [short takeoff and landing] with stealth and high subsonic speed."[53] Thus, by late 2011 the project was hung up in the study phase, with the Air Force balking at providing its share of funding for further research.[54]

In reasonable likelihood, the Army was flogging a dead horse. The JHL concept violated too many time-honored "rules" of airlift aircraft development programs to get all the way through the whole defense research, development, and budgeting processes. Technologically, the aircraft was a high-risk concept. To lift twenty-seven-ton future combat system armored vehicles, it most likely would be a giant helicopter of four- or even six-rotor systems. Everything about the concept—rotor drive systems, multiple engines, connecting shafts, sheer bulk, and so on—smacked of complexity, developmental risk, operational vulnerability, and expense. Estimates for the aircraft, which would fall between the C-130 and the C-17 in size, ran as high as $200 million per copy—about the cost of a C-17 to carry the load of a C-130. The operational value of the aircraft was not clear either. If the Air Force and Navy achieved air dominance in a combat zone—a necessity for any mode of airborne or airlanded operations—then the incremental operational advantage of a JHL aircraft might not offset its opportunity costs within the defense budget. This particularly would be the case if a technologically conservative mix of fixed-wing STOL transports and upgraded helicopters also could provide the Army with enough maneuver dominance to win its campaigns.

Compared to the JHL program, the FCA program met with more success, but not before the Air Force took it over. Regardless of how the Army described the aircraft's intended use as a "direct support" platform, it clearly was a theater airlifter and similar to the C-130 in speed, range, airfield requirements, and missions. It also was exactly like the light transport aircraft sought by the Air Force in a parallel program. In light of these overlaps, the Army and the Air Force entered a memorandum of agreement in June 2006 to seek a common joint cargo aircraft (JCA). In the agreement, the Air Force declared its intention to purchase 70 copies of a "fixed wing airlift platform that performs airlift missions in support of the Joint Force Commander (JFC)." The Army planned to buy at least 75 JCAs as an "on-demand" transport of time-sensitive/mission-critical cargo and key personnel to forward-deployed army units.[55] Moving forward on the JCA agreement, the DOD let a $2.05 billion contract in June 2007 to purchase 78 C-27s as the first batch of an ultimate fleet of 140 or more.[56] By that time, however, the Air Force was pressing for full control of the JCA program. The Army's vice chief of staff, General Richard Cody, rose in defense, declaring that the Army "has a doctrinal right to move vital supplies 'the last tactical mile' . . . [and] can't rely on the USAF system to move supplies with urgency."[57] But Cody and like-minded allies were trying to stem a flooding tide. In April 2009, following months of interservice deliberations, Secretary of Defense Gates released Resource Management Directive 802, which, among many things, transferred full control of the JCA to the Air Force and reduced the buy to 38 aircraft, all of which would go into the Air National Guard.[58]

The logic of transferring the JCA/C-27 program to the Air Force depended on perspective. For army aviators trying to provide responsive airlift over the-ater distances, the aircraft brought capabilities into aviation that helicopters could not provide efficiently. For air force mobility experts, the C-27 was just another airlifter. Indeed, a 2007 RAND report questioned the need for more than a handful of C-27s, if any. Given the inability of the aircraft to provide the short-takeoff-and-landing-rough-field (STOL-RF) capabilities of a true assault airlift aircraft, the study suggested that it offered only marginal improvements in operational flexibility to the fleet. A few might provide some extra "tails" to cover short-notice requests, but otherwise their capabilities were redundant to those of the existing C-130 fleet.[59] Air force field experiments in Afghanistan during 2009 showed that C-130s also could cover most of the direct support missions just as effectively as the C-27. Indeed, the big planes could get into at least 99 percent of the airfields available to the C-27.[60] The fatal blow came from the Mobility Capabilities and Requirements Study-16, which found that the Air Force possessed a surplus of C-130s. That and continued downward pressures on the defense budget led the Air Force in 2011 to cap C-27 acquisition to the thirty-eight already on order. Given its operational characteristics, the JCA had become an attractive but unaffordable adjunct to the primary airlift fleet.[61]

The outcome of the JCA epic through 2011 reaffirmed several "truths" of air mobility policy and force structuring. Among them, perhaps the most impor-tant one was that trespassing interservice roles-and-missions boundaries is bureaucratically dangerous. As worked out during the Vietnam War, the bound-ary between army battlefield airlift and air force theater airlift is artificial and not particularly realistic. It is based on technical attributes—mainly fixed- ver-sus rotary-wing aircraft—rather than on operational needs and continuity. But the issue *was* settled in that way, and that settlement *had* brought interservice peace in a contentious area. Moreover, the seminal document on the issue, the Johnson-McConnell agreement of 1966, provided that "in cases of operational need the CV-2, CV-7 and C-123 type aircraft . . . may be attached to the subordinate tactical echelons of the field army . . . as determined by the appropriate joint/unified commander."[62] So when the Army tried to solve the direct support problem by acquiring the FCA, it set itself up for bureaucratic defeat by stepping out of its doctrinal lane and proposing an expensive technology fix in the presence of a cheaper doctrinal solution to its direct support problem.

Of almost equal importance, the Army virtually guaranteed the failure of the FCA program by proposing a more sophisticated and costly aircraft than it needed to fill the operational void. Had the ground service, instead, sought aircraft equivalent in size and performance to the existing operational support fleet of C-12s and C-23s, it probably could have scooted the FCA in under everyone else's budget radars. Had the proposed aircraft also possessed profound STOL-RF capabilities, the Army's doctrinal case would have been stronger. The Air Force had no plans to acquire STOL-RF aircraft, and such an aircraft would have fit the Army's operating concepts better. But by offering up aircraft that looked and performed like little C-130s, the ground service instituted a turf fight that it could not win.

End State: Air Mobility Forces in 2010

The state of airlift . . . despite a decade of the highest continuous demand since World War II, remains good, meeting ongoing demands from the troop drawdown in Iraq, simultaneous surge in Afghanistan, and humanitarian relief following devastating earthquakes in Haiti and Chile.[63]

As Collin Bakse, the longtime editor of the *Airlift/Tanker Quarterly*, summarized earlier, the American national air mobility system of 2010 had emerged from two decades of full-blown, steady-state, operational surge in remarkably good condition. Most of its airlift aircraft were either relatively new or in line for major upgrades and modernization. The KC-135 fleet was the obvious weak link, but it *was* still functioning. The biggest concern among air force leaders was that the Stratotankers would wear out faster than KC-45s could come on board, starting in 2017. Army battlefield airlift forces also were in generally good shape, with new CH-47Fs flowing steadily into the inventory and a comprehensive modernization program starting up for aviation as a whole.[64] More important, the morale of mobility practitioners generally was high, and they went about their duties with "messianic zeal."[65] In truth, the morale and competence of the mobility community has always been high. Whether they were dropping airborne troopers into Normandy, hauling casualties across the Pacific from Korea, putting whole battalions into the fight in the Ia Drang Valley, sneaking into enemy airspace to pick up fighters with low tanks, or carrying and distributing relief supplies in a hundred different disasters, airlifters and refuelers knew their stuff and were proud of what they did. That all of this capacity and zeal were maintained through twenty years of wartime surge was an accomplishment that would have been inconceivable in 1990.

The reality of surge is critical to grasp. The airlift components did not proceed through the 1990s and 2000s in a series of surges in response to specific events. Rather, the whole system largely stayed at maximum operating tempo year after year. The periods when battlefield, theater, and intertheater mobility components were not fully employed became the infrequent episodes of the operational effort. Particularly for AMC, the essence of force management became the "generation" of every possible aircraft virtually every day and then directed them at the highest-priority requirements of the moment—be they war, natural disaster, routine logistics and passenger carriage, training, maintenance, or whatever. The mobility "fire hose" sprayed every day, only its direction changed. For fliers and ground personnel, this surge translated into being away from home more often than not, losing leaves not taken by the end of the year, and living in a tent in Afghanistan while their wives delivered babies, parents passed on, and children played in soccer leagues. Coming home didn't bring a lot of rest, since they were called on to make up for all of their compatriots taking their turns in "the sandbox." Many of them did this year after year after year. Indeed, master sergeants and lieutenant colonels were retiring from the service in 2010 who had never served in a peacetime military, however that could be described.

Many things contributed to the air mobility community's ability to thrive under such stress. Good leaders worthy of the dedicated people serving under them were essential. Institutional and process reforms, such as developing the Total Force and Air Expeditionary Force programs and exploiting CRAF more thoroughly, did much to spread out the workload and assure individual personnel that they weren't being burdened callously or unequally. Effective engagement in the military policy process by civilian and uniformed leaders was critical to ensuring that the mobility fleets were modernized at least well enough, if not to the satisfaction of all participants. Even periodic mobility studies, like MRS-05 and MRCS-16, made a vital contribution. Grounded as they were on notional guesstimates of ephemeral futures, these studies nevertheless provided starting points for planning and policy. They produced fleets for scenarios that never happened. But the fleets they produced gave the Army and the Air Force the capacity and flexibility needed to respond to actual events that were as unique in many of their details as they were unexpected.

And therein lies probably the most important implication of the past two decades of air mobility history: since no one can predict the future, the essence of planning is to provide flexible capabilities that skilled and brave personnel can use to succeed when unexpected futures suddenly become the present. It is a frequent pretense of many in the public planning and policy processes that they are dealing with certainty in their predictions and numbers. To some degree, the stagecraft of projecting certainty is an essential survival tool in the zero-sum give-and-take of policy development. Convincing illusions of knowing what the future will bring can win funding for projects. But once the policy posturing is over, the true war-fighting strength of the country lies in its communities of professionals who know how things work and can apply the resources at hand quickly and effectively in novel situations.

25. Haiti 2010

The Way It Works

THE RELIEF OF Haiti provides as good a snapshot as any operation of the workings of the air force portion of the American national air mobility system after nearly a century of development and twenty years of a warlike operational tempo. To be sure, the Air Mobility Command (AMC) and the transport and aerial tanker units assigned to overseas joint combatant commands are trained, organized, and equipped for war. But they more frequently lay down their aluminum bridges of support units and aircraft to send relief to people stricken by natural and man-made disasters than for war. These humanitarian relief "global reach lay downs" often are to places visited only rarely by American transports, if at all. Most are small operations involving handfuls of aircraft sorties. The Haitian relief effort, in contrast, involved thousands of sorties moving thousands of people and tens of thousands of tons of cargo. To save lives, the U.S. Air Force (USAF) committed personnel and resources from all over the world. Their success made the Haitian relief effort an exemplar of the elements of American air mobility capabilities and practices.

A Heaving of the Earth in an Unfortunate Place

It would be hard to identify a nation less prepared to handle a major earthquake. Two centuries as a "slave colony" and two more centuries of independence characterized by kleptocratic governments, external exploitation, and overpopulation had left Haiti in deep poverty, unstable politically, and a basket case ecologically. With nine million people crammed into 10,714 square miles, Haiti is one of the most densely populated countries in the world. Most Haitians live on less than $2 per day, while the elite 1 percent of them own over half of the nation's wealth. Corruption in the country is rapacious. Beset by deforestation and erosion, Haiti's agricultural sector cannot feed the country. So poor is the country that many of its schools, medical institutions, and infrastructure and food programs exist only through the largesse of outside donor organizations and governments.

Thus, when the earth heaved at 4:53 p.m. on January 12, 2010, Haiti transitioned from an international welfare case to a prostrate nation in dire need of outside help. Thousands of occupied buildings in the capital of Port-au-Prince collapsed, killing over 200,000 people immediately and injuring over a million. Hundreds of government officials and workers were among the dead, as were members of international aid organizations. The UN Mission alone lost ninety-six workers, including its head of mission, Mr. Hédi Annabi. The city's port also was damaged heavily. Only the single runway of Toussaint L'Ouverture International Airport was available immediately as a gateway for relief assistance. But its control tower was unserviceable, and its parking ramp could handle only eight to ten aircraft at a time. So by the morning of the 14th, the flow of aircraft coming into the airport from all directions quickly overwhelmed its traffic pattern and ground infrastructure. Even as it began, the relief airlift was in danger of clogging to a halt.

Mobilization

Disaster mitigation efforts are routine elements of the domestic responsibilities and foreign affairs of the United States. As a result, the civil and military elements of the United States are practiced in such operations and supported by an array of planning and control organizations, logistical capabilities, and an extensive body of laws, directives, regulations, and other publications to guide their efforts. Thus, America's mobilization to help Haiti was more or less a matter of routine, despite its unique features of scale and location.

Many arms of the government began preparations as soon as news of the disaster hit the wires. The official relief effort began when Ambassador Kenneth H. Merten at Port-au-Prince formally called for help. As the lead agency for the response, the U.S. Agency for International Development (USAID) promptly alerted the U.S. Department of Defense (DOD) that its capabilities would be needed and then directed its own Office of Foreign Disaster Assistance (OFDA) to activate its Response Management Team and command center. On the January 13, President Barack Obama pledged an "aggressive effort" to save lives in response to the "especially cruel and incomprehensible disaster" that had struck a neighboring state.[1] By the time he spoke, an OFDA disaster assistance response team (DART) was en route to Port-au-Prince and expected to arrive at 1615 and assess the situation.

After receiving the USAID alert, the DOD issued a warning order to its subordinate commands. Since Haiti was located in its area of responsibility, the U.S. Southern Command (SOUTHCOM) received overall responsibility for the military effort. The commander in chief of SOUTHCOM (CINCSOUTH), General Douglas Fraser, USAF, activated Joint Task Force–Haiti (JTF-H) to direct operations at Port-au-Prince and placed it under the command of his military deputy, Lieutenant General P. K. (Ken) Keen, USA. Keen actually had been present in Port-au-Prince on SOUTHCOM business at the time of the earthquake and had been providing eyes on the scene for CINCSOUTH since.[2] Simultaneous with the stand-up of JTF-H, the DOD designated the military portion of the U.S. relief effort as Operation Unified Response.

The other joint combatant command with a major role in Haiti would be the U.S. Transportation Command (TRANSCOM). As CINCTRANS, General Duncan J. McNabb, USAF, would direct the efforts of his service components in response to transportation requests from USAID, SOUTHCOM, and other users.[3] His first actions included tasking the AMC to get the airlift under way and establishing a JTF–Port Opening (JTF-PO) to conduct cargo operations at L'Ouverture and the Port-au-Prince Harbor, once it reopened.

As a subordinate command with a large role to play, AMC wasted no time getting its capabilities and forces in motion. Even before formal orders came down from TRANSCOM, the commander, General Raymond E. Johns Jr., and his director of operations, Brigadier General Brooks Bash, began to posture their forces for the operation. With AMC's fleet "pretty much maxing out" in support of routine operations and the surge of nearly 30,000 additional troops and equipment to Afghanistan, Johns requested loans of seven C-17s from Pacific Air Forces and six from the Air Education and Training Command. Johns also activated a crisis action team to meet daily and "accelerate taskings and the information flow through the AMC staff."[4] Bash and his operations staff, meanwhile, were moving additional personnel, equipment, and supplies to Homestead Air Reserve Base, Florida; Pope Air Force Base (AFB), North Carolina; and Charleston AFB, South Carolina, to set them up as the primary aerial ports of *embarkation* for the lift. The 621st Contingency Response Wing, based at McGuire AFB, New Jersey, had a central role to play. It was organized to set up and operate forward aerial ports of *debarkation* (APODs) under contingency conditions.

The 12th Air Force also called on AMC for assistance. As AFSOUTH, the air force component of SOUTHCOM, the 12th would run air operations into Haiti. But to handle such a large mission, AFSOUTH needed augmentation personnel from AMC to flesh out the air mobility division (AMD) of its operational headquarters, the 612th Air and Space Operations Center (612 ASOC). The AFSOUTH commander, Lieutenant General Glenn F. Spears, also asked for the loan of an experienced director of mobility forces (DIRMOBFOR) to advise him on mobility matters and to provide authoritative connectivity into the air mobility community. AMC sent Brigadier General Robert K. Millmann Jr. Millmann normally served as the Air Force Reserve's mobilization assistant to the commander of AMC's 18th Air Force, Major General Mark S. Solo. But he also had filled the DIRMOBFOR role very successfully in several recent domestic weather disasters, notably during the relief of New Orleans after Hurricane Katrina.[5]

General Spears also went to his counterpart at 1st Air Force, Major General Garry C. Dean, for specialized assistance. Within the structure of the AMD of *his* ASOC, General Dean controlled the 601st Regional Air Movement Control Center (601 RAMCC), the only standing unit of its kind in the USAF. In his role as commander of AFNORTH, the air force component of U.S. Northern Command (NORTHCOM), General Dean's spread of responsibilities included assisting civil relief operations within the homeland. Given the unpredictability and time compression of such emergencies, the 1st Air Force established the 601 RAMCC in 2007, with the mission of metering the flow of aircraft into disaster relief airfields. The small crew of mostly reservists in the RAMCC quickly became the locus of most of the Air Force's expertise in its unique mission. So when General Spears recognized that he was going to direct a high-intensity airflow into the restricted infrastructure of L'Ouverture, he asked for a 601 RAMCC expert to show his AMD staff how do the job.[6] But by the time the contingency airflow expert, Major David J. Smith, arrived on the 14th, reports indicated that the traffic situation was in crisis. Major Smith immediately found himself not only helping the 612 AMD rise to the demands of functioning as a RAMCC but also acting as direct adviser and assistant to a three-star general, Spears, regarding operational and international diplomatic matters.[7] Meanwhile, General Spears asked General Dean to let the 601st take over the RAMCC job until the 612th was ready for it.[8]

On the Ground

Beginning on January 13, the mobility "footprint" grew rapidly at L'Ouverture. First on the ground were two Air Force Special Operations Command (AFSOC) MC-130Hs, which landed in the morning with teams of air controllers, medical personnel, and weather observers. Two KC-135s performed the first AMC missions of Operation Unified Response by refueling the Combat Talons during their flights. Led by Chief Master Sergeant Antonio D. Travis, the arriving

AFSOC team found L'Ouverture on the verge of gridlock and the traffic pattern dangerously uncontrolled. Doing what they were trained to do, they started fixing things. Some of these veterans from the 23rd, 21st, and 123rd Special Tactics Squadrons began untangling a knot of forty-five aircraft parked on a ramp designed for ten. Others grabbed handheld radios and a card table and set up a "tower" on the edge of the runway. Twenty-eight minutes after they arrived, the combat controllers cleared their first aircraft to land and then another to take off.[9] The first hint of order was emerging.

AMC began to arrive in strength on the 14th. In the morning a thirteen-member Joint Assessment Team of the 621st Contingency Response Wing arrived to survey L'Ouverture's readiness to handle heavy airlift traffic. A few hours later, the first twenty-one airmen and forty-four tons of equipment from the 621st Wing's 818th Contingency Response Group (818 CRG) arrived to set up APOD operations. They took over ramp operations from the AFSOC team, began aircraft-unloading operations, and set up a makeshift cargo-marshaling area. The pace of operations was such that cargo carried to the marshaling area often went straight onto trucks bound into the city. The daily traffic count grew from about 50 large aircraft arriving on the 14th, to about 70 on the 16th, and reached a peak of 165 on the 19th. The average sortie count for the first two weeks was about 120 large and jumbo aircraft per day, plus many arrivals by smaller aircraft and helicopters. To handle this pace, the 818 CRG eventually grew to about 126 members.[10]

As was a matter of routine in such events, mobility personnel found themselves filling the roles of diplomats in their efforts to get airfield operations in hand. The man on the spot turned out to be remarkably junior in rank. Normally colonels and generals act as the "tea drinkers" who coordinate operations with local officials. But at L'Ouverture the 818 CRG's expert on airfield operations was Captain Donovan Davis. As soon as his feet hit the ground, he engaged in a continual series of meetings with airport officials and other government leaders to clear out the crowds of wandering Haitians, civil relief personnel, reporters, and others from the parking ramp area and to give the 818 CRG full authority over ramp operations. Davis's success and credibility were such that in the midst of an international coordination meeting on the 15th, the prime minister of Haiti pointed to him and said, "You have responsibility for the airfield." From that point on, American authority over airfield access, space allocations, and operations was unassailable, if not beyond the complaints of some other groups.[11]

The arrival of the first fifteen members of the Army's 688th Rapid Port Opening Element (688 RPOE) on September 17 was the next significant addition to the air mobility effort. Based at Fort Eustis, Virginia, the 688 RPOE's task was to ensure the security and efficiency of the air cargo–marshaling yard already opened by the 618 CRG. Indeed, the RPOE and the CRG were the two elements of TRANSCOM's Joint Task Force–Port Opening, a team designed to open up APODs and seaports of debarkation in emergencies. Eventually the 688 RPOE would send about fifty soldiers, sailors, and civilian contractors to Haiti to manage the flow of cargo.[12] It was, noted the JTF-PO commander, Air Force Colonel Patrick "Hoot" Hollrah, the first time "the whole enchilada" of an army–air force–navy port opening task force had ever deployed, but not surprising since the concept was only a few years old at the time.[13]

The Problem of Priorities

In a purely military operation, the prioritization of cargo shipments and aircraft is straightforward. The commanders in chief of combatant commands prioritize their airlift movement requests, and their joint force air component commanders (JFACCs) or AMC's 18 AF make them happen as closely in line with those priorities as possible. Working through their AMDs, JFACCs conduct air movements within their theaters and coordinate intertheater support with the 18 AF. Acting on priorities and movement lists authorized by CINC-TRANS, the 18 AF conducts intertheater air movements, usually in support of every overseas command to some degree all of the time. More complicated than possible to describe here, the delineation and control of airlift priorities consume a great deal of staff efforts during the planning and execution of operations and a lot of text in a number of air force and joint doctrine manuals.[14]

As a humanitarian disaster in a country with only one jet-capable runway and one small parking ramp, the Haiti relief effort placed a premium on the prioritization of cargo and access to L'Ouverture, even as its circumstances complicated the process greatly. Dozens of countries and aid agencies wanted in, and the majority felt that their loads deserved priority access. But particularly in the first days, delays or poor scheduling of critical cargoes and personnel could equate to death for hundreds, maybe thousands. Everyone knew that, and several powerful organizations—particularly SOUTHCOM, USAID, the government of Haiti, and the DOD—felt empowered to set the necessary priorities. In the absence of control of the overall airflow in the first couple of days after the quake, a number of individuals and organizations sent planes into

L'Ouverture without reference to anyone's priority list. The result was a logistician's nightmare, one in which authoritative priority lists were late in coming, changed frequently, and often conflicted and could be ignored by "independent" participants who nevertheless jammed the traffic pattern and took up precious ramp space. It was a situation fraught with danger to the aircrews flying into L'Ouverture and to the lives of the survivors waiting for the right assistance at the right time.

The solution was obvious to many, and Haitian president René Préval took it. Aware of the capabilities of the 818 CRG and AFSOC controllers at L'Ouverture and of the RAMCC at Eglin AFB, he put the Americans in charge of metering the flow of big planes into the parking ramp. On January 15, his prime minister, Jean-Max Bellerive, signed a memorandum of understanding with Ambassador Merten authorizing the DOD to prioritize and supervise the flow of fixed-wing aircraft into Haiti. The Haitian government did not surrender sovereignty over its airspace; it merely attempted to accelerate "the distribution of relief supplies and rendering [of] humanitarian assistance as quickly as possible."[15] Both parties could terminate the agreement at any time, and Préval told the Americans he would resume control if he sensed that his desires and directives were being ignored.[16] But, for the moment, the 601 RAMCC would manage the process of granting access to L'Ouverture, which amounted at least to indirect responsibility for managing priorities, from wherever they came.

Already monitoring the status of L'Ouverture and managing traffic flow in and out of Homestead AFB, the RAMCC went into high gear. Colonel Warren Hurst, the AFNORTH DIRMOBFOR and RAMCC director, began by activating the Haiti Flight Operations Coordination Center (HFOCC) as a temporary office within the RAMCC to handle international requests for arrival slot times. The new name, he hoped, would clarify the purpose and authority of the HFOCC for non-USAF organizations and also allay suspicions that the Americans intended to control actual flight operations.[17] Lieutenant Colonel Bradley Graff, normally the 601 AMD chief, would supervise the HFOCC directly. Once the HFOCC activated at 0700 local time on January 16, its phone bank began ringing. In the first twenty-four hours of operation, the HFOCC team handled over 1,000 slot requests. Ultimately, it would issue over 4,000 arrival slots before handing the HFOCC mission to the 612 AMD on February 22. To handle the load, Graff's team grew from about ten air force reservists to sixty-three individuals drawn from the 1st Air Force, AMC, elsewhere in the Air Force, the Canadian Air Force, and the World Food Programme-

United Nations Humanitarian Air Service (WFP-HAS). What had been a capability incumbent in a few file drawers and the knowledge of a handful of staff officers had, in a few days, become a robust organization brought together from all points of the compass and linked to the world.[18]

The problem for the HFOCC staff was that the process of making rational slot time assignments to so many requesters depended on the availability of clear and authoritative priority lists. Such lists were not available in the first days, so Colonel Hurst filled the gap by directing the HFOCC staff to apportion fifty of the available slots to U.S. military and civilian aircraft and the other fifty to all other international requesters. Arbitrary as it was, Hurst felt that this apportionment would approximate the actual division of effort. Then, when SOUTHCOM began issuing priority lists, so did USAID and the government of Haiti. Generally these lists were similar. But as General Millmann later reported, they "did not line up" precisely. These disconnects obliged the HFOCC staff to adjudicate between them and less formal inputs from the United Nations, the Department of State, the Department of Defense, and a host of smaller agencies that interjected or at least attempted to interject their priorities and/or special permissions into the HFOCC's planning process.[19]

In reality, the press of time tended to trump the HFOCC's best efforts to rationalize priorities and slot time requests. With slot requests coming in every few minutes, HFOCC staffers had to grant them pretty much as they came in. There was no time to put a day's requests in "escrow" until the staff could work out cohesive flow plans. When obviously ill-timed requests came in, say, to deliver clothing in the first days, the staffers could negotiate later arrival times. Otherwise, they were more concerned with keeping the L'Ouverture ramp fully utilized but not saturated rather than with ensuring that every load arrived in precise accordance with a priority list. It wasn't an elegant arrangement, but it made sense in the moment and kept things moving into the stricken city.[20]

The HFOCC staff did establish several procedures to maintain some flexibility to handle unexpected, high-priority slot time requests. Most important, the team withheld 10 percent of all slot times available until they had to release them or risk letting parking spaces go empty. In exceptional cases, the HFOCC also canceled previously awarded slot times to let high-priority missions slip in. If it actually became necessary to divert airborne aircraft, the HFOCC usually sent U.S. military aircraft away. Military operators, HFOCC staffers reasoned, were better able than civil operators to handle the financial and operational impacts of going home to wait for another turn into the field.

When no-shows approached 25 percent of schedule flights, the staff began calling jumbo jet operators for confirmations forty-eight hours before their scheduled slot times. Slots opened up by this procedure could be reassigned to other operators in the queue. Taken together, these procedures markedly reduced wasted parking slots, kept the relief airlift operating in general conformity to higher-level priorities, and helped increase the capacity of L'Ouverture to 170 large aircraft arrivals per day.[21]

For all of its practical success, the HFOCC's involvement in the flow control process was not respected or appreciated by every participant or observer of the relief process. Some foreign officials ignored their slot time obligations by leaving their planes on the L'Ouverture ramp for hours while they visited the disaster scene. At the beginning of operations, a few relief organizations failed or refused to obtain slots from an American military organization. If no parking spaces happened to be available when they showed up in Haiti's airspace, they were sent away.[22] The real firestorm came from governments and organizations philosophically and/or politically unfriendly to the United States. The leaders of Venezuela, Bolivia, and Nicaragua declared that the slot times and the growing numbers of U.S. troops on the ground indicated that, in the words of Venezuelan president Hugo Chávez, "the United States was taking hold of Haiti over the bodies and tears of its people."[23] Individual French and Italian officials also criticized the U.S. "occupation" of Haiti and its alleged refusal to grant landing rights to several relief agencies.[24] Doctors Without Borders claimed that HFOCC turn-backs had caused the death of some of its patients.[25] While not wholly unexpected by the HFOCC's staff, as indicated by its coining of the term "Coordination Center," these criticisms were troubling diplomatically for the United States and SOUTHCOM.

The growing diplomatic pressure led AFSOUTH to take an unprecedented step: it invited specialists from the WFP-HAS into the HFOCC. In previous decades, relations between the UN and the USAF generally had been cool and characterized by a "mutual lack of familiarity" and "little understanding of each other's organization and procedures."[26] But circumstances were pressing, and no civil organization was more qualified to integrate its personnel into the RAMCC than the WFP-HAS. On a routine basis, the organization operates over fifty small and medium-size aircraft and routinely charters larger transports in support of humanitarian operations worldwide. As a common-user airlift provider to the global humanitarian relief community, WFP-HAS personnel are experienced with coordinating and prioritizing transportation requirements from numerous organizations.[27] So bringing its traffic specialists into the HFOCC would provide needed expertise and credibility and buffer the military staff somewhat from the pummeling of international criticism it was enduring. The WFP-HAS responded to the Air Force's invitation by sending three specialists to the HFOCC on January 24: Philippe Martou, deputy chief of the service, and two assistants, Mike Whiting and Albert Riegel. By that time the worst of the crisis was past, but the WFP-HAS team still performed valuable service by coordinating slot times and fielding the complaints of non-U.S. operators, assessing the priority of individual loads, and reducing the number of no-shows in the schedule. Summing it up, Philippe Martou reported, "This unprecedented relationship . . . significantly added to the unity of effort between civil and military aviation."[28]

As an indication with the general satisfaction over the blending of USAF and UN capabilities during Unified Response, most post-event reports endorsed continuation of the practice and refinement of the airflow metering process. Philippe Martou of WFP-HAS proposed the development of civil-military documents and training programs to capture the opportunities revealed by his experience in the HFOCC.[29] The 601 AMD and 612 AMD reports likewise recommended improvements in air force RAMCC capabilities and training programs, many of which the Air Force and various field commands subsequently undertook.[30] An outside analyst endorsed the need for procedural and institutional refinements that emphasized and enabled the sovereign roles of host governments in the distribution of arrival allocations.[31]

Achievements

It will be impossible to ever know precisely how much air cargo was flown into Haiti in the first weeks after the earthquake. In the hectic operations of the first days, much information was lost, as aircraft from many sources swept into and out of L'Ouverture and several smaller fields in the country. No one systematically collected data on the loads brought in by hundreds of light aircraft flights. Still, during the first five weeks, the relief flow averaged around eighty-two large aircraft transiting L'Ouverture per day, of which about thirty-five were commercial charters, thirty-two were international civil and military aircraft, and fifteen were U.S. military aircraft.[32] AMC alone sent 2,677 military and commercial charter missions, carrying 26,781 passengers and 14,135 tons of cargo into and out of the area.[33] The 612 AMD estimated "conservatively" that 3,940 U.S. and international sorties carried 10,151 passengers and 18,194 tons of cargo into L'Ouverture and took out 19,636 passengers and less than 200 tons.[34] Aircraft from over seventy nations contributed to these numbers, but the Royal Canadian Air Force (RCAF) was by far the largest non-AMC contributor. During what the Canadians called Operation Hestia, RCAF C-17s, C-130s, and sea-based helicopters airlifted over 2,800 tons of cargo and 5,447 passengers into and out of Port-au-Prince and Jacmel, a small strip on the southern coast of the country.[35] Thanks to the discipline of all the crews flying into the country, flow control procedures, and disciplined airfield operations, all of this was accomplished without a single significant accident.

At the bottom line, then, the involvement of the USAF, the AMC, and, specifically, the AFSOC combat controllers, the 818 CRG, and the HFOCC in the relief effort saved tens of thousands of Haitian lives. When the dust settled from the initial quake, something like a quarter of a million Haitians—almost 5 percent of the nation's population—lay dead. Perhaps a million lay or stumbled around in and outside of the city with injuries ranging from contusions to compound fractures and crushed organs. As the citizens of a nation that could not provide basic services in normal times, they were doomed without outside help. The flow of help began immediately and just as quickly jammed up at L'Ouverture. Whether the international critics of the United States liked it or not, it was the coordinated team of specialized USAF units and personnel that unjammed the parking ramp in a matter of minutes and, in a matter of hours, brought the flow of aircraft into the main airport to its maximum sustainable rate and kept it there for three weeks without accident or fatality.

The Elements of Greatness

No other air force in the world could have done it, at least not on the scale and with the speed with which the USAF organized the flow of relief into Haiti. There are several high-quality air forces in the world that could have done a similar job on a smaller scale and/or in their regions of influence. But only the USAF has the large global, connected, and responsive national air mobility system needed to activate such a large-scale effort in such a short time. USAID possessed the infrastructure, procedures, and practiced staff needed to direct the relief. SOUTHCOM and AFSOUTH had direct responsibility for the military portions of that effort and had cadres of knowledgeable personnel to initiate operations immediately. They were backed up by a global structure of specialized organizations that included USTRANSCOM, AMC, various logistics commands, NORTHCOM, and the 601 RAMCC. Critically, all of these organizations were staffed by trained professionals who cooperated easily across organizational lines and by individuals of timely initiative who rose to unexpected challenges and filled gaps in guidance and leadership when necessary.

The creation and articulation of so many staffs, organizations, and resources were not and could not have been accidental. They were the product of almost a century of sometimes hit-and-miss development of the professional community, doctrines, and technologies needed to respond so quickly and in such mass to a totally unexpected emergency. The elements of America's air mobility greatness are many, and they operate in an interdependent national system of knowledge and capabilities. At the moment of the Haiti emergency, the system was healthy and working well in all of its parts. But if the history of airlift teaches anything, it is that the national airlift system is sensitive to the degradation or neglect of any of its parts. It can be no more capable than the least capable of its human, ground support, and aviation components. For that reason, any assessment of the future of American airlift capabilities must begin in the sure knowledge that none of its elements can be taken for granted and all must be developed and exercised as a balanced whole, not as a collection of independent parts.

26. The Secret Is People

IT WAS A defining moment, and it happened every year. At the conclusion of the closing awards banquet of the 2011 Airlift/Tanker Association convention, all of the four-star generals in attendance stood on the stage, linked hands, and led over 3,000 members of the American air mobility community in the singing of "God Bless America." This time there were five of them: General Raymond Johns, the current AMC commander; General Thomas Ryan, General Ronald Fogleman, and General Walter Kross, former commanders of MAC or AMC; and General William Begert, the first airlifter to command the Pacific Air Forces. Among those thousands singing along were nineteen-year-old onestripers, midcareer officers and sergeants just back from the wars, active and retired colonels and generals by the hundreds, corporate representatives manning exhibits or patrolling the crowd for business, and "graybeards" back to reconnect. Spouses were there also by the hundreds, some renewing old friendships, and some, perhaps for the first time, getting an insight into the community and mission that drove their spouses to work so hard at such demanding and unpredictable jobs.[1] And there it was before them, a spirit of camaraderie, passion for country, and pride of mission that made it perfectly natural for leaders of high rank, some of them with moistened eyes, to be the song leaders for such a diverse group. They were, as AMC commander Raymond E. Johns Jr. had just said in the keynote address, the people who "answer the call of others, so they can prevail."[2]

The Airlift/Tanker Association is both a product and an underpinning of the unity of the airlift community. Formed as the Airlift Association on the initiative of General William G. Moore and other Vietnam-experienced airlifters in 1969, the organization soldiered through its first decade as a meeting of mainly tactical airlift officers and senior enlisted personnel focused on having a good time over drinks and golf and renewing connections. But they also sat down each year to a growing agenda of meetings that included senior leader panels, discussions of new aircraft programs and tactics, personnel briefings, and other serious matters. Following the consolidation of air force airlift forces in the mid-1970s, the strategic airlift community merged into the association with little difficulty.[3] In 1993 Airlift Association leaders asked the AMC commander General Ronald R. Fogleman to endorse the growing professional content of the annual convention by authorizing military personnel to attend it on funded official orders. Fogleman agreed, subject to continued expansion of the conference agenda and changing the organization's name to include the tanker personnel entering the new command.[4] Thereafter, the Airlift/Tanker Association conventions became massive affairs of meetings, panels, award presentations, vendor exhibits, golf tournaments, and legendary Crud jousts.

Crud is one of two competitive events that simultaneously make enemies and brothers out of air mobility units and people, even if they are women. The other event is the annual Airlift/Tanker rodeo held to allow flying and support units from throughout the American air mobility community and from foreign air forces to compete professionally. But while the rodeo involves a great deal of socialization and after-hours alcohol, it also features flying and firearms, so it tends to be an event overlaid with serious intent and attention to safety. In contrast, the social aspects of Airlift/Tanker Association Crud competitions are less restrained by good judgment and probity. The game itself involves five-person teams jostling around a billiard table trying to knock a target ball into a pocket with a hand-launched object (cue) ball. The action is furious as individual players make "sorties" to and away from the table to make their shots and interfere with the shots of their opponents through mild checking, yelling, wild gestures, and generally uninhibited profanity. Drinking is permitted during play, and the rules basically demand it. So the play gets wilder by the minute. Airmen shove generals aside, the generals shove back, and minor injuries do occur from overly enthusiastic checking or face plants on table edges.[5] But the annual Crud tournament is what everyone has been waiting for, and it is played with zeal worthy of crusaders. Teams honored to represent their units practice for months in their free time to get ready. If the reader finds it hard to understand how an arcane form of billiards can be so important to a community of otherwise serious and accomplished professionals, suffice it here only to accept that Crud is as important to the self-identity and social bonding of the mobility community as football is to Notre Dame.

The points of all of this are that people are the true heart and soul of global air mobility, and the existence of such a large, complex, and dedicated community of practitioners is not accidental. General Johns made that first point the theme of his keynote at the 2011 Airlift/Tanker Association convention. Recounting a dozen vignettes, he described the courage, initiative, skills, and achievements of aircrews and ground teams in war and peace. Dropping supplies to isolated military units and hungry villages in Afghanistan, racing into the Antarctic night to rescue an ailing scientist, carrying radiation hazard teams to Japan, and taking less than forty-eight hours to establish an expeditionary tanker wing in Spain were among many of the things they did to bring help, hope, and fuel where needed. In a particularly moving portion of his presentation, Johns brought the members of a C-17 crew and a critical care air transport team on stage to praise their handling of an injured soldier just clinging to life. Then he called the soldier, Staff Sergeant Thomas Moore, from the crowd and introduced him to the people who had saved his life. The crowd got it. As Johns said at the beginning, "The aircraft has no heart; it's cold steel, titanium, and aluminum; it's really about the people; it's about our airmen, our [aerial] porters, our maintainers, our operators, our intel, our tactics—they are the heart of what we do."[6]

But behind his words, General Johns was making the second point that nothing this big, complex, and effective could have emerged by accident. At the start of his speech, he described an air mobility community of 135,000 active, reserve, guard, and civilian employees. He also extolled the patriotism of the members of the Civil Reserve Airlift Fleet. Behind those obvious elements of the national air mobility system, the general might also have pointed out other military and civil organizations less visible but still indispensable to its effectiveness. Every army unit had personnel, doctrine documents, and loading manuals to enable it to configure for air movement. The Joint Chiefs of Staff and combatant commanders maintained logistics organizations and management systems to facilitate estimates and allocations of air logistics capabilities. Corporations produced the aircraft, materials-handling equipment, and thousands of other items needed by all those people to do their jobs. An extensive body of joint, air force, and Air Mobility Command regulations, doctrine manuals, and instructions encapsulated decades of experience, supported training at dozens of military schools, and enabled units scattered over the world to integrate their activities smoothly. Unquestionably, the air mobility system was an interconnected whole of many parts.

Rather than the product of any distinct set of memorandums and laws, this complex human and material mechanism was more the product of cultural evolution. As described in this book, the basic notion of airlift sparked in the imagination of men well before the dawn of powered flight. In the 110 years following the first flight of the Wright brothers, people nourished that vision into the intellectual, character, and material elements of the modern system. But they were not following any comprehensive plan. Plans were made, often. But no plan for technology or organization refinement retained credibility for more than a few years, if that long. So the air mobility system evolved incrementally as operational experience, technology development, and changeable geopolitics led its practitioners year to year. The really important lessons of dedication, leadership, courage, coordination, and persistent excellence of execution were passed person to person, generation to generation by old hands teaching the new guys in the cockpit, in the classroom, in briefing rooms, or over beers at the club. Consequently, the air mobility arm of the United States evolved not by farsighted fiat but as responses by a history of organizations and thousands of people to the persistent logic of the art and science of moving things by air in war.

And the evolution of air mobility will continue, as the air mobility community faces many challenges. In 2012 America's strategic focus began shifting again from counterinsurgency warfare in the Middle East to the potential of big wars in Asia. At the same time, the country and the world are struggling economically, so the resources available to the U.S. military will shrink. Serious force structure challenges, consequently, face mobility practitioners. It remains anyone's guess as to whether the KC-46 fleet will make it on line as fast as individual KC-135s wear out beyond technical or economic repair. The question of what will follow the C-5 and C-17 fleets is receiving little attention outside of a few planning offices at AMC. But given the predictably protracted development of the next-generation strategic airlifter, the time to energize that process cannot be far off. Meanwhile, fundamental questions remain regarding the future of theater airlift, particularly in light of the Army's commitment to mounted vertical maneuver or something like it. Regardless of whether the answer to these questions is a very large vertical-takeoff-and-landing (VTOL) aircraft or some combination of large helicopters and fixed-wing transports, the C-130 probably will fall short of needs. It will not be able to carry the ground vehicles involved or move the logistics required. Then again, geopolitical realities and modern aerospace power may reduce or even invalidate the logic of moving mechanized units over theater distances by VTOL aircraft in major conflicts. If the principal roles of large ground units under such circumstances remain in the realm of raids in big wars and engagement in low-intensity conflicts, then the C-130s, augmented by C-17s and helicopters, will do just fine.

So unpredictability remains the major element of long-range air mobility planning. The key to succeeding in such uncertainty will be the one thing that seems to be constant in the history of air mobility: the continuity of generation after generation of enthusiastic and competent people showing up to deal effectively with the operational and developmental problems they face. Maintaining that continuity will be as good of an assurance of the future success of the air mobility arm as one could expect. If history teaches anything about air mobility capabilities, it is that the nation never can afford to buy enough of the right aircraft and other things needed to satisfy anticipated requirements and the surprises of the real world. But it always seems to have enough, sometimes just enough, to enable the great people on the scene to make things work. So no matter how stressed or truncated the air mobility system becomes, leaders can do nothing more important for its long-term effectiveness than to ensure that the intergenerational transmission of knowledge, values, and character continues—and *that* is why Crud is so important.

Notes

1. Discovering Air Mobility

1. From Nathan G. Goodman, ed., *The Ingenious Dr. Franklin: Selected Scientific Letters of Benjamin Franklin* (Philadelphia: University of Pennsylvania Press, 1931), 99–105.

2. John Christopher, *Balloons at War: Gasbags, Flying Bombs and Cold War Secrets* (London: Tempus, 2004), 25–26; David W. Wragg, *Flight before Flying* (New York: Frederick Fell, 1974), 52.

3. John Fisher, *Airlift 1870: The Balloon and Pigeon Post in the Siege of Paris* (London: Max Parrish, 1965), 143 and throughout.

4. Octave Chanute, *Progress in Flying Machines* (New York: American Engineer and Railroad Journal, 1894), 266–68.

5. Maurer Maurer, ed., *The U.S. Air Service in World War I*, vol. 2, *Early Concepts of Military Aviation* (Maxwell AFB, AL: Air University Press, 1971), 7, 9, and 32.

6. Edgar S. Gorrell, "Final Report of the Chief of the Air Service," in Maurer, *The U.S. Air Service*, vol. 2, *The Final Report of the Chief of Air Service AEF and a Tactical History*, 79.

2. Military Air Transport in the 1920s

1. The best single source of these after-actions studies and reports remains the Office of Air Force History's four-volume study, *The U.S. Air Service in World War I: Early Concepts of Military Aviation* (Maxwell AFB, AL: Air University Press, 1971).

2. U.S. Air Force Research Studies Institute, *History of the Air Corps Tactical School, 1920–1940* (Maxwell AFB, AL: Air University Press, 1955), 12; U.S. Army, *Training Regulations 440-15: Fundamental Principles for the Employment of the Air Service* (Washington, DC: War Department, January 26, 1926).

3. Charles E. Miller, *Airlift Doctrine* (Maxwell AFB, AL: Air University Press, March 1988), 2–3, 9.

4. "Chart National Airways: But Army Air Service Needs Funds to Put System in Effect," *New York Times*, July 6, 1921.

5. William Mitchell, *Winged Defense: The Development and Possibilities of Modern Air Power—Economic and Military* (New York: G. P. Putnam's Sons, 1925).

6. Maurer Maurer, *Aviation in the United States Army, 1919–1939* (Washington, DC: Office of Air Force History, 1987), 108–11.

7. Except where indicated, all speeds and distances in this book will be given in knots and nautical miles. This will facilitate comparisons between aircraft types, even though knots and nautical miles did not become the common reference in aviation until well after World War II.

8. William C. Sherman, *Air Warfare* (New York: Ronald Press, 1926), 259–63.

9. Cited from Miller, *Airlift Doctrine*, 9.

10. Genevieve Brown, *Development of Transport Airplanes and Air Transport Equipment* (Langley Field, VA: Air Technical Service Command, 1946), 31.

11. K. M. Painter, "Help from the Skies," *Popular Mechanics* 52, no. 5 (1929): 763–65.

12. Thomas C. Turner, "Flying with the Marines in Nicaragua," *The National Aeronautic Magazine* 8, no. 10 (October 1930): 11–32.

13. Aircraft data and production figures drawn from the Air Force Museum's virtual aircraft gallery (www.nationalmuseum.af.mil/factsheets/). But also see Bill Holder and Scott Vadnais, *The "C" Planes: U.S. Cargo Aircraft 1925 to the Present* (China: Holder and Vadnais, 1995). This is a vanity book and contains some factual and numerous typographical errors, but it is a useful small volume, listing data and production figures for all U.S. cargo aircraft.

14. Mason M. Patrick, *The United States in the Air* (New York: Doubleday, 1928), 124–32.

3. Civil Aviation between the Wars

1. Congress, House, *Congressional Record*, vol. 66, pt. 1, December 1 to December 31, 1924, 738, 742, 746.

2. William Mitchell, *Winged Defense: The Development and Possibilities of Modern Air Power—Economic and Military* (New York: G. P. Putnam's Sons, 1925), 88.

3. United States Office of President, *Report of the President's Air Policy Board* (Washington, DC: US Government Printing Office [USGPO], 1925), 8. Also known as the Morrow Report, after the chairman of the study, Dwight W. Morrow.

4. G. Lloyd Wilson, "Express Takes to the Air," in *Air Transportation* (Chicago: Traffic Service Corporation, 1938), 11–12.

5. Nick A. Komons, *Bonfires to Beacons: Federal Civil Aviation Policy under the Air Commerce Act, 1926–1938* (Washington, DC: Smithsonian, 1989), 25.

6. Henry Ladd Smith, *Airways: The History of Commercial Aviation in the United States* (New York: Knopf, 1942), 120; "Air Mail Ace Wins Harmon 1926 Trophy: Aviation Award to Pilot Short Is for Merit of Consistent Flying over Spectacular Performances," *New York Times*, January 14, 1927.

7. U.S. Department of Commerce and the American Engineering Council, *Civil Aviation* (New York: McGraw-Hill, 1926), 1–3.

8. Smith, *Airways*, 118.

9. "Lindbergh's Feat to Fill the Sky with Flyers," *Literary Digest* 93, no. 11 (June 11, 1927): 1–3.

10. Smith, *Airways*, 315.

11. U.S. Government, *United States Statutes at Large, 1938*, vol. 52, 980, 987–93, and 997–98.

12. Edgar S. Gorrell, "The Airline Industry Today," reprint from the Proceedings of the National Aeronautic Association Conference, Chicago, IL, November 30 and December 1, 1936. Gorrell Papers, National Air and Space Museum, box 1 of 1.

13. Smith, *Airways*, 315.

4. Military Air Transport in the 1930s

1. "The Air Corps Exercises at Mather Field," *Air Corps News Letter*, March 31, 1930, 1–2; Genevieve Brown, *Development of Transport Airplanes and Air Transport Equipment* (Langley Field, VA: Air Technical Service Command, 1946), 47.

2. Maurer Maurer, *Aviation in the United States Army, 1919–1939* (Washington, DC: Office of Air Force History, 1987), 246–47.

3. Byron Q. Jones, "Field Exercises of Second Bombardment Wing, Air Corps" and "Detailed Data on Maneuvers of Second Bombardment Group," *Air Corps News Letter*, April 1, 1935, 131–33, and May 1, 1935, 5–6, respectively. Also see "Mobility" in "GHQ Air Force" section of *Air Corps News Letter*, July 1, 1935, 17, for comment on lightweight equipment.

4. Seventh Bomb Group, "Administrative Orders," TD (typewritten document), May 6, 1937, 2, and "Field Orders," April 25, 1937, 2, both in Air Force Historical Research Agency (AFHRA), 145.93–114. Tonnage estimates taken from B.Q. Jones, "Air Forces and War," an Army War College lecture, TD, September 1937, AFHRA, 145.93-115, 76.

5. Norman E. Borden Jr., *Air Mail Emergency, 1934* (Freeport, ME: Bond Wheelwright, 1968), 4–6. Two other useful accounts of the airmail episode are found in Maurer, *Aviation*, 299–317, and John F. Shiner, *Foulois and the U.S. Army Air Corps, 1931–1935* (Washington, DC: Office of Air Force History, 1983), 125–49.

6. Borden, *Air Mail*, 135–36.

7. Lee Arbon, *They Also Flew: The Enlisted Pilot Legacy, 1912–1942* (Washington, DC: Smithsonian, 1991), 82.

8. War Department, *Final Report of the War Department Special Committee on Army Air Corps* (Washington, DC: GPO, 1934), 60.

9. "General Headquarters Air Force Transport," *Air Corps News Letter*, October 15, 1935, 2.

10. Hugh J. Knerr to Chief Air Materiel Division Augustine W. Robins, "Requirements for Transports," TD, January 12, 1937, AFHRA, 145.91-316, 2.

11. Charles E. Miller, *Airlift Doctrine* (Maxwell AFB, AL: Air University Press, 1988), 18.

12. United States Office of President, *Report of the President's Air Policy Board* (Washington, DC: USGPO, 1925), 8. Also known as the Morrow Report, after the chairman of the study, Dwight W. Morrow.

13. Charles H. Lawrance, *Our National Aviation Program* (New York: Aeronautical Chamber of Commerce, 1932), 22–39 and 64; Robert P. White, *Mason Patrick and the Fight for Air Service Independence* (Washington, DC: Smithsonian, 2001), 102–9.

14. United States Congress, Civil Aeronautics Act of 1938, Public Law 706 Sec 2(a), *United States Statutes at Large, 1938*, vol. 52, 980.

15. Hugh B. Cave, *Wings across the World: The Story of the Air Transport Command* (New York: Dodd, Mead, 1945), 3–4; Theodore J. Crackel, *A History of the Civil Reserve Air Fleet* (Washington, DC: Office of Air Force History, 1993), 34–46; Roger E. Bilstein, *Airlift and Airborne Operations in World War II* (Washington, DC: Air Force History and Museums Program, 1998), 11.

16. Crackel, *Civil Reserve Air Fleet*, 34–46.

17. Maurer, *Aviation*, 367–68; War Department, Air Corps Training and Operations Division, Major R. C. Candee, "Memorandum for Executive," TD, August 2, 1935, AFHRA, 145.91-316; and 10th Troop Carrier Group, "History from Date of Activation to December 31, 1940," TD, n.d., AFHRA, Records of 10th Trans Group, frames 1579–80.

18. H. C. Pratt to chief of the Air Corps, "Recommendations for Organizing Transport Squadrons," July 20, 1934, 1; A. W. Robins to chief of the Air Corps, "Redesignation of Certain Transport Units to Create an Active Transport Group," TD, February 10, 1936, AFHRA, 145.91-316, 1; A. W. Robins to chief of Air Corps, "Development of the Transport Group and Squadrons," April 22 and April 30, 1936 (two separate letters), AFHRA, 145.91-316.

19. A. W. Robins to chief of the Air Corps, "Transport Organization," TD, April 15, 1937, AFHRA, 145.91-316, 2, and attached comments by General Arnold.

20. See as the only example of an Air Corps Tactical School student paper on air transport, Ray G. Harris, "Military Air Transport," Student Report, The Air Corps Tactical School, 1938–1939, AFHRC Archives.

21. Henry H. Arnold, staff comments to "Report: Operating Cost Cargo Airplanes," March 1, 1938, AFHRA, 145.91-316.

22. Henry H. Arnold and Ira C. Eaker, *Winged Warfare* (New York: Harper and Brothers, 1941), 14–18.

23. Maurer, *Aviation*, 367–68; War Department, Air Corps Training and Operations Division, Major R. C. Candee, "Memorandum for Executive," TD, August 2, 1935, AFHRA, 145.91-316; 10th Troop Carrier Group, "History from Date of Activation to December 31, 1940," TD, n.d., AFHRC, Records of 10th Trans Group, frames 1579–80; Arbon, *They Also Flew*, 102–3.

24. Arbon, *They Also Flew*, 3.

25. Henry H. Arnold and Ira C. Eaker, *Army Flyer* (New York: Harper and Brothers, 1942), 77, 110–11; Air Corps Personnel Division, "Memorandum for the Chief of Staff, Subject: Commercial Air Transport Pilots Should Be Encouraged to Become Members of the Army Air Corps Reserve," October 15, 1934, AFHRA, 145.93-94, 2–3.

26. Arbon, *They Also Flew*, 104–5.

5. Mobilizing Air Transport for Global War

1. Byron Q. Jones, "Field Exercises of Second Bombardment Wing, Air Corps," and "Detailed Data on Maneuvers of Second Bombardment Group," *Air Corps News Letter*, April 1, 1935, 131–33, and May 1, 1935, 5–6, respectively.

2. Office of the Chief of the Air Corps to the Adjutant General, "Air Corps Balanced Program," TD, June 25, 1937, AFHRA, 145.91-316; Charles E. Miller, *Airlift Doctrine* (Maxwell AFB, AL: Air University Press, 1988), 18.

3. John D. Carter, "The Air Transport Command," in *The Army Air Forces in World War II*, ed. Wesley Frank Craven and James Lea Cate, vol. 7, *Services around the World* (Chicago: University of Chicago, 1958; reprint, Washington, DC: Office of Air Force History, 1983), 5; Alfred Goldberg, "The Production Record," in Craven and Cate, vol. 6, *Men and Planes*, 353.

4. Henry H. Arnold and Ira C. Eaker, *Winged Warfare* (New York: Harper and Brothers, 1941), 13–18, 55–57, and 121–22.

5. James Lee, *Operation Lifeline: History and Development of the Naval Air Transport Service* (Chicago: Ziff Davis, 1947), 8–24.

6. Air Transport Command, *Administrative History of the Air Transport Command: June 1942–March 1943* (Maxwell AFB, AL: AFHRA, November 1945), 66–84; John D. Carter, "The Early Development of Air Transport and Ferrying," in Craven and Cate, vol. 1, *Plans and Early Operations, January 1939 to August 1942*, 352–65; Reginald M. Cleveland, *Air Transport at War* (New York: Harper and Brothers, 1946), 17–20; Oliver La Farge, *Eagle in the Egg* (New York: Arno Press, 1949), 8.

7. Edward V. Rickenbacker, *Rickenbacker* (Englewood Cliffs, NJ: Prentice Hall, 1967), 266–72.

8. Cleveland, *Air Transport*; La Farge, *Eagle in the Egg*, 1–4, 31; Hugh B. Cave, *Wings across the World: The Story of the Air Transport Command* (New York: Dodd, Mead, 1945), 3–4.

9. Cleveland, *Air Transport*, 4.

10. Carter, "Early Development," 351; Cleveland, *Air Transport*, 1.

11. Cleveland, *Air Transport*, 57.

12. Cleveland, *Air Transport*, 13.

13. Carter, "Early Development," 314–17; Geoffrey Perret, *Winged Victory* (New York: Random House, 1993), 46–47; Henry H. Arnold, *Global Mission* (New York: Harper and Brothers, 1949), 294–95.

14. Perret, *Winged Victory*, 202. Dunn went on to command troop carrier operations and wings in North Africa and England and retired as a brigadier general in 1949.

15. See John Warren, *Airborne Operations in World War II, European Theater* (Maxwell AFB, AL: AF Research Studies Institute, 1956), passim; Miller, *Airlift Doctrine*, 80–81, for discussions of the origins and operations of troop carrier forces.

16. Army Air Forces (AAF), Office of Statistical Control, *Army Air Forces Statistical Digest*, December 1945, 1, 7.

17. For discussion of marine air transport forces in World War II, see Robert Sherrod, *History of Marine Corps Aviation in World War II* (San Rafael, CA: Presidio, 1952), 111, 224, 235, 445–71; Jon T. Hoffman, *Silk Chutes and Hard Fighting: U.S. Marine Parachute Units in World War II* (Washington, DC: USMC History and Museums, 1999), throughout.

18. Alfred Goldberg, "The Production Record," in Craven and Cate, vol. 6, *Men and Planes*, 353–54.

6. Air Transport in World War II

1. Air Transport Command (ATC), *Administrative History of the Air Transport Command: June 1942–March 1943* (Maxwell AFB, AL: AFHRA, November 1945), 1.

2. ATC, *Administrative History*, 1–4, 86–91. See also James Lee, *Operation Lifeline: History and Development of the Naval Air Transport Service* (Chicago: Ziff Davis, 1947), 14–22; The Aviation History Unit, OP-519B, Lt. A. R. Buchanan, ed., *The Navy's Air War: A Mission Completed* (New York: Harper and Brothers, 1946), 366–69.

3. Reginald M. Cleveland, *Air Transport at War* (New York: Harper and Brothers, 1946), 170; Matthew Josephson, *Empire of the Air: Juan Trippe and the Struggle for World Airways* (New York: Harcourt Brace, 1943), 162–63.

4. John D. Carter, "The Air Transport Command," in *The Army Air Forces in World War II*, ed. Wesley Frank Craven and James Lea Cate, vol. 7, *Services around the World* (Chicago: University of Chicago, 1958; reprint, Washington, DC: Office of Air Force History, 1983), 22; Genevieve Brown, *Development of Transport Airplanes and Air Transport Equipment* (Langley Field, VA: Air Technical Service Command, 1946), 110–14.

5. Cleveland, *Air Transport*, 29, 55–56; Hugh B. Cave, *Wings across the World: The Story of the Air Transport Command* (New York: Dodd, Mead, 1945), 3–10.

6. ATC, *Administrative History*, supporting documents, 8.

7. Department of the Army, *Army Air Forces Statistical Digest* (Washington, DC: USAAF Office of Statistical Control, December 1945), 310.

8. For insights into this issue, see ATC, *Administrative History*, 136–39, and one of its supporting documents, War Department, Adjutant General, "Air Transport Operations," Memorandum No. W95-19-42, September 21, 1942.

9. The first three commanders of ATC's India-China Division were Colonel Edward H. Alexander (October 21, 1942–October 15, 1943), Brigadier General Earl S. Hoag (October 15, 1943–March 15, 1944), and Brigadier General Thomas O. Hardin (March 15, 1944–September 3, 1944).

10. Herbert Weaver, "The Tenth Air Force," in Craven and Cate, vol. 4, *The Pacific: Guadalcanal to Saipan, August 1942 to July 1944*, 414–31; ATC, *Administrative History*, 76–78; Frank H. Heck, "Airline to China," in Craven and Cate, vol. 7, *Services*, 138–46.

11. William H. Tunner, *Over the Hump* (New York: Duell, Sloan and Pierce, 1964; reprint, Washington, DC: Office of Air Force History, 1985), 17–26, 50. Also see Robert A. Slayton, *Master of the Air: William Tunner and the Success of Military Airlift* (Tuscaloosa: University of Alabama Press, 2010), ch. 2, throughout.

12. Tunner, *Over the Hump*, 34–36.

13. Jacqueline Cochran, "Final Report on Women Pilot Program," Army Air Forces Report 6-12, and 62, Headquarters, AAF, 1945, 18-9. Cochran's final report is a trove of insight into the origins, management, medical issues, and dissolution of the program and is available in numerous libraries and on the Web.

14. ATC, Statistical Control Division, "Women Pilots in the Air Transport Command: October–December 1944," March 1945, 1, 12; AAF Air Surgeon, "Report of the Air Surgeons Office on WASP Personnel," Washington, DC, 1945, 3.

15. See also Molly Merriman, *Clipped Wings: The Rise and Fall of the Women Airforce Service Pilots (WASPs) of World War II* (New York: New York University, 1998), 77–122; Sally Van Wagenen Keil, *Those Wonderful Women in Their Flying Machines: The Unknown Heroines of World War II* (New York: Four Directions Press, 1990), 265–306.

16. War Department, Bureau of Public Relations, "Address by General H. H. Arnold, before Wasp Ceremony, Sweetwater, Texas, Thursday, December 7, 1944," Wings Across America website, wingsacrossamerica.us/records_all/press.htm, March 20, 2010.

17. Tunner, *Over the Hump*, 43–54.

18. Tunner, *Over the Hump*, 114–15.

19. Otha C. Spencer, *Flying the Hump: Memories of an Air War* (College Station: Texas A&M University Press, 1992), 7–8.

20. Tunner, *Over the Hump*, 82.

21. Tunner, *Over the Hump*, 65, 94; Spencer, *Flying the Hump*, 137–44.

22. Spencer, *Flying the Hump*, 55–78; Heck, "Airline to China," 139–51.

23. Tunner, *Over the Hump*, 114–16; Heck, "Airline to China," 140–46. For comparison, the USAF accident rates for the C-17 and C-5 transports in 2006 were 1.7 and 0.95 major accidents per 100,000 flight hours, respectively, per the Air Force Safety Center's web page (http://afsafety.af.mil/stats/f_stats.asp).

24. Tunner, *Over the Hump*, 130–34.

25. Frank H. Heck, "Across the Pacific," in Craven and Cate, vol. 7, *Services*, 201–204.

26. Department of the Army, *Army Air Forces Statistical Digest*, 300; Military Airlift Command, *Anything, Anywhere, Anytime: An Illustrated History of the Military Airlift Command, 1941–1991* (Scott AFB, IL: MAC Office of History, May 1991), 55, 276.

27. Cleveland, *Air Transport*, 4, 316.

28. Henry H. Arnold to Carl Spaatz, letter, no title, December 6, 1945, 2–4.

7. Troop Carrier Aviation in World War II

1. This narrative of Operation Varsity draws on several official and unofficial sources. Among the most important are John Warren, *Airborne Operations in World War II, European Theater* (Maxwell AFB, AL: AF Research Studies Institute, September 3, 1956); Lee Bowen et al., *USAF Airborne Operations: World War II and Korean War* (Washington, DC: USAF Historical Division Liaison Office, 1962); Gerard M. Devlin, *Silent Wings* (New York: St. Martin's, 1985); Martin Wolfe, *Green Light: A Troop Carrier Squadron's War from Normandy to the Rhine* (Washington, DC: Center for Air Force History, 1993); and H. Rex Shama, *Pulse and Repulse: Troop Carrier and Airborne Teams in Europe during World War II* (Austin, TX: Eakin Press, 1995).

2. Bowen et al., *USAF Airborne Operations*, 92.

3. Devlin, *Silent Wings*, 323.

4. Devlin, *Silent Wings*, 318.

5. Bowen et al., *USAF Airborne Operations*, 93.

6. John T. Ellis Jr., *The Airborne Command and Center* (Washington, DC: Army Ground Forces, Historical Section, 1946), 11.

7. "Flying Mules of the Army," *Popular Mechanics*, July 1942, 40–42.

8. Thomas H. Greer, "Combat Crew and Unit Training," in *The Army Air Forces in World War II*, ed. Wesley Frank Craven and James Lea Cate, vol. 6, *Men and Planes* (Chicago: University of Chicago, 1958; reprint, Washington, DC: Office of Air Force History, 1983), 622–25.

9. Ellis, *Airborne Command*, 6.

10. For insights into the workings and culture of troop carrier units, see Martin Wolfe's, *Green Light*; W. L. Brinson, *Three One Five Group: An Account of the Activities of the 315th Troop Carrier Group, United States Army Air Forces, 1942–1945* (Lakemont, GA: Copple House Books, 1984); and *DZ Europe: The 440th Troop Carrier Group* (no author or publisher indicated, but available in the USAF Air University Library).

11. Budd Davisson, "WACO CG-4A: The Flying Cargo Container," *EAA/Sport Aviation Magazine* (December 1994), www.airbum.com/articles/ArticleWACOGliderCG-4A.html.

12. See Genevieve Brown, *Development of Transport Airplanes and Air Transport Equipment* (Langley Field, VA: Air Technical Service Command, 1946), 149–63, for development history and production numbers; see Wolfe, *Green Light*, 404–6, for crewmen's views of aircraft survivability.

13. Brown, *Development of Transport*, 165–84.

14. U.S. Air Force, Air Material Command, *Standard Aircraft Characteristics: C-82A Packet*, 5.

15. Alfred Goldberg, "Logistical Mobility," in Craven and Cate, vol. 2, *Europe: Argument to V-E Day*, 557–62; Roland C. Ruppenthal, *The U.S. Army in World War II: The European Theater of Operations: Logistical Support of the Armies*, vol. 2, *September 1944–May 1945* (Washington, DC: Center of Military History, 1959), 161–64, 424–27; Graham A. Cosmas and Albert E. Cowdrey, *The Medical Department: Medical Service in the European Theater of Operations* (Washington, DC: Center of Military History, 1992), 256–58, 331, 515, 525.

16. Bowen et al., *USAF Airborne Operations*, 27. For troop carrier (combat cargo) operations in Burma, see Gerald A. White Jr., *The Great Snafu Fleet* (Philadelphia, PA: Xlibris, 2000), throughout.

17. U.S. Army, Army Air Forces, Assistant Chief of Staff, Intelligence, "Interview with Brigadier General Ray A. Dunn," October 14, 1943, 18–19.

18. U.S. Army, Headquarters Army Air Forces, Office of Chief of Staff, Intelligence, *Airborne Assault on Holland: An Interim Report* (1945; reprint, Washington, DC: Office of Air Force History, 1992), 8.

19. Office of Chief of Staff, Intelligence, *Airborne Assault on Holland*, 40–42.

20. John N. McVay, "Supply by Air," *Military Review*, August 1945, 38.

21. Office of Chief of Staff, Intelligence, *Airborne Assault on Holland*, 43.

22. Forrest C. Pogue, *The U.S. Army in World War II, European Theater of Operations, the Supreme Command* (Washington, DC: Center of Military History, 1951), 271.

23. Robert F. Futrell, *Ideas, Concepts, Doctrine: Basic Thinking in the United States Air Force*, vol. 1, *1907–1960* (Maxwell AFB, AL: Air University Press, 1989), 179; McVay, "Supply by Air," 40; Office of Chief of Staff, Intelligence, *Airborne Assault on Holland*, 40–42.

24. P. L. Williams, "Organization and Equipment: Troop Carrier Aviation," presentation to the AAF Special Staff School, Orlando, Florida, May 1946, 2.

25. *DZ Europe*.

26. Wolfe, *Green Light*, 102.

27. *DZ Europe*, 8.

8. Airlift Consolidation in the 1940s

1. Army Air Forces, Air Transport Command, *Statistical History of the Air Transport Command*, May 29, 1941–May 31, 1948, 5–6.

2. Robert F. Futrell, *Ideas, Concepts, Doctrine: Basic Thinking in the United States Air Force*, vol. 1, *1907–1960* (Maxwell AFB, AL: Air University Press, 1989), 203; Army Air Forces, Air Transport Command, Deputy Chief of Staff for Planning, "Memo: Survey of Duplications between War and Navy Departments," November 20, 1945, 2.

3. Captain Oliver La Farge to Lieutenant Bingham, letter, "Subject: Mission of the Air Transport Command," July 12, 1943.

4. ATC, "Survey of Duplications," 2, and attachment of same title.

5. General George to General Arnold, August 17, 1942, as quoted in Air Transport Command, *Administrative History of the Air Transport Command: June 1942–March 1943*, TD, AFHRA File 300.01, 136; see also pages 137–39 for detailed discussion of the issue.

6. General H. H. Arnold to Lieutenant General H. L. George, letter, December 5, 1945.

7. General Henry H. Arnold to General Carl Spaatz, letter, December 6, 1945.

8. Colonel Robert Olds to Lieutenant Commander Schildhauer, "Civil Aircraft Allocations," December 22, 1945; John D. Carter, "The Air Transport Command," in *The Army Air Forces in World War II*, ed. Wesley Frank Craven and James Lea Cate, vol. 7, *Services around the World* (Chicago: University of Chicago, 1958; reprint, Washington, DC: Office of Air Force History, 1983), 21.

9. U.S. Air Force, Military Air Transport Service, "The Formation of the Military Air Transport Service," 1949, TD, Kuter Papers, Special Collections, USAF Academy Library, Colorado Springs, Colorado, 1–2.

10. General H. H. Arnold and Vice Admiral F. J. Horne, "Appointment of Joint Army-Navy Air Transport Committee," September 2, 1942, DS, Kuter Papers, USAF Academy Library, Colorado Springs, Colorado.

11. ATC, *Administrative History*, 145–48.

12. U.S. Navy, Commander Air South Pacific (COMAIRSOPAC), "Message: For Improvement of Combat Air Transport Service SOPAC Area," November 24, 1942; attached to Captain Richard M. Davis, assistant to DCS of ATC, "Informal Notes RE: South Pacific Combat Air Transport Command (SCAT)," July 1943, ATC files, Air Mobility Command History Office, Scott AFB, IL.

13. Davis, "Informal Notes," 2.

14. Information on SCAT is scarce. Most specific information here is drawn from Robert J. Allen and Joseph Carney, "The Story of SCAT," *Air Transport Magazine*, part 1, December 1944, and part 2, January 1944; Robert Sherrod, *History of Marine Corps Aviation in World War II* (San Rafael, CA: Presidio, 1952), 111–12; Davis, "Informal Notes," throughout.

15. General Hugh Knerr, who oversaw the service commands of both the 8th and 9th Air Forces, consolidated the 27th and 31st into the 302nd Air Transport Wing on September 1, 1944, though the IX AF Air Service Command retained two of its squadrons to equip the 1st

Air Transport Group (Provisional). See also Alfred Goldberg, "Logistical Mobility," in *The Army Air Forces in World War II*, ed. Craven and Cate, vol. 3, *Europe: Argument to V-E Day January 1944 to May 1945*, 557.

16. Goldberg, "Logistical Mobility," 557–58. IX TCC controlled about 1,400 powered and 2,000 glider aircraft, while the transport groups had about 200 powered aircraft between them. The strength of the two RAF transport groups at the time of the Normandy invasion are given as 460 powered and 1,120 glider aircraft in John Terraine, *The Right of the Line: The Royal Air Force in the European War, 1939–1945* (London: Hodder and Stoughton, 1985), 630.

17. Goldberg, "Logistical Mobility," 561.

18. Roland G. Ruppenthal, *The U.S. Army in World War II: The European Theater of Operations: Logistical Support of the Armies*, vol. 1, *May 1941–September 1944*, and vol. 2, *September 1944–May 1945* (Washington, DC: U.S. Army, 1953; reprint, Washington, DC: Center of Military History, 1959), 161–65, 424–27, 572–83; Charles E. Miller, *Airlift Doctrine* (Maxwell AFB, AL: Air University Press, 1988), 105–6.

19. Cyrus R. Smith, "Consolidation of the Air Transport Command and Naval Air Transport Service into One Air Transportation System," in ATC, *Administrative History of the Air Transport Command: March 1943–July 1944*, 194.

20. ATC *Administrative History: June 1942–March 1943*, 201–5.

21. ATC, *Administrative History: March 1943–July 1944*, 197–201.

22. Futrell, *Ideas, Concepts, Doctrine*, 1:203.

23. HQ USAF, "Summary of List of Studies on Organization and Control of Air Transport"; Miller, *Airlift Doctrine*, 164–65; Futrell, *Ideas, Concepts, Doctrine*, 1:204–5.

24. Herman S. Wolk, *Planning and Organizing the Postwar Air Force, 1943–1947* (Washington, DC: Office of Air Force History, 1984), 70; Arnold to Spaatz, December 6, 1945, 5.

25. AAF, AAF Regulation 20-44, June 28, 1946, paragraph 3a; and ATC Historical Branch, *History of Air Transport Command 1 Aug 1945–31 December 1946* (Washington, DC: HQ ATC, 1950), 10.

26. Cyrus R. Smith, "Elimination of Duplication in Army and Navy Air Transport Services," March 1, 1944, 5.

27. Miller, *Airlift Doctrine*, 205–7.

28. Joint Chiefs of Staff, "Memorandum for the Joint Army-Navy Air Transport Committee," May 4, 1946, TD; Rear Admiral J. W. Reeves Jr. and Lieutenant General H. L. George, "Consolidation of Services of Army Air Forces Air Transport Command and Naval Air Transport Service," June 12, 1946, TD, 2, 6; James Lee, *Operation Lifeline: History and Development of the Naval Air Transport Service* (Chicago: Ziff Davis, 1947), 8–11, 161–62, 165–68.

29. Futrell, *Ideas, Concepts, Doctrine*, 1:203.

30. U.S. Army, "Report of the General Board, United States Forces, European Theater," no. 16, 3–4.

31. Martin Wolfe, *Green Light: Men of the 81st Troop Carrier Squadron Tell Their Story* (Pittsburgh: University of Pennsylvania Press, 1989), 96.

32. Major John N. McVay, "The Troop Carrier Command," *Military Review,* May 1945, 12–15.

33. Miller, *Airlift Doctrine,* 166–69; ATC Historical Branch, *History of Air Transport Command,* 44.

34. Futrell, *Ideas, Concepts, Doctrine,* 1:215.

35. Congress, House Committee on Appropriations, Military Establishment Appropriations Bill for 1948, Hearings before the Subcommittee on Appropriations, 80th Cong., 1st sess., 635.

36. Futrell, *Ideas, Concepts, Doctrine,* 1:215–16, 237–40; General Carl Spaatz, "The Future of the Army Air Forces," *Military Review* 26, no. 4 (July 1946): 3; General George C. Kenney, "Strategic Air Command," *Military Review,* August 1947, 3–7.

37. For discussions of the overweening importance of the institutional independence, see Perry M. Smith, *The Air Force Plans for Peace, 1943–1945* (Baltimore: Johns Hopkins, 1970), 15–18, 20–23, 28, 29, 104; Wolk, *Planning and Organizing,* 46; Futrell, *Ideas, Concepts, Doctrine,* 1:207.

38. Spaatz, "Future of the Army Air Forces," 3–4; Futrell, *Ideas and Concepts,* 1:208.

39. Public Law 253, 61 Stat., chap. 343, 80th Cong., 1st sess., The National Security Act of 1947, July 26, 1947, Sec 202(3); President's Air Policy Board, *Survival,* 37.

40. John Shea, interview by author, August 8, 1990, tape 1A, index 575.

41. For the nature of the National Military Establishment debate and the role of airlift in it, see Steven L. Rearden, *History of the Office of the Secretary of Defense,* vol. 1, *The Formative Years, 1947–1950* (Washington, DC: Historical Office, Office of the Secretary of Defense, 1984), particularly pages 30–36.

42. James Forrestal, Memorandum for the Service Chiefs and JCS, "Organization and Mission of Military Air Transport Service (MATS)," May 3, 1948.

43. Forrestal, "Organization," 1.

44. Forrestal, "Organization," 5.

45. Rearden, *History of the Office of the Secretary of Defense,* 37.

46. Laurence S. Kuter, USAF Oral History interview (Maxwell AFB, AL: Air University), 471–73.

47. Lee, *Operation Lifeline,* 11.

48. Captain M. C. Gurney, "News for Reserve Officers," *Atlantic Wing News Letter* (NAS Patuxent River, Maryland: HQs NATS, May 20, 1948), 1.

49. Rearden, *History of the Office of the Secretary of Defense,* 37.

9. The Berlin Airlift

1. Avi Shlaim, *The United States and the Berlin Blockade, 1948–1949: A Study in Crisis Decision Making* (Berkeley: University of California Press, 1983), 12–34, 202; Andrei Cherny, *The Candy Bombers: The Untold Story of the Berlin Airlift and America's Finest Hour* (New

York: Putnam, 2008), 263; Walter Bedell Smith, *Moscow Mission, 1946–1949* (London: Heineman, 1950), 244.

2. Shlaim, *Berlin Blockade*, 200–201.

3. Harry S. Truman, *Memoirs*, vol. 2, *Years of Trial and Hope, 1946–1953* (London: Hodden and Stoughton, 1956), 130.

4. Shlaim, *Berlin Blockade*, 206.

5. Michael D. Haydock, *City under Siege: The Berlin Blockade and Airlift, 1948–1949* (London: Brassey's, 1999), 155.

6. Haydock, *City under Siege*, 155–56; Collier, *Bridge*, 69–72.

7. James C. Hassdorf, U.S. Air Force Oral History interview, Lieutenant General Joseph Smith, USAF (ret.), July 22–23 and November 16, 1976, 186.

8. Haydock, *City under Siege*, 152–54.

9. Hassdorf, Smith interview, 206; Joseph Smith, interview by Robert C. Owen, April 28, 1991. Smith remained sharp in his memory and feisty regarding his operational and leadership accomplishments during interviews with the author in 1991. Military to the last, he passed his last years in a retirement facility at Ft. Belvoir and died in 1993.

10. Hassdorf, Smith interview, 220.

11. Richard Collier, *Bridge across the Sky: The Berlin Blockade and Airlift, 1948–1949* (New York: McGraw-Hill, 1978), 68–69.

12. Hassdorf, Smith interview, 221.

13. Collier, *Bridge across the Sky*, 91.

14. Collier, *Bridge across the Sky*, 101; William H. Tunner, *Over the Hump* (New York: Duell, Sloan, and Pearce, 1964; reprint, Washington, DC: Office of Air Force History, 1985), 160–61; Haydock, *City under Siege*, 179–81.

15. Tunner, *Over the Hump*, 160.

16. Robert A. Slayton, *Master of the Air: William Tunner and the Success of Military Airlift* (Tuscaloosa: University of Alabama, 2010), 118–22. Slayton's study is both the only major biography of Tunner and the best single study of the workings of Tunner's headquarters and the intra–air force bureaucratic politics of the airlift.

17. Hassdorf, Smith interview, 235.

18. Howell M. Estes Jr., interview by Lieutenant Colonel Robert G. Zimmerman and Lieutenant Colonel Lyn R. Officer, USAF Oral History Program, August 1973, 81–82; Collier, *Bridge across the Sky*, 99–101.

19. Tunner, *Over the Hump*, 166; Haydock, *City under Siege*, 182.

20. Tunner, *Over the Hump*, 152–54.

21. Tunner, *Over the Hump*, 175.

22. Tunner, *Over the Hump*, 172–74.

23. Roger G. Miller, *To Save a City: The Berlin Airlift, 1948–1949* (Washington, DC: Air Force History and Museums, 1998), 50.

24. Tunner, *Over the Hump*, 198.

25. Tunner, *Over the Hump*, 192–96; Haydock, *City under Siege*, 230–31.

26. Tunner, *Over the Hump*, 187–91; Miller, *Save a City*, 52.

27. Slayton, *Master of the Air*, 192–93.

28. Tunner, *Over the Hump*, 195–97, 200–201.

29. Collier, *Bridge across the Sky*, 153.

30. Launius and Cross, *Berlin Airlift*, 49; Tunner, *Over the Hump*, 201, 207–9, 222.

31. "STRATEGY: Precision Operation," *Time*, October 18, 1948; Launius and Cross, *Berlin Airlift*, 15.

32. Slayton, *Master of the Air*, 184–85.

33. William H. Tunner, "The Cargo Plane of the Future," *National Defense Transportation Journal*, January–February 1950, 195–96.

34. Laurence S. Kuter, USAF Oral History interview #810 by Thomas A. Sturm and Hugh N. Ahmann, September 30 and October 1–3, 1974, 444–45; John Shea, interview by author, August 8, 1990, tape 1A, index 106–215.

35. Major General Laurence S. Kuter to Chief of Staff of the Air Force, "Consolidation of the Military Air Transport of the Armed Services," TD, August 24, 1949; Military Air Transport Service, "Consolidation of Military Air Transport Services," TD, August 1949, 5, 8, 11.

36. Major General Laurence S. Kuter, "The Organization and Mission of the Military Air Transport Service: A Speech to the Members of the Air War College, 28 Feb. 1949," TD, n.d., Kuter Papers, Special Collections, USAF Academy Library, Colorado Springs, CO, 7, 11, 15, 17.

37. John P. Whitney, "Remarks before the National Transportation Meeting of the Society of Automotive Engineers," Cleveland, OH, March 29, 1949, 16.

38. "STRATEGY," *Time*.

39. Jacob L. Devers, "Air Transportability of the Infantry Division," *Military Review*, April 1949, 14–18.

40. Robert F. Futrell, *Ideas, Concepts, Doctrine: Basic Thinking in the United States Air Force*, vol. 1, *1907–1960* (Maxwell AFB, AL: Air University Press, 1989), 290–91.

41. Jasper N. Bell, "Air-Head Logistics," *Air University Quarterly Review*, Winter 1949, 39–47.

42. Futrell, *Ideas, Concepts, Doctrine*, 1:215.

43. Congress, House Committee on Appropriations, Military Establishment Appropriations Bill for 1948, Hearings before the Subcommittee on Appropriations, 80th Cong., 1st sess., 635.

44. General George C. Kenney, "Strategic Air Command," *Military Review*, August 1947, 5.

45. Slayton, *Master of the Air*, 202.

46. Charles L. Adams, "Airlines' Mobilization-Day Role in Dispute," *Aviation Week* 52, no. 14 (April 3, 1950): 12–14.

47. *Aviation Week*, April 24, 1950, 7.

10. The Korean War

1. Clay Blair, *The Forgotten War* (New York: Times Books, 1987), ix.

2. Theodore R. Milton, "From the Berlin Airlift to Vietnam and Beyond: A Participant's View," in *Air Power and Warfare: Proceedings of the 8th Military History Symposium, United States Air Force Academy, 18–20 October 1978*, ed. Alfred F. Hurley and Robert C. Ehrhart (Washington, DC: USGPO, 1979). Note: Milton implied that he had commanded airlift operations during Swarmer, but contemporary accounts reported that he had acted as chief of staff. See Fairchild Engine and Airplane Corporation, "An A for an Airhead," *Pegasus Magazine*, June 1950, 4.

3. Ben S. Lee, "Air Transportability Gets a Test," *Aviation Week*, May 1, 1950, 16–17; Charles E. Miller, *Airlift Doctrine* (Maxwell AFB, AL: Air University Press, 1988), 192–94; Fairchild, "An A for an Airhead," 3–5.

4. "Armed Forces: Sunday Punch," *Time*, May 1, 1950.

5. Lee, "Summary of Remarks," in Headquarters Maneuver Commander, Exercise Swarmer "Air Transportability," 16–17.

6. Military Air Transport Service, History Branch, *History of MATS, January to June 1950*, 100; Brigadier General Gerald J. Higgins, "Comments," included in Lieutenant General Lauris Norstad, "Critique: Exercise Swarmer," Fort Bragg, North Carolina, May 1950, 24–25.

7. William H. Tunner, *Over the Hump* (New York: Duell, Sloan and Pearce, 1964; reprint, Washington, DC: Office of Air Force History, 1985), 221; Robert F. Futrell, *Ideas, Concepts, Doctrine: Basic Thinking in the United States Air Force*, vol. 1, *1907–1960* (Maxwell AFB, AL: Air University Press, 1989), 290–91.

8. Milton, "From the Berlin Airlift," 305.

9. Milton, "From the Berlin Airlift," 305.

10. Norstad, "Critique," 5, 7–8.

11. MATS, *History of MATS*, 105; Higgins, "Comments," 5, 8.

12. "Swarmer," *Armor-Cavalry Journal* 59, no. 3 (May–June 1950): 2, 32–33; Higgins, "Comments," 6; "Swarmer Shows Airlift Weakness," *Aviation Week*, May 8, 1950, 12–13.

13. Alexander de Seversky, *Air Power: Key to Survival* (New York: Simon and Schuster, 1950), 287, 338.

14. Howard W. French, "John J. Muccio, 89: Was U.S. Diplomat in Several Countries," *New York Times*, May 22, 1989.

15. William T. Y'Blood, ed., *The Three Wars of Lt. Gen. George E. Stratemeyer: His Korean War Diary* (Washington, DC: Air Force History and Museums, 1999), 50.

16. Y'Blood, *The Three Wars of Lt. Gen. George E. Stratemeyer*, 1–9.

17. For descriptions of early airlift operations in Korea, see Annis G. Thompson, *The Greatest Airlift: The Story of Combat Cargo* (Tokyo: Dai-Nippon, 1954); and Robert F. Futrell, *The United States Air Force in Korea, 1950–1953* (Washington, DC: USGPO, 1983), 77, 155, 268, 557.

18. For discussions of Tunner's arrival in the theater and the stand-up of FEAF CCC, see William H. Tunner, *Over the Hump* (New York: Duell, Sloan and Pierce, 1964; reprint, Washington, DC: Office of Air Force History, 1985), 229–31; Y'Blood, *The Three Wars of Lt. Gen. George E. Stratemeyer*, 135; Futrell, *United States Air Force in Korea*, 556, 561.

19. Y'Blood, *The Three Wars of Lt. Gen. George E. Stratemeyer*, 232.

20. Y'Blood, *The Three Wars of Lt. Gen. George E. Stratemeyer*, 300, 396.

21. Tunner, *Over the Hump*, 231.

22. Futrell, *United States Air Force in Korea*, 156, 557.

23. Y'Blood, *The Three Wars of Lt. Gen. George E. Stratemeyer*, 206; Tunner, *Over the Hump*, 231; Ronald G. Boston, "Doctrine by Default: The Historical Origins of Tactical Airlift," *Air University Review*, May–June 1983, 72.

24. Tunner, *Over the Hump*, 232–34.

25. George E. Stover, "Why Two Air Transport Organizations," *Air University Quarterly Review*, Summer 1950, 79.

26. Leroy M. Stanton, "Why Troop Carrier and MATS Should Not Be Merged," *Air University Quarterly Review*, Fall 1950, 77.

27. Roy E. Appleman, "Up to the Ch'ongch'on," in *U.S. Army in the Korean War: South to the Naktong, North to the Yalu* (Washington, DC: Office of Chief of Military History, 1961), 654–57; Thompson, *The Greatest Airlift*, 70–71.

28. Tunner, *Over the Hump*, 239–42.

29. Y'Blood, *The Three Wars of Lt. Gen. George E. Stratemeyer*, 376.

30. Futrell, *United States Air Force in Korea*, 77, 155, 268, 557.

31. A. W. Jessup, "Korea Points Up Freighter Needs," *Aviation Week*, August 21, 1950, 14–15.

32. Tunner, *Over the Hump*, 228; Miller, *Airlift Doctrine*, 202–5; Military Air Transport Service, "Minutes: Commander's Presentations," August 1, 1950, 5–6.

33. Historical Branch, Military Air Transport Service, *Military Air Transport Service Participation in the Korean Emergency: Pacific Airlift (June–December 1950)*, December 1, 1950, 12.

34. James K. Matthews and Robert C. Owen, *Edward J. Driscoll: Forming a Partnership for National Defense: Commercial Airlines and the Air Force: An Oral History*, (Scott AFB, IL: United States Transportation Command, 2001), 2–5.

35. Herbert M. Levine, "The Politics of Strategic Airlift" (PhD diss., Columbia University, 1970), 133.

36. United States Air Force, DCS Comptroller, *United States Air Force Statistical Digest: Fiscal Year 1951*, 69.

37. Two of the most authoritative histories of the development of American aerial refueling capabilities are Thomas A. Julian, "The Origins of Air Refueling in the United States," in *Technology and the Air Force: A Retrospective Assessment*, ed. Jacob Neufeld et al. (Washington, DC: Air Force History and Museums, 1997); and Richard K. Smith, *Seventy-Five Years of Inflight Refueling* (Washington, DC: Air Force History and Museums, 1998).

38. For a detailed and nearly firsthand account of early marine helicopter experiments and operations in Korea, see Lynn Montross, *Cavalry of the Sky: The Story of U.S. Marine Helicopters* (New York: Harper and Brothers, 1954); and Peter B. Mersky, *U.S. Marine Corps Aviation, 1912 to the Present* (Baltimore: Nautical and Aviation Publishing, 1983), 126–28.

39. Montross, *Cavalry of the Sky*, 162–200.

40. Public Law 253, National Security Act of 1947, 80th Cong., 2nd sess., July 26, 1947; Presidential Executive Order 9877, *Functions of the Armed Forces*, July 26, 1947, sec. 4, para 1e, g.; Steven L. Rearden, *History of the Office of the Secretary of Defense*, vol. 1, *The Formative Years, 1947-1950* (Washington, DC: Historical Office, Office of the Secretary of Defense, 1984), 393-96; Chairman of the Joint Chiefs of Staff, "Functions of the Armed Forces and the Joint Chiefs of Staff," April 21, 1948, sec. VI, para. 1, 4, 5, 6.

41. Richard P. Weinert Jr., *A History of Army Aviation: 1950-1962* (Ft. Monroe, VA: U.S. Army Training and Doctrine Command, 1991), 10; Richard I. Wolf, *The United States Air Force Basic Documents on Roles and Missions* (Washington, DC: Office of Air Force History, 1987), 237.

42. James M. Gavin, *War and Peace in the Space Age* (New York: Harper and Brothers, 1958), 108-11. Also see Frederick A. Bergerson, *The Army Gets an Air Force: Tactics of Insurgent Bureaucratic Politics* (Baltimore: Johns Hopkins University Press, 1978), 3-51, for a discussion of the Army–Air Force dispute over aviation missions and equipage. For a contemporary insight, see Ben S. Lee, "The Army Demands Plane-Buying Power," *Aviation Week*, October 2, 1950, 12-13.

43. Wolf, *The United States Air Force Basic Documents*, 237-46.

44. John J. Tolson, *Airmobility, 1961-1971* (Washington, DC: U.S. Army Center of Military History, 1973), vii.

11. Troop Carrier Aviation in the 1950s

1. Ben S. Lee, "XC-123 Seen in Lead in Evaluation," *Aviation Week*, September 11, 1950, and "Assault Transport Order Goes to Chase," *Aviation Week*, October 23, 1950.

2. "AF Issues Call for Air Freighter," *Aviation Week*, March 5, 1951, 40. For a general discussion of the origins of the resulting aircraft, the C-130, see Joseph E. Dabney, *Herk: Hero of the Skies* (Lakemont, GA: Copple House Books, 1979), 83-89.

3. Robert F. Futrell, *Ideas, Concepts, Doctrine: Basic Thinking in the United States Air Force*, vol. 2, *1961-1984* (Maxwell AFB, AL: Air University Press, 1989), 308, 324, 342. For overview of 18th Air Force history, see 18th Air Force, *A Chronological History of the 18th Air Force* (Langley AFB, VA: TAC History Office, 1956), ii, 1.

4. Annis G. Thompson, "TAC's Global Combat Airlift Air Force," *Fairchild Pegasus*, April 1956, 1.

5. Royal D. Frey, *Case History of the C-119 Airplane: September 1946–June 1953*, Air Materiel Command, Historical Branch, Wright-Patterson AFB, Illinois, September 1953, 12-29.

6. Thompson, "TAC's Global Combat Airlift Air Force," 6.

7. Department of the Air Force, "Standard Aircraft Characteristics, C-124A," *Globemaster*, July 1961; "The C-124," *Air University Quarterly Review* 1, no. 1 (Winter 1951–1952); R. P. Martin, "C-124 Passing Combat Test in Korea," *Aviation Week*, November 17, 1952, 62-68.

8. "AF Issues Call for Air Freighter," *Aviation Week*, March 5, 1951, 40; Alexander McSurely, "AF Orders C-130 into Production," *Aviation Week*, October 6, 1952, 13. For a general discussion of the origins of the C-130, see Dabney, *Herk*, 83-89.

9. National Security Council, "NSC 162/2: Statement of Policy by the National Security Council: Basic National Security Policy, 30 October 1953," in *Foreign Relations of the United States, 1952–1954*, vol. II, *National Security Affairs* (Washington, DC: GPO, 1984), 572, 582–83; McGeorge Bundy, *Death and Survival: Choices about the Bomb in the First Fifty Years* (New York: Random House, 1988), 236–44; "Washington Roundup," *Aviation Week*, June 16, 1952, 9.

10. National Security Council, "NSC 162/2," 591–93.

11. D. D. Eisenhower, "Message of the President to the Congress on the State of the Union, January 7, 1954," and J. F. Dulles, "Outlines of Strategy: Address by the Secretary of State before the Council on Foreign Relations, New York, Jan. 12, 1954," in *Documents on American Foreign Relations, 1954* (New York: Harper and Brothers, for the Council on Foreign Relations, 1955), 5, 9.

12. Thomas D. White, "The Current Concept of American Military Strength," *Air University Quarterly Review* 7 no. 1 (Spring 1954): 4.

13. Nathan F. Twining, "The Air-Atomic Age: Its Perils and Its Opportunities," *Air Force Magazine*, October 1954, 32.

14. Dale O. Smith, "Air Power in Limited War," *Air Force Magazine*, May 1955, 47.

15. O. P. Weyland, "The Role of Tactical Air in the 'Long Pull,'" *Air Force Magazine*, May 1956, 39–41.

16. Edward Timberlake, "Tactical Air Doctrine," *Air Force Magazine*, July 1955, 43.

17. Henry P. Viccellio, "Composite Air Strike Force," *Air University Quarterly Review*, Winter 1956–57, 29–36.

18. Robert A. Doughty, *The Evolution of U.S. Army Tactical Doctrine, 1946–76*, Leavenworth Paper No. 1 (Ft. Leavenworth, KS: U.S. Army Combat Studies Institute, 1979), 12–16.

19. Futrell provides an excellent summary of the Project Vista report in *Ideas, Concepts, Doctrine*, 1:228–31.

20. Frederick C. Krause, "Airborne Operations: Mobility for the Nuclear Age," *Military Review*, November 1959, 68; "Army Requirements for Strategic Mobility," *Army Information Digest*, June 1958, 32.

21. Eighteenth Air Force, *A Chronological History*, 23–24; John B. Wilson, *Army Lineage Series, Maneuver and Firepower: The Evolution of Divisions and Separate Brigades* (Washington, DC: U.S. Army Center of Military History, 1998), 264–69; also see the official film account of Sagebrush, *The Big Picture: Operation Sagebrush*, available on the Web from the National Archives and Records Administration, ARC Identifier 2569597/Local Identifier 111-TV-327.

22. Richard P. Weinert Jr., *A History of the Army Aviation: 1950–1962* (Ft. Monroe, VA: U.S. Army Training and Doctrine Command, 1991), 182–87; James W. Williams, *A History of Army Aviation: From Its Beginnings to the War on Terror* (New York: iUniverse, 2005), 70–72.

23. Army Lieutenant General James M. Gavin, a key member of the Army's so-called airborne club of senior air mobility advocates, confirmed that "the Army was laggard in not forcibly expressing its requirements for airlift before Korea," but it began doing so after

March 1951. See James M. Gavin, *War and Peace in the Space Age* (New York: Harper and Brothers, 1958), 173.

24. I. A. Edwards, "Joint Airborne Operations," *Military Review*, November 1953, 16–17.

25. Major General Earle G. Wheeler, "Strategic Mobility," *Army Information Digest*, January 1957, 2–12.

26. United States Air Force, *Statistical Digest*, fiscal year 1955, 545–49, and 1960, 354, 359.

27. Viccellio, "Composite Air Strike Force," 29.

28. Thompson, "TAC's Global Combat Airlift Air Force," 3.

29. James I. Baginski, interview by Robert C. Owen, March 29, 1993, tape 1, side A, 025-111.

30. Congress, House Committee on Appropriations, Subcommittee on Air Force Appropriations, Department of the Air Force Appropriations for 1957, Hearings before Subcommittee, 84 Cong., 2nd sess., April 1956, 1547.

31. Department of Defense, *DOD Directive 5160.2: Single Manager Assignment for Airlift Service*, December 7, 1956.

32. "Secretary Stevens Says Aircraft Lack Bars Army from Crossing Mobility 'Threshold,'" *Army, Navy, Air Force Journal*, September 25, 1954, 97.

33. General Matthew B. Ridgway, "We Need a Powerful Army," *Ordnance*, September–October 1955, 232–36.

34. "The Status Quo in Airlift," *Army*, August 1956, 16, 55–57.

35. "The Army's Atomic Dilemma," *Air Force Magazine*, May 1956, 40.

36. Congress, Senate Committee on Armed Services, Study of Air Power, Hearings before the Subcommittee on the Air Force, 84th Cong., 2nd sess., April 1956, 520–21, 771, 833–35, 839–42, 849–53.

37. Congress, House Committee on Appropriations, Subcommittee on Army Appropriations, Department of the Army Appropriations for 1957, Hearings before Subcommittee, 84th Cong., 2nd sess., August 3, 1956, 342.

38. Congress, House Committee on Appropriations, Subcommittee on Army Appropriations, Department of the Army Appropriations for 1957, Hearings before Subcommittee, 84th Cong., 2nd sess., August 3, 1956, 342; and Committee on Appropriations, AF Appropriations for 1957, 1464, 1479–81, 1493–504, 1539, 1544–55, 1593–604.

39. Roger J. Spiller's, *"Not War but Like War": The American Intervention in Lebanon*, Leavenworth Paper No. 3 (Ft. Leavenworth, KS: U.S. Army Combat Studies Institute, 1981), is a concise and thorough assessment of operations overall, particularly on the land side.

40. Numbers derived from Spiller, *"Not War but Like War,"* appendix 3; Futrell, *Ideas, Concepts, Doctrine*, 1:612.

41. Brigadier General Thomas R. Phillips, "Inter-Service Rivalry Seen in Middle East Marine Airlift," *Army-Navy-Air Force Register*, August 2, 1958, 3.

42. Twelfth Air Force Information Services Office, "Tactical Air Command's Formosa Composite Air Strike Force," TD, c. 1959, TAC Office of History, Langley AFB, VA, 7–12; also see Laurence S. Kuter, "The Meaning of the Taiwan Strait Crisis," *Air Force Magazine*, March 1959.

43. Kuter, "The Meaning of the Taiwan Strait Crisis," 110.

44. Viccellio, "The Composite Air Strike Force," 14.

45. Editorial, "Army's Urgent Need: Adequate, Modern Airlift," *American Aviation*, March 9, 1959, 25; Frederick C. Krause, "Airborne Operations: Mobility for the Nuclear Age," *Military Review*, November 1959, 65–78.

46. Laurence S. Kuter, USAF Oral History interview #810 by Thomas A. Sturm and Hugh N. Ahmann, September 30 and October 1–3, 1974, 473; Futrell, *Ideas, Concepts, Doctrine*, 311.

47. William H. Tunner, "Address to Air Force Association Convention," September 5, 1959.

48. USAF, *Statistical Digest*, fiscal year 1960, 3–10.

12. Army Aviation in the 1950s

1. Hanson Baldwin, "The Atom Bomb and Future War: There May Be Devastating 'Push Button' Battles," *Life*, August 20, 1945, 17–20.

2. Richard P. Weinert Jr., *A History of Army Aviation: 1950–1962* (Ft. Monroe, VA: U.S. Army Training and Doctrine Command, 1991), 10; Richard I. Wolf, *The United States Air Force Basic Documents on Roles and Missions* (Washington, DC: Office of Air Force History, 1987), 237.

3. Department of the Air Force, "Standard Aircraft Characteristics, YC-125B, Raider," October 20, 1950.

4. Performance data extracted from *Jane's All the World's Aircraft, 1951–1952* (London: Sampson Low, 1952), 214c–216c; Ben S. Lee, "XC-123 Seen in Lead in Evaluation," *Aviation Week*, September 11, 1950, 15, and "Assault Transport Order Goes to Chase," October 23, 1950, 11.

5. James M. Gavin, *War and Peace in the Space Age* (New York: Harper and Brothers, 1958), 108–11; "Army Sets New Plans to Operate Aircraft," *Aviation Week*, December 10, 1951, 13–14.

6. Ben S. Lee, "Army Demands Plane-Buying Power," *Aviation Week*, October 2, 1950, 12–13.

7. Ben S. Lee, "Is USAF Troop Support Adequate?,"*Aviation Week*, February 12, 1951, 14.

8. "The Army's Role in Air Power," *Aviation Week*, February 26, 1951, 17.

9. For insights into army internal and external advocacy of the aviation arm in the 1950s, see Frederick A. Bergerson, *The Army Gets an Air Force: Tactics of Insurgent Bureaucratic Politics* (Baltimore: Johns Hopkins University Press, 1978), 3–51.

10. "Army Plane Purchases to Grow" *Aviation Week*, April 16, 1951, 13, and "Army Sets New Plans to Operate Aircraft," December 10, 1951, 13.

11. "Army Buying," *Aviation Week*, March 5, 1951, 17.

12. James W. Williams gives a valuable inside look at these negotiations in *A History of Army Aviation: From Its Beginnings to the War on Terror* (New York: iUniverse, 2005), 52–53. The tests of the agreements themselves are in Wolf, *The United States Air Force Basic Documents*, 237–46.

13. Jake Culpepper, "Airpower in the News: Army Aviation," *Air Force Magazine*, January 1953, 11.

14. Robert F. Futrell, *Ideas, Concepts, Doctrine: Basic Thinking in the United States Air Force*, vol. 1, *1907–1960* (Maxwell AFB, AL: Air University Press, 1989), 297–337; "Army Aviation: Directing Artillery to Directing Traffic," *Air Force Magazine*, April 1952, 14.

15. Alexander McSurely, "Army Shows Off Its Air Power," *Aviation Week*, September 29, 1952, 15–16.

16. Futrell, *Ideas, Concepts, Doctrine*, 228–3; Robert A. Doughty, *The Evolution of U.S. Army Tactical Doctrine, 1946–76*, Leavenworth Paper No. 1 (Ft. Leavenworth, KS: U.S. Army Combat Studies Institute, 1979), 12–16.

17. Lieutenant Colonel Louise F. Hamele, "Inside the Infantry Division," *Military Review*, June 1953, 37–39; Lieutenant Colonel John M. Kinzer, "Airborne Assault by an Infantry Division," *Military Review*, October 1953, 46–49; Lieutenant Colonel I. A. Edwards, "Joint Airborne Operations," *Military Review*, November 1953, 16–17. Edwards made the call for a three-division lift, and the estimate for the size of that lift is extracted from discussions in John B. Wilson, Army Lineage Series, *Maneuver and Firepower: The Evolution of Divisions and Separate Brigades* (Washington, DC: U.S. Army Center of Military History, 1998), 222–26.

18. James M. Gavin, "Cavalry, and I Don't Mean Horses," *Harper's Magazine*, April 1954, 54–60.

19. Futrell, *Ideas, Concepts, Doctrine*, 454–55.

20. National Security Council, "NSC 162/2: Statement of Policy by the National Security Council: Basic National Security Policy, 30 October 1953," in *Foreign Relations of the United States, 1952–1954*, vol. II, *National Security Affairs* (Washington, DC: GPO, 1984), 595.

21. Gavin, *War and Peace*, 150–57.

22. Matthew B. Ridgway, "We Need a Powerful Army," *Ordnance*, September–October 1955, 232–36.

23. Maxwell D. Taylor, *The Uncertain Trumpet* (New York: Harper and Brothers, 1959), 29–36; Gavin, *War and Peace*, 152.

24. Kalev I. Sepp, "The Pentomic Puzzle: The Influence of Personality and Nuclear Weapons on U.S. Army Organization 1952–1958," *Army History*, Winter 2001, 1–11; Wilson, *Maneuver and Firepower*, 264–79.

25. Bergerson, *The Army Gets an Air Force*, 54–56; Weinert, *A History of Army Aviation*, ch. 3, throughout.

26. Weinert, *A History of Army Aviation*, 41–44.

27. Williams, *A History of Army Aviation*, 73.

28. "Army Looks to Sage Brush's SkyCav Operation as Basis of Permanent Unit," *Army, Navy, Air Force Journal*, December 10, 1955, 1, 3.

29. Eighteenth Air Force, *A Chronological History of the 18th Air Force* (Langley AFB, VA: TAC History Office, 1956), 23–24; Wilson, *Maneuver and Firepower*, 264–69; also see the official film account of Sagebrush, *The Big Picture: Operation Sagebrush*, available on the

Web from the National Archives and Records Administration, ARC Identifier 2569597/Local Identifier 111-TV-327.

30. Maxwell D. Taylor, "The Army Needs Mobility," *Military Review*, November–December, 1955, 50–51.

31. John W. Oswalt, "Why and How Army Aviation Arms for Battle," *Army Magazine*, May 1958, 39–42; John J. Tolson, *Airmobility, 1961–1971* (Washington, DC: U.S. Army Center of Military History, 1973), 6–7; Williams, *A History of Army Aviation*, 74–76.

32. Weinert, *A History of Army Aviation*, 160–66.

33. Tolson, *Airmobility*, 7–10; Congress, House Committee on Armed Services, Military Airlift: Hearings before the Subcommittee on Military Airlift, 91st Cong., 2nd sess., January–February 1970, 6405.

34. Congress, House Committee on Appropriations, Department of Defense Appropriations for 1961, Pt. 1, Hearings before the Subcommittee on Department of Defense Appropriations, 86th Cong., 2nd sess., 380–81, 421.

35. Tolson, *Airmobility*, 8–9; Weinert, *A History of Army Aviation*, 115–19.

13. Air Transport in the 1950s

1. Charles E. Miller, *Airlift Doctrine* (Maxwell AFB, AL: Air University Press, 1988), 166–69; ATC Historical Branch, *History of Air Transport Command, 1 Aug 1945–31 December 1946* (Washington, DC: HQ ATC, 1950), 44.

2. Secretary of Defense, "Organization and Mission of Military Air Transport Service (MATS)," May 3, 1948, 1–5.

3. Laurence S. Kuter, "The Organization and Mission of the Military Air Transport Service: A Speech to the Members of the Air War College," February 28, 1949.

4. Laurence S. Kuter, USAF Oral History interview #810 by Thomas A. Sturm and Hugh N. Ahmann, September 30 and October 1–3, 1974, 444–45; John Shea, interview by Robert Owen, August 8, 1990, tape 1A, index 106–215; see also George E. Stover, "Why Two Air Transport Organizations?," *Air University Quarterly Review*, Summer 1950, 77, 80.

5. Laurence S. Kuter to Chief of Staff of the Air Force, "Consolidation of the Military Air Transport of the Armed Services," July 10, 1950, 5, 8, 11; and Miller, *Airlift Doctrine*, 202.

6. William H. Tunner, *Over the Hump* (New York: Duell, Sloan and Pearce, 1964; reprint, Washington, DC: Office of Air Force History, 1985), 264.

7. Major General William H. Tunner to Lieutenant General George E. Stratemeyer, untitled end-of-tour report, February 7, 1951, 3–9.

8. See United States Air Force, *Statistical Digest*, fiscal year 1952, 92; Robert F. Futrell, *Ideas, Concepts, Doctrine: Basic Thinking in the United States Air Force*, vol. 1, *1907–1960* (Maxwell AFB, AL: Air University Press, 1989), 317–19.

9. Richard E. Maltais, *History of the Warner Robins Air Materiel Area, 1 July 1971–30 June 1972, Pt I: Weapon Systems, C-133 Cargomaster, 1953–1971* (Warner Robins AFB, GA: WRAMA Hist Study No. 26, 1973), 4–8.

10. Douglas Aircraft, "The XC-132 Logistic Transport and In-Flight Refueler," 1953, info

brochure; Congress, House Committee on Appropriations, Subcommittee on Department of Defense Appropriations, Strategic Mobility, 85th Cong., 1st sess., March 1957, 2075; RAND Corp., *Transport Aircraft Characteristics and Performance,* RAND Report 256 (Santa Monica, CA: RAND, 1956), 55–56.

11. Finletter's quote extracted from Leroy M. Stanton, "Why Troop Carrier and MATS Should Not Be Merged," *Air University Quarterly Review,* Fall 1950, 80.

12. Joseph Smith, interview by James C. Hassdorf, July 22–23, 1976, USAF Oral History interview no. 906 (Maxwell AFB, AL: AF Historical Research Agency), 264–68; Futrell, *Ideas, Concepts, Doctrine,* 1:311.

13. Futrell, *Ideas, Concepts, Doctrine,* 1:308, 324, 342; Eighteenth Air Force, *A Chronological History of the 18th Air Force* (Langley AFB, VA: TAC History Office, 1956), 1–4.

14. Cannon's letter and Vandenberg's quote extracted from Futrell, *Ideas, Concepts, Doctrine,* 1:311–12.

15. Smith, Hassdorf interview, 264.

16. Smith, Hassdorf interview, 264–68.

17. Smith, Hassdorf interview, 265.

18. Smith, Hassdorf interview, 265–72; Joseph Smith, telephone interview by Robert C. Owen, April 28, 1991, notes in author's files.

19. Smith, Hassdorf interview, 278–84; Joseph Smith, letter to Robert C. Owen, November 11, 1992.

20. MATS, *History of the Military Air Transport Service, January–June 1952, Narrative* (Scott AFB, IL: AMC History Office), 122–29.

21. MATS, *History, January–June 1952,* 125–27.

22. Smith, Hassdorf interview, 284.

23. MATS, *History, January–June 1952,* 123–24; MATS, *History of the Military Air Transport Service, July–December 1952, Narrative,* 334–35; Smith letter, November 11, 1992.

24. MATS, *History, July–December 1952,* 108, 292, 305–6.

25. "MATS Still Hoping for Jet Transport," *Aviation Week,* December 15, 1952, 79.

26. Smith, Hassdorf interview, 277–78.

27. Joseph Smith, "The Mission of MATS," *Defense Transportation Journal,* November–December 1954, 54.

28. Congress, House Committee on Armed Services, Special Subcommittee on National Military Airlift, Hearings on National Military Airlift, 86th Cong., 2nd sess, March–April 1960, 4177; and House Committee on Appropriations, Department of the Air Force Appropriations for 1957, 84th Cong., 2nd sess., April 1956, 1431.

29. SAC support data taken from MATS Semi-Annual, and Annual History Reports: January–June 1954, 15; July–December 1954, 13; July 1956–June 1957, 14; and from Special Subcommittee on National Military Airlift, 4177. Smith's estimate of a SAC wing's mobility requirements comes from Congress, House Committee on Appropriations, Department of the Air Force Appropriations for 1957, 84th Cong., 2nd sess., April 1956, 1431.

30. See in particular, "Functions of the Armed Forces and the Joint Chiefs of Staff," April 21,

1948, sec VI, para A5 and A6, in Richard I. Wolf, *The United States Air Force Basic Documents on Roles and Missions* (Washington, DC: Office of Air Force History, 1987), 159–63.

31. Futrell, *Ideas, Concepts, Doctrine*, 1:328; Robert A. Doughty, *The Evolution of U.S. Army Tactical Doctrine, 1946–76*, Leavenworth Paper No. 1 (Ft. Leavenworth, KS: U.S. Army Combat Studies Institute, 1979), 12–16, 159–60.

32. Figures assembled from USAF, *Statistical Digest*, fiscal year 1952, 92–93; Military Airlift Command, *Anything, Anywhere, Anytime: An Illustrated History of the Military Airlift Command, 1941–1991* (Scott AFB, IL: MAC Office of History, 1991), 280.

33. See, in particular, John M. Kinzer, "Airborne Assault by an Infantry Division," *Military Review*, October 1953, 46–49; I. A. Edwards, "Joint Airborne Operations," *Military Review*, November 1953, 16–17; James M. Gavin, *War and Peace in the Space Age* (New York: Harper and Brothers, 1958), 173; "Secretary Stevens Says Aircraft Lack Bars Army from Crossing Mobility Threshold," *Army, Navy, Air Force Journal*, September 25, 1954, 97.

34. President's Air Coordinating Committee, *Civil Air Policy: A Report by Direction of the President*, May 1, 1954, 2 ("Murray Report").

35. Murray Report, 17; Frederick C. Thayer, *Air Transport Policy and National Security: A Political, Economic and Military Analysis* (Chapel Hill: University of North Carolina, 1965), 123; Miller, *Airlift Doctrine*, 236.

36. Herbert M. Levine, "The Politics of Strategic Airlift" (PhD diss., Columbia University, 1970), 133; John Shea, telephone interview by author, May 22, 1991.

37. Congress, House Commission on Organization of the Executive Branch of the Government, Subcommittee on Transportation, Report on Transportation, March 1955, 236 ("Hoover Report").

38. Hoover Report, 251; Committee on Organization of Executive Branch of the Government, Transportation: A Report to the Congress, March 1955, 7, 53, 274–75, 295.

39. Congress, Senate Committee on Armed Services, Study of Air Power, Hearings before the Subcommittee on the Air Force, 84th Cong., 2nd sess., April 1956, 520–21, 771, 833–35, 839–42, 849, 852–53.

40. *Newsweek*, February 13, 1980, 20–21.

41. Congress, House Committee on Appropriations, Subcommittee on Army Appropriations, Department of the Air Force Appropriations for 1957, Hearings before Subcommittee, 84th Cong., 2nd sess., October 10, 1956, 1493.

42. Committee on Appropriations, AF Appropriations for 1957, 1464, 1479–81, 1493–504, 1539, 1544–45, 1593–604; *Air Force Magazine*, August 1957, 285. Also see William C. Kashatus, *Dapper Dan Flood: The Controversial Life of a Congressional Power Broker* (University Park: Pennsylvania State University Press, 2010), for insights into Flood's personality and character.

43. Committee on Appropriations, Department of the AF Appropriations, 1415, 1515, 1543–47.

44. Smith, Hassdorf interview, 340–41; Smith to author, June 11, 1991.

45. "The Status Quo in Airlift," *Army*, August 1956, 16, 55–57.

46. Major General Earle G. Wheeler, "Strategic Mobility," *Army Information Digest*, January 1957, 2–12.

47. Congress, House Committee on Appropriations, Department of Defense Appropriation Bill, 1957, Report no. 2104, 84th Cong., 2nd sess., May 3, 1957, 46.

48. HQ USAF, Directorate of Plans, *History of the Directorate of Plans, Deputy Chief of Staff, Plans and Programs*, vol. 16, January 1, 1958–June 30, 1958, 163–64.

49. Congress, House Committee on Government Operations, Military Operations Subcommittee, Hearings on Military Air Transportation, 85th Cong., 2nd sess., June 26, 1958, 472–73; and Commission on Organization of the Executive Branch of the Government, *Final Report to the Congress*, June 1955, 28–29, 35, 81–82.

50. Congress, Senate Committee on Interstate and Foreign Commerce, Study of Military Air Transport Service, Hearings before a Special Subcommittee, 85th Cong., 2nd sess., May 19, 1958, 20.

51. Transport Service, Hearings before a Special Subcommittee, 1, 20, 102.

52. Congress, House Committee on Armed Services, Hearings before Subcommittee No. 4, Investigation of National Defense: Phase II, 85th Cong., 2nd sess., March–July 1958, 3–5, 17–18, 74, 230; Smith, Hassdorf interview, 341–42; John Shea, and interview by author, August 8, 1990, tape 1B, indexes 115, 117.

53. "Army Requirements for Strategic Mobility," *Army Information Digest*, June 1958, 36–37.

54. Committee on Armed Services, Hearings before Subcommittee No. 4, 209–10.

55. "Air Lift: Does the Army Have Enough?," *Army, Navy, Air Force Register*, August 31, 1957, 27.

56. Military Air Transport Service, "MATS Comments Relative to the Task Force Recommendations Contained in the Staff Study on Air Force Air Transportation" (Scott AFB, IL: Air Mobility Command Office of History, 1958); HQ USAF, Directorate of Plans, *History of the Directorate of Plans, Deputy Chief of Staff, Plans and Programs, HQ USAF*, vol. 19, July 1, 1959–December 31, 1959, 50.

57. Dwight D. Eisenhower, "Memorandum for the Secretary of Defense," July 23, 1958, in Department of Defense, Assistant Secretary (Supply and Logistics), *The Role of Military Air Transport Service in Peace and War* (February 1960), appendix.

14. The National Military Airlift Hearings

1. Congress, House Committee on Armed Services, Hearings before a Special Subcommittee on National Military Airlift, 88th Cong., 1st sess., July 1963, 6164.

2. Congress, House Committee on Armed Services, Report of Special Subcommittee on National Military Airlift, 4028.

3. Maxwell D. Taylor, *The Uncertain Trumpet* (New York: Harper and Brothers, 1959), 191.

4. Henry Kissinger, *Nuclear Weapons and Foreign Policy* (Garden City, NY: Doubleday, 1958), 180.

5. B. H. Liddell Hart, *Deterrent or Defense* (New York: Praeger, 1960), 126–27.

6. William H. Tunner, *Over the Hump* (New York: Duell, Sloan and Pearce, 1964; reprint, Washington, DC: Office of Air Force History, 1985), 315.

7. Tunner expressed his self-perceptions in Tunner, *Over the Hump*, 281, 287–91. General Brett was a respected fighter commander who met Tunner on several occasions and told the

author during an interview on February 23, 1991, that the airlifter was a prima donna who "went back on his wartime buddies." For Curtis E. LeMay's assessment, see Curtis E. LeMay and MacKinlay Kantor, *Mission with LeMay: My Story* (New York: Doubleday, 1965), 416.

8. Tunner, *Over the Hump*, 300; John Shea, interview by Robert Owen, August 8, 1990, tape 1B, index 249; Robert J. Hohenberg, "United States Military Airlift: A Report to the Secretary of the Air Force on the Military Air Transport Service," July 1959, 5, 29.

9. Tunner, *Over the Hump*, 307; Rebecca Y. Noell, *Exercise Big Slam/Puerto Pine 14-28, March 1960*, MATS Historical Division report, March 1961, 1–11.

10. Tunner, *Over the Hump*, 299; Robert F. Futrell, *Ideas, Concepts, Doctrine: Basic Thinking in the United States Air Force*, vol. 1, *1907-1960* (Maxwell AFB, AL: Air University Press, 1989); Edward Kolodziej, *The Uncommon Defense and Congress, 1945-1963* (Columbus: Ohio State University Press, 1966), 200–203, 300.

11. Congress, House Committee on Government Operations, Subcommittee on Military Operations, Military Air Transportation (Executive Action in Response to Committee Recommendations), 86th Cong., 1st sess., May 1959, 2–4; Subcommittee on Armed Services, Adequacy of Transportation, 435; Frederick C. Thayer, *Air Transport Policy and National Security: A Political, Economic and Military Analysis* (Chapel Hill: University of North Carolina, 1965), 170, 191; Wayne W. Parrish, "Personal View: Quesada 0, Douglas 0, Cargo 0," *Airlift*, September 1959, 7.

12. Congress, House Committee on Appropriations, Department of Defense Appropriations for 1961, Pt 1, Hearings before the Subcommittee on Department of Defense Appropriations, 86th Cong., 2nd sess., 380–81, 421.

13. Shea, Owen interview, tape 1B, index 408–13.

14. Department of Defense, Assistant Secretary (Supply and Logistics), report, "The Role of Military Air Transport Service in Peace and War," February 1960. The report is included in Congress, House Committee on Government Operations, Hearings before Military Operations Subcommittee, 86th Cong., 2nd sess., 6, 11–14.

15. Shea, Owen interview, tape 1B, index 422; Congress, House Committee on Armed Services, Special Subcommittee on National Military Airlift, Hearings on National Military Airlift, 86th Cong., 2nd sess., 4055–57, 4352.

16. Shea, Owen interview, tape 2A, indexes 133 and 650, and tape 1B, index 422.

17. Tunner, *Over the Hump*, 307.

18. Committee on Armed Services, Hearings on National Military Airlift, 4058.

19. Shea, Owen interview, tape 1B, index 565; Tunner, *Over the Hump*, 306.

20. Committee on Armed Services, Hearings on National Military Airlift, 4062, 4075, 4164, 4335. The detailed movement requirements were classified in 1960, but they can be inferred from a table of army division "weights" in Congress, House Committee on Armed Services, Hearings before a Special Subcommittee on National Military Airlift, 88th Cong., 1st sess., July 1963, 6022.

21. Committee on Armed Services, Hearings on National Military Airlift, 4164, 4169–71, 4334, 4345–46, 4355.

22. Committee on Armed Services, Hearings on National Military Airlift, 4791–95; Tunner, *Over the Hump*, 310; Noell, *Exercise Big Slam*, 38–42.

23. Tunner, *Over the Hump*, 309–11; Committee on Armed Services, Hearings on National Military Airlift, 4168; Noell, *Exercise Big Slam*, 40. For examples of the commercial press articles generated by the exercise, see "Airlift Test Emphasizes Need for MATS Modernization," *Army, Navy, Air Force Journal*, March 26, 1960, 13; "Big Slam Pushes MATS to Near War Capability," *Air Force Times*, March 26, 1960, 18; "Airlift," *Army*, May 1960, 18; Clay Blair Jr., "Uncle Sam's Orphan Airline," *Saturday Evening Post*, June 4, 1960, 5F–8F.

24. Committee on Armed Services, Hearings on National Military Airlift, 4410.

25. Committee on Armed Services, Hearings on National Military Airlift, 4510, 4522, 4532–39, 4558, 4563, 4573, 4581, 4617, 4683.

26. Committee on Armed Services, Hearings on National Military Airlift, 4787–802; Noell, *Exercise Big Slam*, 12.

27. Committee on Armed Services, Hearings on National Military Airlift, 4056–57, 4409, 4880–905; HQ USAF, Directorate of Plans, *History of the Directorate of Plans, Deputy Chief of Staff, Plans and Programs, HQ USAF*, vol. 20, January 1, 1960–June 30, 1960, 23, Air Force History Office; "Army Sparks Air Buildup to Ease Airlift Gap," *Army, Navy, Air Force Journal*, April 23, 1960, 20.

28. Charles E. Miller, *Airlift Doctrine* (Maxwell AFB, AL: Air University Press, 1988), 271.

15. Inventing the Civil Reserve Airlift Fleet

1. Congress, Merchant Marine Act, 1936, *U.S. Statutes at Large, January 1935–June 1936*, vol. 69, sections 101, 212, 301, 302, and throughout.

2. "Transport: Kennedy's Clippers," *Time*, November 29, 1937, 35.

3. See chapter 5 (this text), "Mobilizing the Air Transport for Global War," for details.

4. Reginald M. Cleveland, *Air Transport at War* (New York: Harper and Brothers, 1946), vii.

5. Army Air Forces, AAF Regulation 20-44, June 28, 1946, 27.

6. Air Transport Command Historical Branch, *History of Air Transport Command 1 Aug 1945–31 December 1946* (Washington, DC: HQ ATC, 1950), 259–82.

7. The rest of ATC's aircraft were assigned to auxiliary services, such as weather and rescue; Air Transport Command, *Statistical History of the Air Transport Command, 29 May 1941–31 May 1948* (Washington, DC: Headquarters ATC, 1949), 5–6.

8. Air Transport Command, *History of Air Transport Command 1 Aug 1945–31 December 1946*, 10, 45–48; ATC, *Statistical History*, 82–84.

9. R. E. G. Davis, *Airlines of the United States since 1914* (Washington, DC: Smithsonian, 1972), 448.

10. Richard Malkin, *Boxcars in the Sky* (New York: Import Publications, 1951), 195–214.

11. Frederick C. Thayer, *Air Transport Policy and National Security: A Political, Economic and Military Analysis* (Chapel Hill: University of North Carolina Press, 1965), 90–116.

12. Call contracts allowed the government to make a "requisition of any kind of service which . . . [the contracted carrier] could possibly render," simply by issuing a service order for a specific requirement. Air Transport Command, *Administrative History of the Air Transport Command: March 1943–July 1944*, 205–6.

13. Air Transport Command, *Statistical History*, 86–93; *History of Air Transport Command: 1 Aug 1945–31 December 1946*, 79–80, 247–48.

14. United States. Congress. The Civil Aeronautics Act, PL 706, 23 June 1938, in U.S. *Statutes at Large, 1938*, vol. 52, 973–1032.

15. Army Air Forces, AAF Regulation 20-44, June 28, 1946, paragraph 3a.

16. Robert Webster to Carl A. Spaatz, letter, "Subject: Mission of the Air Transport Command, December 12, 1946"; extracted from Charles E. Miller, *Airlift Doctrine* (Maxwell AFB, AL: Air University Press, 1988), 166.

17. Congress, House Committee on Appropriations, Military Establishment Appropriations Bill for 1948, Hearings before the Subcommittee on Appropriations, 80th Cong., 1st sess., 635.

18. General Carl Spaatz, "The Future of the Army Air Forces," *Military Review*, July 1946, 3–4; General George C. Kenney, "Strategic Air Command," *Military Review*, August 1947, 3–7.

19. Miller, *Airlift Doctrine*, 169; President's Air Policy (Finletter) Commission, *Survival in the Air Age: Report of the President's Air Policy Commission* (Washington, DC: GPO, 1948), 37.

20. Charles J. Kelly Jr., *The Sky's the Limit* (New York: Coward-McCann, 1963), 174.

21. For the struggling state of the airline industry and the proscription of ATC and NATS competition with them, see Finletter Commission, *Survival*, 37, 99.

22. Miller, *Airlift Doctrine*, 170; Finletter Commission, *Survival*, 97–114; Congress, House Committee on Armed Services, Hearings on H.R. 6501, To Provide for the Development of Civil Transport Aircraft Adaptable for Auxiliary Military Service, R&D Program Established, 87th Cong., 2nd sess., May 1948, 7105, 7140; Herbert M. Levine, "The Politics of Strategic Airlift" (PhD diss., Columbia University, 1970), 47–48.

23. Theodore J. Crackel's unpublished "History of the Civil Reserve Air Fleet" (Washington, DC: Office of Air Force History, 1993) remains the best available discussion of the issue. See also Thayer, *Air Transport Policy*, 122–23; and Levine, "The Politics of Strategic Airlift," 117. For Kuter's view on the issue, see Joseph Smith, interview by James C. Hassdorff, USAF Oral History interview, July and November 1976, Office of Air Force History, 343; Charles L. Adams, "Airlines' Mobilization-Day Role in Dispute," *Aviation Week*, 52, no. 14 (April 3, 1950): 12.

24. Charles Adams, "Airlines Ease into Mobilization," *Aviation Week*, July 17, 1950, 45.

25. Staff Journal, MATS Plans and Ops Weekly Diary, July 12, 1950, CRAF Papers, Box 14, Folder IV-13, AMC/HO, taken from Crackel, "History of the Civil Reserve Air Fleet," 149–50.

26. Crackel, "History of the Civil Reserve Air Fleet," 156–57.

27. President, Executive Order 10219, "Defining Certain Responsibilities of Federal Agencies with Respect to Transportation and Storage," *Federal Register* 16, no. 42 (March 2, 1951): 1.

28. Deparment of Commerce, "Establishing the Defense Air Transportation Administration," *Federal Register* 16, no. 11 (November 10, 1951): 11511.

29. James H. Douglas, "Report on Utilization of Airlines for Wartime Airlift and Proposals to Aid Expansion of Civil Air Fleet," Air Mobility Command History Office, 1950.

30. Secretary of the Air Force, *Semi-annual Report of the Secretary of the Air Force, 1 January 1954*, 262; Joseph Smith, *Semiannual Report to the Secretary of Defense, July thru December 1954: Military Air Transport Service*, 1955, 15.

31. "Airline M-Day Is Given Approval," *Aviation Week*, December 24, 1951, 18.

32. Crackel, "History of the Civil Reserve Air Fleet," 171–75; MATS, "Civil Reserve Air Fleet Plan: Summary of Implementing Actions (Jan 1952–Jan 1953)," 7–9, and "Civil Reserve Air Fleet Plan," both in MATS Office of History, *History of MATS*, July–December 1952, 325–31.

33. Crackel, "History of the Civil Reserve Air Fleet," 175–76.

34. "Statement of the Secretary of the Air Force, the Honorable Thomas K. Finletter," in "Report to the Airline Presidents on Civil Aviation Mobilization," March 26, 1952, AMC/HO; see also the "Department of Defense Plan for the Civil Reserve Fleet," March 20, 1952, 6–7; Smith, *Semiannual Report to the Secretary of Defense*, 15.

35. "Secretary Stevens Says Aircraft Lack Bars Army from Crossing Mobility Threshold," *Army, Navy, Air Force Journal*, September 25, 1954, 97.104–107, 117–45.

36. President's Air Coordinating Committee, *Civil Air Policy: A Report by Direction of the President*, May 1, 1954, 2, 16, 17.

37. Congress, House Commission on Organization of the Executive Branch of the Government, Subcommittee on Transportation, Report on Transportation, March 1955, 25 and 236; and Transportation: A Report to the Congress, March 1955, 7, 53, 274.

38. Commission on Organization of the Executive Branch of the Government, Report on Transportation, 295.

39. Congress, House Committee on Appropriations, Subcommittee on Army Appropriations, 322–56, 703; *Air Force Magazine*, August 1957, 285.

40. Congress, House Committee on Government Operations, Military Operations Subcommittee. Hearings on Military Air Transportation, 85th Cong., 2nd sess., June 26, 1958, 472–73; *Final Report to the Congress*, 28–29, 35, 81–82; HQ USAF, Directorate of Plans, *History of the Directorate of Plans, Deputy Chief of Staff, Plans and Programs*, vol. 16, January 1, 1958–June 30, 1958, Office of Air Force History, 163–64.

41. Congress. Senate Committee on Interstate and Foreign Commerce. Study of Military Air Transport Service, Hearings before a Special Subcommittee, 85th Cong., 2nd sess., May 19, 1958, 1, 20, 102.

42. Congress, House Committee on Government Operations, Subcommittee on Military Operations, Military Air Transportation (Executive Action in Response to Committee Recommendations), 86th Cong, 1st sess., 1959, 16–17.

43. Subcommittee on Military Operations, Military Air Transportation, 45–47, 79.

44. Subcommittee on Military Operations, Military Air Transportation, 120–62.

45. Subcommittee on Military Operations, Military Air Transportation, 202–7.

46. William H. Tunner, *Over the Hump* (New York: Duell, Sloan and Pearce, 1964; reprint, Washington, DC: Office of Air Force History, 1985), 285.

47. Subcommittee on Military Operations, Military Air Transportation, 228.

48. Department of Defense, Assistant Secretary (Supply and Logistics), report, "The Role of Military Air Transport Service in Peace and War," February 1960, 3, 5–6, 11–13. The report is included in Congress, House Committee on Government Operations, Hearings before Military Operations Subcommittee, 86th Cong., 2nd sess., 133–74.

49. Congress, House Committee on Armed Services, Hearings on National Military Airlift, 86th Cong., 2nd sess., 4410, 4489, 4495, 4538.

50. Congress, House Committee on Armed Services, Hearings on National Military Airlift (1963), 6164.

51. Congress, House Committee on Armed Services, Hearings on National Military Airlift, 4510, 4502–3, 4522, 4532–39, 4558, 4560–65, 4573, 4581, 4617–23, 4565, 4683.

52. Congress, House Report of the Special Subcommittee on National Military Airlift, 86th Cong., 2nd sess., 4051–55.

53. Secretary of the Air Force, Committee to Study MATS, "The Reed Committee Report," by Gordon W. Reed, in House Committee on Government Operations, Military Air Transport Hearings (1960), 196.

54. The CAB director's cancellation of overseas rate exemptions, along with the Air Force comptroller general's supporting decision and affiliated correspondence are included in House Committee on Government Operations, Military Air Transportation (1961), 88, 147–49.

55. HQ USAF, "The Air Force Program of Implementation of the Presidentially-Approved Courses of Action Contained in the Department of Defense Report 'Role of Military Air Transport Service in Peace and War,'" May 1, 1960, in Congress, House Committee on Government Operations, Military Air Transportation (1961), Hearings before the Military Operations Subcommittee, 87th Cong., 1st sess., June 1961, 177–81, 188.

56. President, Executive Order 10999, "Assigning Emergency Preparedness Functions to the Secretary of Commerce," *Code of Federal Regulations, Title 3, Executive Orders 1959–1963*.

57. House Committee on Government Operations, Military Air Transportation Hearings (1963), 9–11, 108–9; House Committee on Armed Services, Military Airlift Hearings (1965), 6661, 6721.

58. House Committee on Armed Services, Airlift Hearings (1965), 6930–37.

59. Robert F. Futrell, *Ideas, Concepts, Doctrine: Basic Thinking in the United States Air Force*, vol. 1, *1907–1960* (Maxwell AFB, AL: Air University Press, 1989), 634–35; MATS, *Short History of the Military Airlift Command* (Scott AFB, IL: MAC Office of History, 1977), 20–21.

60. House Committee on Government Operations, Military Air Transportation (1961), 7–10, 29–30, 34, 128.

61. HQ USAF, Directorate of Plans, *History of the Directorate of Plans, Deputy Chief of Staff, Plans and Programs*, vol. 22, July 1, 1961–December 31, 1961, 248–49; House Committee on Armed Services, Richmond Air Crash, November 8, 1961, Hearings before the Special Subcommittee to Investigate Imperial Airlines Plane Crash near Richmond, Virginia, November 8, 1961, 87th Cong., 2nd sess., 2863–64; Department of Defense, "The Role of

Military Air Transport," 6, 11–14; James K. Matthews and Robert C. Owen, *Edward J. Driscoll: Forming a Partnership for National Defense: Commercial Airlines and the Air Force: An Oral History* (Scott AFB, IL: U.S. Transportation Command, 2001), 18–20.

62. House Committee on Government Operations, Military Air Transportation Hearings (1963), 57; House Committee on Gonvernment Operations, Military Air Transportation (1963), 6; House Committee on Armed Services Hearings on National Military Airlift (1963), 5988.

63. House Committee on Armed Services, Richmond Air Crash, 3104; House Committee on Armed Services, Hearings on National Military Airlift (1963), 6181.

64. Richard J. Kent Jr., *Safe, Separated and Soaring: A History of Federal Civil Aviation Policy, 1961–1972* (Washington, DC: Department of Transportation, 1980), 82–83; PL 87-528, "An Act to Amend the Federal Aviation Act of 1958," *Statutes at Large*, 76, 143 (1962).

65. House Committee on Armed Services, Hearings on National Military Airlift (1963), 6178–79; House Committee on Government Operations, Military Air Transportation (1963), 5, 63; Committee on Government Operations, Military Air Transportation Hearings (1963), 2–43.

66. Congress, House Committee on Armed Services, Military Airlift, Hearings before the Special Subcommittee on Military Airlift, 89th Cong., 1st and 2nd sess., October 1965–January 1966, 6722, 6725.

67. House Committee on Armed Services, Military Airlift Hearings (1966), 6665, 6722–26; House Committee on Government Operations, Military Air Transportation (1963), 45.

68. House Committee on Armed Services, Military Airlift: Hearings before the Subcommittee on Military Airlift, 91st Cong., 2nd sess., January–February 1970, 6295; House Committee on Armed Services, Military Airlift Hearings (1965), 6727–28.

16. Vietnam

1. Department of Defense, *Annual Report for Fiscal Year 1964*, 297, and *Annual Report for Fiscal Year 1965* (Washington, DC: Department of Defense, 1965), 323.

2. Aircraft numbers from Military Airlift Command, *Anything, Anywhere, Anytime: An Illustrated History of the Military Airlift Command, 1941–1991* (Scott AFB, IL: Military Airlift Command History Office, 1991), 120–21, 182–83.

3. For the best general histories of Army Aviation during this period see, Richard P. Weinert Jr., *A History of Army Aviation: 1950–1962* (Ft. Monroe, VA: U.S. Army Training and Doctrine Command, 1991), and James W. Williams, *A History of Army Aviation: From Its Beginnings to the War on Terror* (New York: iUniverse, 2005). For background to McNamara's decision, see John J. Tolson, *Air Mobility, 1961–1971* (Washington, DC: U.S. Army Center of Military History, 1973), 20–25. Also for a useful, if somewhat acerbic summary of the Army–Air Force dispute over airlift concepts, see Sheridan Stuart, "Air Concepts on a Collision Course?," *Air Force Magazine*, August 1964, 34–39.

4. U.S. Strike Command, "Development of a Joint Test Plan to Improve Army Tactical Mobility," February 14, 1963, TAC Office of History, 1.

5. U.S. Strike Command, "Joint Test Plan," attachment 1, 1–2.

6. Tolson, *Air Mobility*, 21–23.

7. Gabriel P. Disosway, "Talking Paper on Logistic Concepts (Air Line of Communications)," in *Report of the Tactical Air-Support Evaluation Board*, TD, August 1962, Air Combat Command History Office, Langley AFB, VA, I-23.

8. Lieutenant General C. W. G. Rich, "Final Report: Field Test Program Army Air Mobility Concept," vol. 1, January 15, 1965, 1–37.

9. William G. Moore, interview by Robert C. Owen, March 3, 1994, tape 1, side A, 011-027.

10. B. Sheehan, "Tailored by TAWC," *Airman*, March 1965, 7; Robert G. Sparkman, "Exercise Gold Fire I," *Air University Review*, March–April 1965, 32–44; Charles R. Shrader, *History of Operations Research in the United States Army*, vol. 2, *1961–1973* (Washington, DC: U.S. Army Center for Military History, 2008), 278–82.

11. "LeMay Blasts Army 'Duplication,'" *Air Force Times*, April 15, 1964, 1, 46.

12. Tolson, *Air Mobility*, 51–58; Congress, House Committee on Armed Services, Military Airlift, Hearings before the Special Subcommittee on Military Airlift, 89th Cong., 1st and 2nd sess., October 1965–January 1966, 6833–34.

13. Rich, "Final Report," 42. Also see Williams, *A History of Army Aviation*, 107–12; Tolson, *Air Mobility*, 51–58.

14. MATS, *History, Military Air Transport Service*, January 1–June 30, 1962, 1:6; John Shea, telephone interview by Robert C. Owen, May 22, 1991; Kennith Blan, interview by Robert C. Owen, March 14, 2001, tape 1, side A, index 195, and side B, index 100; Joe W. Kelly, "Address by Lt Gen Joe W. Kelly, Commander MATS, to Aviation/Space Writers Association (AWA), National Meeting and News Conference, San Francisco, California, 25 May 1962," TD, General Kelly file, MAC Office of History, Scott AFB, IL, May 1962, 3–5.

15. Royce E. Eckwright and Gerald T. Cantwell, "The Congo Airlift: 1960," Historical Division, Office of Information, Headquarters, United States Air Forces in Europe, 1961; Kennith Blan, Owen interview, March 14, 2001, tape 1, side B, index 000-030.

16. Glen R. Birchard, "Anatomy of an Airlift," *Air University Review*, May–June 1964, 17–34; D. M. Parker, "Analysis of C-141 Capability to Perform MATS 'Big Lift' Deployment," Lockheed Aircraft Corp. Project Memorandum ASP 7208-503/63-1, April 1964, ii, 4.

17. Charles E. Miller, *Airlift Doctrine* (Maxwell AFB, AL: Air University Press, 1988), 327–33.

18. John Shea, interview by Robert C. Owen, August 8, 1991, tape 2A, index 500; Committee on Armed Services, Military Airlift (1970), 6260.

19. Department of Defense, *Annual Report for Fiscal Year 1965*, 321; Howell M. Estes Jr., "Address to the National Defense Transportation Association," Atlanta, Georgia, August 11, 1966, 9.

20. Military Airlift Command, *Anything, Anytime, Anywhere*, 124.

21. Department of Defense, *Annual Report for Fiscal Year 1965*, 27; Charles Joseph Gross, *Prelude to the Total Force: The Air National Guard, 1943–1969* (Washington, DC: Office of Air Force History, 1985), 117–18, 147–51; Gerald T. Cantwell, *Citizen Airmen: A History of the Air Force Reserve, 1946–1994* (Washington, DC: Air Force History and Museums, 1994), 209–10, 216.

22. The reserve associate program is described in Congress, House Committee on Armed

Services, Military Airlift: Hearings before the Subcommittee on Military Airlift, 91st Cong., 2nd sess., January–February 1970, 6259–69.

23. CRAF tonnages from Congress, Senate Committee on Commerce, Economic Condition of the Air Transportation Industry, Hearings before the Subcommittee on Aviation, 92nd Cong., 1st sess., February and May 1971, 1031; Estes, "Address to the National Defense Transportation Association," 9.

24. Aircraft fleet composition and tonnage statistics from Dick J. Burkard, *Military Airlift Command: Historical Handbook, 1941–1984* (Scott AFB, IL: Military Airlift Command History Office, 1984), 7, 100.

25. Miller, *Airlift Doctrine*, 334–35; Harold K. Brown, "The Revolution in Airlift," *Air Force and Space Digest*, June 1968, 114–15.

26. Ray L. Bowers, *The United States Air Force in Southeast Asia: Tactical Airlift* (Washington, DC: Office of Air Force History, 1983), 675–83, 691.

27. Bowers, *Tactical Airlift*, 246.

28. Bernard W. Rogers, *Vietnam Studies, Cedar Falls–Junction City: A Turning Point* (Washington, DC: Department of the Army, 1989), 84, 101–2.

29. Shelby L. Stanton, *Vietnam Order of Battle* (New York: Galahad Books, 1986), 54.

30. Bowers, *Tactical Airlift*, 68–110.

31. Ray Bowers, "USAF Airlift and the Airmobility Idea in Vietnam," *Air University Review*, November–December 1974, 65.

32. Bowers, "USAF Airlift," 66.

33. The best descriptions of air force operations in this battle are in Bernard C. Nalty, *Air Power and the Fight for Khe Sanh* (Washington, DC: Office of Air Force History, 1986), 42–59, and Bowers, *Tactical Airlift*, 295–316.

34. Bowers, *Tactical Airlift*, 689.

35. There are many accounts available in literature and on the Web of the courageous and almost miraculous deed of Colonel Jackson and his crew. He gave an interview in 2008, which the author found on the Web in 2011 at www.youtube.com/watch?V=1SSVi7pf9tk.

36. Robert C. Mason, *Chickenhawk* (New York: Viking Press, 1983), 78.

37. Stanton, *Vietnam Order of Battle*, 109.

38. Tolson, *Airmobility*, 39, 103–4.

39. Tolson, *Airmobility*, 169–79.

40. James R. Ebert, *A Life in a Year: The American Infantryman in Vietnam, 1965–1972* (Novato, CA: Presidio, 1993), 334–43.

17. Nickel Grass

1. General Paul K. Carlton's personal characteristics were common grist during the author's early years as a MAC crewman. In good humor, the general and his wife confirmed the stories to me during an interview conducted in August 1991.

2. Paul K. Carlton, U.S. Air Force Academy (USAFA) Oral History interview no. 348, December 8, 1983, 32–34.

3. Carlton, USAFA interview, 34; John Shea, interview by Robert C. Owen, August 8, 1991, tape 1A, index 534, and tape 3B, index 010.

4. Carlton, USAFA interview, 37–41, 64–68.

5. Carlton, Owen interview, tape 1A, index 600.

6. Walter J. Boyne, *The Two O'clock War: The 1973 Yom Kippur Conflict and the Airlift That Saved Israel* (New York: St. Martin's, 2002), 67.

7. Boyne, *Two O'clock War*, 85–87.

8. General Accounting Office, *Airlift Operations of the Military Airlift Command during the 1973 Middle East War* (Washington, DC: Government Printing Office, April 16, 1975), 11.

9. Department of State, "Secretary's Staff Meeting, Tuesday, October 23, 1973–4:35 P.M.," 6. This and other Department of State documents referenced in this chapter are found in George Washington University (GWU) Online National Security Archives.

10. "Black October: Old Enemies at War Again," *Time*, October 10, 1973, 32.

11. U.S. Department of State, "Memorandum of Conversation," October 9, 1973, GWU Archive.

12. Boyne, *Two O'clock War*, 75–77; Carlton, interview, tape 1, side A, index 535.

13. Lift numbers and distances for American and Soviet lifts are from General Accounting Office, *Strategic Airlift to Israel* (Washington, DC: GPO, 1973); Military Airlift Command, *Strategic Airlift to Israel* (Scott AFB, IL: MAC Office of History, November 30, 1973), 139–41.

14. Boyne, *Two O'clock War*, 168.

15. General Accounting Office, *Strategic Airlift to Israel*, 20–22.

16. P. K. Carlton, "Fly Me . . . I'm MAC," *Sealift*, n.p., March 1974.

17. Boyne, *Two O'clock War*, 280.

18. Boyne, *Two O'clock War*, 88.

19. Department of State, "Secretary's Staff Meeting."

20. Leonid Brezhnev, letter to Richard M. Nixon, October 24, 1973, 2, GWU Archive.

21. Richard M. Nixon, letter to Leonid Brezhnev, October 25, 1973, 1, GWU Archive.

22. General Accounting Office, *Strategic Airlift to Israel*, i–iii, 30; P. K. Carlton, letter to General George S. Brown, subject: Quarterly Report, January 14, 1974, 1.

23. Jeffery S. Underwood, *Military Airlift Comes of Age: Consolidation of Strategic and Tactical Airlift Forces under the Military Airlift Command, 1974–1977* (Scott AFB, IL: MAC Office of History, 1990), 9.

24. Carlton, "Fly Me," n.p.

18. Airlift Consolidation in the 1970s

1. Commander Air South Pacific (COMAIRSOPAC), Message: For Improvement of Combat Air Transport Service SOPAC Area, November 24, 1942; attached to Captain Richard M. Davis, assistant to DCS of ATC, "Informal Notes RE: South Pacific Combat Air Transport Command (SCAT)," July 1943, ATC files, Air Mobility Command History Office, Scott AFB, IL.

2. Alfred Goldberg, "Logistical Mobility," in *The Army Air Forces in World War II*, ed.

Wesley Frank Craven and James Lea Cate, vol. 3, *Europe: Argument to V-E Day January 1944 to May 1945* (Chicago: University of Chicago, 1951; reprint, Washington, DC: Office of Air Force History, 1983), 557–61; Roland G. Ruppenthal, *The U.S. Army in World War II: The European Theater of Operations: Logistical Support of the Armies*, vol. 1, *May 1941–September 1944* (Washington, DC: Center of Military History, 1959), 161–65, 424–27, and vol. 2, *September 1944–May 1945*, 572–83.

3. Military Air Transport Service, "The Formation of the Military Air Transport Service," 1949, Kuter Papers, USAFA Library, Colorado Springs, CO, 1–2.

4. General H. H. Arnold and Vice Admiral F. J. Horne, "Appointment of Joint Army–Navy Air Transport Committee," September 2, 1942, Kuter Papers; Air Transport Command, *Administrative History of the Air Transport Command: June 1942–March 1943*, 145–48.

5. Major General Laurence S. Kuter to Chief of Staff USAF, "Consolidation of the Military Air Transport of the Armed Services," July 10, 1950, Air Mobility Command History Office, Scott AFB, IL, 1–2; Rear Admiral John P. Whitney to Director of Manpower and Organization, HQ USAF, "Proposed Organization Structures for Combining Troop Carrier and MATS Units," October 10, 1950, Air Mobility Command History Office, Scott AFB, IL, 202.

6. Major General William H. Tunner to Lieutenant General George E. Stratemeyer, untitled end-of-tour report, February 7, 1951, 3–9, Air Mobility Command History Office, Scott AFB, IL.

7. Charles E. Miller, *Airlift Doctrine* (Maxwell AFB, AL: Air University Press, 1988), 209, 218–19, 240; Futrell, *Ideas, Concepts, Doctrine*, 1:390–91; Congress, House Commission on Organization of the Executive Branch of the Government, Report on Transportation, March 1955, 239.

8. Commission on Organization of the Executive Branch, Report on Transportation, 239.

9. William H. Tunner, *Over the Hump* (New York: Duell, Sloan and Pearce, 1964; reprint, Washington, DC: Office of Air Force History, 1985), 230–32.

10. George E. Stover, "Why Two Air Transport Organizations?," *Air University Quarterly Review*, Summer 1950, 77, 80.

11. Leroy M. Stanton, "Why Troop Carrier and MATS Should Not Be Merged," *Air University Quarterly Review*, Fall 1950, 74–77.

12. Congress, House Committee on Armed Services, Hearings before the Special Subcommittee on National Military Airlift, 88th Cong., 1st sess., July 1963, 5968.

13. HQ USAF, Directorate of Plans, *History of the Directorate of Plans, Deputy Chief of Staff, Plans and Programs, HQ USAF*, vol. 23, July 1–December 31, 1962, 221.

14. Military Airlift Command, *Strategic Airlift Input to Project Corona Harvest Jan 1965–Mar 1968* (Scott AFB, IL: Air Mobility Command History Office, 1970), I-IV-15.

15. Ray L. Bowers, *The United States Air Force in Southeast Asia: Tactical Airlift* (Washington, DC: Office of Air Force History, 1983), 383; MAC, *Strategic Airlift Input to Project Corona Harvest*, II-I-1 through 3.

16. Bowers, *United States Air Force in Southeast Asia*, 384–85.

17. James I. Baginski, interview by Robert C. Owen, March 29, 1993, tape 1, side A, index 458, and side B, index 014.

18. Tactical Air Command, "Tactical Airlift Study, Volume 1," January 1966, Air Combat Command History Office, Langley AFB, VA, 145, 148–49.

19. United States Air Force, Air Force Manual 2-4, *Tactical Airlift*, August 1966, 5; Brigadier General William G. Moore Jr., Commander, 834th Air Division, "End of Tour Report, October 1966 to November 1967: Tactical Airlift," 1967, AFHRA, Maxwell AFB, AL, 33–36.

20. Major General William G. Moore, interview by Colonel Louis P. Lindsay, May 4, 1970, *Corona Harvest Report 466*, 40–48, 52, 59–60; William G. Moore, interview by Robert C. Owen, March 3, 1994, tape 1, side A, index 200.

21. Major General Burl W. McLaughlin, interview by Colonel Louis P. Lindsay, April 20, 1970, *Corona Harvest Report 265*, AFHRA, Maxwell AFB, AL; Bowers, *United States Air Force in Southeast Asia*, 649–50; Baginski, Owen interview, tape 2, side A, index 014.

22. Baginski, Owen interview, tape 1, side B, index 135-336.

23. William W. Momyer, *Airpower in Three Wars* (Washington, DC: Office of Air Force History, 1978), 41–45.

24. William W. Momyer, "End-of-Tour Report," 1968, Corona Harvest files, AFHRA, Maxwell AFB, AL, 12.

25. Tactical Airlift Center, "TALC Absorbed," *Tactical Airlift*, July 1971, 4; LeRoy M. Stanton, "Review and Analysis of USAF Tactical Airlift Center Mission Responsibilities, Organization and Command and Control Relationship with Headquarters Tactical Air Command," April 21, 1967, Air Combat Command History Office, Langley AFB, VA, 2–4.

26. HQ TAC, "TAC Doctrinal Positions," April 15, 1972, Air Combat Command History Office, Langley AFB, VA, 19–21, 35.

27. Ray Bowers, telephone interview by Robert C. Owen, January 10, 1992; William W. Momyer, interview by Robert C. Owen, February 2, 1992, 1.

28. HQ USAF, *USAF Airlift Activities in Support of Operations in Southeast Asia, 1 January 1965–31 March 1968* (Maxwell AFB, AL: Air University Press, 1973), 3–4a.

29. Bowers, *United States Air Force in Southeast Asia*, 650.

30. President Nixon articulated the doctrine for the American public in a television broadcast on November 9, 1969, which is available at many sites on the Web. Also see Jeffrey P. Kimball, "The Nixon Doctrine: A Saga of Misunderstanding," *Presidential Studies Quarterly* 36, no. 1 (2006): 27–44.

31. Roger R. Trask, *The Secretaries of Defense: A Brief History, 1947-1985* (Washington, DC: Historical Office of the Secretary of Defense, 1985), 41; Paul K. Carlton, U.S. Air Force Academy Oral History interview no. 348, December 8, 1983, 87–88; Paul K. Carlton, interview by Robert C. Owen, August 9, 1991, tape 1, side A, index 300.

32. Congress, House Committee on Armed Services, The Posture of the U.S. Military Airlift, Hearings before the Committee on Armed Services, 95th Cong., 1st sess., September 19–20, 1977, 122–25.

33. Department of Defense, Program Decision Memorandum, July 29, 1974, *Consolidation of Airlift Forces*, as found in Richard I. Wolf, *The United States Air Force Basic Documents in Roles and Missions* (Washington, DC: Office of Air Force History, 1987), 391.

34. Department of Defense, *Consolidation of Airlift Forces*, 391.

35. Carlton, USAFA interview, 47-48; Carlton, Owen interview, tape 1, side A, index 200. The best general discussion of airlift consolidation is Jeffery S. Underwood, *Military Airlift Comes of Age: Consolidation of Strategic and Tactical Airlift Forces under the Military Airlift Command, 1974-1977* (Scott AFB, IL: MAC Office of History, 1990).

36. Willard J. Webb and Ronald H. Cole, *The Chairmen of the Joint Chiefs of Staff* (Washington, DC: Historical Division Joint Chiefs of Staff, 1989), 89-91; Edgar F. Puryear Jr., *George S. Brown, General U.S. Air Force: Destined for Stars* (Novato, CA: Presidio, 1983), 53-55, 125-31.

37. HQ USAF, "Point Paper on Consolidation of USAF Airlift Capabilities," August 7, 1974, Pentagon, DC, 3, 7, author's files. Note: Files held in "author's files" and cited in this chapter were extracted in 1991 from microfiche files held in the HQ USAF Doctrine Division (XOXD) and in the Joint Chiefs of Staff Information Management Office, file #2165/101. The author does not know the current disposition of those original microfiche, if they still exist.

38. Robert E. Huyser, interview by Robert C. Owen, April 7, 1992; John Shea, interview, tape 1, side B, index 405, and tape 3, side B, index 010-025.

39. John Shea, telephone interview by Robert C. Owen, May 22, 1991.

40. Ed Kelley, interview by Robert C. Owen, July 27, 1990; Thomas Package, interview by author, December 1990. Both individuals were MAC staff officers during this period and were involved directly in the planning.

41. Underwood, *Military Airlift Comes of Age*, 14.

42. Brigadier General John E. Ralph, Director of Doctrine, Concepts and Objectives (AF/XOD), to Lieutenant General Robert E. Huyser, DCS Plans and Operations (AF/XO), "MAC 10 December Briefing to Air Force Council on Airlift Consolidation," December 17, 1974, author's files.

43. HQ USAF, "USAF Conceptual Plan for Consolidation of Airlift Resources," February 7, 1975.

44. HQ MAC and HQ USAFE, "Agreement between Headquarters US Air Forces Europe and Headquarters Military Airlift Command for the Operational Command, Control and Management of EUCOM Theater Airlift," October 25, 1975, Air Mobility Command History Office, Scott AFB, IL, sec. 3, 1, and attachment 1, "Operational Control Relationship."

45. J. William Middendorf II, Secretary of the Navy, to Assistant Secretary of Defense (Programs and Analysis), "Air Force Plan for Consolidation of Airlift Resources," May 20, 1975, and attached "Marine Corps Comments on the Conceptual Plan for Consolidation of Airlift Resources," Air Mobility Command History Office, Scott AFB, IL. For Hebert's long association and promotion of the Navy, see F. Edward Hebert with John McMillan, *Last of the Titans: The Life and Times of Congressman F. Edward Hebert of Louisiana* (Lafayette: University of South West Louisiana, 1976).

46. Fred J. Shafer, director, General Accounting Office, to James R. Schlesinger, March 24, 1975, author's files.

47. Colonel George Riedel, Acting Deputy Assistant Secretary of Defense (Plans and Analysis), "Memorandum for Record: Subject, Airlift Consolidation," April 28, 1975, Air Mobility Command History Office, Scott AFB, IL; Congress, House Committee on Armed Services, Research and Development Subcommittee, the Posture of Military Airlift, 94th Cong., 2nd sess., April 9, 1976, 13.

48. General Paul K. Carlton to General David C. Jones, November 16, 1974, Air Mobility Command History Office, Scott AFB, IL.

49. General David C. Jones to General Paul K. Carlton, December 17, 1974, Air Mobility Command History Office, Scott AFB, IL.

50. General Paul K. Carlton to General Robert J. Dixon, January 28, 1975, and General Dixon to General Carlton, January 28, 1975, both in Air Mobility Command History Office, Scott AFB, IL.

51. General George S. Brown to Service Chiefs, "Airlift Consolidation," November 8, 1975; General George S. Brown to Secretary of Defense, "Air Force Plan for Consolidation of Airlift Resources," November 12, 1975; General George S. Brown to Secretary of Defense, "Airlift Consolidation," November 12, 1975—all at Air Mobility Command History Office, Scott AFB, IL.

52. Frank A. Schrontz, "Talking Paper: Subject, Should MAC Remain a Single Manager or Become a Specified Command?," January 30, 1976, Air Mobility Command History Office, Scott AFB, IL.

53. Lieutenant Colonel Lewis M. Israelitt, Mobility Operations Division, J4 Joint Staff, "Precis: Airlift Consolidation," April 23, 1976, author's files; Colonel Lippert, JCS Legal Counsel, "Memorandum for General Brown: Subject, Legal Aspects of Establishing MAC as a Specified Command," April 20, 1976, author's files.

54. House Committee on Armed Services, Posture of Military Airlift, 571; Leonard Sullivan Jr., "Airlift Consolidation—Action Memorandum," March 25, 1976, author's files.

55. Edward C. Aldridge Jr. to William P. Clements, "Memorandum for Deputy Secretary of Defense Clements, Subject: Airlift Consolidation—Action Memorandum," March 25, 1976, author's files.

56. Aldridge to Clements, memorandum; Futrell, *Ideas, Concepts, Doctrine*, 2:641; George S. Brown to William P. Clements, "Military Airlift Command," May 14, 1975, author's files.

57. George S. Brown to Frank A. Schrontz, "Memorandum for Asst Secty of Defense (I&L): Subject, Airlift Consolidation," April 5, 1976, author's files.

58. George S. Brown to David Jones, "Industrially Funded C-130 Airlift Operations," April 6, 1976, author's files.

59. Lewis M. Israelitt, "Memorandum for General Casey: Subject, Airlift Consolidation," and attached "Draft Memorandum" and "Precis," April 23, 1976, author's files.

60. William P. Clements, Undersecretary of Defense, "Memorandum, Military Airlift Command," May 5, 1976, author's files.

61. William P. Clements, "Memorandum for [several addressees]: Subject: Airlift Consolidation," June 9, 1976, author's files.

62. Admiral J. L. Holloway, Chief of Naval Operations, to Chairman, Joint Chiefs of Staff, "Memorandum: Subject, Airlift Consolidation," June 28, 1976, author's files.

63. Richard A. Wiley to Secretary of Defense, "Memorandum: Subject, Establishment of a Specified Command for Military Airlift—Action Memorandum," August 6, 1976, author's files.

64. HQ USAF, Deputy Chief of Staff, Operations, letter, "Subject: Implementation Plan for Consolidation of DOD Airlift Resources," July 15, 1976, author's files.

65. Secretary of Defense to Chairman, JCS, "Memorandum: Subject, Detailed Implementation Plan for the Consolidation of DOD Airlift Resources," September 20, 1976, author's files.

19. Airlift in the 1980s

1. The author was a first lieutenant copilot in the 37th TAS briefing room that day.

2. William P. Schlitz, "The Prime Mover," *Air Force Magazine*, February 1979, 47.

3. William G. Moore, "CINCMAC to JCS, message, Subject: REFORGER and CRESTED CAP 1978," November 4, 1978, 1–9; Military Airlift Command, *History of Military Airlift Command, 1 January–31 December 1978*, vol. 1, *Narrative and Appendices*, 92–98, both from Air Mobility Command History Office, Scott AFB, IL.

4. Schlitz, "Prime Mover," 52.

5. John W. Leland and Kathryn A. Wilcoxson, *The Chronological History of the C-5 Galaxy* (Scott AFB, IL: Air Mobility Command, 2003), 18–19.

6. "C-141 Stretch Passes 150 Mark," [MAC] *Command Post*, August 1981, 18; William Head, *Reworking the Workhorse: The C-141B Stretch Modification Program* (Robins AFB, GA: Air Force Logistics Command, Office of History, 1984), throughout.

7. William G. Palmby, "Enhancement of the Civil Reserve Air Fleet: An Alternative for Bridging the Airlift Gap" (thesis, School of Advanced Airpower Studies, Maxwell AFB, AL, 1995), 28–31.

8. Military Airlift Command, *History of Military Airlift Command, 1 January–31 December 1979*, vol. 1, *Narrative and Appendices* (Scott AFB, IL: Air Mobility Command History Office, 1980), 1. The aircraft were the Boeing YC-14 and the McDonnell Douglas YC-15.

9. Schlitz, "Prime Mover," 52.

10. Paul K. Carlton, U.S. Air Force Academy Oral History interview no. 348, December 8, 1983, 87–88; Paul K. Carlton, interview by Robert C. Owen, August 9, 1991, tape 1, side A, index 300.

11. John F. Shea, Deputy Director of Plans, Military Airlift Command, "MAC 04-79, Statement of Operational Need (SON) for Intertheater Airlift Vehicle," August 10, 1979, 1–2; MAC, "Mission Element Need Analysis," August 10, 1979, attachment 1, 1–4.

12. Military Airlift Command, *History of Military Airlift Command, 1 January–31 December 1979*, 70.

13. Department of Defense, "Congressionally Mandated Mobility Study, Vol. 2, [SECRET]," 2-1 (material used is unclassified); Major Thomas R. Mikolajcik, AFXOFL, "Point Paper on Congressionally Mandated Mobility Study (CMMS)," April 30, 1981, 1—both in Air Mobility Command History Office, Scott AFB, IL.

14. Major Duncan McNabb, "Point Paper, Subject: Congressionally Mandated Mobility Study (CMMS)," HQ MAC/XPPB, February 12, 1986, Air Mobility Command History Office, Scott AFB, IL.

15. McNabb, "Point Paper"; John Shea, interview by Robert C. Owen, August 8, 1990, tape 3A, index 409; Military Airlift Command, *History of Military Airlift Command, 1 January–31 December 1982*, vol. 1, *Narrative and Appendices* (Scott AFB, IL: Air Mobility Command History Office), 80; Military Airlift Command, *History, Calendar Year 1981*, vol. 1, *Narrative and Appendices* (Scott AFB, IL: Air Mobility Command History Office), 68–70.

16. Military Airlift Command, *History, January 1–December 31, 1979*, 77; and *Military Airlift Command, History, January 1–December 31, 1982*, 84.

17. U.S. Air Force *Airlift Master Plan* (Washington, DC: Headquarters USAF, September 29, 1983), III-10, V-5–V-10.

18. Department of Defense, Office of the Inspector General, *Civil Reserve Air Fleet*, Audit Report Number 92-068, April 3, 1992, 13; Ronald N. Priddy, *A History of the Civil Reserve Air Fleet in Operations Desert Shield, Desert Storm, and Desert Sortie* (Washington, DC: DOD Policy Board on Federal Aviation, 1993), 32–33.

19. Russell Murray II, Assistant Secretary of Defense for Program Analysis and Evaluation, to Hans Mark, Secretary of the Air Force, "CX Analysis," March 3, 1980; Rudy DeLeon, Undersecretary of Defense, to Frank Carlucci, Secretary of Defense, Memorandum, "Subject: Airlift Acquisition–DECISION MEMORANDUM," November 27, 1981.

20. U.S. General Accounting Office, "The Department of Defense Should Resolve Certain Issues Concerning the C-X Aircraft," October 10, 1980, 2.

21. Dina Rasor, Director, Project on Military Procurement, "Assessment of C-5N vs. KC-10 and 747F," March 15, 1982, 12.

22. Steven V. Roberts, "Effort to Shoot Down C-X Cargo Plane Intensifies," *New York Times*, December 9, 1981, 26; George C. Wilson, "City Hall Style Politics Spill Over into Pentagon Plane Selection," *Washington Post*, November 28, 1981, 2; Joseph Albright, "Airlines Ask Pentagon to Purchase Their 747s," *Atlanta Constitution*, April 2, 1982, 1.

23. William R. Richardson and Thomas M. Ryan, "Memorandum of Understanding for the Development of Joint Airlift Concepts and Doctrine," August 16, 1984, 1.

24. Susan Mercer Williams, *An Airlift Odyssey: A History of Tactical Airlift Modernization, 1955–1983* (Marietta, GA: Lockheed-Georgia Company, 1983), 147–56 and throughout.

25. Military Airlift Command and U.S. Army Training and Doctrine Command, Airlift Concepts and Requirements Agency (ACRA), "Qualitative Intratheater Airlift Requirements Study," 1985, xviii. Also see the "Phase II" iteration of the report, which ACRA released in 1986 and that reinforced the salient conclusions and recommendations of the initial study.

26. Military Airlift Command, Deputy Chief of Staff of Plans, "Advanced Tactical Transport (ATT) Concept Paper," November 1985.

27. Editor's note on Peter W. Russo, "Small and Sure: A New Concept in Theater Airlift," *Air Force Journal of Logistics*, Winter 1985, 21.

28. Military Airlift Command, *History of Military Airlift Command, Calendar Year 1990*, vol. 1, *Narrative and Appendices* (Scott AFB, IL: Air Mobility Command History Office), 389–90; HQ USAF, Directorate of Plans, Airlift Forces Division (AF/XOXFL), Staff Summary Sheet, "Subject: C-130E Replacement Aircraft," January 1990; Point Paper on C-130E Replacement, January 16, 1990, AMC History Office, Scott AFB, IL, 1991.

29. Military Airlift Command, *Anything, Anywhere, Anytime: An Illustrated History of the Military Airlift Command, 1941–1991* (Scott AFB, IL: AMC History Office, 1991), 183.

30. MAC, *Anything, Anywhere, Anytime*, 180–83.

31. Robert B. Patterson, interview by Robert C. Owen, August 9, 2002, tape 1, side A, index 130–250.

32. General Duane Cassidy, interview with Robert C. Owen, tape 1, side B, index 030.

33. James A. Kitfield, "A Better Way to Run a War," *Air Force Magazine*, October 2006, 37.

34. David Packard to General Duane H. Cassidy, letter without subject, June 26, 1986, AMC History Office, Scott AFB, IL, 1991, 1.

35. Congress, PL 99-433—Oct. 1, 1986, Goldwater-Nichols Department of Defense Reorganization Act of 1986, sec. 212 (a) (3).

36. R. Cody Phillips, *Operation Just Cause: The Incursion into Panama* (Washington, DC: U.S. Army Center of Military History, 2004), 49.

37. Ronald H. Cole, *Operation JUST CAUSE: The Planning and Execution of Joint Operations in Panama, February 1988–January 1990* (Washington, DC: Joint History Office, 1995), 30.

38. David Fulghum, "The Air Force Role in Panama," *Air Force Times*, January 8, 1990, 15.

39. Account of Rio Hato attack given by Major Joe Bob Stuka in Fulghum, "Air Force Role," 14.

40. Michael Coman, interview by Robert C. Owen, May 4, 2011. Coman is a retired USAF colonel and participated in the C-141 airdrops.

41. Fulghum, "Air Force Role," 15.

42. MAC, *Anything, Anywhere, Anytime*, 195–98.

20. Acquisition of the C-17

1. Betty R. Kennedy, *Globemaster III: Acquiring the C-17* (Scott AFB, IL: Air Mobility Command Office of History, 2004), xiv.

2. David M. Walsh, *The Military Balance in the Cold War: U.S. Perceptions and Policy, 1976–85* (London: Routledge, 2008), 36–41, 109–28.

3. Congress of the United States, Congressional Budget Office (CBO), *Assessing the NATO/Warsaw Pact Military Balance* (Washington, DC: CBO, December 1977), 43–44.

4. CBO, *Assessing the Military Balance*, 25; Department of Defense, "Report of Secretary of Defense Donald H. Rumsfeld to the Congress on the FY 1978 Budget and Its Implications for

the FY 1978 Authorization Request and the FY 1977–1981 Defense Programs," January 27, 1976, 94–96.

5. "Report of Secretary of Defense James R. Schlesinger to the Congress on the FY 1976 and Transition Budgets, FY 1977 Authorization Request and FY 1976–1980 Defense Programs," February 5, 1975, III-122–III-129.

6. Department of Defense, "Report of Secretary of Defense on the FY 1978 Defense Budget," January 17, 1976, v–vii.

7. W. E. Hoehn et al., *Stategic Mobility Alternatives for the 1980s*, vol. 1, *Executive Summary* (Santa Monica, CA: RAND, 1977), 2, 9–11.

8. United States Air Force, Directorate of Operations, "Airlift Study: New Factors Influencing Airlift Enhancement," March 31, 1977, II-1–II-14, III-8.

9. Shea, "MAC 04-79, Statement of Operational Need (SON) for Intertheater Airlift Vehicle"; MAC, "Mission Element Need Analysis," August 10, 1979, attachment 1, 1–4.

10. Summary and quotations extracted from Military Airlift Command, *History of Military Airlift Command, 1 January–31 December 1979* (Scott AFB, IL: AMC History Office, 1980), 68–70. See also Kennedy, *Globemaster III*, 17-20. The Secretary of Defense's actions were Program Management Directives R-Q6131(3) and R-C-0020(1).

11. "Report of Secretary of Defense Harold Brown to the Congress on the FY 1981 Budget, FY 1982 Authorization Request and FY 1981–1985 Defense Programs," January 29, 1980, 207, 211–12.

12. Kennedy, *Globemaster III*, 24–28.

13. Charles E. Miller, *Airlift Doctrine* (Maxwell AFB, AL: Air University Press, 1988), 388–96.

14. Russell Murray II, Assistant Secretary of Defense for Program Analysis and Evaluation, to Hans Mark, Secretary of the Air Force, "CX Analysis," March 3, 1980; Rudy DeLeon, Undersecretary of Defense, to Frank Carlucci, Secretary of Defense, Memorandum, "Subject: Airlift Acquisition—DECISION MEMORANDUM," November 27, 1981.

15. Kennedy, *Globemaster III*, 24–43.

16. Kennedy, *Globemaster III*, 41, 53–55.

17. Department of Defense, "Congressionally Mandated Mobility Study, Vol. 2, [SECRET]," 2-1 (material used is unclassified); Major Thomas R. Mikolajcik, AFXOFL, "Point Paper on Congressionally Mandated Mobility Study (CMMS)," April 30, 1981, 1; John Shea, interview by Robert C. Owen, August 8, 1990, tape 3A, index 409.

18. Lieutenant General Robert F. Coverdale, Vice Commander, Military Airlift Command, to HQ USAF, Msg, "SUBJ: C-5N and C-17 Comparative Performance Characteristics," October 12, 1981, 1. See also Steven V. Roberts, "Effort to Shoot Down C-X Cargo Plane Intensifies," *New York Times*, December 9, 1981, 26; George C. Wilson, "City Hall Style Politics Spill Over into Pentagon Plane Selection," *Washington Post*, November 28, 1981, 2; M. Lynn Olason, VP-Gen Mgr, Government Programs, Boeing Commercial Airplane Company, to HQ AF Logistics Command, Attn: Col. William H. Glendenning, "Subject: Request for Quotation," AMC History Office, March 5, 1981.

19. Kennedy, *Globemaster III*, 40–64.

20. Lieutenant General Thomas M. Ryan Jr., Vice Commander, Military Airlift Command, to Lieutenant General Lawrence A. Skantze, Commander, Aeronautical Systems Division, letter, "SUBJECT: Commercial Freighters as a Near-Term Solution to the Airlift Shortfall," August 7, 1980.

21. Jeffrey Record, *U.S. Strategic Airlift: Requirements and Capabilities*, National Security Paper 2 (Washington, DC: Institute for Foreign Policy Analysis, January 1986), 21–24.

22. Congress, Congressional Budget Office, *Improving Strategic Mobility: The C-17 Program and Alternatives* (Washington, DC: CBO, September 1986), 39.

23. General Duane H. Cassidy, "A Case for the C-17 Aircraft," *National Security Newsletter of the Reserve Officers Association of the United States*, September 1986, 3.

24. Kennedy, *Globemaster III*, 76.

25. U.S. General Accounting Office, *Military Airlift: Air Force Analysis Supports Acquisition of C-17 Aircraft* (Washington, DC: USGPO, March 1987), 20.

26. Kennedy, *Globemaster III*, 92–103.

27. Kennedy, *Globemaster III*, 119–21, 127; Air Mobility Command, *History, 1 June 1992–31 December 1994*, 336; John D. Morrocco, "C-17 Put on Final Notice as Pentagon Mulls Options," *Aviation Week and Space Technology*, May 17, 1993, 62.

28. Paul Proctor, "USAF Starts Off-the-Shelf Airlifter Competition," *Aviation Week and Space Technology*, November 22, 1993, 37; James K. Matthews and John W. Leland, *General Ronald R. Fogleman, Commander in Chief United States Transportation Command and Commander Air Mobility Command: An Oral History* (Scott AFB, IL: AMC History Office, 1995), 46.

29. David A. Fulghum, "Joint Chiefs to Push C-17, C-33 Mix," *Aviation Week and Space Technology*, October 2, 1995, 63.

30. "DOD Announces C-17/NDAA Aircraft Decision," U.S. Department of Defense News Release No. 587-95, February 28, 1995, 1.

31. Military Airlift Command, *History of Military Airlift Command, Calendar Year 1990*, vol. 1, *Narrative and Appendices* (Scott AFB, IL: AMC/HO), 400–401.

32. Kennedy, *Globemaster III*, 133–35, 160.

33. Sandy Detering, "Point Paper: Mobility Requirements Study—Bottom-Up Review Update (MRS-BURU)," July 6, 1995, 1; Air Mobility Command, *History of Air Mobility Command, 1 January–31 December 1995*, vol. 1, *Narrative and Appendices* (Scott AF, IL: AMC/HO), 145, supporting document 3-72, "Strategic Airlift Force Mix Analysis," November 1, 1995.

34. Paul S. Killingsworth and Laura Melody, *Should C-17s Be Used to Carry In-Theater Cargo during Major Deployments?* (Santa Monica, CA: RAND, 1997), 37.

35. Matthews and Leland, *General Ronald R. Fogleman*; John D. Morrocco, "Deutch Raps House Plan to Buy C-17 Alternatives," *Aviation Week and Space Technology*, May 23, 1995, 22–23.

36. Brigadier Thomas R. Mikolajcik, interview by Robert C. Owen, March 15, 2001, tape 1, side a, index 022-050 and index 098-160.

37. Robert C. Owen, "A Structural and Operational Future for Global Airlift," *Comparative Strategy*, October–December 1993; "The Airlift System: A Primer," *Airpower Journal*, Fall 1995, 16–29.

38. President of the United States, "Statement of National Airlift Policy," National Security Decision Directive number 280, October 24, 1987; Kennedy, *Globemaster III*, 122.

39. Kennedy, *Globemaster III*, 55–56, 137–44.

40. "Rutherford on Lift," *Air Force Magazine*, November 1995, 46.

41. Air Mobility Command, *History of Air Mobility Command, 1 January–31 December 1995*, 1:149–51; General Duane Cassidy, interview with Robert C. Owen, May 28, 2002, tape 1, side A, index 290.

42. Cassidy, Owen interview, tape 1, side A, index 255.

21. The First Gulf War

1. Military Airlift Command, *History of Military Airlift Command, Calendar Year 1991*, vol. 1, *Narrative and Appendices* (Scott AFB, IL: AMC/HO), 175.

2. Jean R. Gebman, Louis J. Batchelder, and Katherine M. Poehlmann, *Finding the Right Mix of Military and Civil Airlift, Issues and Implications*, vol. 1, *Executive Summary* (Santa Monica, CA: RAND, 1994), 13–14; RAND Corporation, "Project Air Force Analysis of the Air War in the Gulf: An Assessment of Strategic Airlift Operational Efficiency" (Santa Monica, CA: RAND, 1993), 33, 91; Military Airlift Command, *History of Military Airlift Command, Calendar Year 1991*, 181–83.

3. James K. Matthews and Cora J. Holt, *So Many, So Much, So Far, So Fast: United States Transportation Command and Strategic Deployment for Operation Desert Shield/Desert Storm* (Washington, DC: USGPO, 1996), 45–46.

4. Military Airlift Command, *History of Military Airlift Command, Calendar Year 1990*, vol. 1, *Narrative and Appendices* (Scott AFB, IL: AMC/HO), 160–79.

5. Matthews and Holt, *So Many, So Much*, 267.

6. Matthews and Holt, *So Many, So Much*, 13; Frank N. Shubert and Theresa L. Kraus, eds., *The Whirlwind War: The United States Army in Operations DESERT SHIELD and DESERT STORM* (Washington, DC: U.S. Army Center of Military History, 1995), 80–81. The C-5 calculation is a rough estimate based on the sixty-ton average payloads, about ten-hour daily flying rate, and average of about 70 percent availability rate actually achieved during Desert Shield, per Lieutenant Colonel Bill Ewing and Lieutenant John Walker, MAC Command Analysis Group, "MAC: Eight Months of Desert Storm/Shield," Scott AFB, IL, June 1991, 8–10.

7. Edwin H. Simmons, *The United States Marines: A History*, 4th ed. (Washington, DC: Marine History and Museums Division, 1992), 286–96; David Tretler and Daniel Kuehl, "U.S. Army Deployment by Unit and Location," in *The Gulf War Airpower Survey*, ed. Eliot A. Cohen, vol. 1, part 1, *A Statistical Compendium* (Washington, DC: USGPO, 1993), 65–69, table 18.

8. Matthews and Holt, *So Many, So Much*, 41.

9. Shubert and Kraus, *Whirlwind War*, 55.

10. D. F. Bond, "Desert Shield Airlift Slackens," *Aviation Week and Space Technology*, October 8, 1990, 76.

11. David A. Fulghum, "MAC 'Desert Express' Rushes Priority Supplies to Mideast," *Aviation Week and Space Technology*, December 3, 1990, 20–21.

12. MAC, *History of Military Airlift Command, Calendar Year 1990*, 193; Matthews and Holt, *So Many, So Much*, 47.

13. MAC, *History of Military Airlift Command, Calendar Year 1991*, 185–87.

14. Richard L. Olson, "Deploying to the Theater," in *The Gulf War Airpower Survey*, ed. Eliot A. Cohen, vol. 3, part 1, *Logistics* (Washington, DC: USGPO, 1993), 109, 132.

15. MAC, *History, 1 January 1991–31 May 1992*, 198–99.

16. Arthur J. Lichte, interview by Robert C. Owen, 1 October 2010 tape 1, side A, index 120-40.

17. Matthews and Holt, *So Many, So Much*, 50–51.

18. Matthews and Holt, *So Many, So Much*, 13.

19. Simmons, *Statistical Compendium*, 59–62.

20. MAC, *History, 1 January 1991–31 May 1992*, 193–94.

21. Edwin E. Tenoso, interview by Robert C. Owen, October 13, 2011, tape 1, side A, index 037.

22. William G. Pagonis, *Moving Mountains: Lessons in Leadership and Logistics from the Gulf War* (Boston: Harvard, 1992), 140.

23. MAC, *History, 1 January 1991–31 May 1992*, 206–9; AMC History Office, "C-130 Support of the 'Hail Mary Pass' during Operation DESERT STORM," November 10, 1992, supporting document 3-37.

24. Olson, "Deploying to the Theater," 153.

25. James W. Williams, *A History of Army Aviation: From Its Beginnings to the War on Terror* (New York: iUniverse, 2005), 243–56.

26. Tenoso, Owen interview, 165.

27. Pagonis, *Moving Mountains*, 125.

28. Ewing, "Eight Months," 7, 9, 11, 17; Military Airlift Command, *History of Military Airlift Command, Calendar Year 1990*, 180–82; Shubert and Kraus, *Whirlwind War*, 57; Pagonis, *Moving Mountains*, 87.

29. MAC, *History, 1 January 1991–31 May 1992*, appendix 3–6, 489.

30. Tenoso, Owen interview, 067-130.

31. Tenoso, Owen interview, 209-400.

32. Ronald N. Priddy, *A History of the Civil Reserve Air Fleet in Operations Desert Shield, Desert Storm, and Desert Sortie* (Washington DC: DOD Policy Board on Federal Aviation, 1993), appendix N; Gebman, Batchelder, and Poehlmann, *Finding the Right Mix*, 13–14; U.S. General Accounting Office, *Military Airlift: Changes Underway to Ensure Continued Success of Civil Reserve Air Fleet* (Washington, DC: GAO, 1992), 8; Department of Defense, Office of

the Inspector General, *Civil Reserve Air Fleet*, Audit Report Number 92-068, April 3, 1992, 14; MAC, *History, Calendar Year 1992* (Scott AFB, IL: AMC/HO), 204.

33. As an early example of a proposal to base an army war-fighting concept on "C-5 loads," see Patrick J. Bodelson and Kevin B. Smith, "Design for Tempo," *U.S. Army Aviation Digest*, March–April 1991, 2–16.

22. Messing with Success

1. Secretary of the Air Force, *The Air Force and U.S. National Security: Global Reach—Global Power* (Washington, DC: Department of the Air Force, June 1990), 1–2, 15.

2. Air Mobility Command, *History of Air Mobility Command, 1 June 1992–31 December 1992*, vol. 1, *Narrative* (Scott AFB, IL: AMC/HO), 52.

3. General Merrill A. McPeak, "Remarks at the Air Force Association National Symposium Los Angeles," October 24, 1991, 1–5.

4. Anonymous, "TAC-umsizing the Air Force: The Emerging Vision of the Future," August 1991.

5. Julie Bird, "Fighter Mafia: Some View Balance of Power as Skewed within Air Force," *Air Force Times*, February 1, 1993, 12–13.

6. Russell E. Dougherty, "Roots and Wings: A Perspective on Reorganization," *Airpower Journal*, Summer 1992, 4–14.

7. James K. Matthews and Jay H. Smith, *Hansford T. Johnson, United States Transportation Command and Air Mobility Command: An Oral History* (Scott AFB, IL: Offices of AMC and U.S. Transportation Command History, 1992), 52–59.

8. Air Mobility Command, *History, 1 June 1992–31 December 1992*, 69–80.

9. Air Mobility Command, *History, 1 June 1992–31 December 1992*, 83.

10. Lieutenant Colonel Dave Snyder, AMC Doctrine Division (AMC/XPD), "White Paper: A Review of Today's Airlift System," n.d. (early 1996), 4; James K. Matthews and Robert T. Cossaboom, *General Robert L. Rutherford: An Oral History* (Scott AFB, IL: U.S. Transportation Command Research Center, 1996), 37.

11. David Hughes, "Heavy Jets Key to Airlift," *Aviation Week and Space Technology*, January 15, 1996, 46–47.

12. Air Mobility Command, *History of Air Mobility Command, 1 January–31 December 1996*, vol. 1, *Narrative* (Scott AFB, IL: AMC/HO), 118–21. See also Chris Krisinger, "Airlift to the Balkans: Something New, Something Old," *Defense Transportation Journal*, June 1996, 16–17.

13. Air Mobility Command, *History of the Air Mobility Command, 1 January 1995–31 December 1995*, vol. 1, *Narrative and Appendices* (Scott AFB, IL: AMC/HO), 52–53.

14. Robert C. Owen, "The Airlift System: A Primer," *Air Power Journal*, Fall 1995, 28.

15. Chris J. Krisinger, "Towards a Seamless Mobility System: The C-130 and Air Force Reorganization," *Air Power Journal*, Fall 1995, 6, 44.

16. Chris J. Krisinger, letter, "Response to CSAF Letter, Dated 12 October 1995," n.d., author's files.

17. Matthews and Cossaboom, *General Robert L. Rutherford*, 37–38, 48; Air Mobility Command, *History of Air Mobility Command, 1 January–31 December 1998*, vol. 1, *Narrative and Appendices* (Scott AF, IL: AMC/HO), 211.

18. Steven Watkins, "C-130s Are Headed Back to Air Mobility Command," *Air Force Times*, November 4, 1996, 3.

19. Air Mobility Command, *History, 1 January–31 December 1996*, 20.

23. The 1990s

1. Air Mobility Command, *History of Air Mobility Command, 1 January–31 December 1999*, vol. 1, *Narrative and Appendices* (Scott AFB, IL: AMC/HO), 184.

2. James K. Matthews and John W. Leland, *General Ronald R. Fogleman, Commander in Chief United States Transportation Command and Commander Air Mobility Command: An Oral History*, (Scott AFB, IL: AMC History Office, 1995), 8–11; Military Airlift Command, *History of Military Airlift Command, Calendar Year 1991*, vol. 1, *Narrative and Appendices* (Scott AFB, IL: AMC/HO), 43.

3. Steward M. Powell, "They Deliver," *Air Force Magazine*, August 1991, 54.

4. David J. Lynch, "The C-17 Fights the Headwinds," *Air Force Magazine*, July 1993, 32–40; David F. Bond, "MAC Faces Widening Gap in Peacetime, Crisis Needs," *Aviation Week and Space Technology*, September 9, 1991, 48–50.

5. James Kitfield, "Airlift at High Tempo," *Air Force Magazine*, January 1995, 59.

6. Air Mobility Command, *History of Air Mobility Command, 1 June 1992–31 December 1994*, vol. 1, *Narrative and Appendices* (Scott AFB, IL: AMC/HO), 128, 132–34.

7. Thomas R. Mikolajcik, interview by Robert C. Owen, March 15, 2001, tape 1, side A, index 740-900.

8. Tony Capaccio, "Bosnia Airdrop," *Air Force Magazine*, July 1993, 53–55; Kurt Schork, Reuters News Agency, "Bosnian Muslims Cling to Lifeline: Once-Maligned Airdrops Now Keeping Six Enclaves Alive," *Washington Times*, September 14, 1993, 18.

9. Air Mobility Command, *History of Air Mobility Command, 1 January–31 December 1995*, vol. 1, *Narrative and Appendices*, (Scott AFB, IL: AMC/HO), 43, 59.

10. William J. Allen, "Crisis in Southern Iraq: Operation Southern Watch," in *Short of War: Major USAF Contingency Operations, 1947-1997*, ed. A. Timothy Warnock (Maxwell AFB, AL: Air University Press, 2000), 189–95; Kitfield, "Airlift at High Tempo," 57; AMC, *History, 1 January–31 December 1999*, 180–82.

11. As chief of AMC's Policy and Doctrine Division (AMC/XPD), the author was involved directly in setting up the TACON transfer and almost daily coordination with General Bishop on command relations issues. See also William J. Begert, "Kosovo and Theater Air Mobility," *Aerospace Power Journal*, Winter 1999, 17; AMC, *History of Air Mobility Command, 1 January–31 December 1998*, vol. 1, *Narrative and Appendices* (Scott AFB, IL: AMC/HO), 182–83.

12. Air Mobility Command, *History, 1998*, 89–96, and *History, 1999*, 96–100.

13. Lieutenant Colonel Rowayne A. Schatz, "Theater Airlift Lessons from Kosovo," *Air and*

Space Power Chronicles, July 10, 2000, 8, retrieved November 7, 2011, from www.airpower .maxwell.af.mil/airchronicles/cc/schatz.html.

14. Robert C. Owen, AMC Doctrine and Policy Division (AMC/XPD), "Mobility Data for the 'Air War over Serbia' Fact Sheet," July 1, 1999, 1–8; Air Mobility Command, *History, 1999*, 203, 268, 371; Schatz, "Theater Airlift Lessons," 5.

15. United States Air Forces of Europe, 86th Contingency Response Group, "Case Study on the 86th Contingency Response Group (CRG), Rinas Airport, Tirana, Albania Deployment," 3–10.

16. Lieutenant Colonel Richard D. Simpson, Deputy Chief, Air Mobility Command Doctrine Division (AMC/XPD), "Allied Force DM4 Set-up," e-mail to Major Peter A. Hirneise, 437th Airlift Wing, November 18, 1999.

17. Schatz, "Theater Airlift Lessons," 15, 19.

18. Department of Defense, *Report to Congress: Kosovo/Operation Allied Force After-Action Report*, January 31, 2000, 120–21.

19. "One War Too Many," *Jane's Defence Weekly*, December 8, 1999, throughout.

20. Air Mobility Command, *History, 1995*, 4–8, 147, 259; Kitfield, "Airlift at High Tempo," 587; Air Mobility Command, *History, 1999*, 8–16.

21. General John J. Jumper, Commander, Air Combat Command, message, "Spring '99 CAF/MAF Commanders Videoconference," June 11, 1999, 5; General Tony Robertson, "Air War over Serbia: A Mobility Perspective," briefing to the Air Force Doctrine Center Kosovo Doctrine Summit, July 7, 1999, slide 9; Department of Defense, *Kosovo After-Action Report*, 33; Simpson, "Allied Force DM4 Set-up."

22. Air Mobility Command, *History, 1999*, 259–61.

23. Chuck McCutcheon, "Despite Leaner Pentagon Budgets, a Venerable Plane Still Flies High," *Congressional Quarterly Weekly*, August 22, 1998, 2296.

24. Eric Schmitt, "Joint Chiefs Accuse Congress of Weakening U.S. Defense," *New York Times*, September 30, 1998, 1.

25. U.S. General Accounting Office, *Intratheater Airlift: Information on the Air Force's C-130 Aircraft*, April 1998, 6; "Pentagon Mulling Proposed Kill of Air Force's C-130J Program," *Inside the Pentagon*, December 16, 1999, 1.

26. Hansford T. Johnson, Commander, Air Mobility Command, "White Paper on Incentives for the Civil Reserve Air Fleet (CRAF)," August 20, 1992, 3–6.

27. James K. Matthews and Robert T. Cossaboom, *General Robert L. Rutherford: An Oral History* (Scott AFB, IL: U.S. Transportation Command Research Center, 1996), 23–24.

28. Colonel Murrell D. Porter, Chief AMC CRAF Division (AMC/DOF), interview by Robert C. Owen, June 6, 1995; U.S. GAO, *Military Airlift: Changes Underway to Ensure Continued Success of Civil Reserve Air Fleet* (Washington, DC: GAO, 1992), 7–13; William G. Palmby, "Enhancement of the Civil Reserve Air Fleet: An Alternative for Bridging the Airlift Gap" (thesis, School of Advanced Airpower Studies, Maxwell AFB, AL, 1995), 57–59.

29. Vago Muradian, "Aging Fleets Are Pushed to the Limit, Plan Says," *Air Force Times*, December 12, 1994, 22; Kitfield, "Airlift at High Tempo," 60.

30. Air Mobility Command, *History, 1999*, 179–207. See also General Michael E. Ryan, "DOD News Conference," August 4, 1998, 1–2.

31. Matthews and Cossaboom, *General Robert L. Rutherford*, 15–17.

32. AMC, *History, 1999*, 189–200.

33. Colonel Gary Phipps, Chief AMC Operational Plans Division (AMC/DOX), to Major General John D. Hopper, AMC Deputy Director of Operations (AMC/DO), e-mail, "CSAF Reconstitution Brief," June 1, 1999.

34. Colonel Robert C. Owen, Chief AMC Doctrine and Policy Division (AMC/XPD), to Major General Nick Williams, Deputy Director of Plans (AMC/XP), e-mail, "Initiating Reconstitution Team (R-Team)," May 25, 1999.

35. Joint Chiefs of Staff, *Mobility Requirements Study* (unclassified), vol. 1, January 23, 1992, ES-2–ES-6, I-2.

36. Office of Secretary of Defense, "Report on the Bottom-Up Review," October 1993, 7, 20.

37. Christopher Bowie et al., *The New Calculus: Analyzing Airpower's Changing Role in Joint Theater Campaigns* (Santa Monica, CA: RAND, 1993), xix.

38. USAF, Scientific Advisory Board, *New World Vistas: Air and Space Power for the 21st Century*, 1995, 29, 57.

39. James A. Fellows et al., "Airlift 2025: The First with the Most—A Research Paper Presented to Air Force 2025," August 1996, 7.

40. Sandy Detering, HQ AMC/XPDIJ, Point Paper, July 6, 1995; John Borsi, HQ AMCSAF, "Mobility Requirements Study—Bottom-Up Review Update," March 30, 1995, 2.

41. Congressional Budget Office, *Moving U.S. Forces: Options for Strategic Mobility* (Washington, DC: CBO, 1997), 45–46.

24. The 2000s

1. Daniel L. Haulman, "Intertheater Airlift Challenges of Operation Enduring Freedom," Air Force Historical Research Agency, November 14, 2002, 11; "War Using 70% of Active Duty Tankers," *U.S. News and World Report*, November 12, 2001; "War Drains U.S. Military's Aircraft and Munitions," *Aviation Week and Space Technology*, February 18, 2002, 31.

2. John A. Tirpak, "The Squeeze on Air Mobility," *Air Force Magazine*, July 2003, 25.

3. U.S. Central Air Force (USCENTAF), "Operation Iraqi Freedom—by the Numbers," April 30, 2003, 7–8, 25.

4. John A. Tirpak, "More Airlift, Fewer Convoys," *Air Force Magazine*, February 2005, 8; Amy Butler, "U.S. Air Force Crafts Cargo, Refueler Fleet Plans While Shifting Approach in Iraq," *Aviation Week and Space Technology*, November 13, 2006, 29–30.

5. Adam J. Hebert, "Air Mobility's Never-Ending Surge," *Air Force Magazine*, September 2006, 48; John A. Tirpak, "Air Mobility in the Doldrums," *Air Force Magazine*, August 2005, 33–37.

6. Tirpak, "The Squeeze on Air Mobility," 22–29.

7. For an early discussion of this, see Dennis Steele, "A U.S. Army Line Battalion in the War on Terrorism," *Army*, June 2002, 22.

8. The earliest official U.S. doctrine for theater airlift in counterinsurgencies is found in U.S. Marine Corps, "Aviation," in *Small Wars Manual* (Washington, DC: USGPO, 1940), 21–24, which remains remarkably useful in contemporary operations.

9. Joseph Kapinos, "C-130 Crew Proves New Airdrop Method," *Airlift/Tanker Quarterly*, Spring 2010, 14; Duncan J. McNabb, "We Measure Success through the Eyes of the War Fighter," *Air and Space Power Journal*, Winter 2011, 10.

10. James W. Williams, *A History of Army Aviation: From Its Beginnings to the War on Terror* (New York: iUniverse, 2005), 386.

11. Frank Tiboni, "U.S. Army Aviation Leaders Call for Improved Intra-Theater Airlift," *Defense News.com*, May 13, 2002.

12. William Matthews, "New Wings: Army Guard Prepares for New Light Cargo Aircraft to Replace Sherpa, but with Joint Operations in Mind," *National Guard*, November 2005, 22–23.

13. Association of the United States Army, *U.S. Army Aviation: Balancing Current and Future Demands*, AUSA January 2008, 5–8.

14. Matthews, "New Wings," 24–25; "C-27 Gets a 'J' from Alenia, Lockheed Martin," *Aviation Week and Space Technology*, February 12, 1996, 27–28; David A. Fulghum, "Crying Foul: Lockheed Martin Protests First Down Select in the New Army/Air Force Cargo Aircraft Competition," *Aviation Week and Space Technology*, August 21–28, 2006, 34.

15. Secretary of Defense, *Mobility Requirements Study (MRS) Executive Summary*, (Washington, DC: Department of Defense, December 2000), 4.

16. "GAO: Military 30% Short of Airlift Requirement for War," *Defense Week*, December 18, 2000, 1.

17. "Ryan: 'We Will Never Have Enough Lift' for Two Regional Wars," *Aerospace Daily*, June 22, 2000, 1.

18. "Despite Heavy Demands, AMC Predicts No Change in Airlift Requirement," *Inside the Air Force*, March 8, 2002, 1.

19. Robert Wall, "Demand Pressure: Despite Funding Uncertainty Transcom Chief Expects More C-17s," *Aviation Week and Space Technology*, August 2, 2004, 3; John A. Tirpak, "The Airlift Gap," *Air Force Magazine*, October 2004, 34.

20. Department of Defense, *Executive Summary: Mobility Capabilities and Requirements Study 2016*, n.d. (c. May 2010), 1–4, 8–9.

21. Tirpak, "Air Mobility in the Doldrums," 34.

22. U.S. Government Accountability Office, *Defense Transportation: Study Limitations Raise Questions about the Adequacy and Completeness of the Mobility Capabilities Study and Report*, GAO-06-938, September 2006, 2–13.

23. U.S. Government Accountability Office, "Testimony before the House Committee on Armed Services, Air and Land Forces Subcommittee," March 7, 2007.

24. Department of Defense, *Executive Summary: Mobility Capabilities and Requirements Study*, 3–6; John A. Tirpak, "The Double Life of Air Mobility," *Air Force Magazine*, July 2010, 31.

25. "World News Roundup," *Aviation Week and Space Technology*, September 19, 2008, 20; Jack Jackson, *Mobility Capabilities and Requirements Study 2016 Accreditation Report*, vol. 1,

Summary, Institute for Defense Analyses, Paper P-4475 (Alexandria, VA: IDA, September 2009), 1–10.

26. "Wyatt Says Mobility Study Off on Tactical Airlift Needs," *Air Force Magazine*, June 2010, 16; and Congress, House Committee on Armed Services, House Armed Services Subcommittee on Air and Land Forces Holds Hearing on the Army and Air Force National Guard and Reserve Components, CQ Congressional Transcripts, April 22, 2010, 11–12, 15–17.

27. H. Thomas Fields Jr., "The Air-Maneuver and Transport Concept: Can It Transform the Nature of Rapid Contingency Operations?" *Army*, January 2004, 21–23; U.S. Congress, "Joint Statement before the House Armed Services Committee by the Honorable Thomas E. White, Secretary of the Army, and General Eric K. Shinseki, Chief of Staff, United States Army, on the Fiscal Year 2002 Army Budget Request," July 18, 2001.

28. Scott R. Gourley, "Army Aviation and Army Transformation," *Army*, January 2003, 28–33.

29. See chapter 20 (this text), "Acquisition of the C-17," for detailed discussion of the plane's early development.

30. Air Mobility Command, *History of Air Mobility Command, 1 January–31 December 1997*, vol. 1, *Narrative and Appendices* (Scott AF, IL: AMC/HO), 240, 242–43; William R. Richardson, Burdeshaw Associates, Ltd., Briefing to General Walter Kross, "Final Report on C-17 Briefing Results," June 4, 1997.

31. Tirpak, "Air Mobility in the Doldrums," 33–37; David A. Fulghum, "Plans Adrift," *Aviation Week and Space Technology*," August 8, 2005, 35.

32. Amy C. Butler, "A+ for Effort" and "Sunset for Airlifters: New Pentagon Study Could Spell Doom for C-17 and C-130J Production Lines," *Aviation Week and Space Technology*, June 27, 2005, 20, and October 31, 2005, 22–23, respectively; Tirpak, "The Squeeze on Air Mobility," 22–30; "Save the C-17, Says Senate," *Air Force Magazine*, January 2006, 10; Adam J. Hebert, "Air Mobility's Never-Ending Surge," *Air Force Magazine*, 51.

33. Amy Butler, "Down and Dirty," *Aviation Week and Space Technology*, February 23, 2009, 30; John A. Tirpak, "Washington Watch," *Air Force Magazine*, December 2009, 10, 15.

34. See chapter 23 (this text), "The 1990s: Years of Steady-State Surge," for details of early C-130J program.

35. Jonathan Karp, "Rumsfeld Restores Lockheed's C-130 to Defense Budget," *Wall Street Journal*, May 12, 2005; Tirpak, "Air Mobility in the Doldrums," 36.

36. Amy Butler, "RevAMPed," *Aviation Week and Space Technology*, January 18, 2010, 30; U.S. Transportation Command, "Statement of General Duncan J. McNabb, USAF, Commander, United States Transportation Command before the Senate Armed Services Committee," April 7, 2011, 13.

37. "Boeing C-17 Cargo Plane Doesn't Perform as Advertised, General Kross Says," *St Louis Post-Dispatch*, November 27, 1999.

38. Air Mobility Command, *History, 1997*, 261–62; Air Mobility Command, *History of Air Mobility Command, 1 January–31 December 1999*, vol. 1, *Narrative and Appendices* (Scott AF, IL: AMC/HO), 259–61.

39. John A. Tirpak, "The Super Galaxy," *Air Force Magazine*, March 2010, 51; Bruce

Rolfsen, "C-5M Aircrews Crow about New Engines, Avionics," Air Force News Service, April 29, 2009, retrieved December 19, 2011, from www.airforcetimes.com/news/2009/04/airforce _c5m_dover_042909.

40. John M. Doyle, "CRAF Fair," Aviation Week and Space Technology, June 1, 2009; John A. Tirpak, "Washington Watch," Air Force Magazine, February 2009, 8.

41. For discussions of the origins of FTF, see John T. Correll, "Future Total Force," Air Force Magazine, July 1999, 28–33; James A. Jernig, "Flying Operations in Total Force Integration Environment," research paper, Air Command and Staff College, Maxwell AFB, AL, 35–38. The author was the AMC lead for FTF from 1999 to 2001.

42. Kristin F. Lynch et al., Supporting the Future Total Force: A Methodology for Evaluating Potential Air National Guard Mission Assignments (Santa Monica, CA: RAND, 2007), 35–53.

43. John A. Tirpak, "Integrated Total Force," Air Force Magazine, March 2008, 24–29; U.S. Air Force, "Air Force Weapon System Roadmap Released," January 16, 2008, retrieved December 19, 2011, from www.af.mil/news/story.asp?id=123082420.

44. Department of Defense, "Final Report, Commission on the National Guard and Reserves: Transforming the National Guard and Reserves into a 21st-Century Operational Force," January 31, 2008, 367–68 and throughout.

45. Glenn W. Goodman Jr., "General John W. Handy, U.S. Air Force," Armed Forces Journal, October 2003, 28.

46. U.S. Government Accounting Office to Senator Carl Levin, Chair, Committee on Armed Services, and others, letter, "Subject: Air Force Aircraft: Preliminary Information on Air Force Tanker Leasing," May 15, 2002, 13, 18.

47. "Even during Hill Recess, Tanker Wars Rage," Defense Week, August 12, 2002, 1.

48. "Watchdogs Criticize Former Air Force Official Hired by Boeing," Federal Times, January 13, 2003, 9; William Matthews, "Tanker Lease Program: Air Force 'Done Deal' Gets Undone," Armed Force Journal, October 2003, 12; U.S. Senate, "Statement of Senator McCain on S.2559, the Fiscal Year 2005 Defense Appropriations Act," June 24, 2004, 1–2; John A. Tirpak, "Washington Watch: Druyun's Downfall," Air Force Magazine, November 2004, 10.

49. John McCain to Robert M. Gates, letter, "Re: Tanker Replacement Program," December 1, 2006.

50. Amy Butler, "Competitive Edge?," Aviation Week and Space Technology, November 30, 2009, 30; John M. Doyle, "Gathering Storm," Aviation Week and Space Technology, March 17, 2008; Daniel I. Gordon, Deputy General Counsel, U.S. Government Accountability Office, "Testimony before the Air and Land Forces Subcommittee, Committee on Armed Services, House of Representatives: Aerial Refueling Tanker Protest," July 10, 2008, 2–8.

51. John T. Bennett, "Murtha Wants Speedy Mixed Air Force Tanker Buy," Defense News, March 12, 2009, retrieved December 1, 2011, from www.defensenews.com/story.php?i=3986371.

52. Graham Warwick, "Herculean Task," Aviation Week and Space Technology, May 12, 2008, 29; Robert Quackenbush, "U.S. Army, Joint Heavy Lift: Past Present and Compelling Future," Aviation Today: Rotor and Wing, August 1, 2008.

53. Graham Warwick, "U.S. Army Moves on Next-Gen Helo," *Aviation Week and Space Technology*, April 19, 2011.

54. Stew Magnuson, "Inter-Service Rivalry Surrounds Joint Heavy Lift Aircraft Program," *National Defense*, March 2009; USAF, Aeronautical Systems Center, "Joint Future Theater Lift (JFTL) Technology Study (JTS): Capability Request for Information," October 20, 2010, 3–4.

55. Department of Defense, "Memorandum of Agreement between the Department of the Army and the Department of the Air Force, Subject: Way Ahead for the Convergence of the Army Future Cargo Aircraft (FCA) and the Air Force Light Cargo Aircraft (LCA) Programs," June 16, 2006, 2, 3, 6.

56. Gayle S. Putrich, "C-27J Tapped for Joint Cargo Aircraft," *Army Times*, June 14, 2008.

57. Amy Butler, "Line in the Sky," *Aviation Week and Space Technology*, April 2, 2007, 52; Robert S. Dudney, "The Last Tactical Mile and Other Tales," *Air Force Magazine*, December 2007, 2.

58. Kenneth Horn et al., *Use of the C-27 Fixed-Wing Aircraft for Conducting Army Mission Critical, Time Sensitive Missions in Counterinsurgency Operations* (Santa Monica, CA: RAND, 2010), 1; A. Fulghum et al., "Airlift Angst," *Aviation Week and Space Technology*, February 18, 2008, 43.

59. Robert Owen and Karl Mueller, *Airlift Capabilities for Future U.S. Counterinsurgency Operations* (Santa Monica, CA: RAND, 2007), 39, 47–48.

60. Megan Scully, "The Little Airlifter That Could," *Air Force Magazine*, July 2010, 58–61.

61. Amy Butler et al., "Facing the Music," *Aviation Week and Space Technology*, April 27, 2009, 28; Horn et al., *Use of the C-27*, 8, 17.

62. Richard I. Wolf, *The United States Air Force Basic Documents on Roles and Missions* (Washington, DC: Office of Air Force History, 1987), 382.

63. Collin R. Bakse, ed., "Cover Story," *Airlift/Tanker Quarterly*, Summer 2010, 6.

64. Graham Warwick, "Advancing Edge: U.S. Army Next-Generation Rotorcraft Plans Raise Questions about Industry's Ability to Innovate," *Aviation Week and Space Technology*, July 2010, 29.

65. David Wood, "The Airlifter's War," *Air Force Magazine*, February 2010, 38–42.

25. Haiti 2010

1. Michael D. Shear, "Obama Orders Rapid Mobilization of U.S. Rescue, Relief Efforts for Haiti," *Washington Post*, January, 14, 2010, A01; Mark Thompson, "The U.S. Military in Haiti: A Compassionate Invasion," *Time*, January 16, 2010.

2. Lieutenant General Ken Keen, Commander JTF-H, briefing, "JTF-Haiti Forming a Joint Task Force in a Crisis: Observations and Recommendations," n.d. (probably mid-April 2010), slide 11 of 15.

3. Ellery D. Wallwork et al., *Operation Unified Response: Air Mobility Command's Response to the 2010 Haiti Earthquake Crisis* (Scott AFB, IL: Air Mobility Command, 2010), 26.

4. Wallwork et al., *Operation Unified Response*, 10, 25; Staff Sergeant LuCelia Ball, "Team

Hickam, PACAF Aircraft Depart to Assist Haiti Relief Effort," Pacific Air Forces News Release, January 21, 2010, retrieved June 17, 2010, from www.15wing.af.mil/news/story.asp?id=123186711.

5. Major General Richard K. Millmann Jr., interview by Robert C. Owen, July 19, 2011, tape 1, side A, index 030.

6. Captain Justin A. Longmire et al., 612 Air and Space Operations Center/Air Mobility Division, Haiti Flight Operations Coordination Center, "After Action Report," March 2010, 12. RAMCCs had been activated in Europe and the Middle East to handle airflows into Bosnia, Iraq, and Afghanistan, but they were all temporary.

7. Major David J. Smith, e-mail to Robert C. Owen, "Re: Interview Follow-Up," August 17, 2011. In the 601 AMD, Smith was the Air Mobility Control Team chief.

8. 601 Air and Space Operations Center/Air Mobility Division, Haiti Flight Operations Coordination Center, "After Action Report," March 2010, 8–12; Colonel Warren Hurst and others, interview by Robert C. Owen, August 10, 2011, tape 1, side A, index 024-58.

9. Major David Small, "Airman Named to *Time Magazine*'s '100 Most-Influential People' List for Haiti Airfield Efforts," Air Force National Media Outreach Office, April 30, 2010, retrieved August 23, 2011, from www.southcom.mil/appssc/news.php?storyId=2319. The 612 AMD history indicates that only eighteen minutes passed between the AFSOC's arrival and the start of tower operations.

10. Captain Dustin Doyle, "Contingency Response Airmen Return Home after Haiti Relief Operations," Joint Base McGuire-Dix-Lakehurst Web page, March 1, 2010, retrieved June 17, 2011, from www.jointbasemdl.af.mil/news/story.asp?id=123192689; Longmire et al., "After Action Report," A4.

11. Parker Gyokeres, "Air Force Captain Looks Back on Efforts to Re-establish Air Ops in Haiti," 621st Contingency Response Wing Public Affairs Office, McGuire AFB, NJ, retrieved August 23, 2011, from www.southcom.mil/appssc/news.php?storyId=2262.

12. Scott R. Gourley, "JTF Port Opening for Operation Unified Response," January 29, 2011, U.S. Army Materiel Command, 2010–2011 edition, Faircount Media, retrieved September 3, 2011, from www.defensemedianetwork.com/stories/jtf-port-opening-for-operation-unified-response/.

13. Jim Garamone, "Joint Task Force Organizes Haitian Airport," American Forces Press Service, January 28, 2010, retrieved August 23, 2011, www.defense.gov/news/newsarticle.aspx?id=57776.

14. For detailed discussions of logistics planning and airlift command and control, see Joint Publication (JP) 3-17, *Air Mobility Operations*, October 2, 2009, chapters 2 and 3; JP 4-0, *Joint Logistics*, July 18, 2008, chapter 5; Air Force Doctrine Document (AFDD 2-6), *Air Mobility Operations*, March 1, 2006, chapters 2 and 6.

15. "Memorandum of Understanding Regarding the Use and Management of Haitian Airspace between the Government of the United States of America and the Government of Haiti," January 14, 2011, extracted from 601 AOC, "After Action Report," appendix 1.

16. 601 AOC, "After Action Report," 23.

17. Lieutenant Colonel J. J. Grindrod, e-mail to Robert C. Owen, "601 AOC Comments," August 16, 2011.

18. 601 AOC, "After Action Report," 4–7.

19. Millmann, Owen interview, tape 1, side A, index 149-64.

20. Colonel Warren Hurst and others, interview by Robert C. Owen, August 10, 2011, tape 1, side A, index 189-359.

21. Wallwork et al., *Operation Unified Response*, 32; Longmire et al., "After Action Report," 45–46, A-12.

22. Martha Mendoza, "Haiti Flight Logs Detail Early Chaos," Associated Press, February 18, 2010.

23. Agence France-Presse, "U.S. Rejects Latin American Claim It Is 'Occupying' Haiti," January 22, 2010, retrieved June 10, 2011, from www.google.com/hostednews/afp/article/ALeqM5hx
PFjXRHzg1A1D9UuUAKhbd7j98A.

24. David Williams, "U.S. Criticised over Haiti Relief Effort as Italian Disaster Expert Brands It 'Badly Managed,'" *Daily Mail* (London), January 26, 2010; and "France Criticises U.S. Occupation," *The Telegraph*, January 18, 2010.

25. Doctors Without Borders, "Doctors Without Borders Plane with Lifesaving Medical Supplies Diverted Again from Landing in Haiti," Press Release, January 19, 2010, retrieved July 12, 2011, from www.doctorswithoutborders.org/press/release.cfm?id=4176.

26. Daniel Bymann et al., *Strengthening the Partnership: Improving Military Coordination with Relief Agencies and Allies in Humanitarian Operations* (Santa Monica, CA: RAND, 2000), xvii, 114.

27. United Nations, *World Food Program Aviation Annual Report 2009* (Geneva, Switzerland: WFP Information Unit, 2009), summary page and throughout.

28. Philippe Martou, "Executive Summary," in 601 AOC, "After Actions Report," 2.

29. Martou, "Executive Summary," 26–27.

30. Grindrod, e-mail.

31. Robert C. Owen, "United States Air Force and United Nations Cooperation in Future High Intensity Humanitarian Airlift Operations: Honing the Partnership" (for the conference On the Wings of Peace: Air Power in United Nations Operations, RCAF Air Warfare Center, Trenton, Ontario, June 17, 2011), 18–19.

32. Longmire et al., "After Action Report," A4; Wallwork et al., *Operation Unified Response*, 23–24.

33. These are figures updated in an e-mail between the author and AMC historian Mark Morgan on June 7, 2011, and are slightly higher than those contained in the official AMC history; Wallwork et al., *Operation Unified Response*, 97.

34. Longmire et al., "After Action Report," A4.

35. National Defense and the Defense Forces of Canada, "Factsheet, Operation and Joint Task Force Haiti," n.d., retrieved June 10, 2011, from www.cefcom-comfec.forces.gc.ca/pa-ap/ops/fs-fr/hestia-eng.asp.

26. The Secret Is People

1. The 2011 Airlift/Tanker Association convention was held at the Gaylord Palms Convention Center, Nashville, Tennessee, and was attended by well over 4,000 people.

2. As of January 28, 2012, General Johns's address was available online at www.youtube. com/watch?v=TOxjhy8BfQc.

3. Robert Ellington, interview by Robert C. Owen, July 18, 2007, tape 1, side B, index 790-960; James I. Baginski, interview by Robert C. Owen, July 5, 2007, tape 1, side A, index 023-155.

4. "Association Round-up: Golden Bear Chapter," *Airlift/Tanker Quarterly*, Spring 2007, 7.

5. For those wishing to cast caution to the wind and learn the game, Wikipedia provides a useful generic discussion of the rules at http://en.wikipedia.org/wiki/Crud_%28game%29, and the Airlift/Tanker Association has published "Concept of Operations for Airlift/Tanker Association Crud Operations, 28–31 Oct. 10," which can be found at http://atalink.org/Forms/2010_CRUD_CONOPs.pdf, at least as of January 27, 2012.

6. Johns, address, indexes 06:34 and 32:25.

Selected Bibliography

Arbon, Lee. *They Also Flew: The Enlisted Pilot Legacy, 1912–1942.* Washington, DC:
Smithsonian, 1991.

Arnold, Henry H. *Global Mission.* New York: Harper and Brothers, 1949.

Arnold, Henry H., and Ira C. Eaker. *Army Flyer.* New York: Harper and Brothers, 1942.

——. *Winged Warfare.* New York: Harper and Brothers, 1941.

Bergerson, Frederick A. *The Army Gets an Air Force: Tactics of Insurgent Bureaucratic Politics.*
Baltimore: Johns Hopkins University Press, 1978.

Bilstein, Roger E. *Airlift and Airborne Operations in World War II.* Washington, DC: Air
Force History and Museums Program, 1998.

Blair, Clay. *The Forgotten War.* New York: Times Books, 1987.

Borden Jr., Norman E. *Air Mail Emergency, 1934.* Freeport, ME: Bond Wheelwright, 1968.

Bowers, Ray L. *The United States Air Force in Southeast Asia: Tactical Airlift.* Washington,
DC: Office of Air Force History, 1983.

Bowie, Christopher, and others. *The New Calculus: Analyzing Airpower's Changing Role in
Joint Theater Campaigns.* Santa Monica, CA: RAND, 1993.

Boyne, Walter J. *The Two O'clock War: The 1973 Yom Kippur Conflict and the Airlift That Saved
Israel.* New York: St. Martin's, 2002.

Brinson, W. L. *Three One Five Group: An Account of the Activities of the 315th Troop Carrier
Group, United States Army Air Forces, 1942–1945.* Lakemont, GA: Copple House Books, 1984.

Brown, Genevieve. *Development of Transport Airplanes and Air Transport Equipment.*
Langley Field, VA: Air Technical Service Command, 1946.

Buchanan, A. R., ed. *The Navy's Air War: A Mission Completed.* New York: Harper and
Brothers, 1946.

Bundy, McGeorge. *Death and Survival: Choices about the Bomb in the First Fifty Years.* New
York: Random House, 1988.

Burkard, Dick J. *Military Airlift Command: Historical Handbook, 1941–1984.* Scott AFB, IL:
Military Airlift Command History Office, 1984.

Cantwell, Gerald T. *Citizen Airmen: A History of the Air Force Reserve, 1946–1969.*
Washington, DC: Air Force History and Museums, 1994.

Cave, Hugh B. *Wings across the World: The Story of the Air Transport Command.* New York:
Dodd, Mead, 1945.

Chanute, Octave. *Progress in Flying Machines.* New York: American Engineer and Railroad
Journal, 1894.

Cherny, Andrei. *The Candy Bombers: The Untold Story of the Berlin Airlift and America's
Finest Hour.* New York: Putnam, 2008.

Christopher, John. *Balloons at War: Gasbags, Flying Bombs and Cold War Secrets.* London: Tempus, 2004.

Cleveland, Reginald M. *Air Transport at War.* New York: Harper and Brothers, 1946.

Cohen, Eliot A. *The Gulf War Airpower Survey.* 5 vols. Washington, DC: USGPO, 1993.

Cole, Ronald H. *Operation JUST CAUSE: The Planning and Execution of Joint Operations in Panama, February 1988–January 1990.* Washington, DC: Joint History Office, 1995.

Collier, Richard. *Bridge across the Sky: The Berlin Blockade and Airlift, 1948–1949.* New York: McGraw-Hill, 1978.

Congress, Congressional Budget Office. *Improving Strategic Mobility: The C-17 Program and Alternatives.* Washington, DC: Congressonal Budget Office, 1986.

Cosmas, Graham A., and Albert E. Cowdrey. *The Medical Department: Medical Service in the European Theater of Operations.* Washington, DC: Center of Military History, 1992.

Crackel, Theodore J. *A History of the Civil Reserve Air Fleet.* Washington, DC: Office of Air Force History, 1993.

Craven, Wesley Frank, and James Lea Cate, eds. *The Army Air Forces in World War II.* 7 vols. Chicago: University of Chicago, 1958; reprint, Washington, DC: Office of Air Force History, 1983.

Dabney, Joseph E. *Herk: Hero of the Skies.* Lakemont, GA: Copple House Books, 1979.

Davis, R. E. G. *Airlines of the United States since 1914.* Washington, DC: Smithsonian, 1972.

De Seversky, Alexander. *Air Power: Key to Survival.* New York: Simon and Schuster, 1950.

Devlin, Gerard M. *Silent Wings.* New York: St. Martin's, 1985.

Doughty, Robert A. *The Evolution of U.S. Army Tactical Doctrine, 1946–76.* Ft. Leavenworth, KS: U.S. Army Combat Studies Institute, 1979.

Ebert, James R. *A Life in a Year: The American Infantryman in Vietnam, 1965–1972.* Novato, CA: Presidio, 1993.

Fisher, John. *Airlift 1870: The Balloon and Pidgeon Post in the Siege of Paris.* London: Max Parrish, 1965.

Frey, Royal D. *Case History of the C-119 Airplane: September 1946–June 1953.* Wright-Patterson AFB, OH: Air Material Command Historical Branch, 1953.

Futrell, Robert F. *Ideas, Concepts, Doctrine: Basic Thinking in the United States Air Force.* 2 vols. Maxwell AFB, AL: Air University Press, 1989.

———. *The United States Air Force in Korea, 1950–1953.* Washington, DC: USGPO, 1983.

Gavin, James M. *War and Peace in the Space Age.* New York: Harper and Brothers, 1958.

Gebman, Jean R., Louis J. Batchelder, and Katherine M. Poehlmann. *Finding the Right Mix of Military and Civil Airlift, Issues and Implications:* Vol. 1, *Executive Summary.* Santa Monica, CA: RAND, 1994.

Goodman, Nathan G., ed. *The Ingenious Dr. Franklin: Selected Scientific Letters of Benjamin Franklin.* Philadelphia: University of Pennsylvania Press, 1931.

Gross, Charles Joseph. *Prelude to the Total Force: The Air National Guard, 1943–1969.* Washington, DC: Office of Air Force History, 1985.

Haydock, Michael D. *City under Siege: The Berlin Blockade and Airlift, 1948–1949*. London: Brassey's, 1999.

Head, William. *Reworking the Workhorse: The C-141B Stretch Modification Program*. Robins AFB, GA: Air Force Logistics Command, Office of History, 1984.

Hebert, Edward, and John McMillan. *Last of the Titans: The Life and Times of Congressman F. Edward Hebert of Louisiana*. Lafayette: University of South West Louisiana, 1976.

Hoehn, W. E., et al. *Strategic Mobility Alternatives for the 1980s*. Vol. 1, *Executive Summary*. Santa Monica, CA: RAND, 1977.

Hoffman, Jon T. *Silk Chutes and Hard Fighting: U.S. Marine Parachute Units in World War II*. Washington, DC: USMC History and Museums, 1999.

Horn, Kenneth, and others. *Use of the C-27 Fixed-Wing Aircraft for Conducting Army Mission Critical, Time Sensitive Missions in Counterinsurgency Operations*. Santa Monica, CA: RAND, 2010.

Josephson, Matthew. *Empire of the Air: Juan Trippe and the Struggle for World Airways*. New York: Harcourt Brace, 1943.

Kashatus, William C. *Dapper Dan Flood: The Controversial Life of a Congressional Power Broker*. University Park: Pennsylvania State University Press, 2010.

Keil, Sally Van Wagenen. *Those Wonderful Women in Their Flying Machines: The Unknown Heroines of World War II*. New York: Four Corners Press, 1990.

Kelly Jr., Charles J. *The Sky's the Limit*. New York: Coward-McCann, 1963.

Kennedy, Betty R. *Globemaster III: Acquiring the C-17*. Scott AFB, IL: Air Mobility Command History Office, 2004.

Kent Jr., Richard J. *Safe, Separated and Soaring: A History of Federal Civil Aviation Policy, 1961–1972*. Washington, DC: USGPO, 1980.

Killingsworth, Paul S., and Laura Melody. *Should C-17s Be Used to Carry In-Theater Cargo during Major Deployments?* Santa Monica, CA: RAND, 1997.

Kissinger, Henry. *Nuclear Weapons and Foreign Policy*. Garden City, NY: Doubleday, 1958.

Kolodziej, Edward. *The Uncommon Defense and Congress, 1945–1963*. Columbus: Ohio State University Press, 1966.

Komons, Nick A. *Bonfires to Beacons: Federal Civil Aviation Policy under the Air Commerce Act, 1926–1938*. Washington, DC: Smithsonian, 1989.

La Farge, Oliver. *Eagle in the Egg*. New York: Arno Press, 1949.

Lawrance, Charles H. *Our National Aviation Program*. New York: Aeronautical Chamber of Commerce, 1932.

Lee, Bowen, and others. *USAF Airborne Operations: World War II and Korean War*. Washington, DC: USAF Historical Division, 1962.

Lee, James. *Operation Lifeline: History and Development of the Naval Air Transport Service*. Chicago: Ziff Davis, 1947.

Leland, John W., and Kathryn A. Wilcoxson. *The Chronological History of the C-5 Galaxy*. Scott AFB, IL: Air Mobility Command History Office, 2003.

LeMay, Curtis E., and MacKinlay Kantor. *Mission with LeMay: My Story.* New York: Doubleday, 1965.

Levine, Herbert M. "The Politics of Strategic Airlift." PhD diss., Columbia University, 1970.

Liddell Hart, B.H. *Deterrent or Defense.* New York: Praeger, 1960.

Lynch, Kristin F., and others. *Supporting the Future Total Force: A Methodology for Evaluating Potential Air National Guard Mission Assignments.* Santa Monica, CA: RAND, 2007.

Malkin, Richard. *Boxcars in the Sky.* New York: Import Publications, 1951.

Maltais, Richard E. *History of the Warner Robbins Air Material Area, 1 July 1971–30 June 1972, Pt. I: Weapon Systems, C-133 Cargomaster, 1953–1971.* Warner Robins AFB, GA: WRAMA History Study No. 26, 1973.

Mason, Robert C. *Chickenhawk.* New York: Viking Press, 1983.

Matthews, James K., and Robert T. Cossaboom. *General Robert L. Rutherford: An Oral History.* Scott AFB, IL: U.S. Transportation Command Research Center, 1996.

Matthews, James K., and Cora J. Holt. *So Many, So Much, So Far, So Fast: United States Transportation Command and Strategic Deployment for Operation Desert Shield/Desert Storm.* Washington, DC: USGPO, 1996.

Matthews, James K., and John W. Leland. *General Ronald R. Fogleman, Commander in Chief United States Transportation Command and Commander Air Mobility Command: An Oral History.* Scott AFB, IL: AMC History Office, 1995.

Matthews, James K., and Robert C. Owen. *Edward J. Driscoll: Forming a Partnership for National Defense: Commercial Airlines and the Air Force: An Oral History.* Scott AFB, IL: U.S. Transportation Command, 2001.

Matthews, James K., and Jay H. Smith. *Hansford T. Johnson, United States Transportation Command and Air Mobility Command: An Oral History.* Scott AFB, IL: Offices of AMC and U.S. Transportation Command History, 1992.

Maurer, Maurer. *Aviation in the United States Army, 1919–1939.* Washington, DC: Office of Air Force History, 1987.

———. *The U.S. Air Service in World War I.* 4 vols. Maxwell AFB, AL: Air University Press, 1971.

Merriman, Molly. *Clipped Wings: The Rise and Fall of the Women Airforce Service Pilots (WASPs) of World War II.* New York: New York University, 1998.

Mersky, Peter B. *U.S. Marine Corps Aviation, 1912 to the Present.* Baltimore: Nautical and Aviation Publishing, 1983.

Military Airlift Command. *Anything, Anywhere, Anytime: An Illustrated History of the Military Airlift Command, 1941–1991.* Scott AFB, IL: Military Airlift Command History Office, 1991.

———. *Strategic Airlift to Israel.* Scott AFB, IL: MAC History Office, 1973.

Miller, Charles E. *Airlift Doctrine.* Maxwell AFB, AL: Air University Press, 1988.

Miller, Roger G. *To Save a City: The Berlin Airlift, 1948–1949.* Washington, DC: Air Force History and Museums, 1998.

Mitchell, William. *Winged Defense: The Development and Possibilities of Modern Air Power—Economic and Military.* New York: G. P. Putnam's Sons, 1925.

Momyer, William W. *Airpower in Three Wars*. Washington, DC: Office of Air Force History, 1978.

Montross, Lynn. *Cavalry of the Sky: The Story of U.S. Marine Helicopters*. New York: Harper and Brothers, 1954.

Nalty, Bernard C. *Air Power and the Fight for Khe Sanh*. Washington, DC: Office of Air Force History, 1986.

Owen, Robert, and Karl Mueller. *Airlift Capabilities for Future U.S. Counterinsurgency Operations*. Santa Monica, CA: RAND, 2007.

Pagonis, William G. *Moving Mountains: Lessons in Leadership and Logistics from the Gulf War*. Boston: Harvard, 1992.

Palmby, William G. "Enhancement of the Civil Reserve Air Fleet: An Alternative for Bridging the Airlift Gap." Thesis, School of Advanced Airpower Studies, Maxwell AFB, AL, 1995.

Patrick, Mason M. *The United States in the Air*. New York: Doubleday, 1928.

Perret, Geoffrey. *Winged Victory*. New York: Random House, 1993.

Phillips, R. Cody. *Operation Just Cause: The Incursion into Panama*. Washington, DC: U.S. Army Center of Military History, 2004.

Pogue, Forrest C. *The U.S. Army in World War II, European Theater of Operations, the Supreme Command*. Washington, DC: Center of Military History, 1951.

Priddy, Ronald N. *A History of the Civil Reserve Air Fleet in Operations Desert Shield, Desert Storm, and Desert Sortie*. Washington, DC: DOD Policy Board on Federal Aviation, 1993.

Puryear Jr., Edgar F. *George S. Brown, General U.S. Air Force: Destined for Stars*. Novato, CA: Presidio, 1983.

RAND Corporation. *Transport Aircraft Characteristics and Performance, RAND Report-294*. Santa Monica, CA: RAND, 1956.

Rearden, Steven L. *History of the Office of the Secretary of Defense*. Washington, DC: Historical Office, Office of the Secretary of Defense, 1984.

Rickenbacker, Edward V. *Rickenbacker*. Englewood Cliffs, NJ: Prentice Hall, 1967.

Rogers, Bernard W. *Vietnam Studies, Cedar Falls–Junction City: A Turning Point*. Washington, DC: Department of the Army, 1989.

Ruppenthal, Roland C. *The U.S. Army in World War II: The European Theater of Operations: Logistical Support of the Armies*. 2 vols. Washington, DC: Center of Military History, 1959.

Shama, H. Rex. *Pulse and Repulse: Troop Carrier and Airborne Teams in Europe during World War II*. Austin, TX: Eakin Press, 1995.

Sherman, William C. *Air Warfare*. New York: Ronald Press, 1926.

Sherrod, Robert. *History of Marine Corps Aviation in World War II*. San Rafael, CA: Presidio, 1952.

Shiner, John F. *Foulois and the U.S. Army Air Corps, 1931–1935*. Washington, DC: Office of Air Force History, 1983.

Shlaim, Avi. *The United States and the Berlin Blockade, 1948–1949: A Study in Crisis Decision Making*. Berkeley: University of California Press, 1983.

Shrader, Charles R. *History of Operations Research in the United States Army.* Vol. 2, *1961–1973.* Washington, DC: U.S. Army Center for Military History, 2008.

Shubert, Frank N., and Theresa L. Kraus, eds. *The Whirlwind War: The United States Army in Operations DESERT SHIELD and DESERT STORM.* Washington, DC: U.S. Army Center of Military History, 1995.

Simmons, Edwin H. *The United States Marines: A History.* 4th ed. Washington, DC: Marine History and Museums Division, 1992.

Slayton, Robert A. *Master of the Air: William Tunner and the Success of Military Airlift.* Tuscaloosa: University of Alabama, 2010.

Smith, Henry Ladd. *Airways: The History of Commercial Aviation in the United States.* New York: Knopf, 1942.

Smith, Perry M. *The Air Force Plans for Peace, 1943–1945.* Baltimore: Johns Hopkins, 1970.

Smith, Richard K. *Seventy-Five Years of Inflight Refueling.* Washington, DC: Air Force History and Museums, 1998.

Smith, Walter Bedell. *Moscow Mission, 1946–1949.* London: Heineman, 1950.

Spencer, Otha C. *Flying the Hump: Memories of an Air War.* College Station: Texas A&M University, 1992.

Stanton, Shelby L. *Vietnam Order of Battle.* New York: Galahad Books, 1986.

Taylor, Maxwell D. *The Uncertain Trumpet.* New York: Harper and Brothers, 1959.

Terraine, John. *The Right of the Line: The Royal Air Force in the European War, 1939–1945.* London: Hodder and Stoughton, 1985.

Thayer, Frederick C. *Air Transport Policy and National Security: A Political, Economic and Military Analysis.* Chapel Hill: University of North Carolina, 1965.

Thompson, Annis G. *The Greatest Airlift: The Story of Combat Cargo.* Tokyo: Dai-Nippon, 1954.

Tolson, John J. *Airmobility, 1961–1971.* Washington, DC: U.S. Army Center of Military History, 1973.

Trask, Roger R. *The Secretaries of Defense: A Brief History, 1947–1985.* Washington, DC: Historical Office of the Secretary of Defense, 1985.

Truman, Harry S. *Memoirs.* Vol. 2: *Years of Trial and Hope, 1946–1953.* London: Hodden and Stoughton, 1956.

Tunner, William H. *Over the Hump.* New York: Duell, Sloan and Pierce, 1964; reprint, Washington, DC: Office of Air Force History, 1985.

Underwood, Jeffery S. *Military Airlift Comes of Age: Consolidation of Strategic and Tactical Airlift Forces under the Military Airlift Command, 1974–1977.* Scott AFB, IL: MAC Office of History, 1990.

United States Air Force, Research Studies Institute. *History of the Air Corps Tactical School, 1920–1940.* Maxwell AFB, AL: Air University Press, 1955.

U.S. Army. *Training Regulations 440-15, Air Service: Fundamental Principles for the Employment of the Air Service.* Washington, DC: War Department, 1926.

U.S. Department of Commerce and the American Engineering Council. *Civil Aviation.* New York: McGraw-Hill, 1926.

U.S. General Accounting Office. *Airlift Operations of the Military Airlift Command during the 1973 Middle East War.* Washington, DC: USGPO, 1975.

———. *Military Airlift: Air Force Analysis Supports Acquisition of C-17 Aircraft.* Washington, DC: USGPO, 1987.

———. *Military Airlift: Changes Underway to Ensure Continued Success of Civil Reserve Air Fleet.* Washington, DC: U.S. General Accounting Office, 1992.

———. *Strategic Airlift to Israel.* Washington, DC: USGPO, 1973.

Wallwork, Ellery D., Kathy S. Gunn, and others. *Operation Unified Response: Air Mobility Command's Response to the 2010 Haiti Earthquake Crisis.* Scott AFB, IL: Air Mobility Command, 2010.

Walsh, David M. *The Military Balance in the Cold War: U.S. Perceptions and Policy, 1976–85.* London: Routledge, 2008.

Warnock, A. Timothy, ed. *Short of War: Major USAF Contingency Operations, 1947–1997.* Maxwell AFB, AL: Air University Press, 2000.

Warren, John. *Airborne Operations in World War II, European Theater.* Maxwell AFB, AL: AF Research Studies Institute, 1956.

Webb, Willard J., and Ronald H. Cole. *The Chairmen of the Joint Chiefs of Staff.* Washington, DC: Historical Division Joint Chiefs of Staff, 1989.

Weinert Jr., Richard P. *A History of Army Aviation: 1950–1962.* Ft. Monroe, VA: U.S. Army Training and Doctrine Command, 1991.

White Jr., Gerald A. *The Great Snafu Fleet.* Philadelphia, PA: Xlibris, 2000.

White, Robert P. *Mason Patrick and the Fight for Air Service Independence.* Washington, DC: Smithsonian, 2001.

Williams, James W. *A History of Army Aviation: From Its Beginnings to the War on Terror.* New York: iUniverse, 2005.

Williams, Susan Mercer. *An Airlift Odyssey: A History of Tactical Airlift Modernization, 1955–1983.* Marietta, GA: Lockheed-Georgia Company, 1983.

Wilson, John B. *Army Lineage Series, Maneuver and Firepower: The Evolution of Divisions and Separate Brigades.* Washington, DC: U.S. Army Center of Military History, 1998.

Wolf, Richard I. *The United States Air Force Basic Documents on Roles and Missions.* Washington, DC: Office of Air Force History, 1987.

Wolfe, Martin. *Green Light: Men of the 81st Troop Carrier Squadron Tell Their Story.* Pittsburgh: University of Pennsylvania Press, 1989.

———. *Green Light: A Troop Carrier Squadron's War from Normandy to the Rhine.* Washington, DC: Center for Air Force History, 1993.

Wolk, Herman S. *Planning and Organizing the Postwar Air Force, 1943–1947.* Washington, DC: Office of Air Force History, 1984.

Wragg, David W. *Flight before Flying.* New York: Frederick Fell, 1974.

Y'Blood, Thomas. *The Three Wars of Lt. Gen. George E. Stratemeyer: His Korean War Diary.* Washington, DC: Air Force History and Museums, 1999.

Index

About the Author

ROBERT C. OWEN is a professor in the Department of Aeronautical Science at Embry-Riddle Aeronautical University, Daytona Beach Campus. He teaches courses in manned and unmanned aviation operations, law, and history and conducts research in national defense policy issues. Professor Owen joined the Embry-Riddle faculty in 2002, following a twenty-eight-year career with the U.S. Air Force. His military career included a mix of operational, staff, and advanced education assignments. He is both an air force command pilot and a commercial pilot with instrument and multiengine ratings. He flew over 3,400 hours in the Air Force and over 1,000 hours in various civilian aircraft. Professor Owen also served on the HQ Air Force Staff and as the chief of the Policy and Doctrine Division of HQ Air Mobility Command. His academic assignments included tours as an assistant professor of history at the U.S. Air Force Academy and as dean of the USAF's School of Advanced Airpower Studies, the service's graduate school for strategic planners. Professor Owen lives in Port Orange, Florida, and is the fortunate husband of the former Adrienne Goodman and the proud father of two great adults, Heather and Robert.

CPSIA information can be obtained
at www.ICGtesting.com
Printed in the USA
LVOW12*1920101117

555817LV00005B/6/P